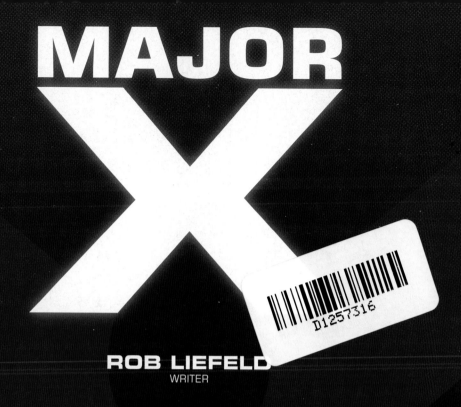

MAJOR X

ROB LIEFELD
WRITER

ROB LIEFELD (#1 & #6), **BRENT PEEPLES** (#2, #4 & #5)
AND **WHILCE PORTACIO** (#3)
PENCILERS

ROB LIEFELD WITH
ADELSO CORONA & **DAN FRAGA** (#1); **SCOTT HANNA** (#2);
WHILCE PORTACIO (#3); **ADELSO CORONA** (#4-5);
ROB LIEFELD, **CORY HAMSCHER** & **ADELSO CORONA** (#6)
INKERS

ROMULO FAJARDO JR.
COLOR ARTIST

VC's JOE SABINO
LETTERER

ROB LIEFELD & **ROMULO FAJARDO JR.**
COVER ARTISTS

ANNALISE BISSA
ASSISTANT EDITOR

JORDAN D. WHITE
EDITOR

COLLECTION EDITOR **MARK D. BEAZLEY** • ASSISTANT EDITOR **CAITLIN O'CONNELL** • ASSOCIATE MANAGING EDITOR **KATERI WOODY**
ASSOCIATE MANAGER, DIGITAL ASSETS **JOE HOCHSTEIN** • SENIOR EDITOR, SPECIAL PROJECTS **JENNIFER GRÜNWALD**
VP PRODUCTION & SPECIAL PROJECTS **JEFF YOUNGQUIST** • RESEARCH & LAYOUT **JEPH YORK**
PRODUCTION **JERRON QUALITY COLOR, COLORTEK** & **JOE FRONTIRRE** • BOOK DESIGNERS **SALENA MAHINA** & **ADAM DEL RE**

SVP PRINT, SALES & MARKETING **DAVID GABRIEL** • DIRECTOR, LICENSED PUBLISHING **SVEN LARSEN**
EDITOR IN CHIEF **C.B. CEBULSKI** • CHIEF CREATIVE OFFICER **JOE QUESADA**
PRESIDENT **DAN BUCKLEY** • EXECUTIVE PRODUCER **ALAN FINE**

MAJOR X. Contains material originally published in magazine form as MAJOR X #0-6. First printing 2019. ISBN 978-1-302-91741-8. Published by MARVEL WORLDWIDE, INC., a subsidiary of MARVEL ENTERTAINMENT, LLC. OFFICE OF PUBLICATION: 135 West 50th Street, New York, NY 10020. **Printed in the U.S.A.** DAN BUCKLEY, President, Marvel Entertainment; JOHN NEE, Publisher; JOE QUESADA, Chief Creative Officer; TOM BREVOORT, SVP of Publishing; DAVID BOGART, Associate Publisher & SVP of Talent Affairs; DAVID GABRIEL, SVP of Sales & Marketing, Publishing; JEFF YOUNGQUIST, VP of Production & Special Projects; DAN CARR, Executive Director of Publishing Technology; ALEX MORALES, Director of Publishing Operations; DAN EDINGTON, Managing Editor; SUSAN CRESPI, Production Manager; STAN LEE, Chairman Emeritus. For information regarding advertising in Marvel Comics or on Marvel.com, please contact Vit DeBellis, Custom Solutions & Integrated Advertising Manager, at vdebellis@marvel.com. For Marvel subscription inquiries, please call 888-511-5480. **Manufactured between 8/9/2019 and 9/10/2019 by LSC COMMUNICATIONS INC., KENDALLVILLE, IN, USA.**

10 9 8 7 6 5 4 3 2 1

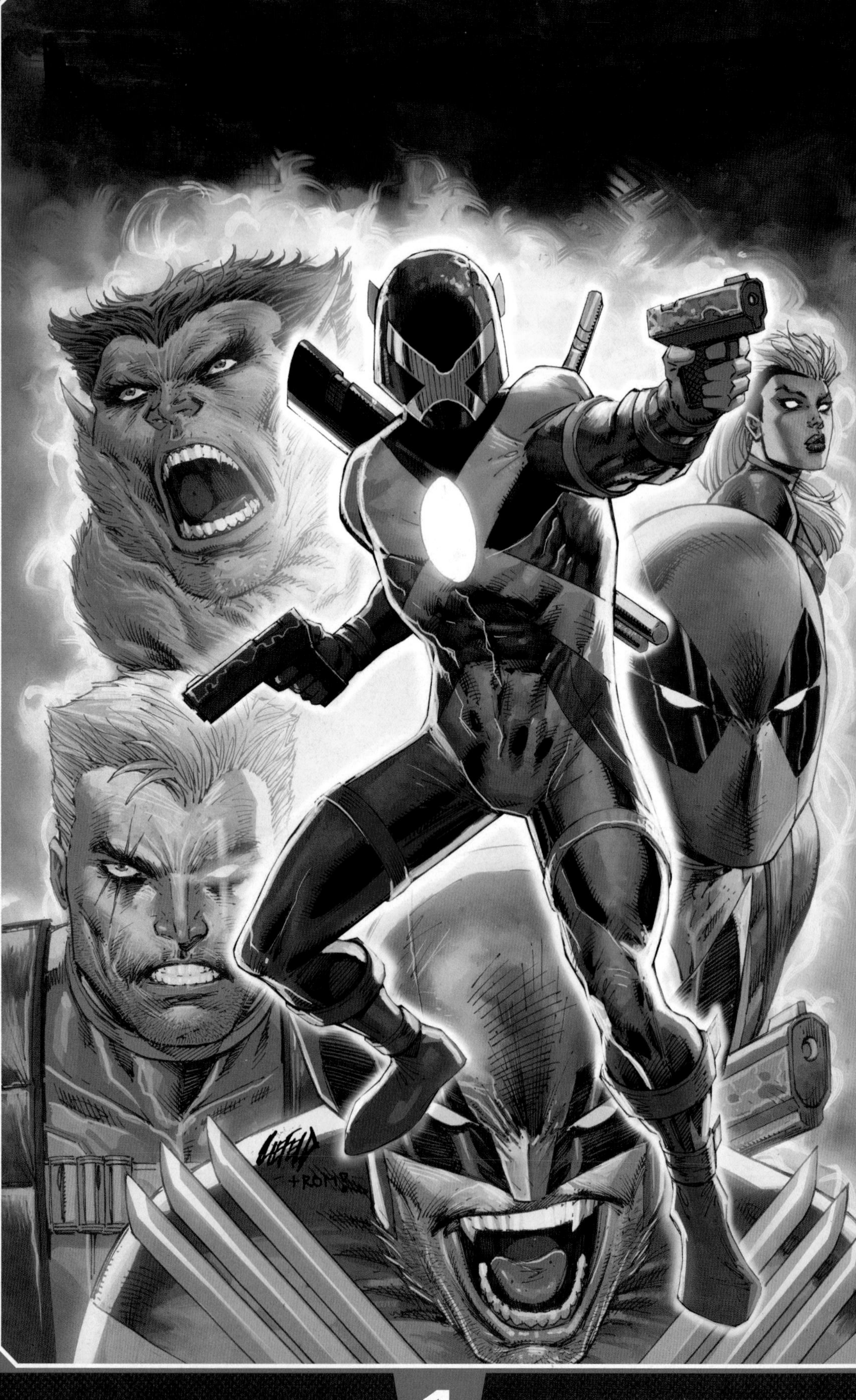

1

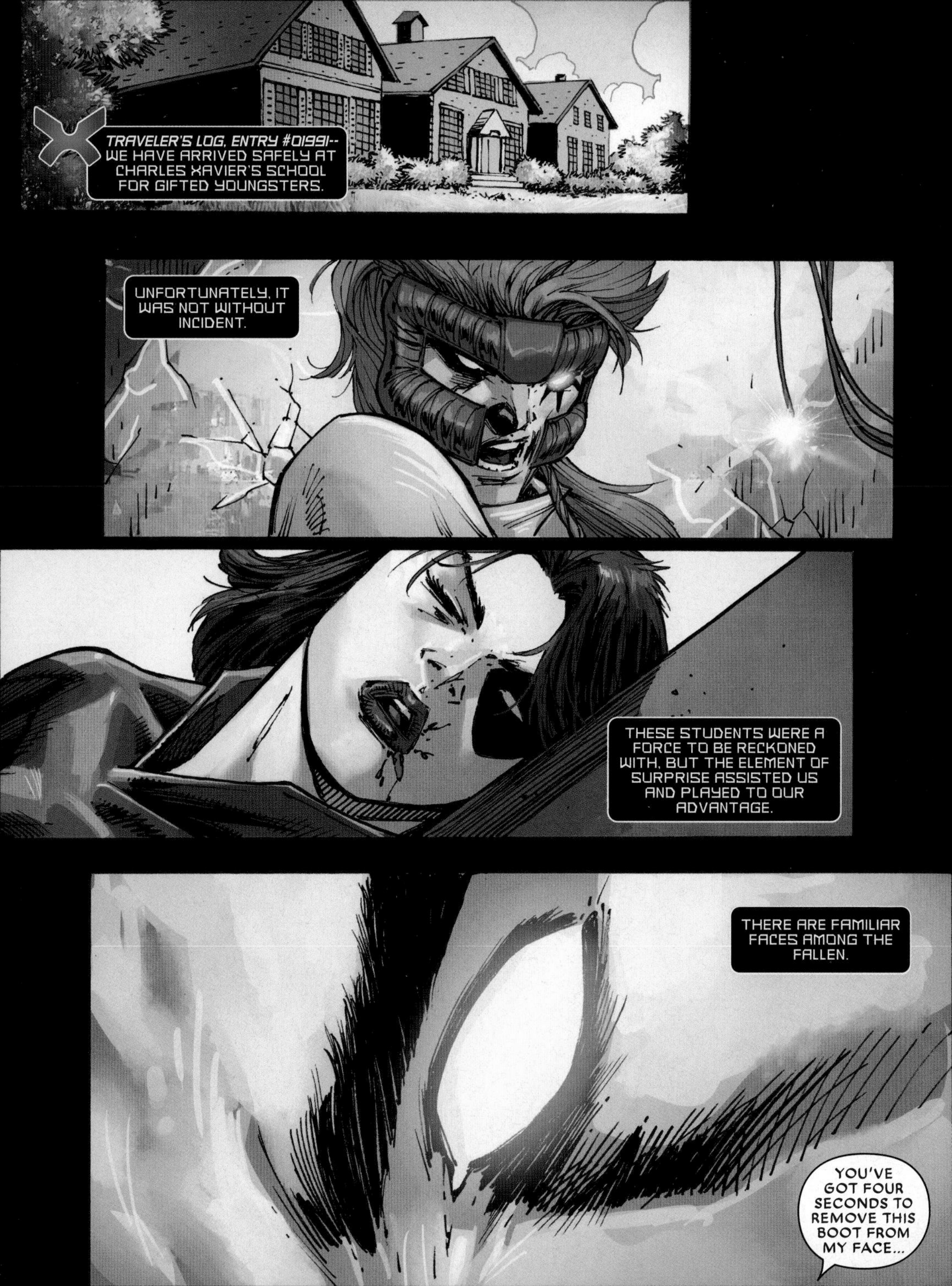
TRAVELER'S LOG, ENTRY #01991-- WE HAVE ARRIVED SAFELY AT CHARLES XAVIER'S SCHOOL FOR GIFTED YOUNGSTERS.
UNFORTUNATELY, IT WAS NOT WITHOUT INCIDENT.
THESE STUDENTS WERE A FORCE TO BE RECKONED WITH, BUT THE ELEMENT OF SURPRISE ASSISTED US AND PLAYED TO OUR ADVANTAGE.
THERE ARE FAMILIAR FACES AMONG THE FALLEN.
YOU'VE GOT FOUR SECONDS TO REMOVE THIS BOOT FROM MY FACE...

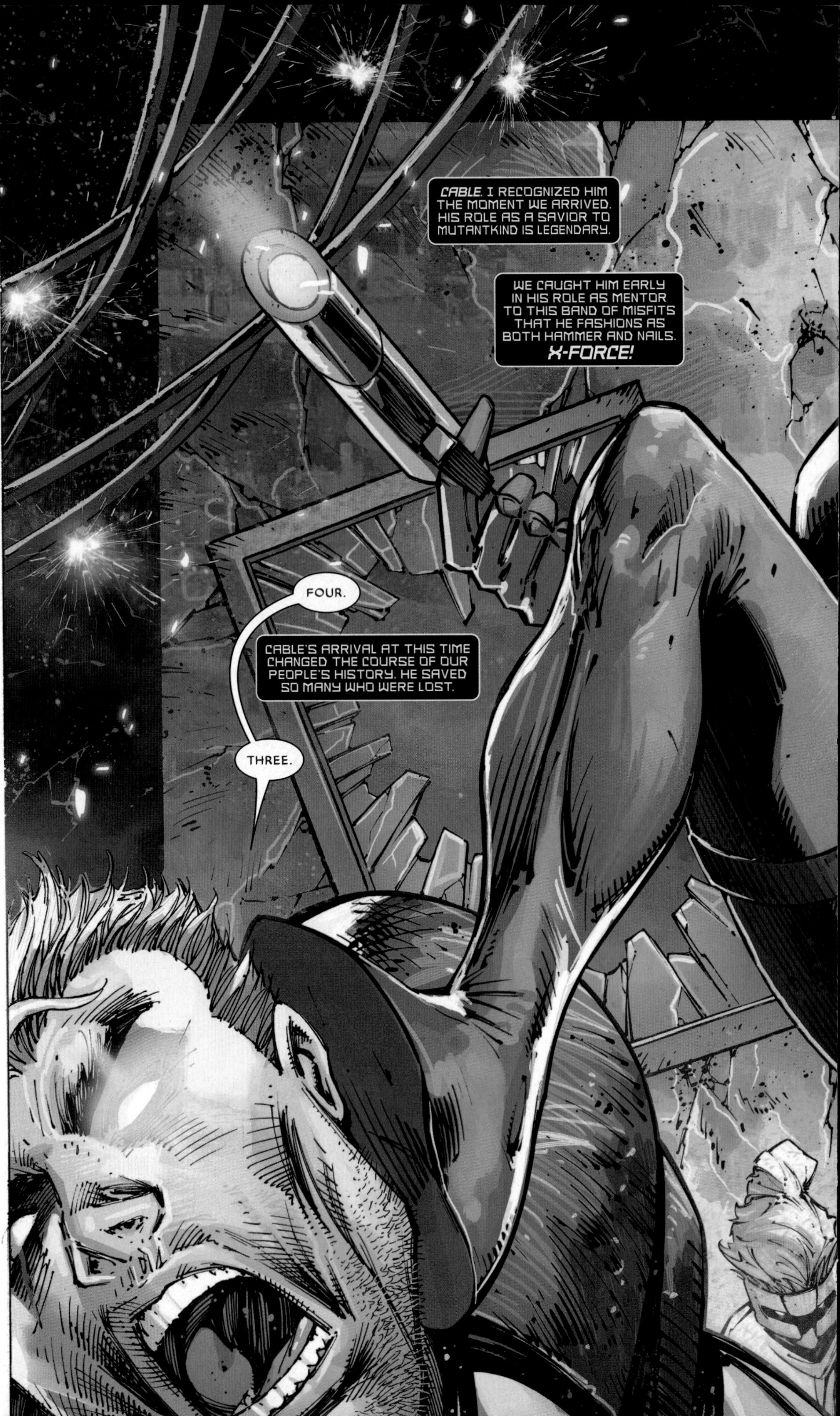
CABLE. I RECOGNIZED HIM THE MOMENT WE ARRIVED. HIS ROLE AS A SAVIOR TO MUTANTKIND IS LEGENDARY.
WE CAUGHT HIM EARLY IN HIS ROLE AS MENTOR TO THIS BAND OF MISFITS THAT HE FASHIONS AS BOTH HAMMER AND NAILS. X-FORCE!
FOUR.
CABLE'S ARRIVAL AT THIS TIME CHANGED THE COURSE OF OUR PEOPLE'S HISTORY. HE SAVED SO MANY WHO WERE LOST.
THREE.

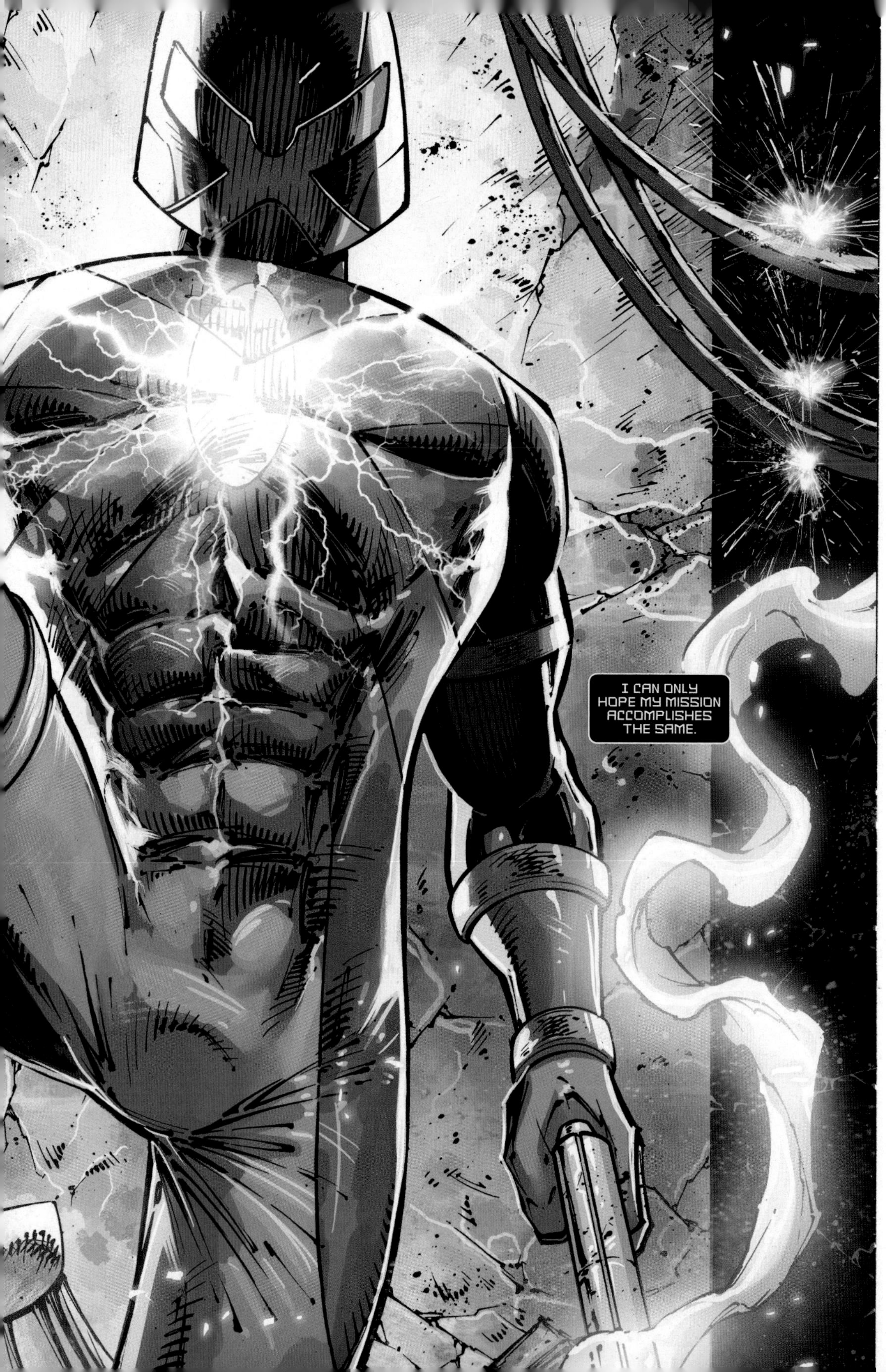
I CAN ONLY HOPE MY MISSION ACCOMPLISHES THE SAME.

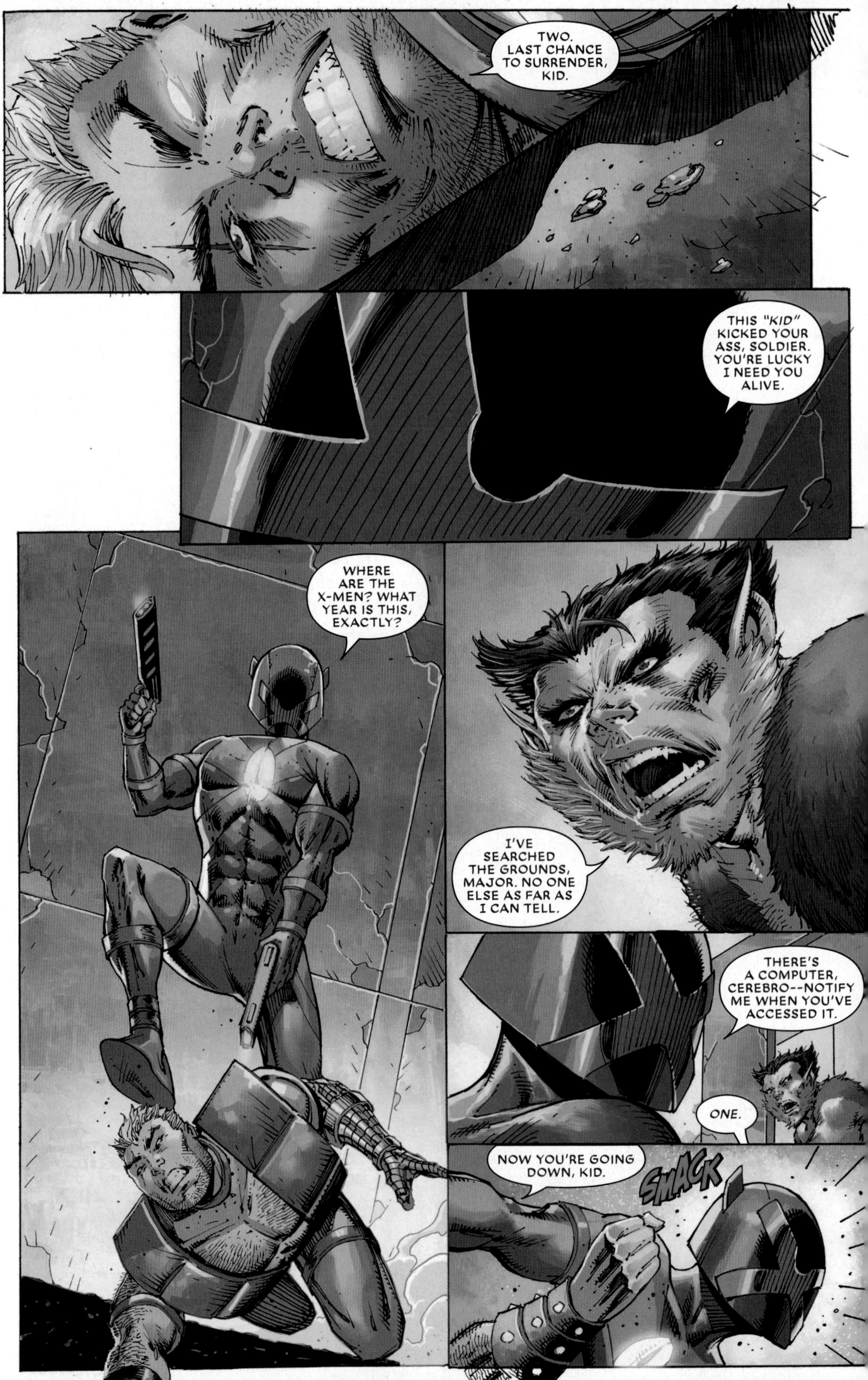
TWO. LAST CHANCE TO SURRENDER, KID.
THIS "KID" KICKED YOUR ASS, SOLDIER. YOU'RE LUCKY I NEED YOU ALIVE.
WHERE ARE THE X-MEN? WHAT YEAR IS THIS, EXACTLY?
I'VE SEARCHED THE GROUNDS, MAJOR. NO ONE ELSE AS FAR AS I CAN TELL.
THERE'S A COMPUTER, CEREBRO--NOTIFY ME WHEN YOU'VE ACCESSED IT.
ONE.
NOW YOU'RE GOING DOWN, KID.
SMACK

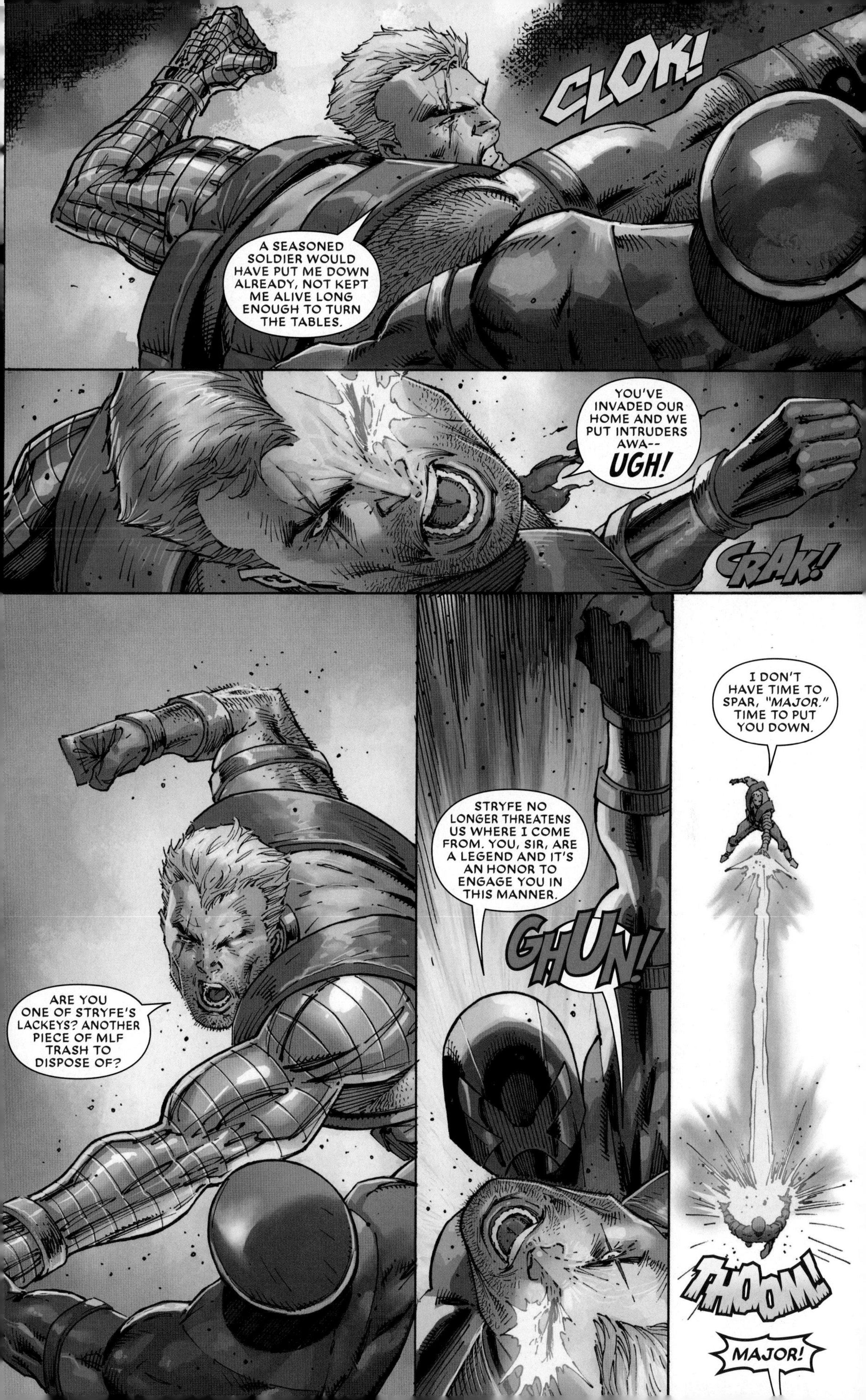
CLOK!
A SEASONED SOLDIER WOULD HAVE PUT ME DOWN ALREADY, NOT KEPT ME ALIVE LONG ENOUGH TO TURN THE TABLES.
YOU'VE INVADED OUR HOME AND WE PUT INTRUDERS AWA-- UGH!
CRAK!
ARE YOU ONE OF STRYFE'S LACKEYS? ANOTHER PIECE OF MLF TRASH TO DISPOSE OF?
STRYFE NO LONGER THREATENS US WHERE I COME FROM. YOU, SIR, ARE A LEGEND AND IT'S AN HONOR TO ENGAGE YOU IN THIS MANNER.
GHUN!
I DON'T HAVE TIME TO SPAR, "MAJOR." TIME TO PUT YOU DOWN.
THOOM!
MAJOR!

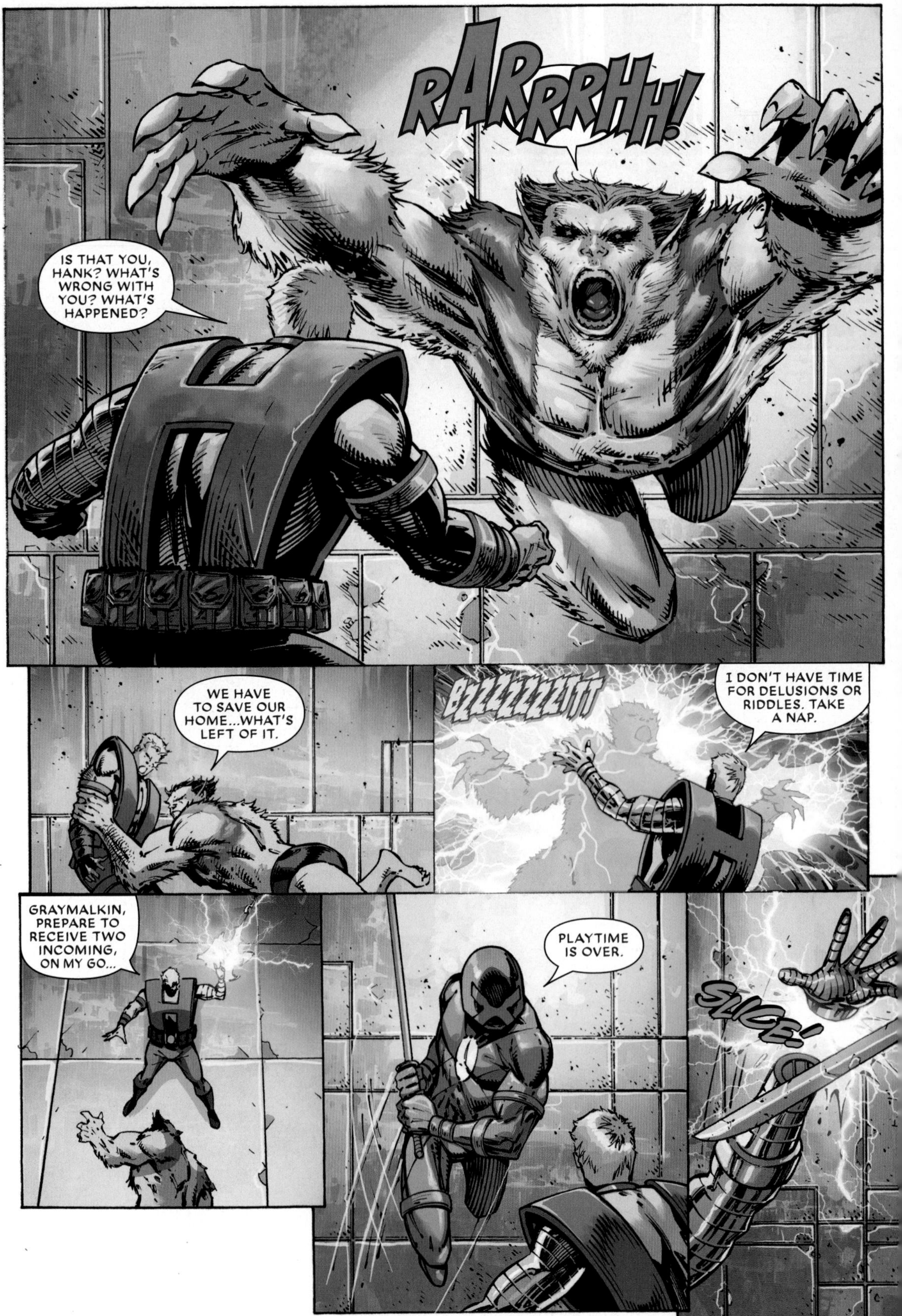
RARRRHH!
IS THAT YOU, HANK? WHAT'S WRONG WITH YOU? WHAT'S HAPPENED?
WE HAVE TO SAVE OUR HOME...WHAT'S LEFT OF IT.
BZZZZZZZZTTT
I DON'T HAVE TIME FOR DELUSIONS OR RIDDLES. TAKE A NAP.
GRAYMALKIN, PREPARE TO RECEIVE TWO INCOMING, ON MY GO...
PLAYTIME IS OVER.
SLICE!

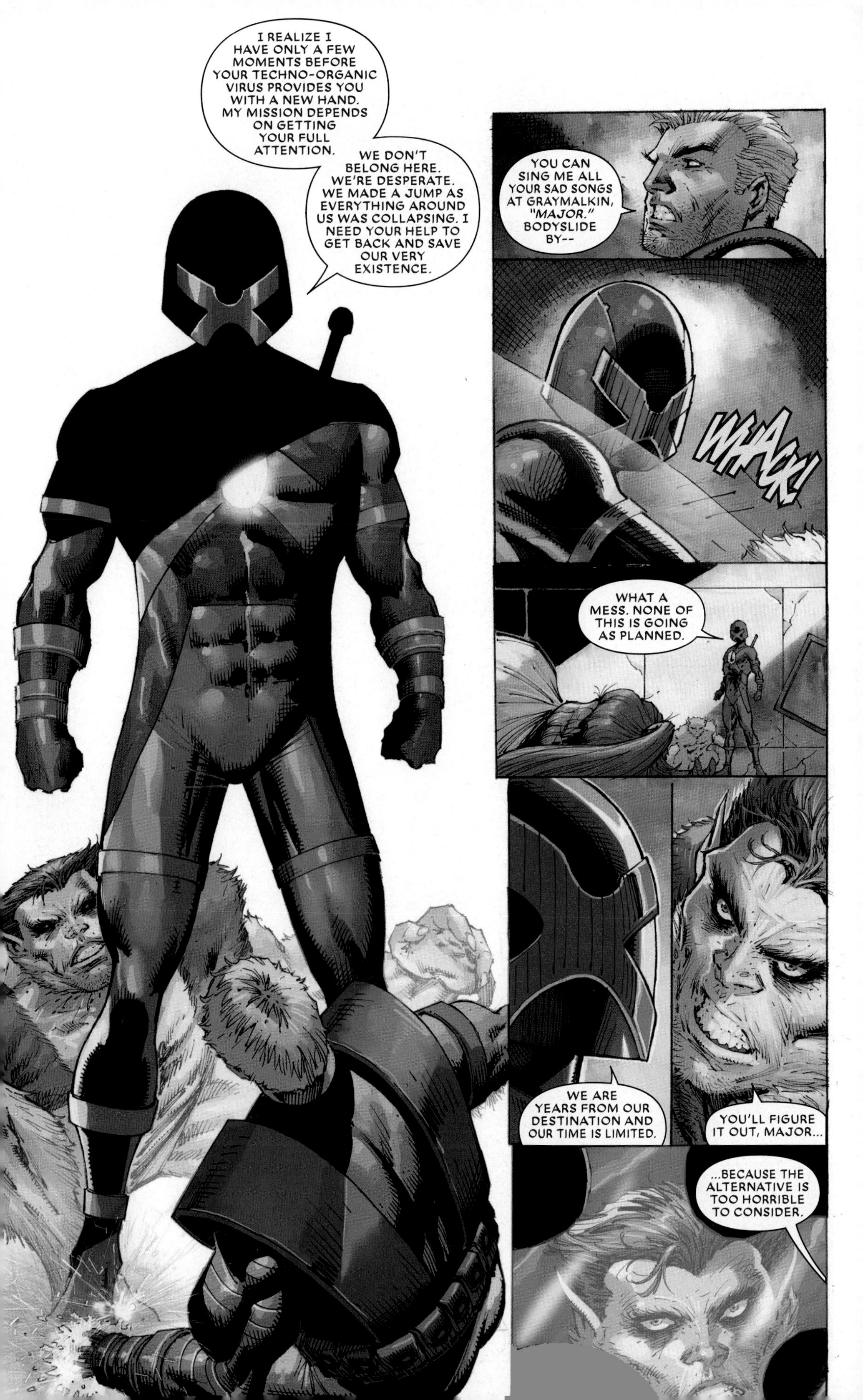
I REALIZE I HAVE ONLY A FEW MOMENTS BEFORE YOUR TECHNO-ORGANIC VIRUS PROVIDES YOU WITH A NEW HAND. MY MISSION DEPENDS ON GETTING YOUR FULL ATTENTION.
WE DON'T BELONG HERE. WE'RE DESPERATE. WE MADE A JUMP AS EVERYTHING AROUND US WAS COLLAPSING. I NEED YOUR HELP TO GET BACK AND SAVE OUR VERY EXISTENCE.
YOU CAN SING ME ALL YOUR SAD SONGS AT GRAYMALKIN, "MAJOR." BODYSLIDE BY--
WHACK!
WHAT A MESS. NONE OF THIS IS GOING AS PLANNED.
WE ARE YEARS FROM OUR DESTINATION AND OUR TIME IS LIMITED.
YOU'LL FIGURE IT OUT, MAJOR...
...BECAUSE THE ALTERNATIVE IS TOO HORRIBLE TO CONSIDER.

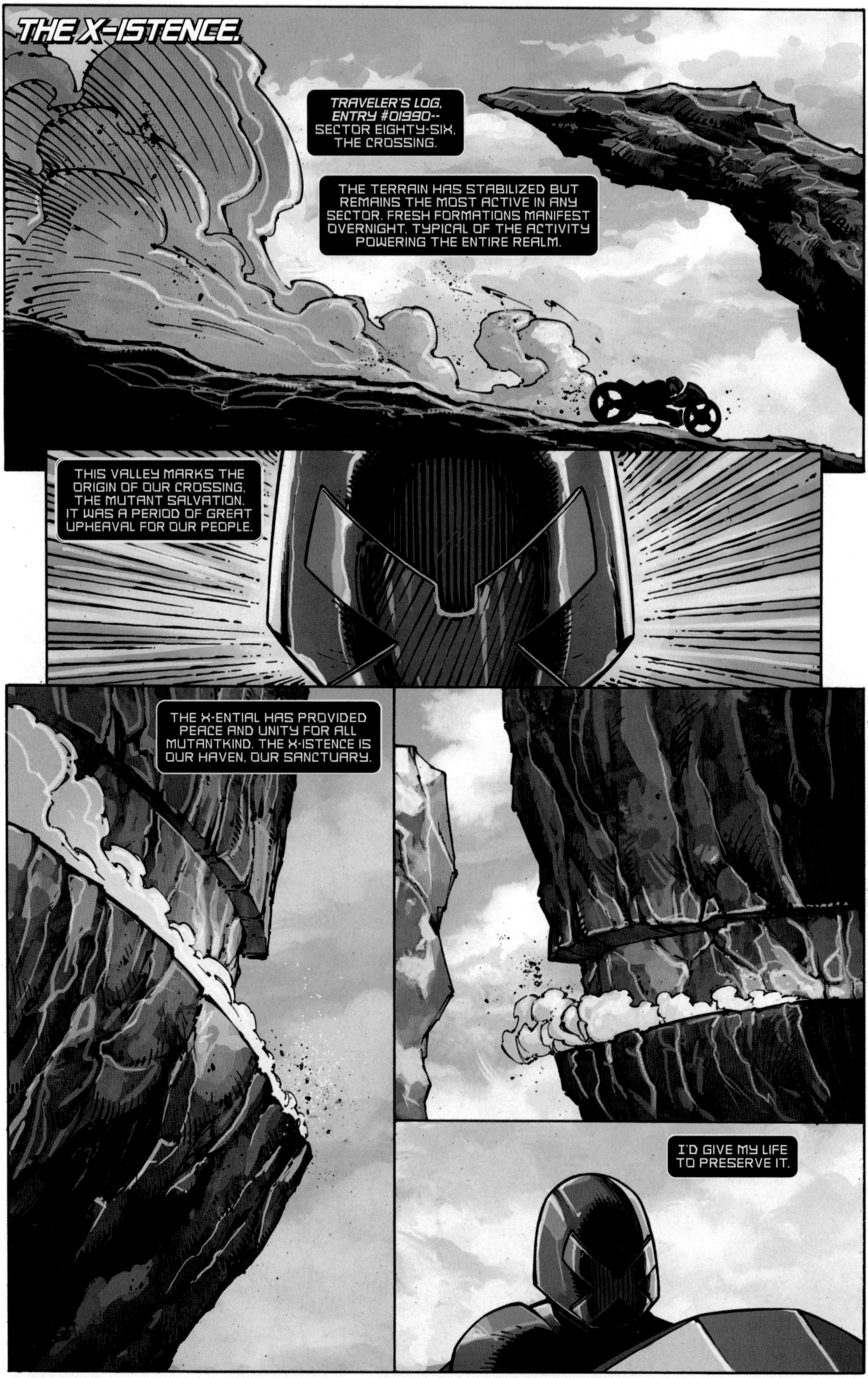
THE X-ISTENCE.
TRAVELER'S LOG, ENTRY #01990-- SECTOR EIGHTY-SIX, THE CROSSING.
THE TERRAIN HAS STABILIZED BUT REMAINS THE MOST ACTIVE IN ANY SECTOR. FRESH FORMATIONS MANIFEST OVERNIGHT, TYPICAL OF THE ACTIVITY POWERING THE ENTIRE REALM.
THIS VALLEY MARKS THE ORIGIN OF OUR CROSSING, THE MUTANT SALVATION. IT WAS A PERIOD OF GREAT UPHEAVAL FOR OUR PEOPLE.
THE X-ENTIAL HAS PROVIDED PEACE AND UNITY FOR ALL MUTANTKIND. THE X-ISTENCE IS OUR HAVEN, OUR SANCTUARY.
I'D GIVE MY LIFE TO PRESERVE IT.

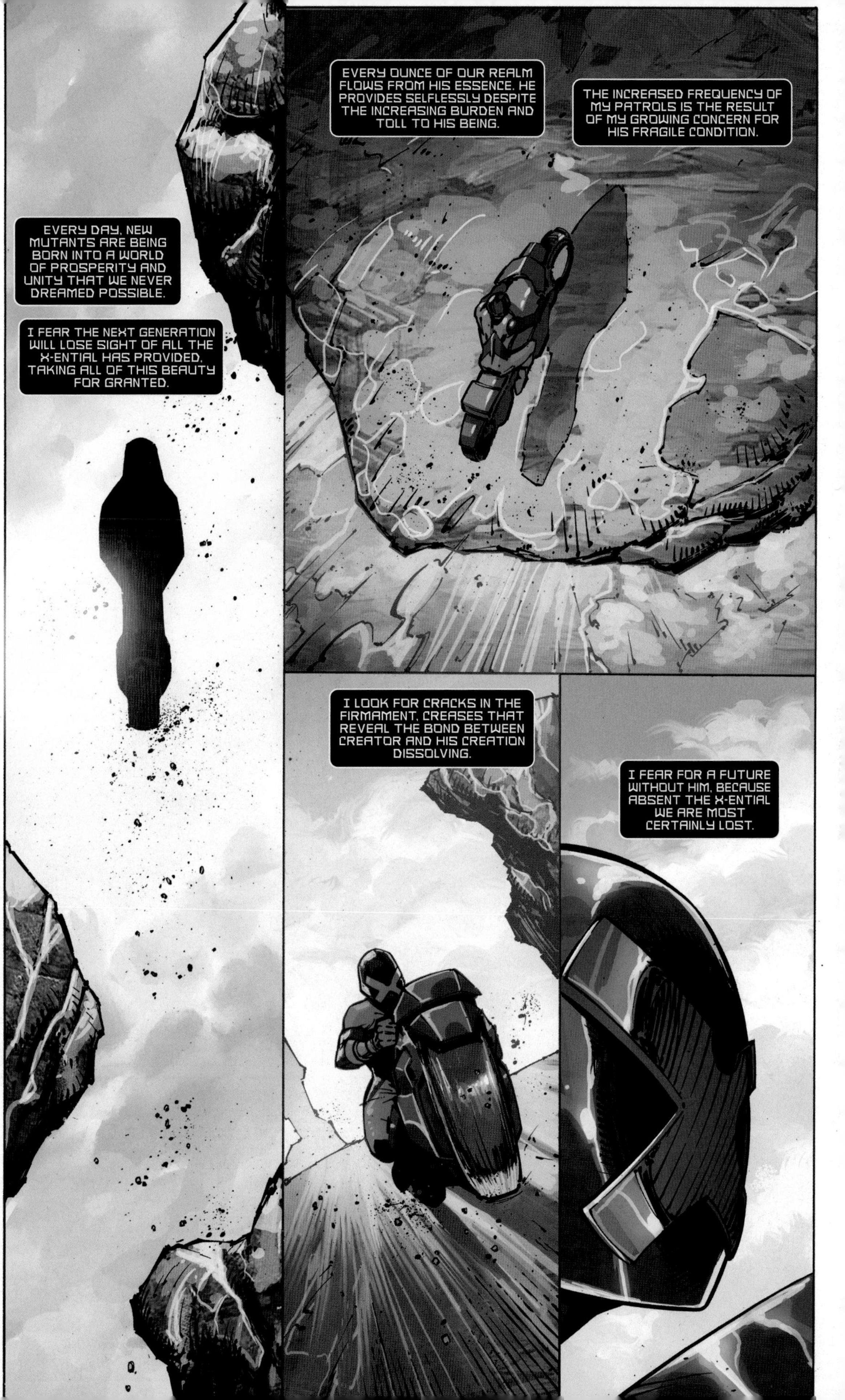
EVERY DAY, NEW MUTANTS ARE BEING BORN INTO A WORLD OF PROSPERITY AND UNITY THAT WE NEVER DREAMED POSSIBLE.
I FEAR THE NEXT GENERATION WILL LOSE SIGHT OF ALL THE X-ENTIAL HAS PROVIDED, TAKING ALL OF THIS BEAUTY FOR GRANTED.
EVERY OUNCE OF OUR REALM FLOWS FROM HIS ESSENCE. HE PROVIDES SELFLESSLY DESPITE THE INCREASING BURDEN AND TOLL TO HIS BEING.
THE INCREASED FREQUENCY OF MY PATROLS IS THE RESULT OF MY GROWING CONCERN FOR HIS FRAGILE CONDITION.
I LOOK FOR CRACKS IN THE FIRMAMENT, CREASES THAT REVEAL THE BOND BETWEEN CREATOR AND HIS CREATION DISSOLVING.
I FEAR FOR A FUTURE WITHOUT HIM, BECAUSE ABSENT THE X-ENTIAL WE ARE MOST CERTAINLY LOST.

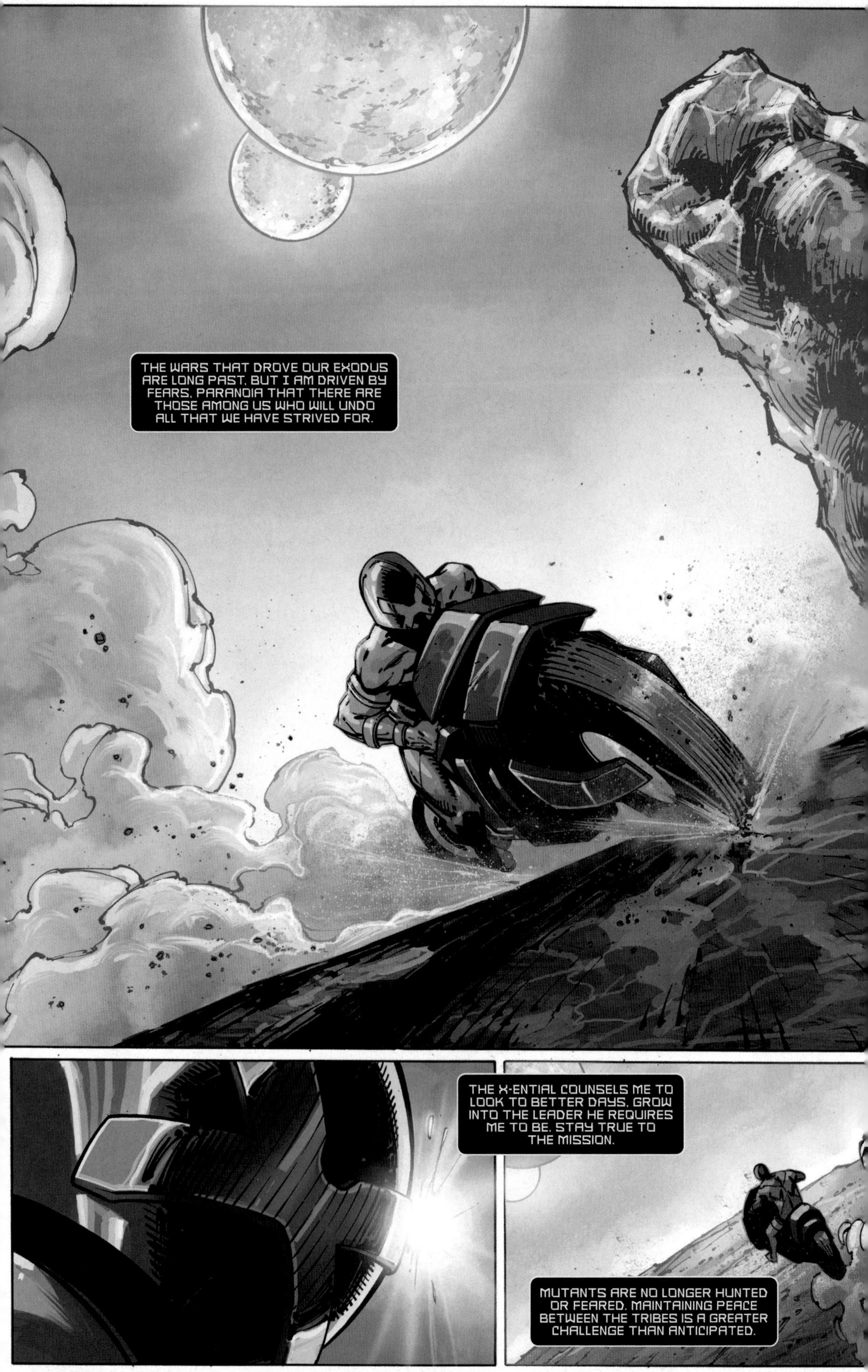
THE WARS THAT DROVE OUR EXODUS ARE LONG PAST, BUT I AM DRIVEN BY FEARS, PARANOIA THAT THERE ARE THOSE AMONG US WHO WILL UNDO ALL THAT WE HAVE STRIVED FOR.
THE X-ENTIAL COUNSELS ME TO LOOK TO BETTER DAYS, GROW INTO THE LEADER HE REQUIRES ME TO BE. STAY TRUE TO THE MISSION.
MUTANTS ARE NO LONGER HUNTED OR FEARED. MAINTAINING PEACE BETWEEN THE TRIBES IS A GREATER CHALLENGE THAN ANTICIPATED.

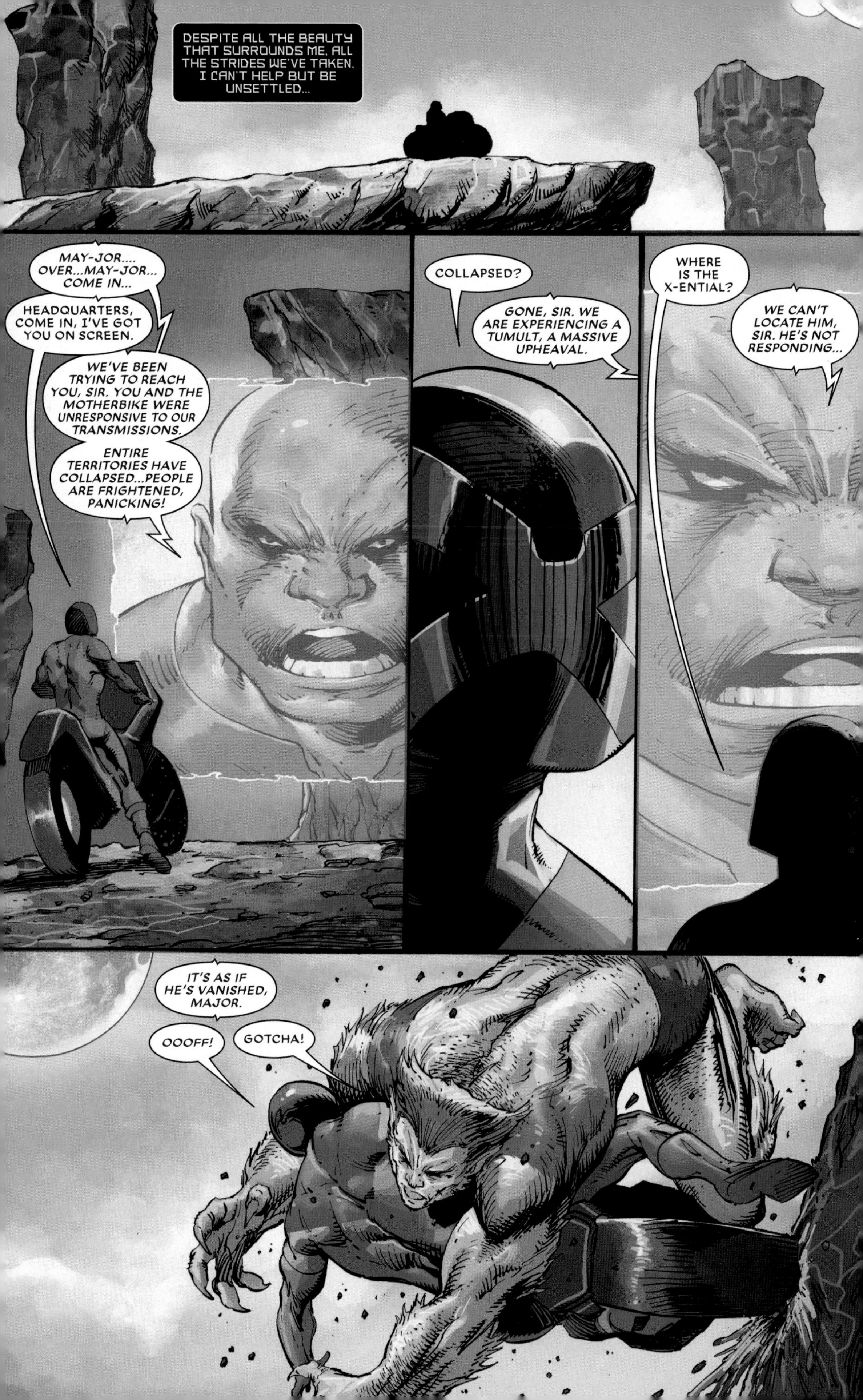
DESPITE ALL THE BEAUTY THAT SURROUNDS ME, ALL THE STRIDES WE'VE TAKEN, I CAN'T HELP BUT BE UNSETTLED...
MAY-JOR.... OVER...MAY-JOR... COME IN...
HEADQUARTERS, COME IN, I'VE GOT YOU ON SCREEN.
WE'VE BEEN TRYING TO REACH YOU, SIR. YOU AND THE MOTHERBIKE WERE UNRESPONSIVE TO OUR TRANSMISSIONS.
ENTIRE TERRITORIES HAVE COLLAPSED...PEOPLE ARE FRIGHTENED, PANICKING!
COLLAPSED?
GONE, SIR. WE ARE EXPERIENCING A TUMULT, A MASSIVE UPHEAVAL.
WHERE IS THE X-ENTIAL?
WE CAN'T LOCATE HIM, SIR. HE'S NOT RESPONDING...
IT'S AS IF HE'S VANISHED, MAJOR.
OOOFF!
GOTCHA!

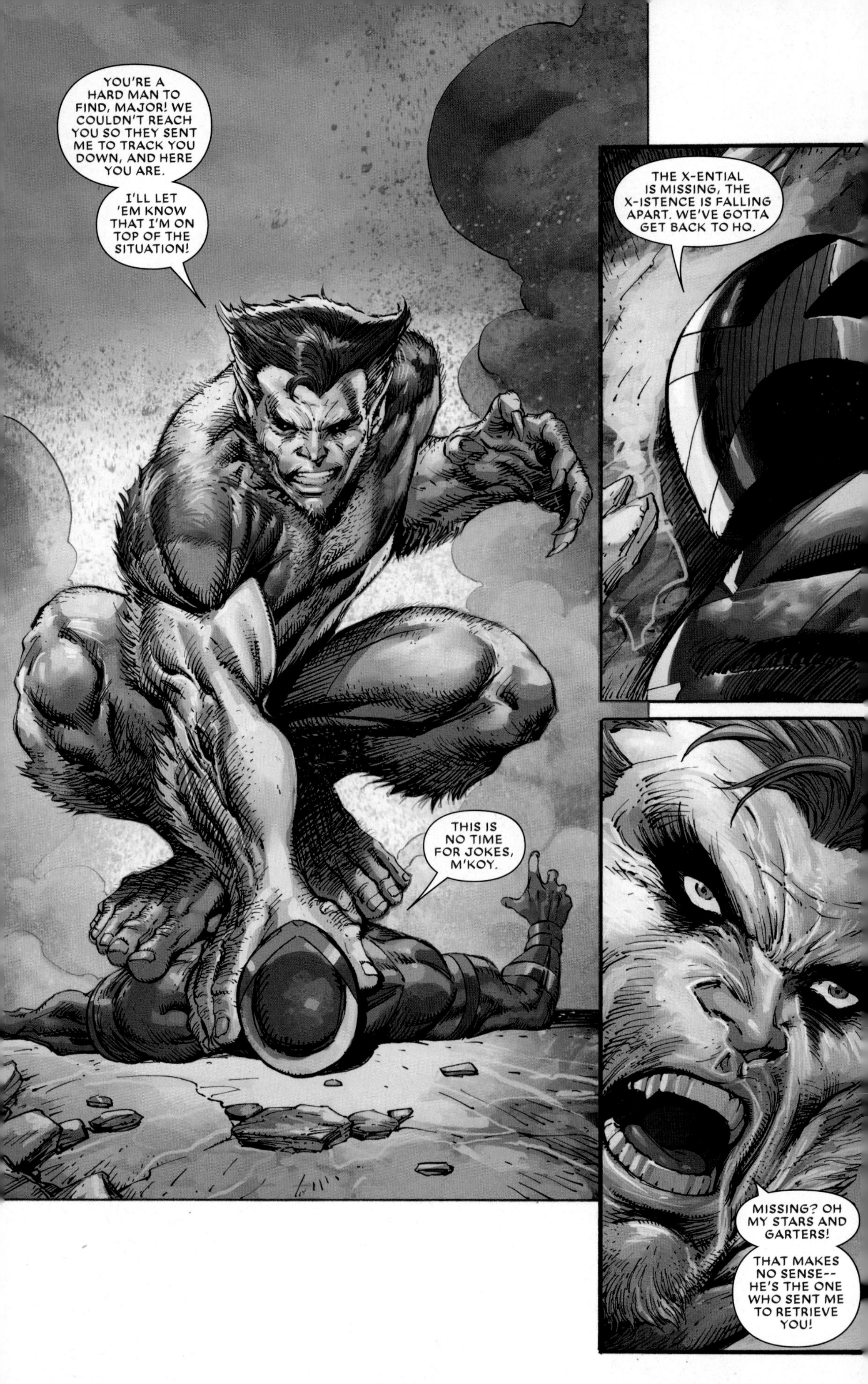
YOU'RE A HARD MAN TO FIND, MAJOR! WE COULDN'T REACH YOU SO THEY SENT ME TO TRACK YOU DOWN, AND HERE YOU ARE.
I'LL LET 'EM KNOW THAT I'M ON TOP OF THE SITUATION!
THIS IS NO TIME FOR JOKES, M'KOY.
THE X-ENTIAL IS MISSING, THE X-ISTENCE IS FALLING APART. WE'VE GOTTA GET BACK TO HQ.
MISSING? OH MY STARS AND GARTERS!
THAT MAKES NO SENSE-- HE'S THE ONE WHO SENT ME TO RETRIEVE YOU!

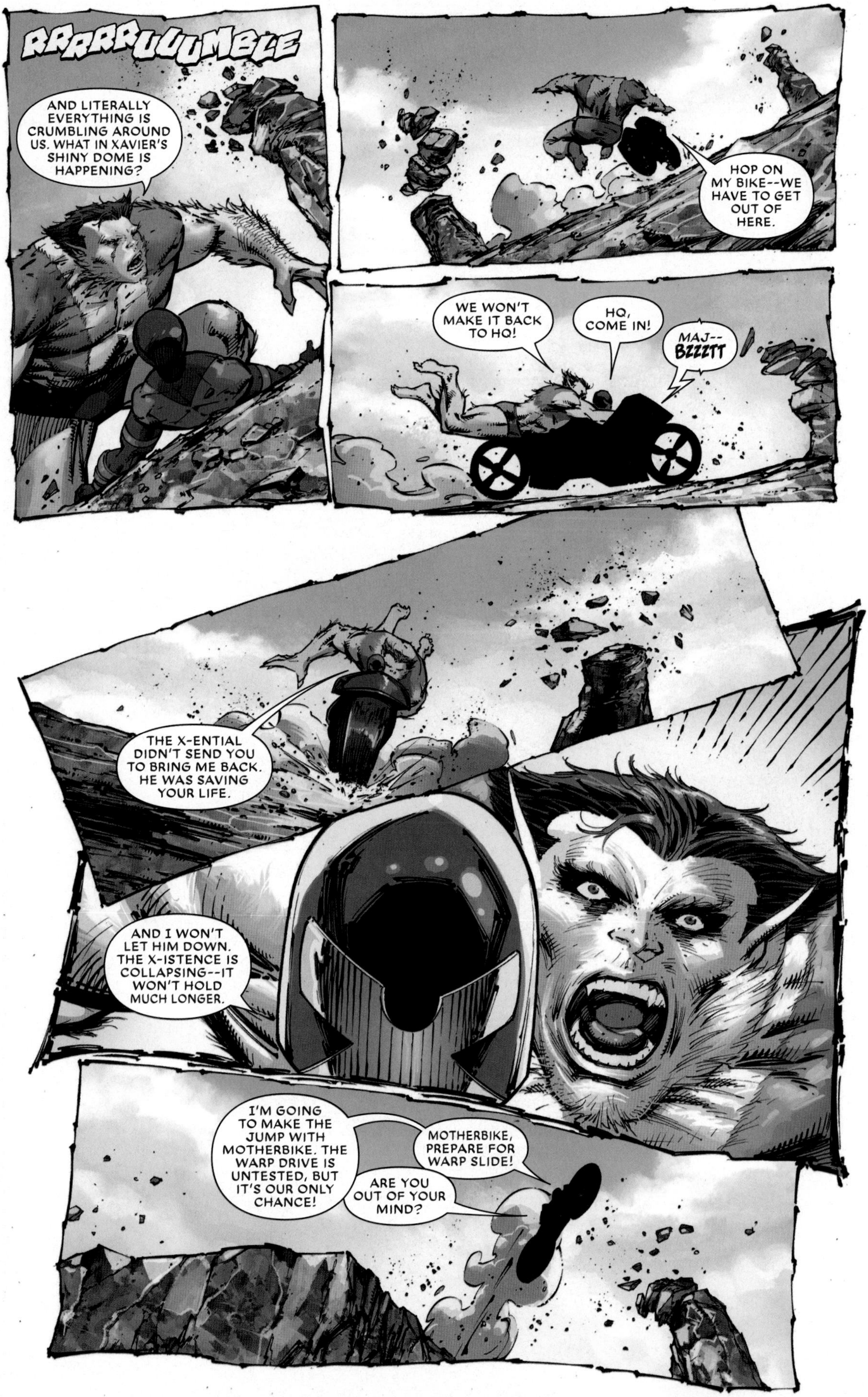
RRRRRUUUMBLE
AND LITERALLY EVERYTHING IS CRUMBLING AROUND US. WHAT IN XAVIER'S SHINY DOME IS HAPPENING?
HOP ON MY BIKE--WE HAVE TO GET OUT OF HERE.
WE WON'T MAKE IT BACK TO HQ!
HQ, COME IN!
MAJ-- BZZZTT
THE X-ENTIAL DIDN'T SEND YOU TO BRING ME BACK. HE WAS SAVING YOUR LIFE.
AND I WON'T LET HIM DOWN. THE X-ISTENCE IS COLLAPSING--IT WON'T HOLD MUCH LONGER.
I'M GOING TO MAKE THE JUMP WITH MOTHERBIKE. THE WARP DRIVE IS UNTESTED, BUT IT'S OUR ONLY CHANCE!
MOTHERBIKE, PREPARE FOR WARP SLIDE!
ARE YOU OUT OF YOUR MIND?

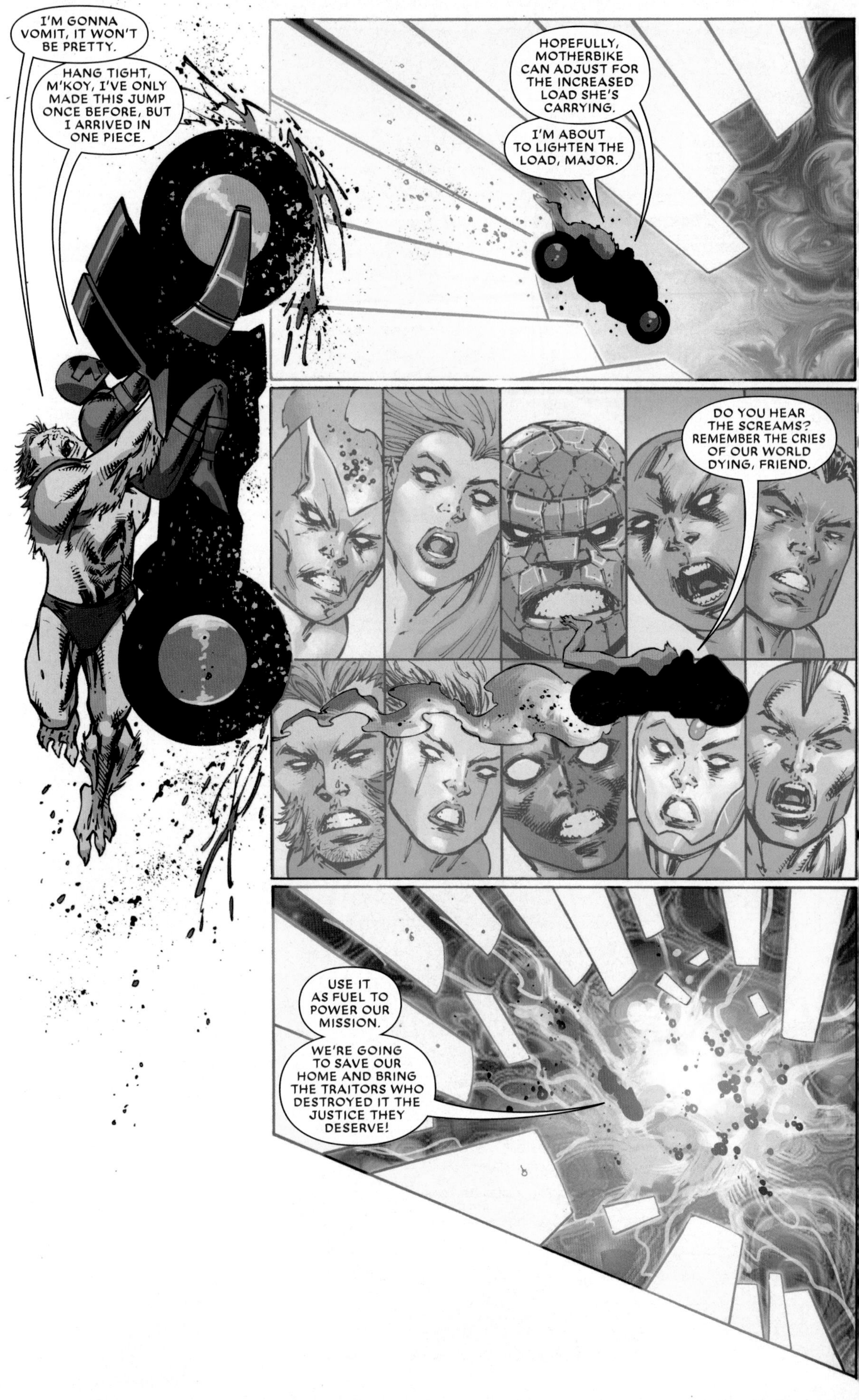

I'M GONNA VOMIT, IT WON'T BE PRETTY.
HANG TIGHT, M'KOY, I'VE ONLY MADE THIS JUMP ONCE BEFORE, BUT I ARRIVED IN ONE PIECE.
HOPEFULLY, MOTHERBIKE CAN ADJUST FOR THE INCREASED LOAD SHE'S CARRYING.
I'M ABOUT TO LIGHTEN THE LOAD, MAJOR.
DO YOU HEAR THE SCREAMS? REMEMBER THE CRIES OF OUR WORLD DYING, FRIEND.
USE IT AS FUEL TO POWER OUR MISSION.
WE'RE GOING TO SAVE OUR HOME AND BRING THE TRAITORS WHO DESTROYED IT THE JUSTICE THEY DESERVE!

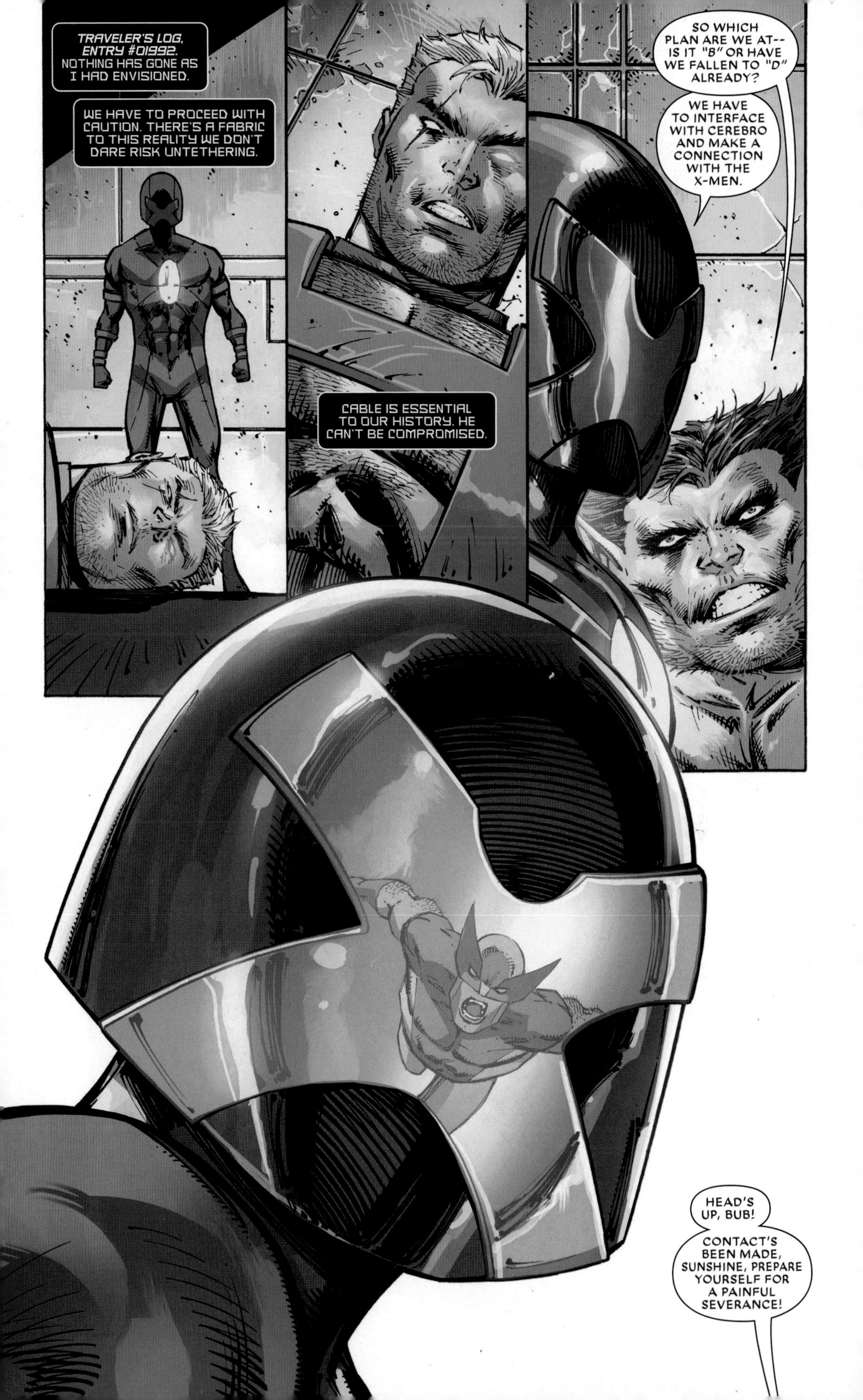
TRAVELER'S LOG, ENTRY #01992. NOTHING HAS GONE AS I HAD ENVISIONED.
WE HAVE TO PROCEED WITH CAUTION. THERE'S A FABRIC TO THIS REALITY WE DON'T DARE RISK UNTETHERING.
CABLE IS ESSENTIAL TO OUR HISTORY. HE CAN'T BE COMPROMISED.
SO WHICH PLAN ARE WE AT-- IS IT "B" OR HAVE WE FALLEN TO "D" ALREADY?
WE HAVE TO INTERFACE WITH CEREBRO AND MAKE A CONNECTION WITH THE X-MEN.
HEAD'S UP, BUB!
CONTACT'S BEEN MADE, SUNSHINE, PREPARE YOURSELF FOR A PAINFUL SEVERANCE!

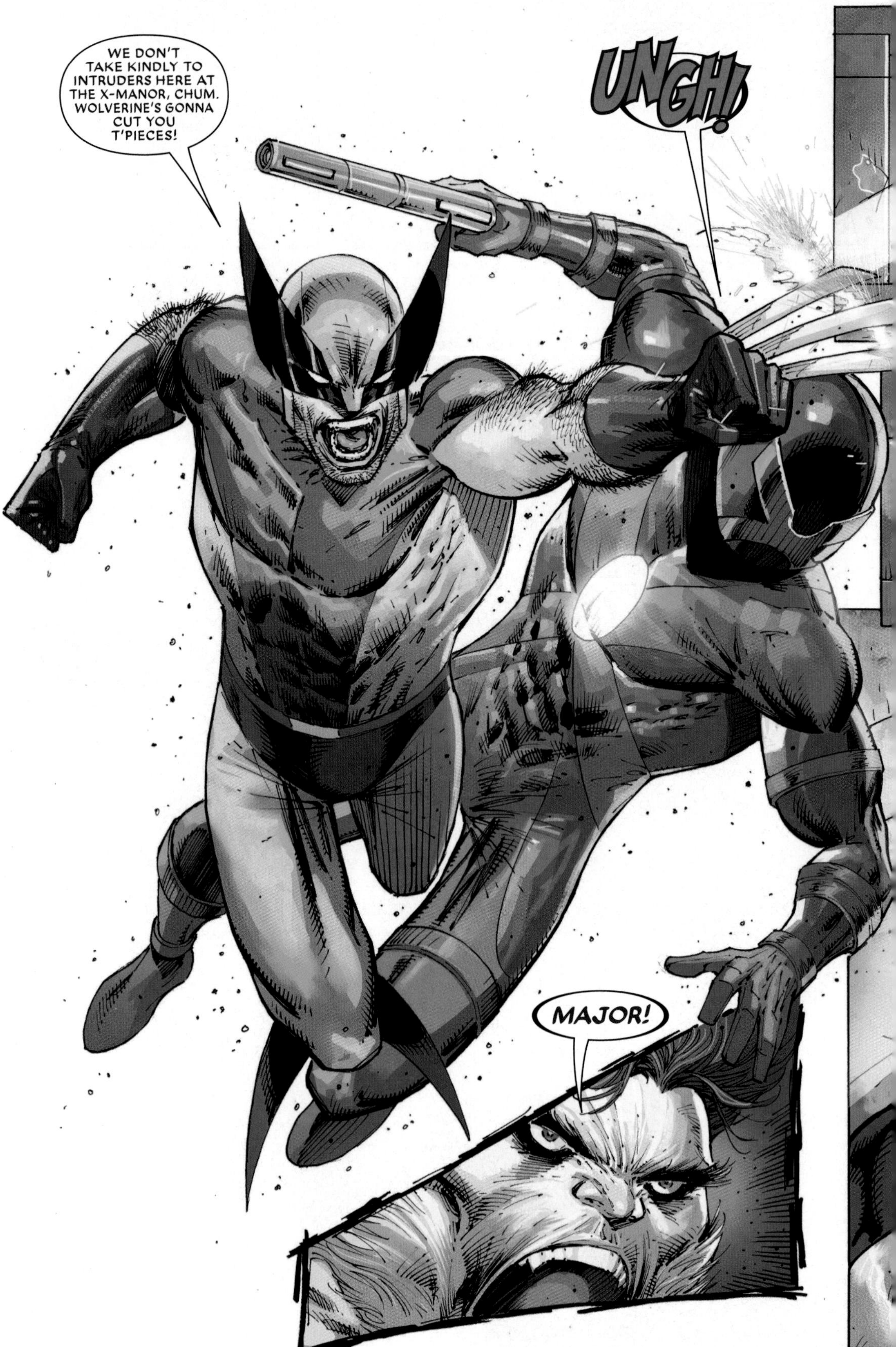
WE DON'T TAKE KINDLY TO INTRUDERS HERE AT THE X-MANOR, CHUM. WOLVERINE'S GONNA CUT YOU T'PIECES!
UNGH!
MAJOR!

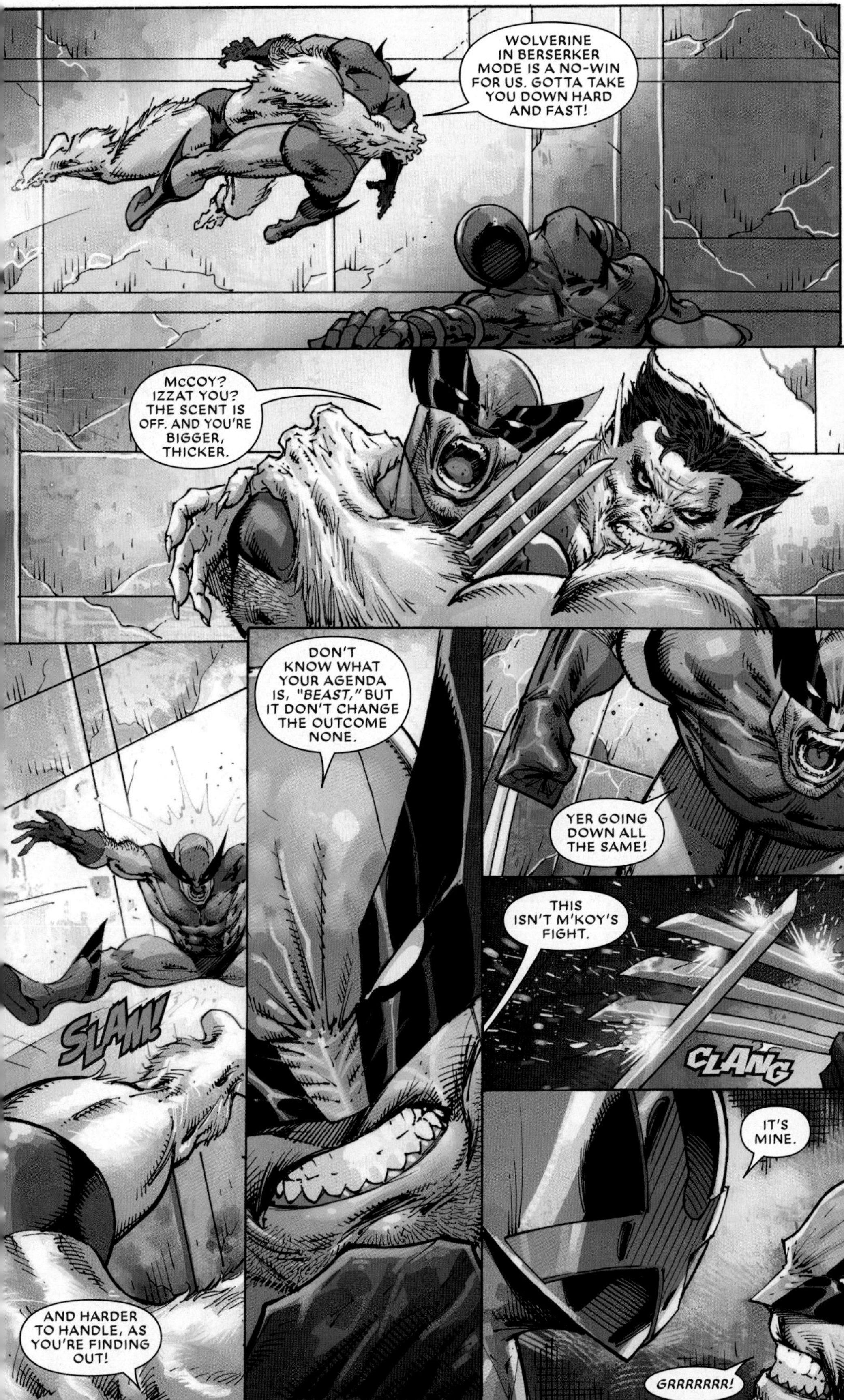
WOLVERINE IN BERSERKER MODE IS A NO-WIN FOR US. GOTTA TAKE YOU DOWN HARD AND FAST!
McCOY? IZZAT YOU? THE SCENT IS OFF. AND YOU'RE BIGGER, THICKER.
SLAM!
AND HARDER TO HANDLE, AS YOU'RE FINDING OUT!
DON'T KNOW WHAT YOUR AGENDA IS, "BEAST," BUT IT DON'T CHANGE THE OUTCOME NONE.
YER GOING DOWN ALL THE SAME!
THIS ISN'T M'KOY'S FIGHT.
CLANG
IT'S MINE.
GRRRRRRR!

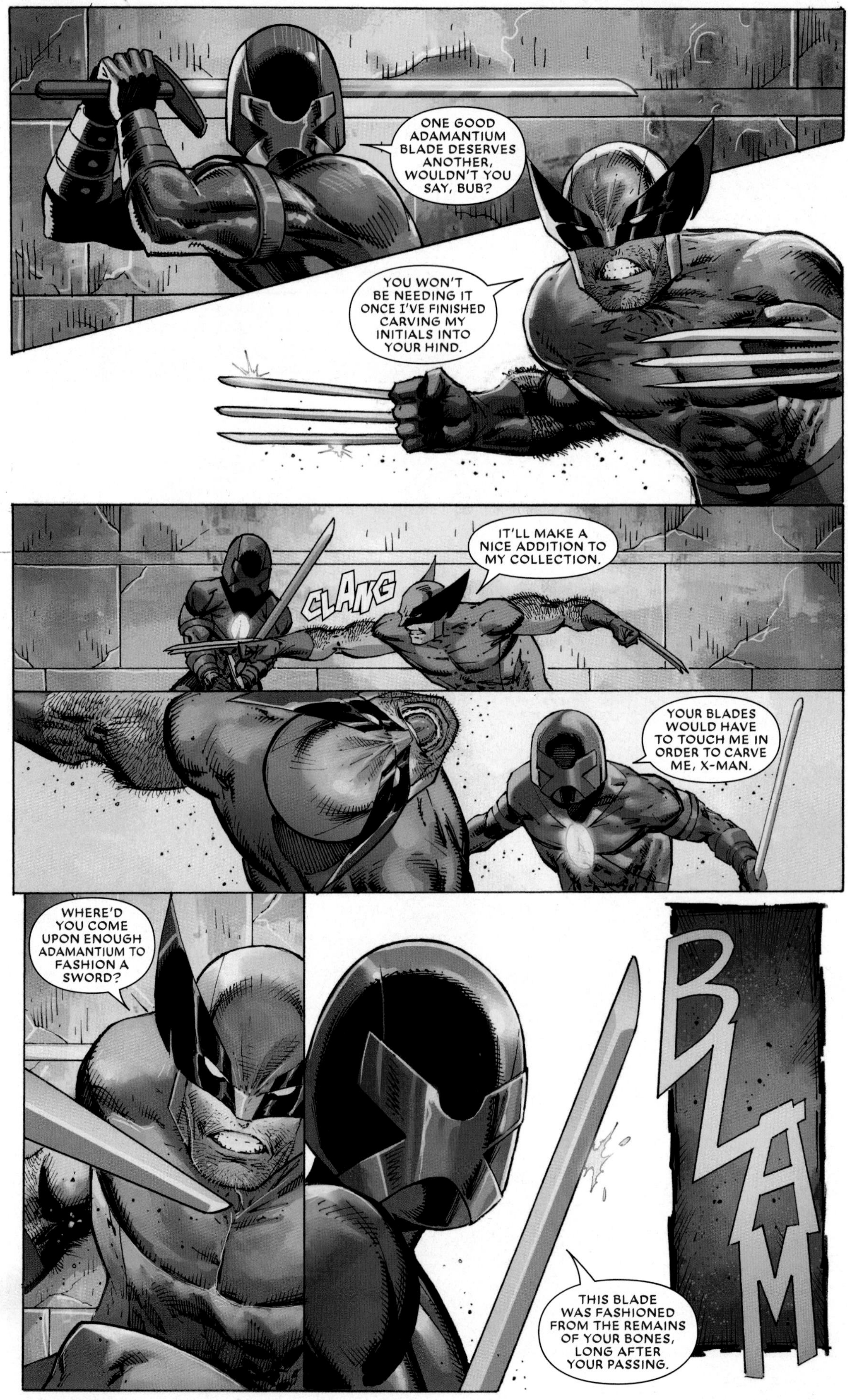
ONE GOOD ADAMANTIUM BLADE DESERVES ANOTHER, WOULDN'T YOU SAY, BUB?
YOU WON'T BE NEEDING IT ONCE I'VE FINISHED CARVING MY INITIALS INTO YOUR HIND.
IT'LL MAKE A NICE ADDITION TO MY COLLECTION.
CLANG
YOUR BLADES WOULD HAVE TO TOUCH ME IN ORDER TO CARVE ME, X-MAN.
WHERE'D YOU COME UPON ENOUGH ADAMANTIUM TO FASHION A SWORD?
BLAM
THIS BLADE WAS FASHIONED FROM THE REMAINS OF YOUR BONES, LONG AFTER YOUR PASSING.

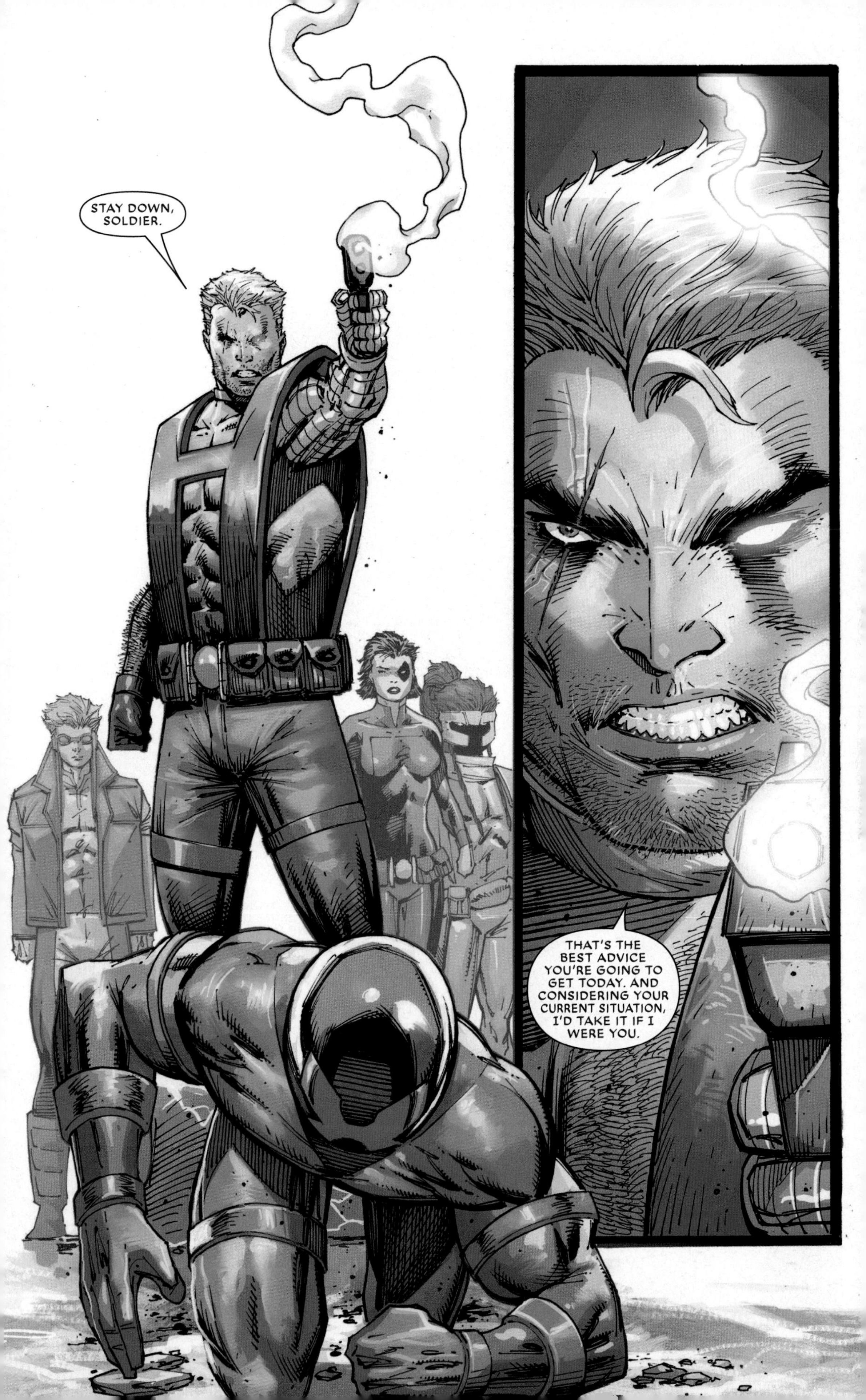
STAY DOWN, SOLDIER.
THAT'S THE BEST ADVICE YOU'RE GOING TO GET TODAY. AND CONSIDERING YOUR CURRENT SITUATION, I'D TAKE IT IF I WERE YOU.

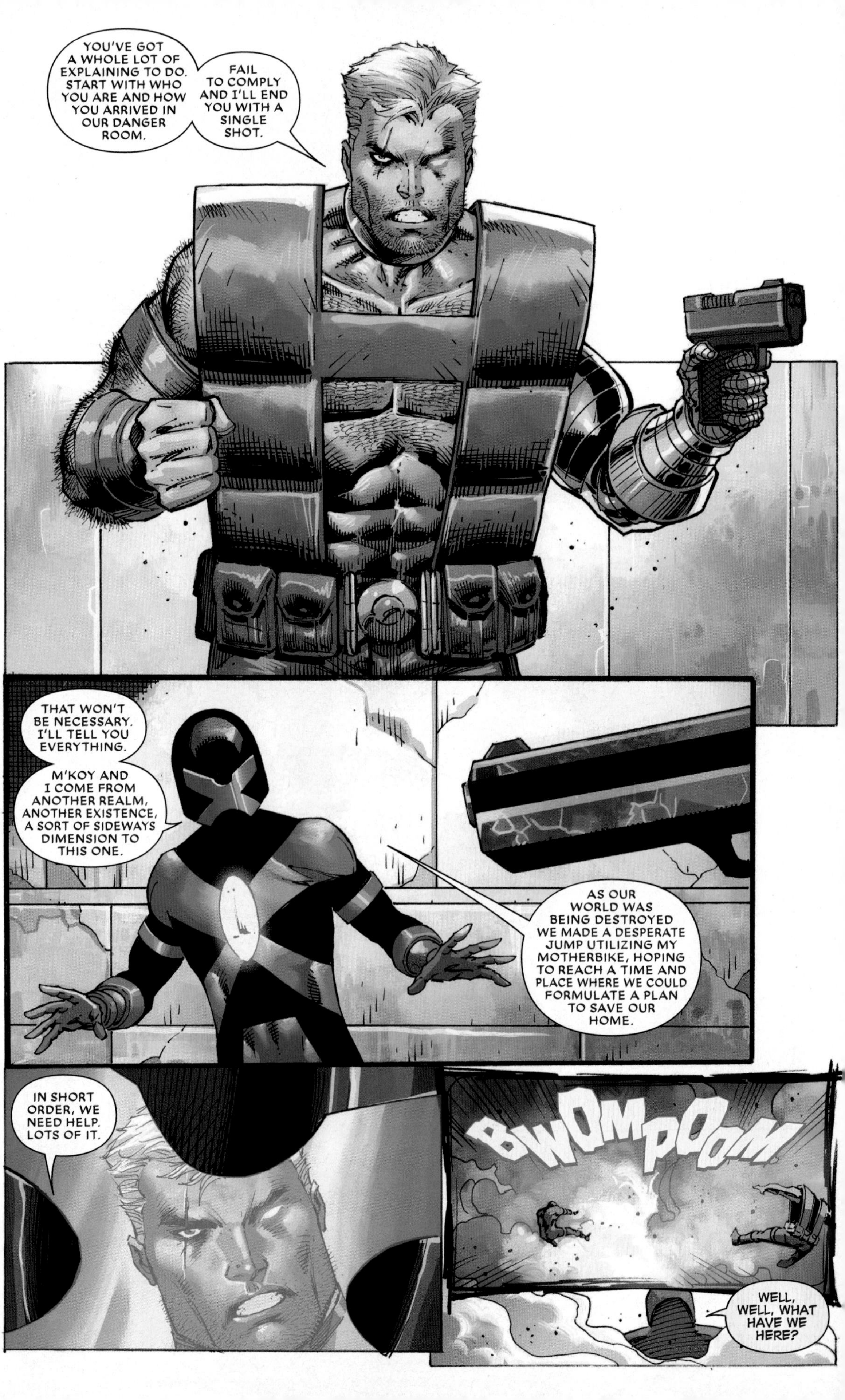
YOU'VE GOT A WHOLE LOT OF EXPLAINING TO DO. START WITH WHO YOU ARE AND HOW YOU ARRIVED IN OUR DANGER ROOM.
FAIL TO COMPLY AND I'LL END YOU WITH A SINGLE SHOT.
THAT WON'T BE NECESSARY. I'LL TELL YOU EVERYTHING.
M'KOY AND I COME FROM ANOTHER REALM, ANOTHER EXISTENCE, A SORT OF SIDEWAYS DIMENSION TO THIS ONE.
AS OUR WORLD WAS BEING DESTROYED WE MADE A DESPERATE JUMP UTILIZING MY MOTHERBIKE, HOPING TO REACH A TIME AND PLACE WHERE WE COULD FORMULATE A PLAN TO SAVE OUR HOME.
IN SHORT ORDER, WE NEED HELP. LOTS OF IT.
BWOMPOOM
WELL, WELL, WHAT HAVE WE HERE?

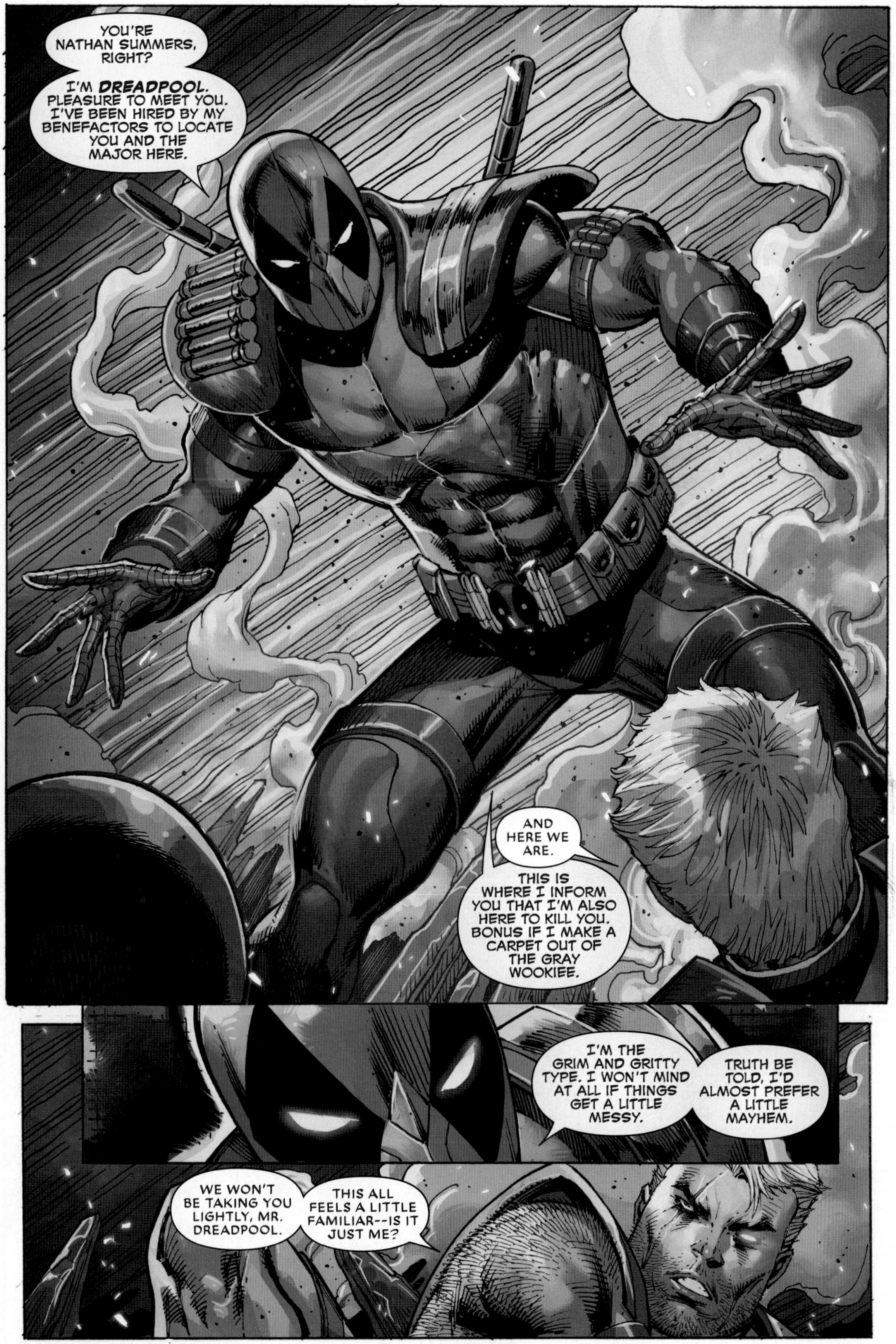
YOU'RE NATHAN SUMMERS, RIGHT?
I'M DREADPOOL. PLEASURE TO MEET YOU. I'VE BEEN HIRED BY MY BENEFACTORS TO LOCATE YOU AND THE MAJOR HERE.
AND HERE WE ARE.
THIS IS WHERE I INFORM YOU THAT I'M ALSO HERE TO KILL YOU. BONUS IF I MAKE A CARPET OUT OF THE GRAY WOOKIEE.
I'M THE GRIM AND GRITTY TYPE. I WON'T MIND AT ALL IF THINGS GET A LITTLE MESSY.
TRUTH BE TOLD, I'D ALMOST PREFER A LITTLE MAYHEM.
WE WON'T BE TAKING YOU LIGHTLY, MR. DREADPOOL.
THIS ALL FEELS A LITTLE FAMILIAR--IS IT JUST ME?

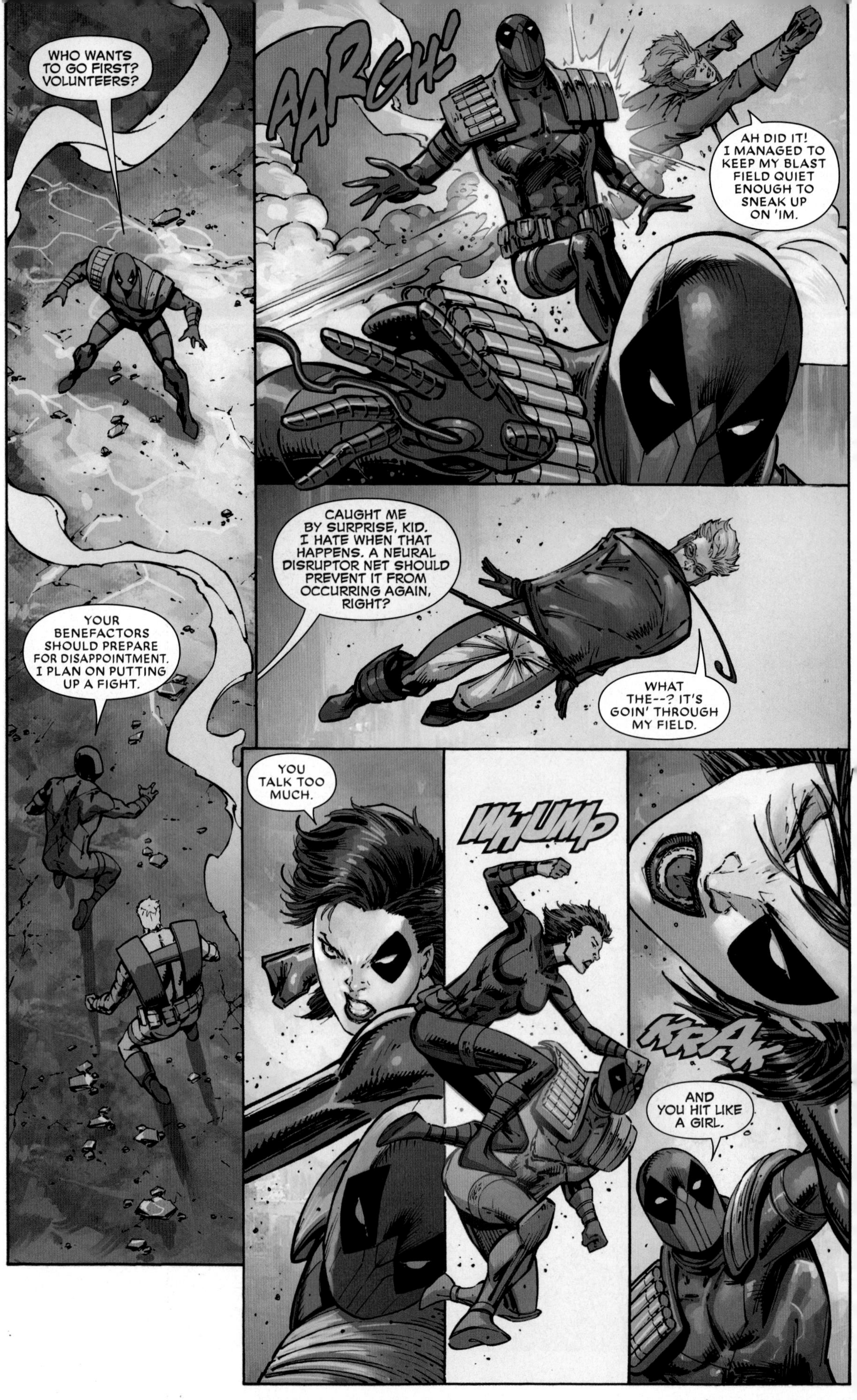
WHO WANTS TO GO FIRST? VOLUNTEERS?
YOUR BENEFACTORS SHOULD PREPARE FOR DISAPPOINTMENT. I PLAN ON PUTTING UP A FIGHT.
AARGH!
AH DID IT! I MANAGED TO KEEP MY BLAST FIELD QUIET ENOUGH TO SNEAK UP ON 'IM.
CAUGHT ME BY SURPRISE, KID. I HATE WHEN THAT HAPPENS. A NEURAL DISRUPTOR NET SHOULD PREVENT IT FROM OCCURRING AGAIN, RIGHT?
WHAT THE--? IT'S GOIN' THROUGH MY FIELD.
YOU TALK TOO MUCH.
WHUMP
KRAK
AND YOU HIT LIKE A GIRL.

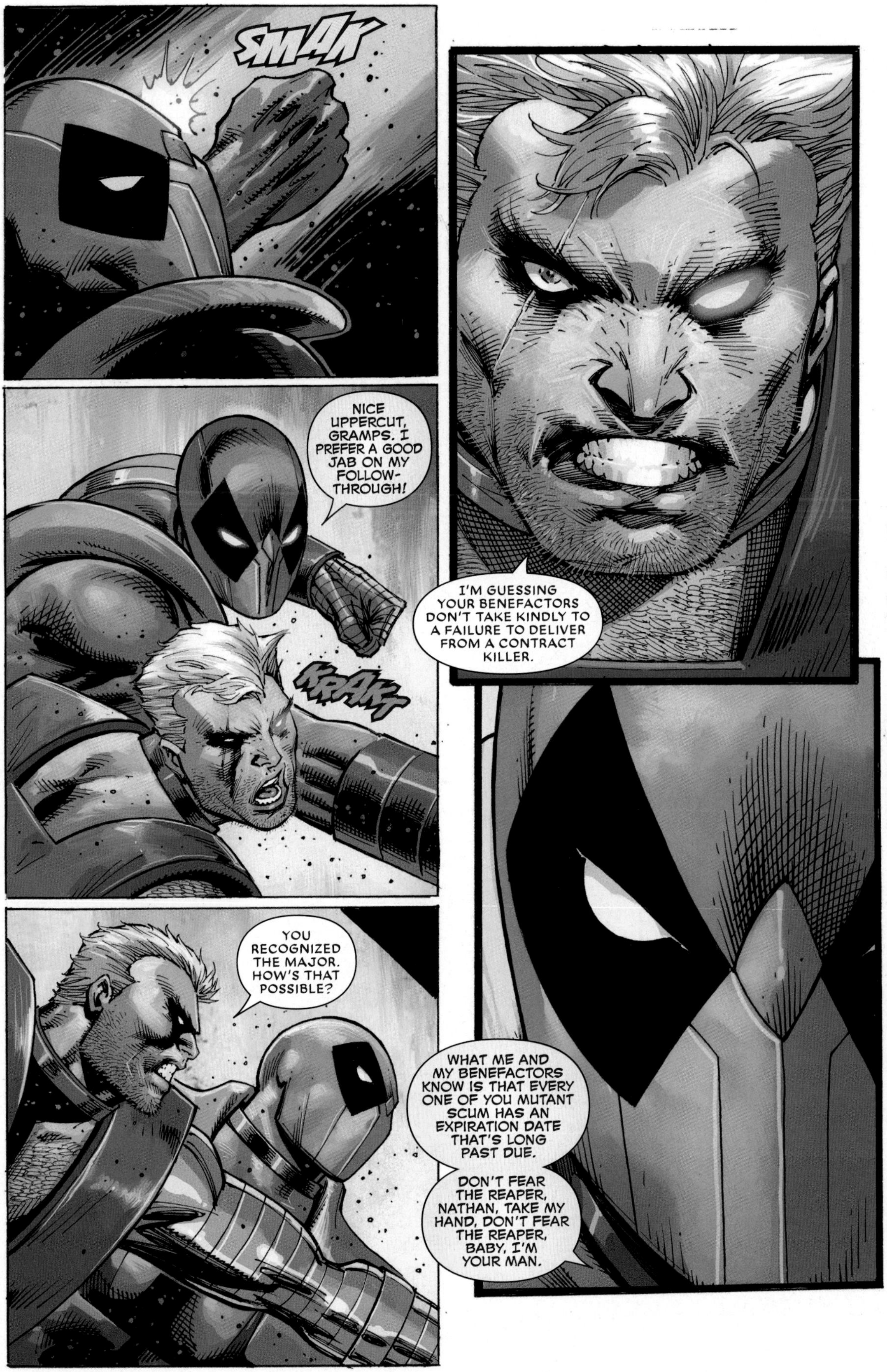
SMAK
NICE UPPERCUT, GRAMPS. I PREFER A GOOD JAB ON MY FOLLOW-THROUGH!
KRAKT
YOU RECOGNIZED THE MAJOR. HOW'S THAT POSSIBLE?
I'M GUESSING YOUR BENEFACTORS DON'T TAKE KINDLY TO A FAILURE TO DELIVER FROM A CONTRACT KILLER.
WHAT ME AND MY BENEFACTORS KNOW IS THAT EVERY ONE OF YOU MUTANT SCUM HAS AN EXPIRATION DATE THAT'S LONG PAST DUE.
DON'T FEAR THE REAPER, NATHAN, TAKE MY HAND, DON'T FEAR THE REAPER, BABY, I'M YOUR MAN.

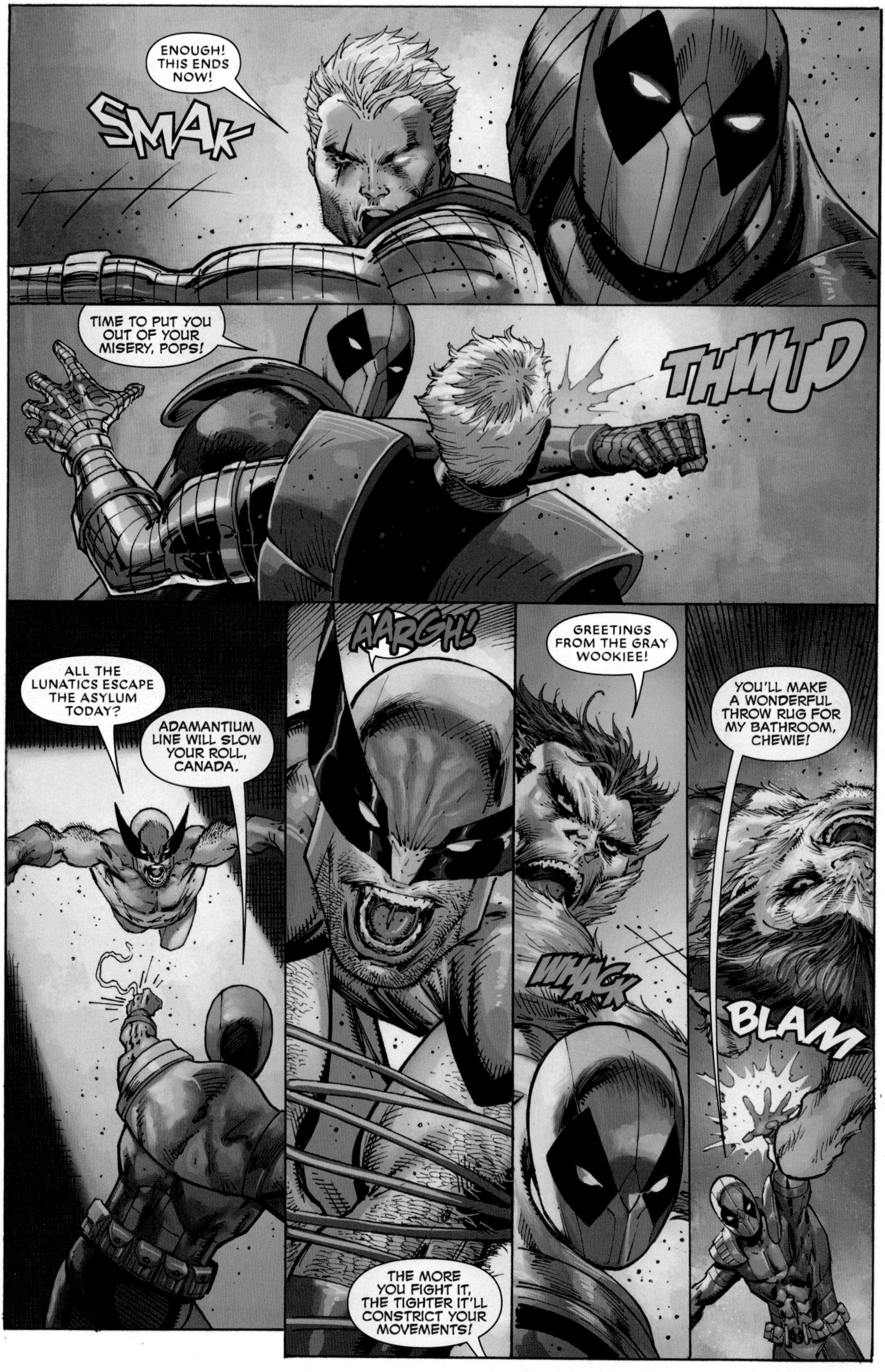
ENOUGH! THIS ENDS NOW!
SMAK
TIME TO PUT YOU OUT OF YOUR MISERY, POPS!
THWUD
ALL THE LUNATICS ESCAPE THE ASYLUM TODAY?
ADAMANTIUM LINE WILL SLOW YOUR ROLL, CANADA.
AARGH!
THE MORE YOU FIGHT IT, THE TIGHTER IT'LL CONSTRICT YOUR MOVEMENTS!
GREETINGS FROM THE GRAY WOOKIEE!
WHACK
YOU'LL MAKE A WONDERFUL THROW RUG FOR MY BATHROOM, CHEWIE!
BLAM

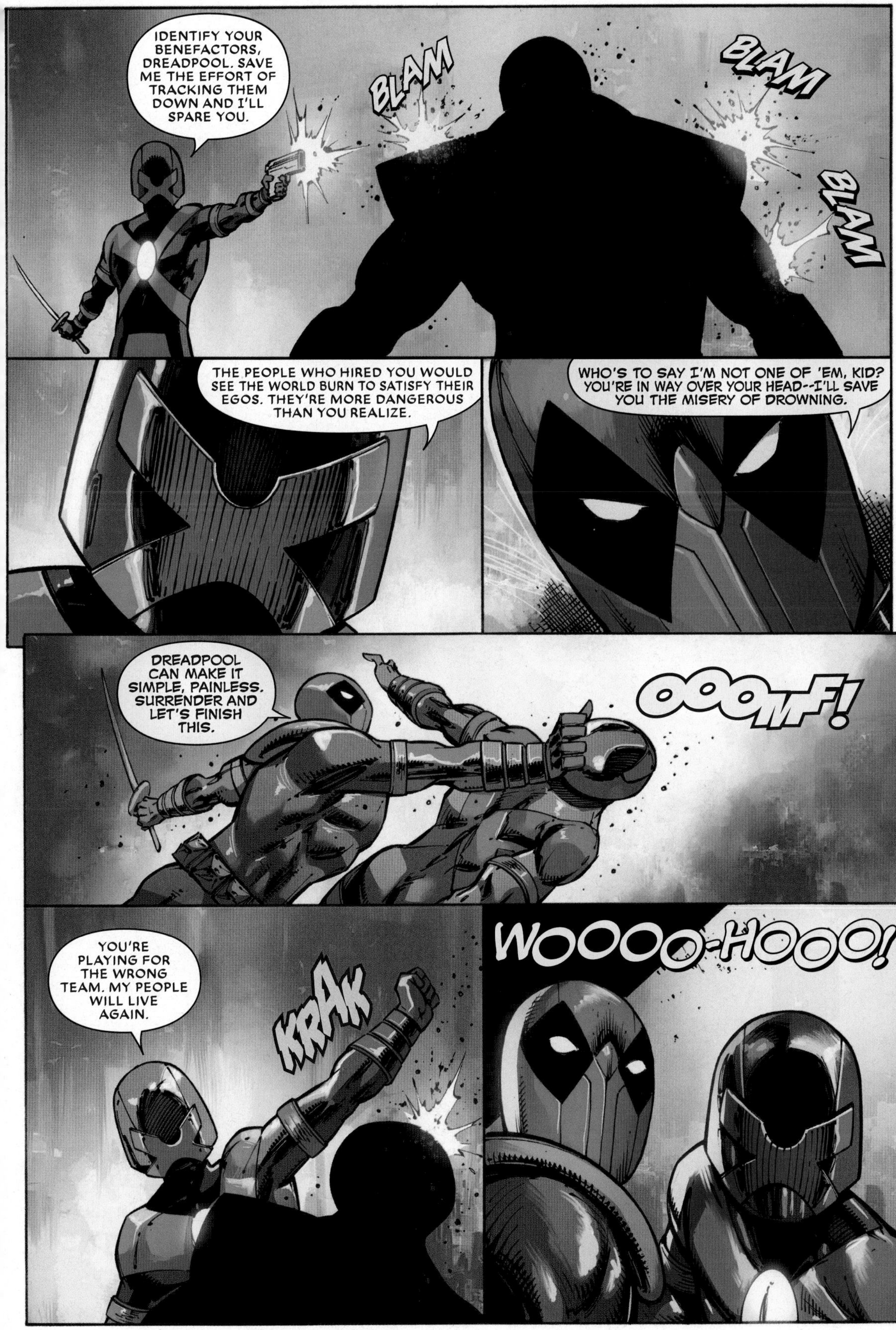
IDENTIFY YOUR BENEFACTORS, DREADPOOL. SAVE ME THE EFFORT OF TRACKING THEM DOWN AND I'LL SPARE YOU.
BLAM
BLAM
BLAM
THE PEOPLE WHO HIRED YOU WOULD SEE THE WORLD BURN TO SATISFY THEIR EGOS. THEY'RE MORE DANGEROUS THAN YOU REALIZE.
WHO'S TO SAY I'M NOT ONE OF 'EM, KID? YOU'RE IN WAY OVER YOUR HEAD--I'LL SAVE YOU THE MISERY OF DROWNING.
DREADPOOL CAN MAKE IT SIMPLE, PAINLESS. SURRENDER AND LET'S FINISH THIS.
OOOMF!
YOU'RE PLAYING FOR THE WRONG TEAM. MY PEOPLE WILL LIVE AGAIN.
KRAK
WOOOO-HOOOO!

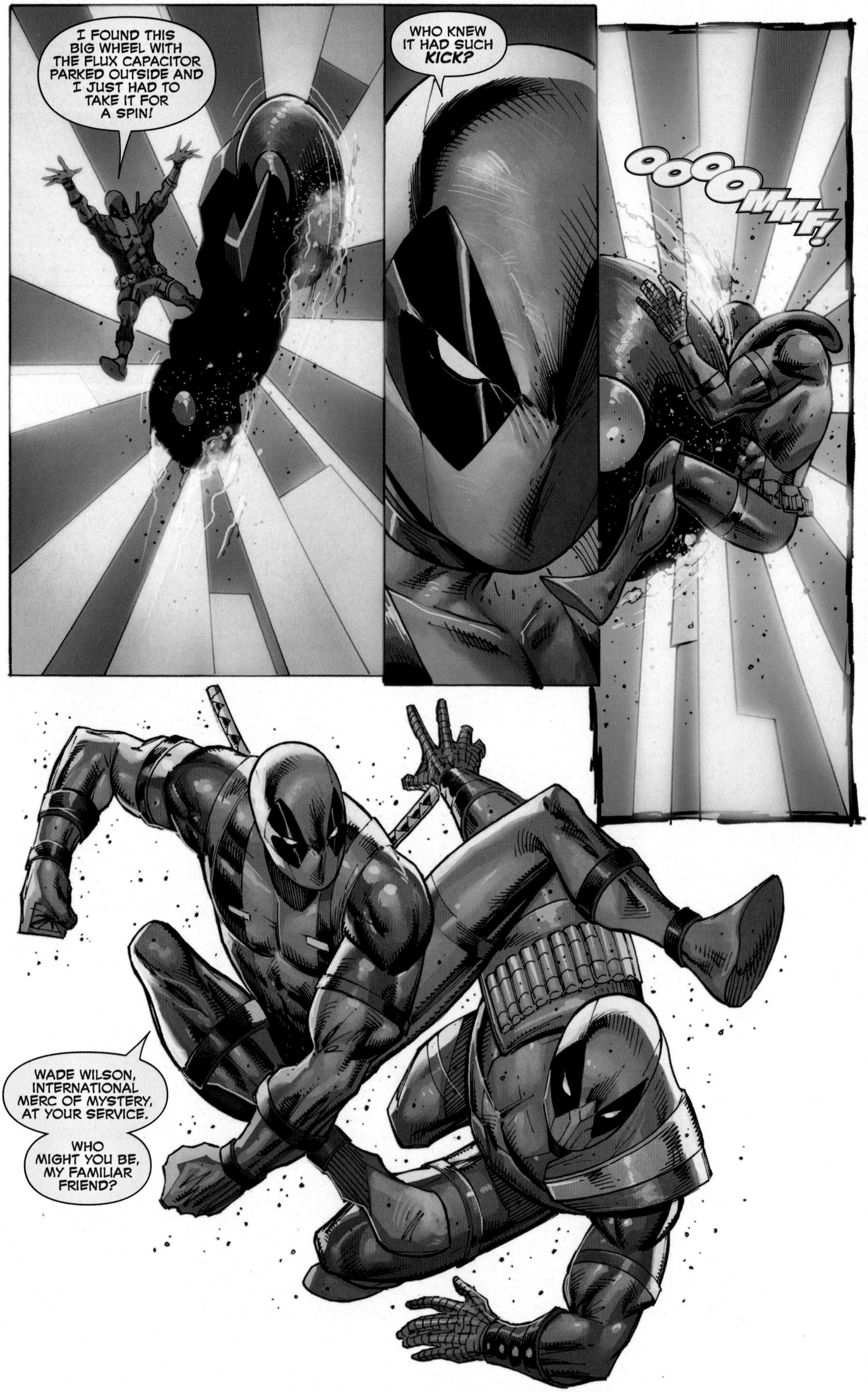
I FOUND THIS BIG WHEEL WITH THE FLUX CAPACITOR PARKED OUTSIDE AND I JUST HAD TO TAKE IT FOR A SPIN!
WHO KNEW IT HAD SUCH KICK?
OOOOMMF!
WADE WILSON, INTERNATIONAL MERC OF MYSTERY, AT YOUR SERVICE.
WHO MIGHT YOU BE, MY FAMILIAR FRIEND?

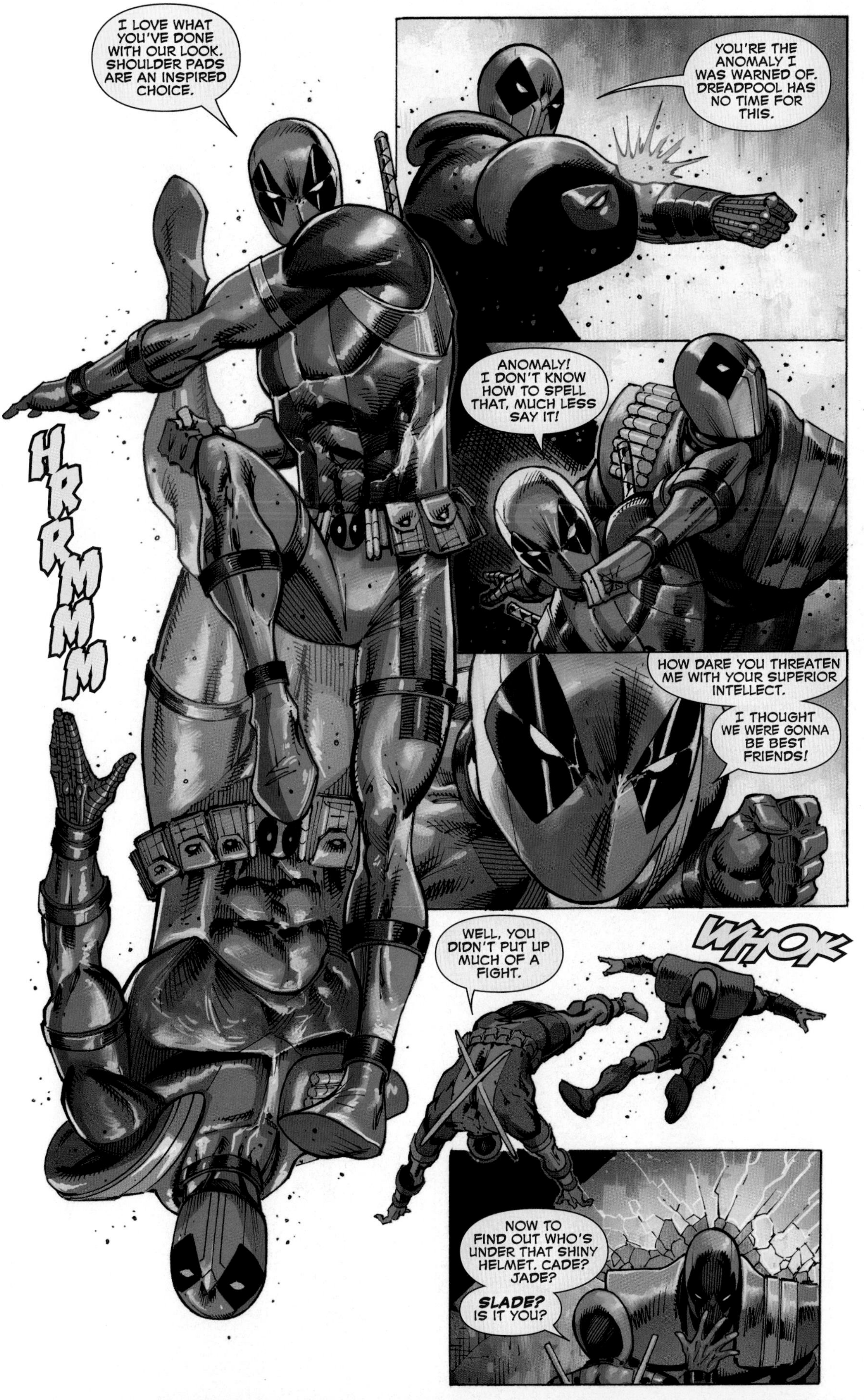

I LOVE WHAT YOU'VE DONE WITH OUR LOOK. SHOULDER PADS ARE AN INSPIRED CHOICE.
YOU'RE THE ANOMALY I WAS WARNED OF. DREADPOOL HAS NO TIME FOR THIS.
HRRMMM
ANOMALY! I DON'T KNOW HOW TO SPELL THAT, MUCH LESS SAY IT!
HOW DARE YOU THREATEN ME WITH YOUR SUPERIOR INTELLECT.
I THOUGHT WE WERE GONNA BE BEST FRIENDS!
WHOK
WELL, YOU DIDN'T PUT UP MUCH OF A FIGHT.
NOW TO FIND OUT WHO'S UNDER THAT SHINY HELMET. CADE? JADE?
SLADE? IS IT YOU?

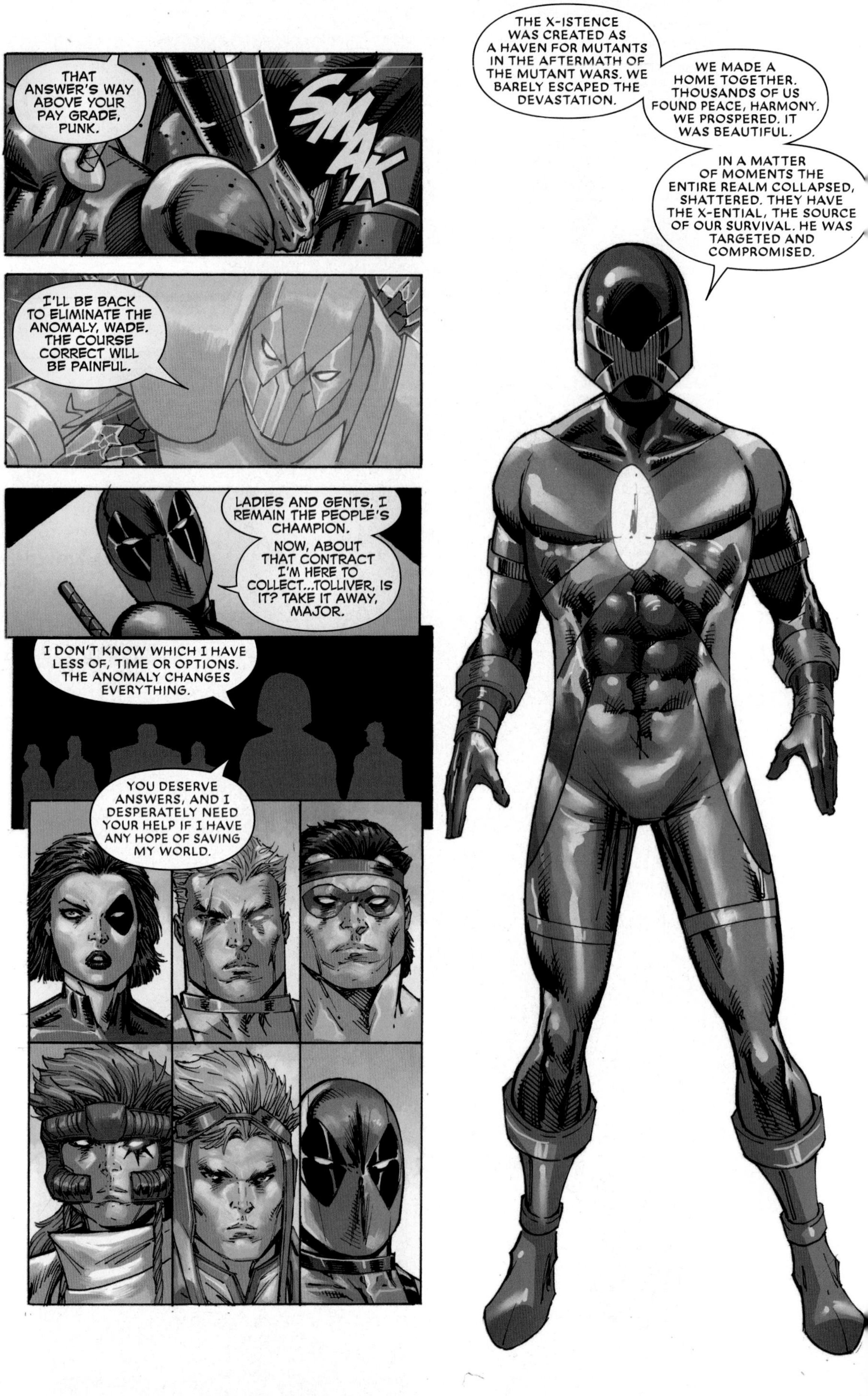
THAT ANSWER'S WAY ABOVE YOUR PAY GRADE, PUNK.
SMAK
I'LL BE BACK TO ELIMINATE THE ANOMALY, WADE. THE COURSE CORRECT WILL BE PAINFUL.
LADIES AND GENTS, I REMAIN THE PEOPLE'S CHAMPION.
NOW, ABOUT THAT CONTRACT I'M HERE TO COLLECT...TOLLIVER, IS IT? TAKE IT AWAY, MAJOR.
I DON'T KNOW WHICH I HAVE LESS OF, TIME OR OPTIONS. THE ANOMALY CHANGES EVERYTHING.
YOU DESERVE ANSWERS, AND I DESPERATELY NEED YOUR HELP IF I HAVE ANY HOPE OF SAVING MY WORLD.
THE X-ISTENCE WAS CREATED AS A HAVEN FOR MUTANTS IN THE AFTERMATH OF THE MUTANT WARS. WE BARELY ESCAPED THE DEVASTATION.
WE MADE A HOME TOGETHER. THOUSANDS OF US FOUND PEACE, HARMONY. WE PROSPERED. IT WAS BEAUTIFUL.
IN A MATTER OF MOMENTS THE ENTIRE REALM COLLAPSED, SHATTERED. THEY HAVE THE X-ENTIAL, THE SOURCE OF OUR SURVIVAL. HE WAS TARGETED AND COMPROMISED.

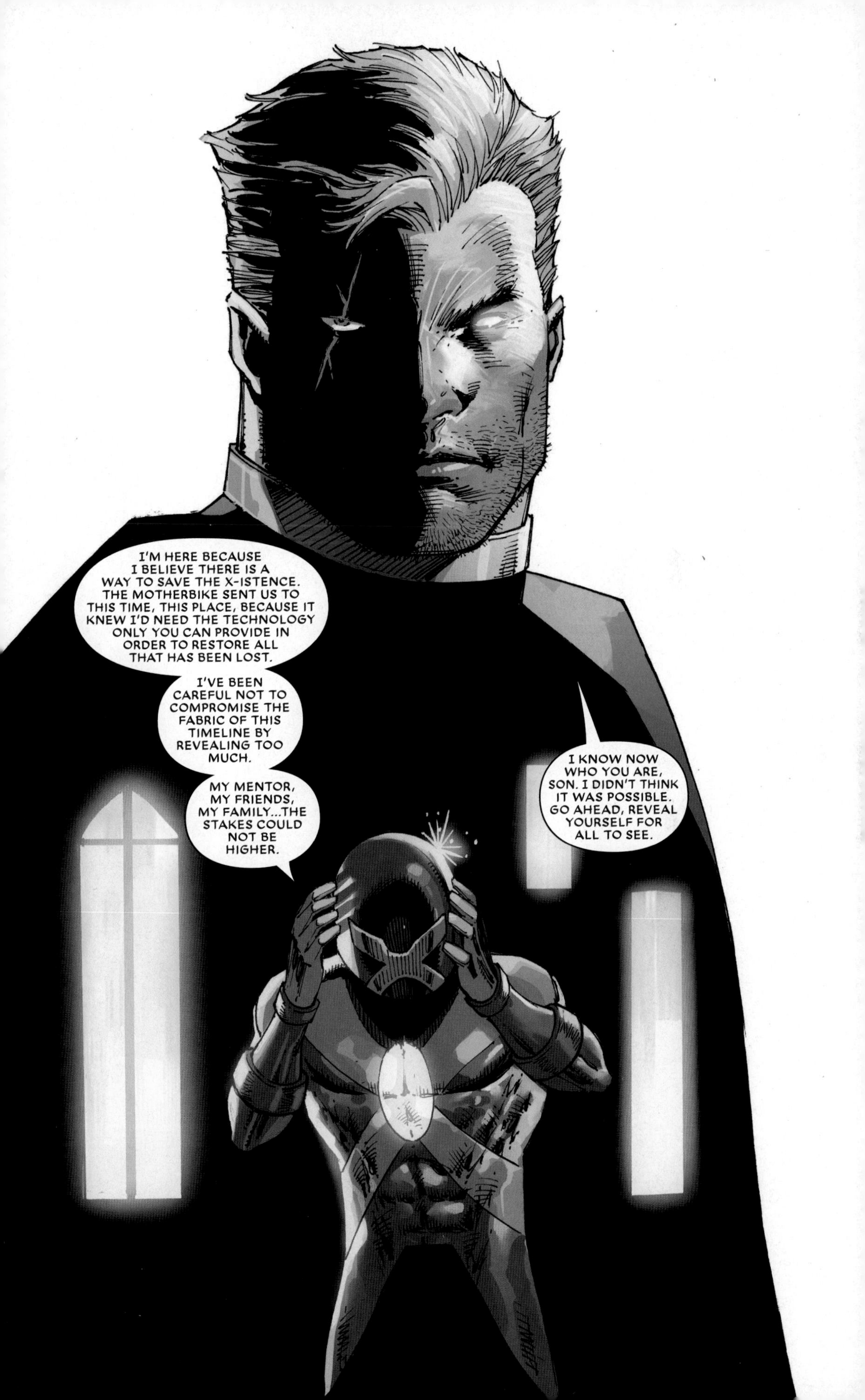
I'M HERE BECAUSE I BELIEVE THERE IS A WAY TO SAVE THE X-ISTENCE. THE MOTHERBIKE SENT US TO THIS TIME, THIS PLACE, BECAUSE IT KNEW I'D NEED THE TECHNOLOGY ONLY YOU CAN PROVIDE IN ORDER TO RESTORE ALL THAT HAS BEEN LOST.
I'VE BEEN CAREFUL NOT TO COMPROMISE THE FABRIC OF THIS TIMELINE BY REVEALING TOO MUCH.
MY MENTOR, MY FRIENDS, MY FAMILY...THE STAKES COULD NOT BE HIGHER.
I KNOW NOW WHO YOU ARE, SON. I DIDN'T THINK IT WAS POSSIBLE. GO AHEAD, REVEAL YOURSELF FOR ALL TO SEE.

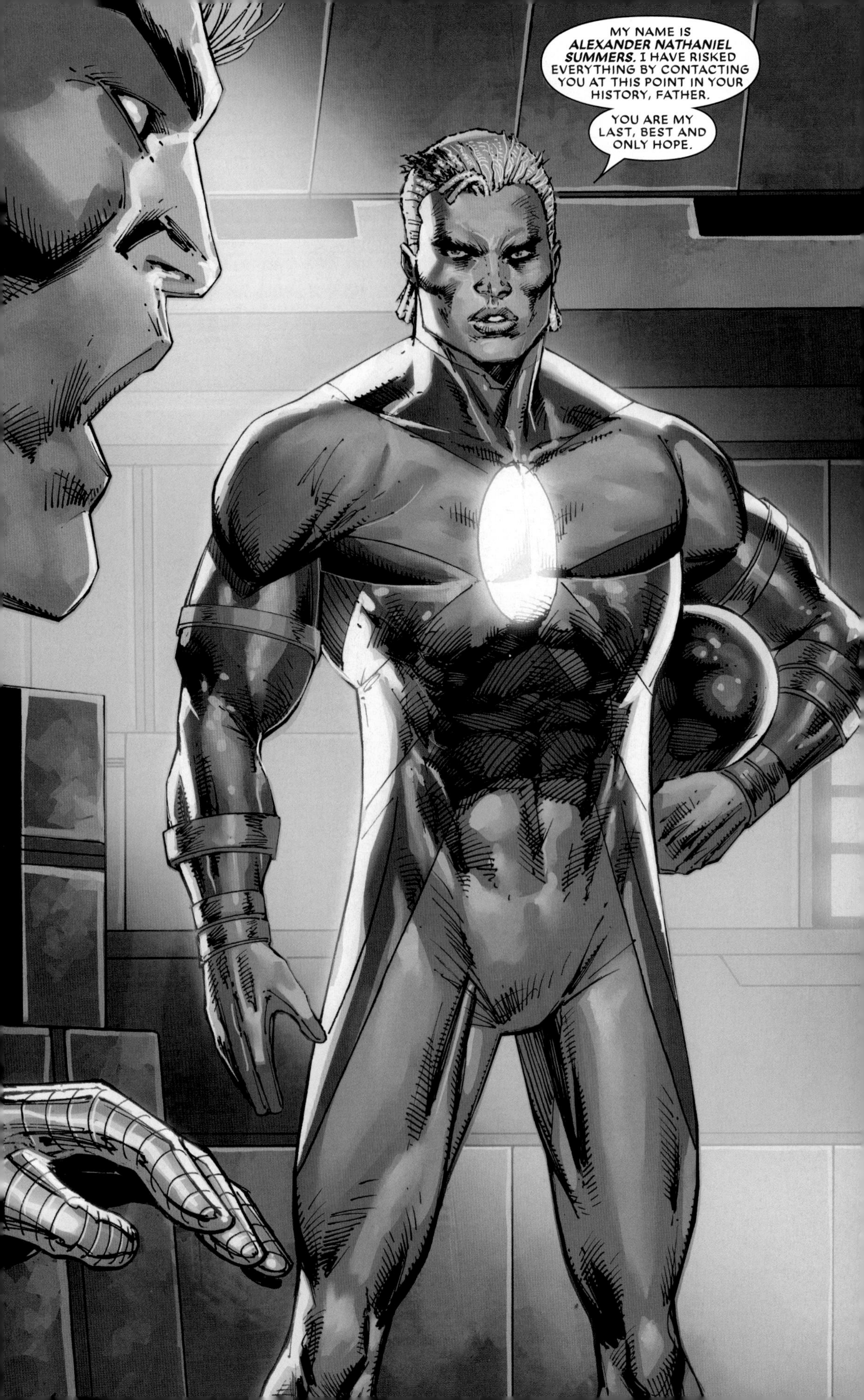
MY NAME IS ***ALEXANDER NATHANIEL SUMMERS.*** I HAVE RISKED EVERYTHING BY CONTACTING YOU AT THIS POINT IN YOUR HISTORY, FATHER.
YOU ARE MY LAST, BEST AND ONLY HOPE.

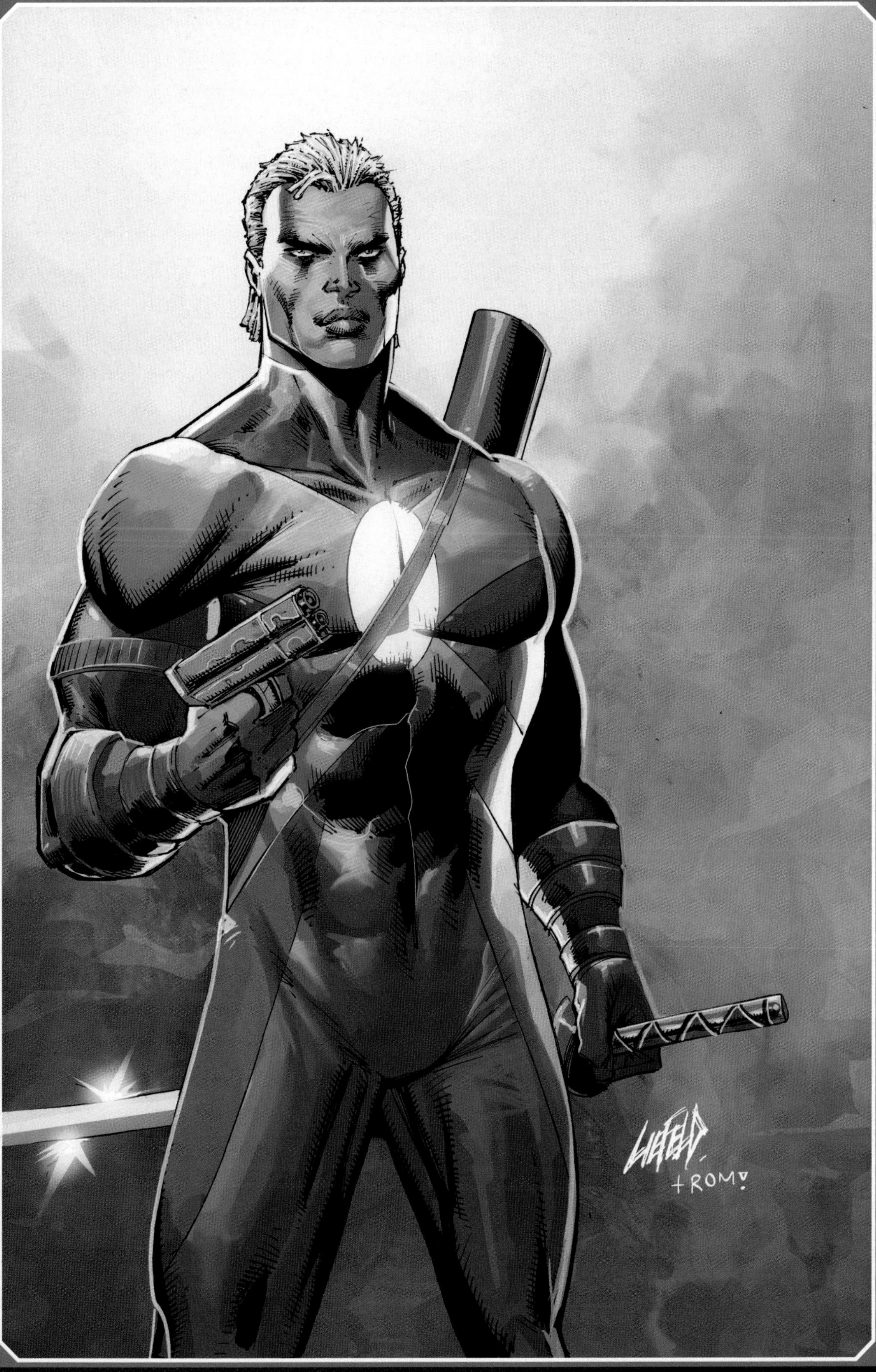

ROB LIEFELD & ROMULO FAJARDO JR.

#1 SECOND PRINTING COVER

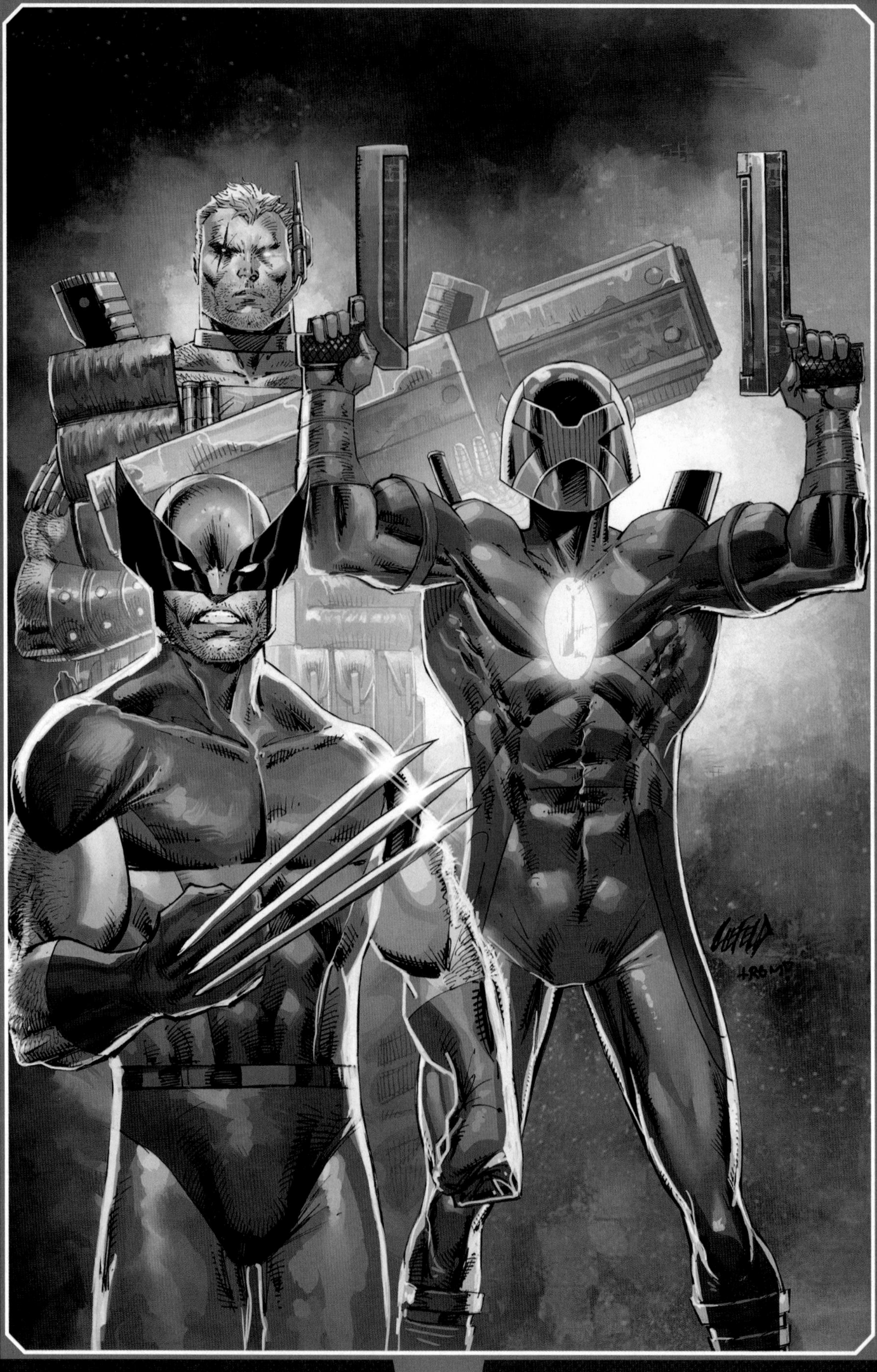

2

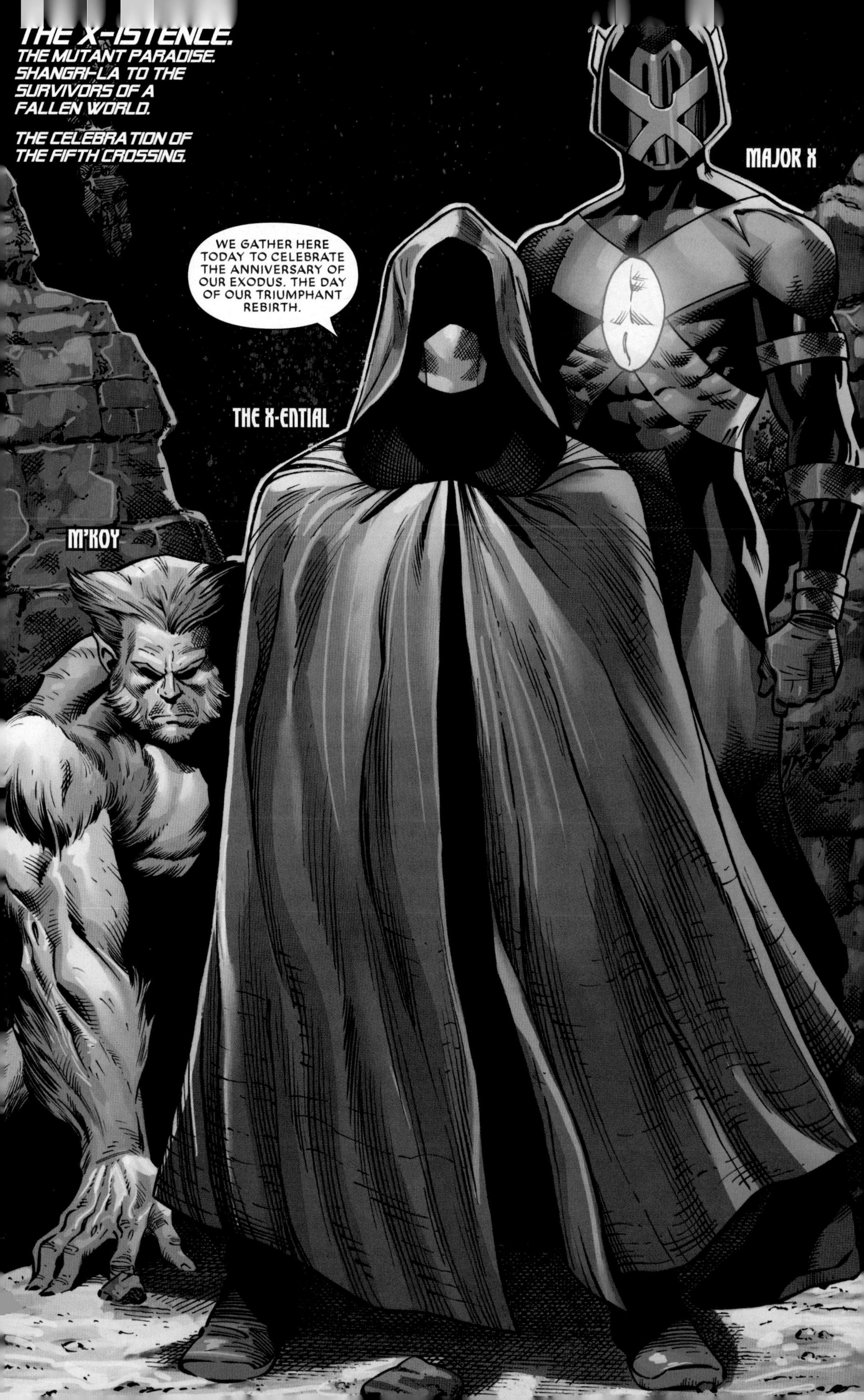
THE X-ISTENCE.
THE MUTANT PARADISE. SHANGRI-LA TO THE SURVIVORS OF A FALLEN WORLD.
THE CELEBRATION OF THE FIFTH CROSSING.
MAJOR X
WE GATHER HERE TODAY TO CELEBRATE THE ANNIVERSARY OF OUR EXODUS. THE DAY OF OUR TRIUMPHANT REBIRTH.
THE X-ENTIAL
M'KOY

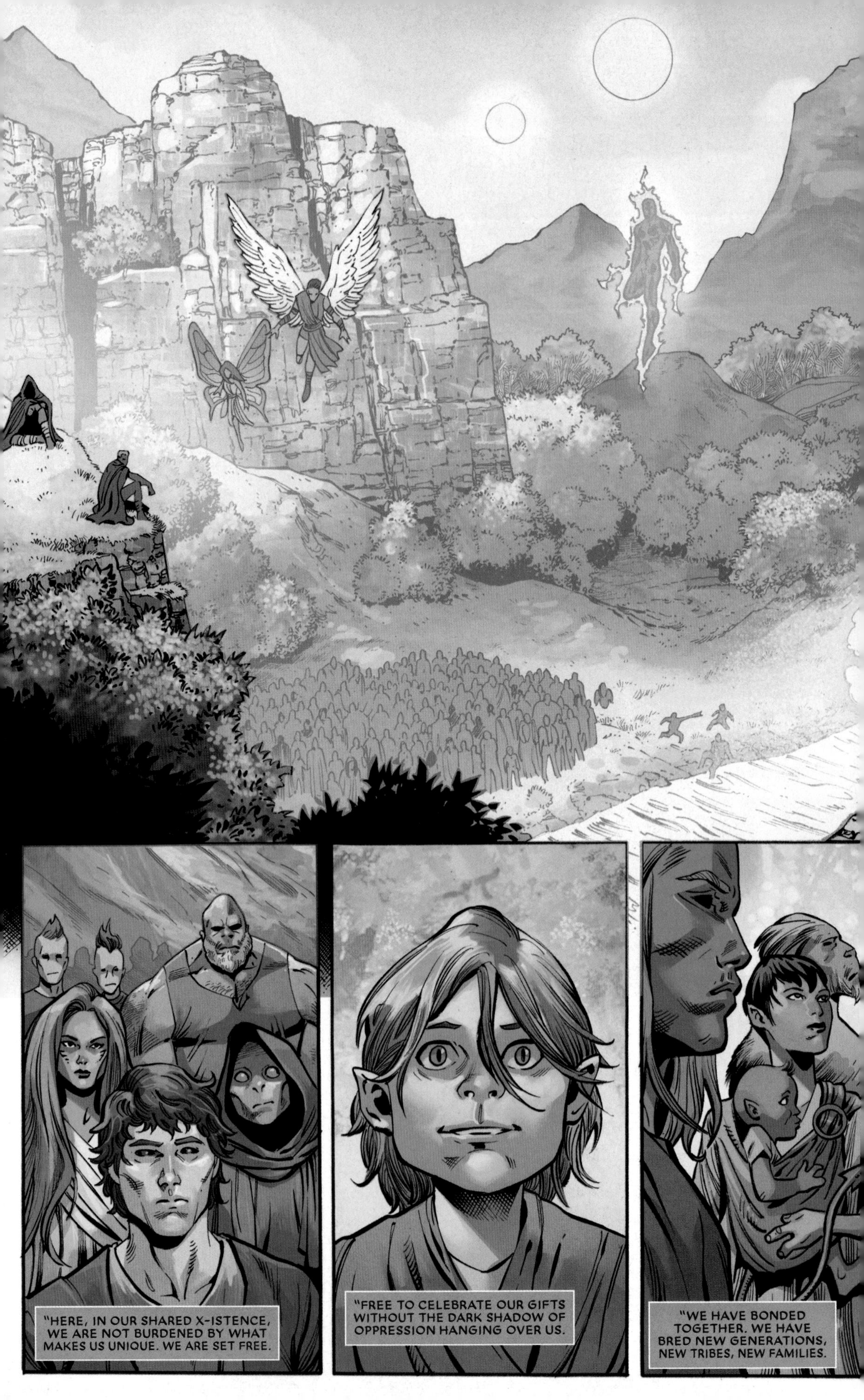
"HERE, IN OUR SHARED X-ISTENCE, WE ARE NOT BURDENED BY WHAT MAKES US UNIQUE. WE ARE SET FREE.
"FREE TO CELEBRATE OUR GIFTS WITHOUT THE DARK SHADOW OF OPPRESSION HANGING OVER US.
"WE HAVE BONDED TOGETHER. WE HAVE BRED NEW GENERATIONS, NEW TRIBES, NEW FAMILIES.

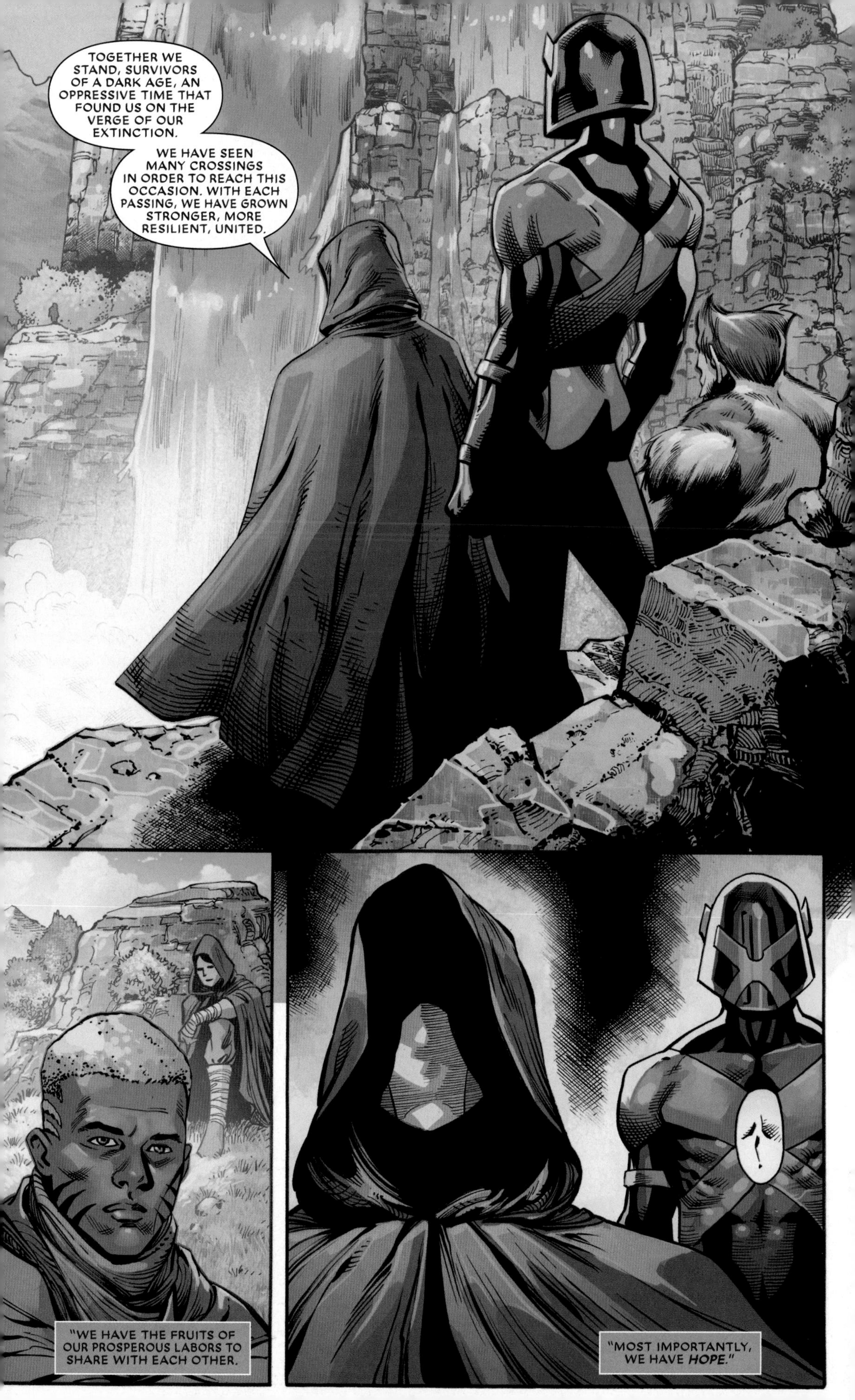
TOGETHER WE STAND, SURVIVORS OF A DARK AGE, AN OPPRESSIVE TIME THAT FOUND US ON THE VERGE OF OUR EXTINCTION.
WE HAVE SEEN MANY CROSSINGS IN ORDER TO REACH THIS OCCASION. WITH EACH PASSING, WE HAVE GROWN STRONGER, MORE RESILIENT, UNITED.
"WE HAVE THE FRUITS OF OUR PROSPEROUS LABORS TO SHARE WITH EACH OTHER.
"MOST IMPORTANTLY, WE HAVE *HOPE*."

"THE WORLD WAS BURNING. THE TIME OF MUTANTS WAS AT AN END.

"ALLIANCES WERE SHATTERED. FEAR WAS THE ONLY CONSTANT.

CHERISH THE HOPE WE SHARE. IT CAME AT A STEEP PRICE, WITH GREAT SACRIFICES FROM THE FALLEN.

"*THE CATALYST* HAD BROUGHT RUIN AND DEVASTATION TO ALL MUTANTKIND.

MUTANT FILTH! YOUR TIME AMONG US IS FINISHED. THE CLEANSING WILL PURGE YOUR DISEASE!

"I HELD THE PORTAL AT THE CHECKPOINT FOR AS LONG AS I WAS PHYSICALLY CAPABLE. ONE AFTER ANOTHER, THEY CAME.

"SALVATION MERE MOMENTS AWAY.

"TIME WAS GROWING SHORT. THE CATALYST WAS CLOSING IN.

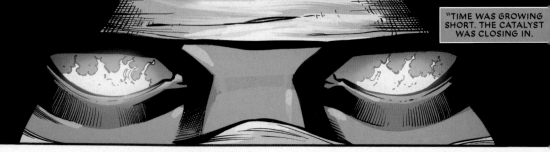

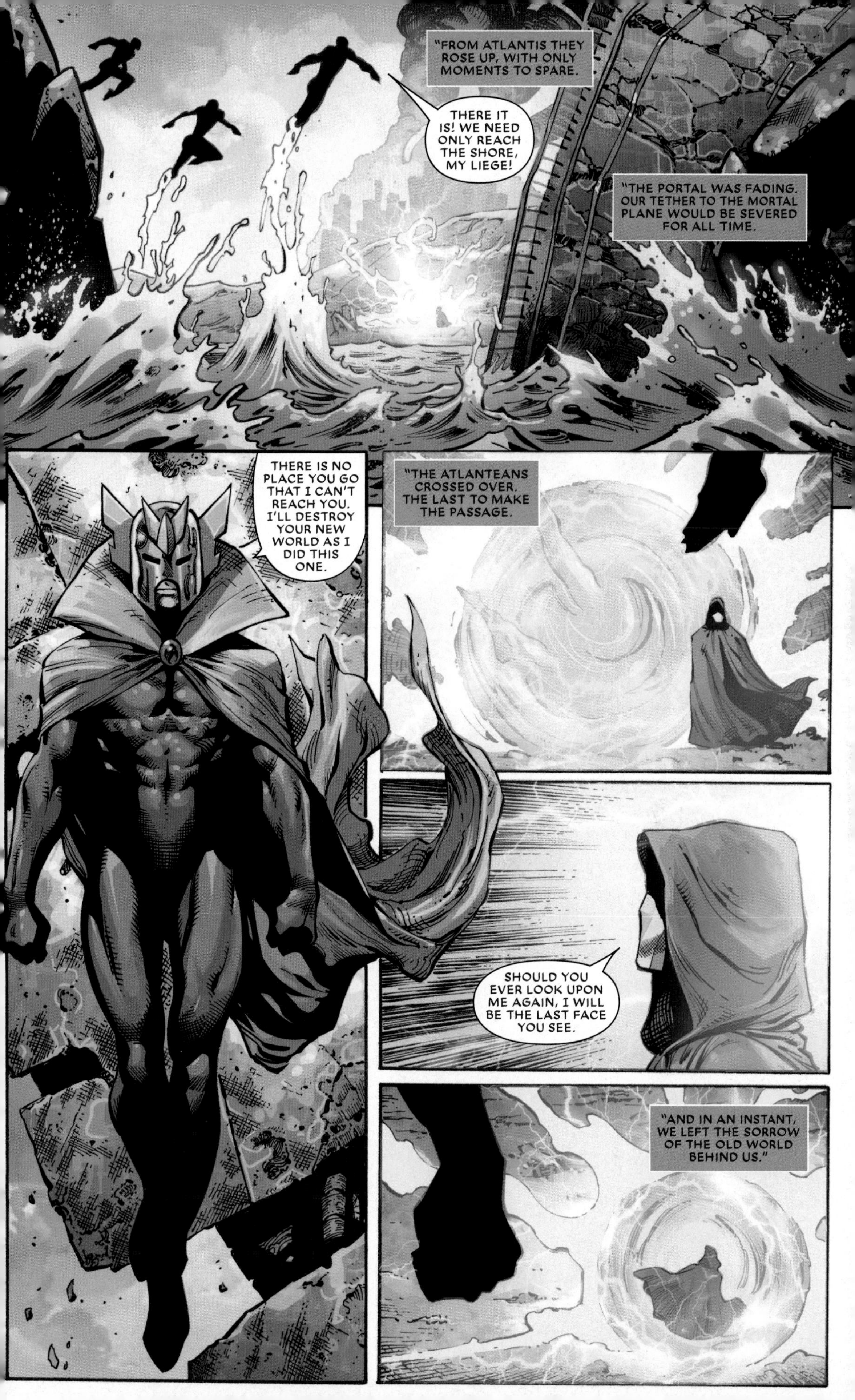
"FROM ATLANTIS THEY ROSE UP, WITH ONLY MOMENTS TO SPARE.
THERE IT IS! WE NEED ONLY REACH THE SHORE, MY LIEGE!
"THE PORTAL WAS FADING. OUR TETHER TO THE MORTAL PLANE WOULD BE SEVERED FOR ALL TIME.
THERE IS NO PLACE YOU GO THAT I CAN'T REACH YOU. I'LL DESTROY YOUR NEW WORLD AS I DID THIS ONE.
"THE ATLANTEANS CROSSED OVER. THE LAST TO MAKE THE PASSAGE.
SHOULD YOU EVER LOOK UPON ME AGAIN, I WILL BE THE LAST FACE YOU SEE.
"AND IN AN INSTANT, WE LEFT THE SORROW OF THE OLD WORLD BEHIND US."

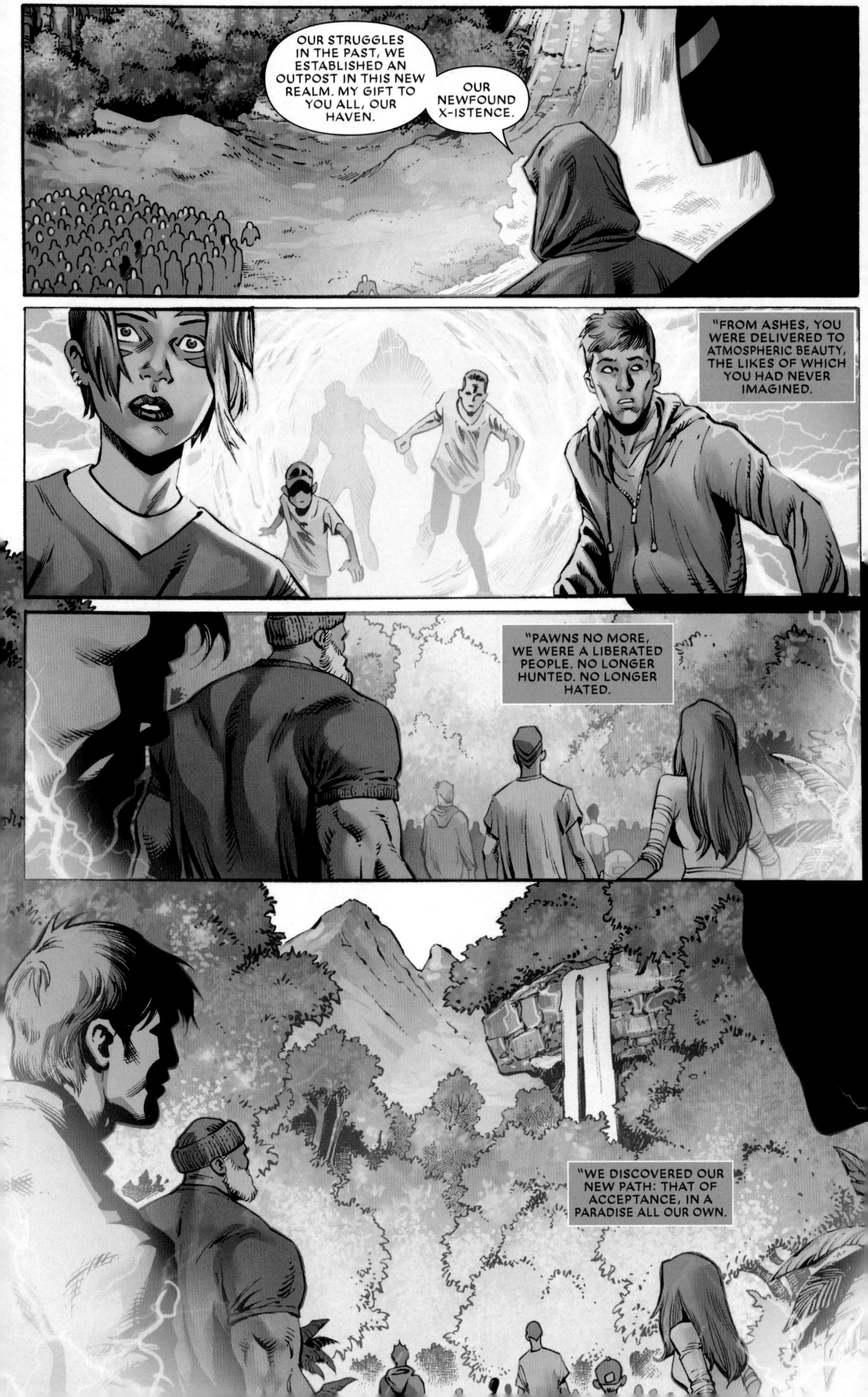

OUR STRUGGLES IN THE PAST, WE ESTABLISHED AN OUTPOST IN THIS NEW REALM. MY GIFT TO YOU ALL, OUR HAVEN.
OUR NEWFOUND X-ISTENCE.
"FROM ASHES, YOU WERE DELIVERED TO ATMOSPHERIC BEAUTY, THE LIKES OF WHICH YOU HAD NEVER IMAGINED.
"PAWNS NO MORE, WE WERE A LIBERATED PEOPLE. NO LONGER HUNTED. NO LONGER HATED.
"WE DISCOVERED OUR NEW PATH: THAT OF ACCEPTANCE, IN A PARADISE ALL OUR OWN.

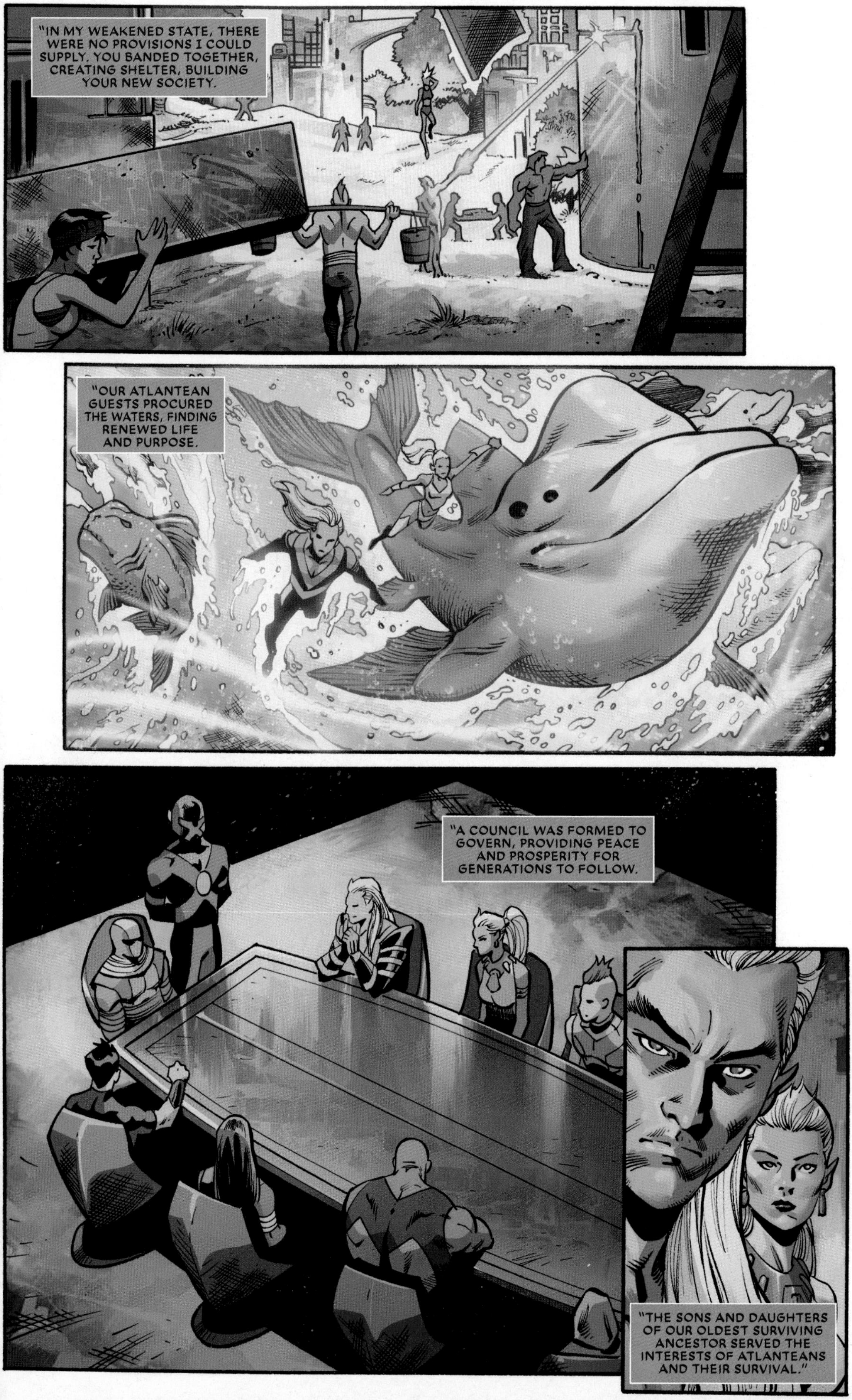
"IN MY WEAKENED STATE, THERE WERE NO PROVISIONS I COULD SUPPLY. YOU BANDED TOGETHER, CREATING SHELTER, BUILDING YOUR NEW SOCIETY.
"OUR ATLANTEAN GUESTS PROCURED THE WATERS, FINDING RENEWED LIFE AND PURPOSE.
"A COUNCIL WAS FORMED TO GOVERN, PROVIDING PEACE AND PROSPERITY FOR GENERATIONS TO FOLLOW.
"THE SONS AND DAUGHTERS OF OUR OLDEST SURVIVING ANCESTOR SERVED THE INTERESTS OF ATLANTEANS AND THEIR SURVIVAL."

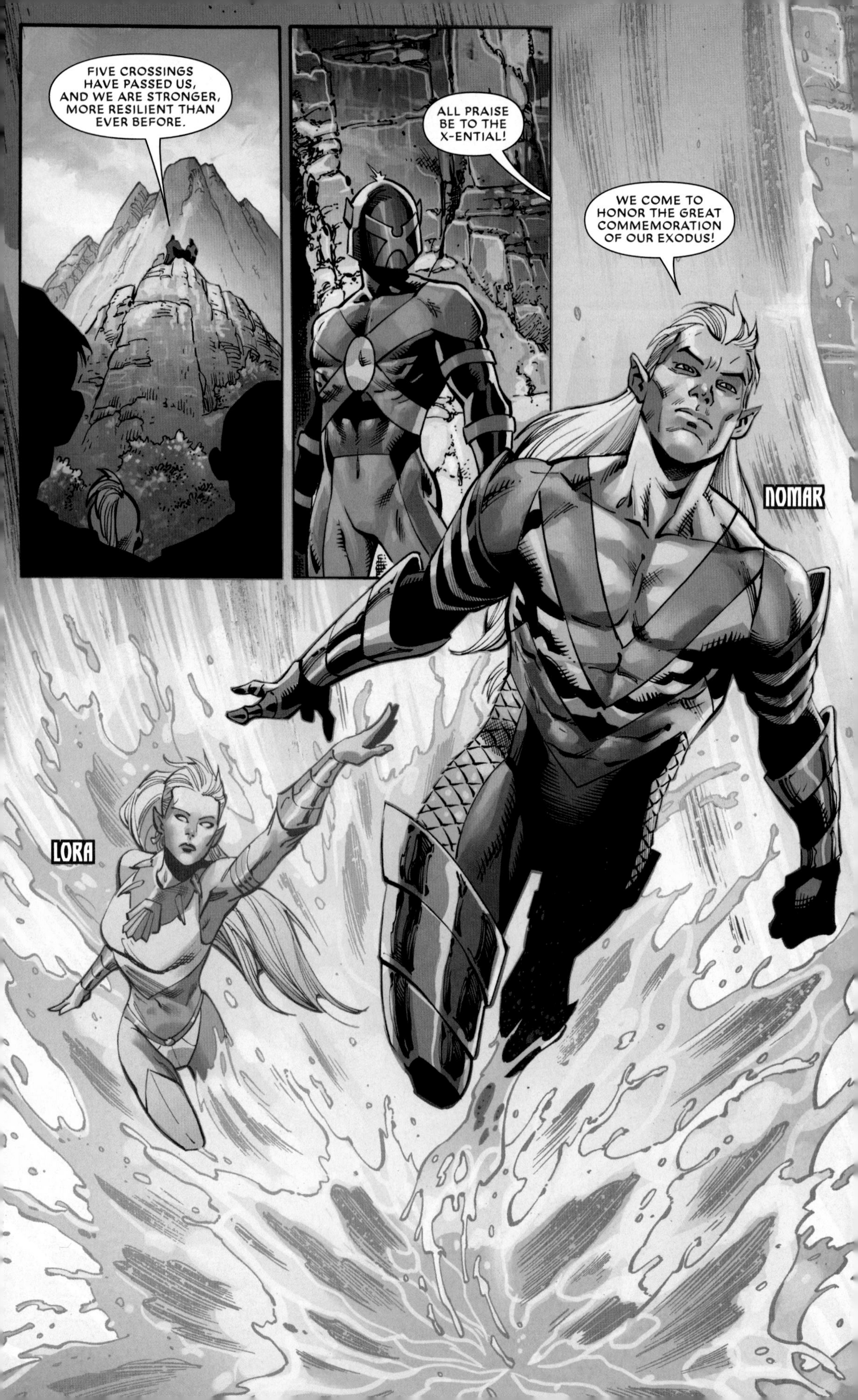
FIVE CROSSINGS HAVE PASSED US, AND WE ARE STRONGER, MORE RESILIENT THAN EVER BEFORE.
ALL PRAISE BE TO THE X-ENTIAL!
WE COME TO HONOR THE GREAT COMMEMORATION OF OUR EXODUS!
NOMAR
LORA

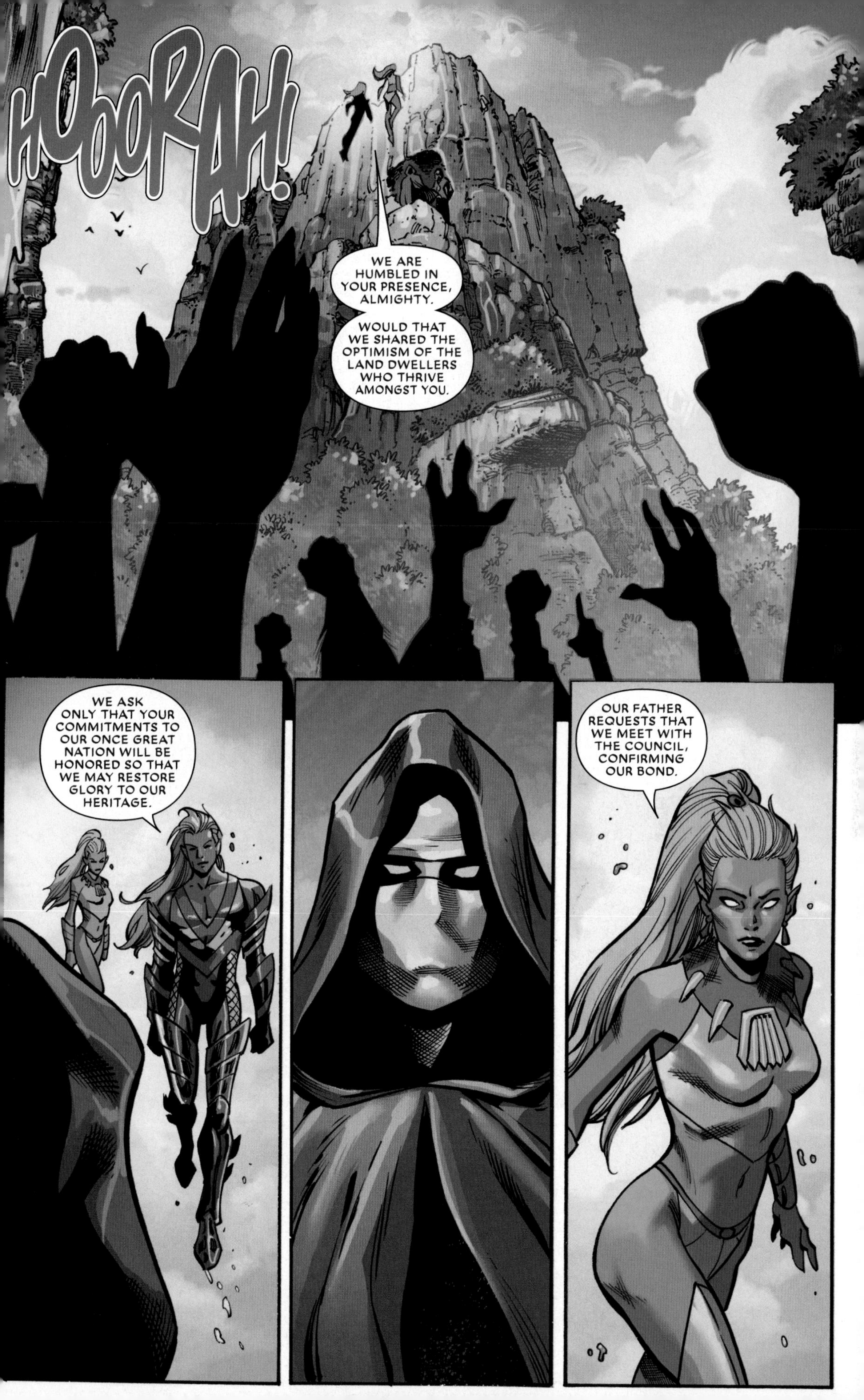
HOOORAH!
WE ARE HUMBLED IN YOUR PRESENCE, ALMIGHTY.
WOULD THAT WE SHARED THE OPTIMISM OF THE LAND DWELLERS WHO THRIVE AMONGST YOU.
WE ASK ONLY THAT YOUR COMMITMENTS TO OUR ONCE GREAT NATION WILL BE HONORED SO THAT WE MAY RESTORE GLORY TO OUR HERITAGE.
OUR FATHER REQUESTS THAT WE MEET WITH THE COUNCIL, CONFIRMING OUR BOND.

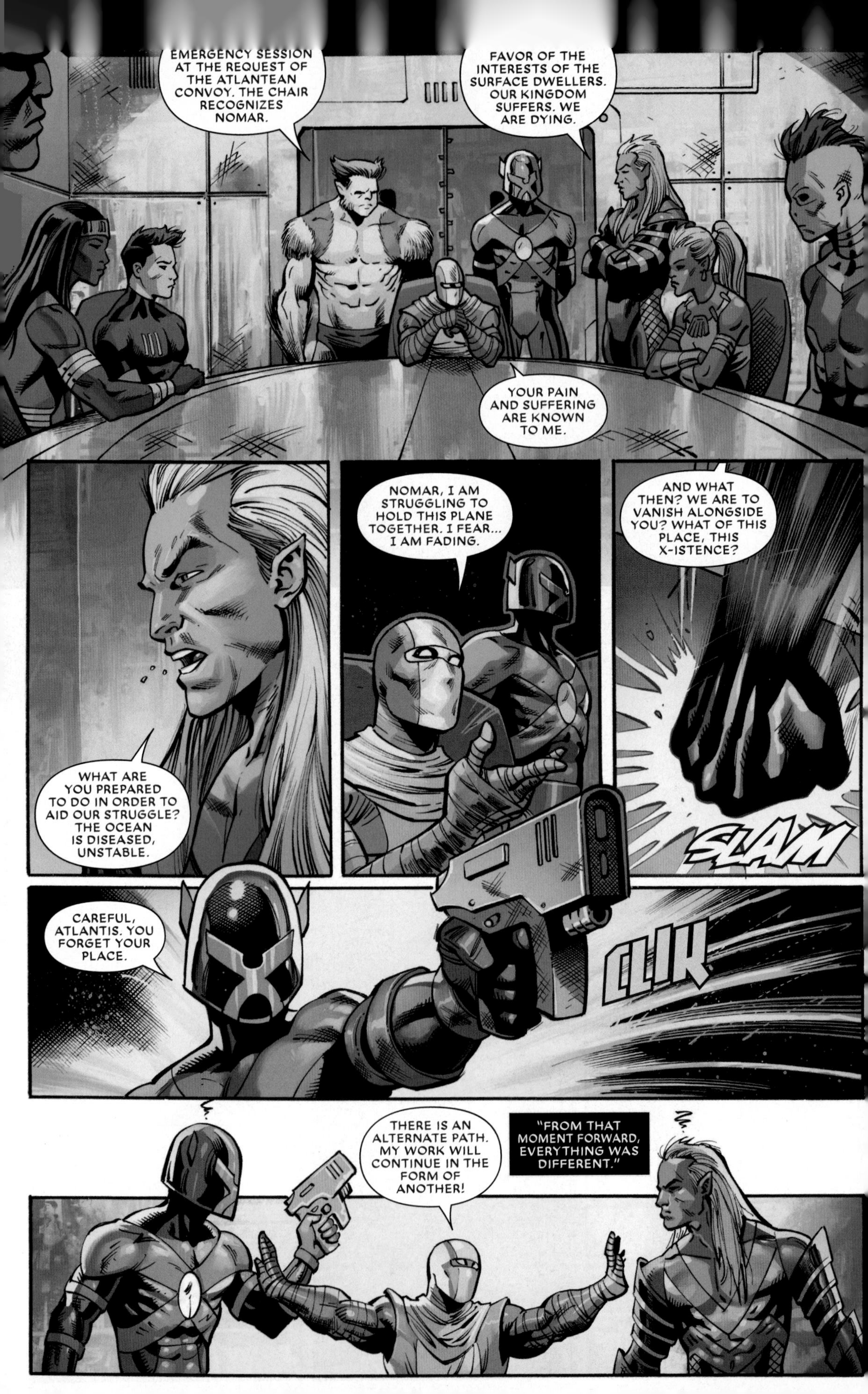
EMERGENCY SESSION AT THE REQUEST OF THE ATLANTEAN CONVOY. THE CHAIR RECOGNIZES NOMAR.
FAVOR OF THE INTERESTS OF THE SURFACE DWELLERS. OUR KINGDOM SUFFERS. WE ARE DYING.
YOUR PAIN AND SUFFERING ARE KNOWN TO ME.
WHAT ARE YOU PREPARED TO DO IN ORDER TO AID OUR STRUGGLE? THE OCEAN IS DISEASED, UNSTABLE.
NOMAR, I AM STRUGGLING TO HOLD THIS PLANE TOGETHER. I FEAR... I AM FADING.
AND WHAT THEN? WE ARE TO VANISH ALONGSIDE YOU? WHAT OF THIS PLACE, THIS X-ISTENCE?
SLAM
CAREFUL, ATLANTIS. YOU FORGET YOUR PLACE.
CLIK
THERE IS AN ALTERNATE PATH. MY WORK WILL CONTINUE IN THE FORM OF ANOTHER!
"FROM THAT MOMENT FORWARD, EVERYTHING WAS DIFFERENT."

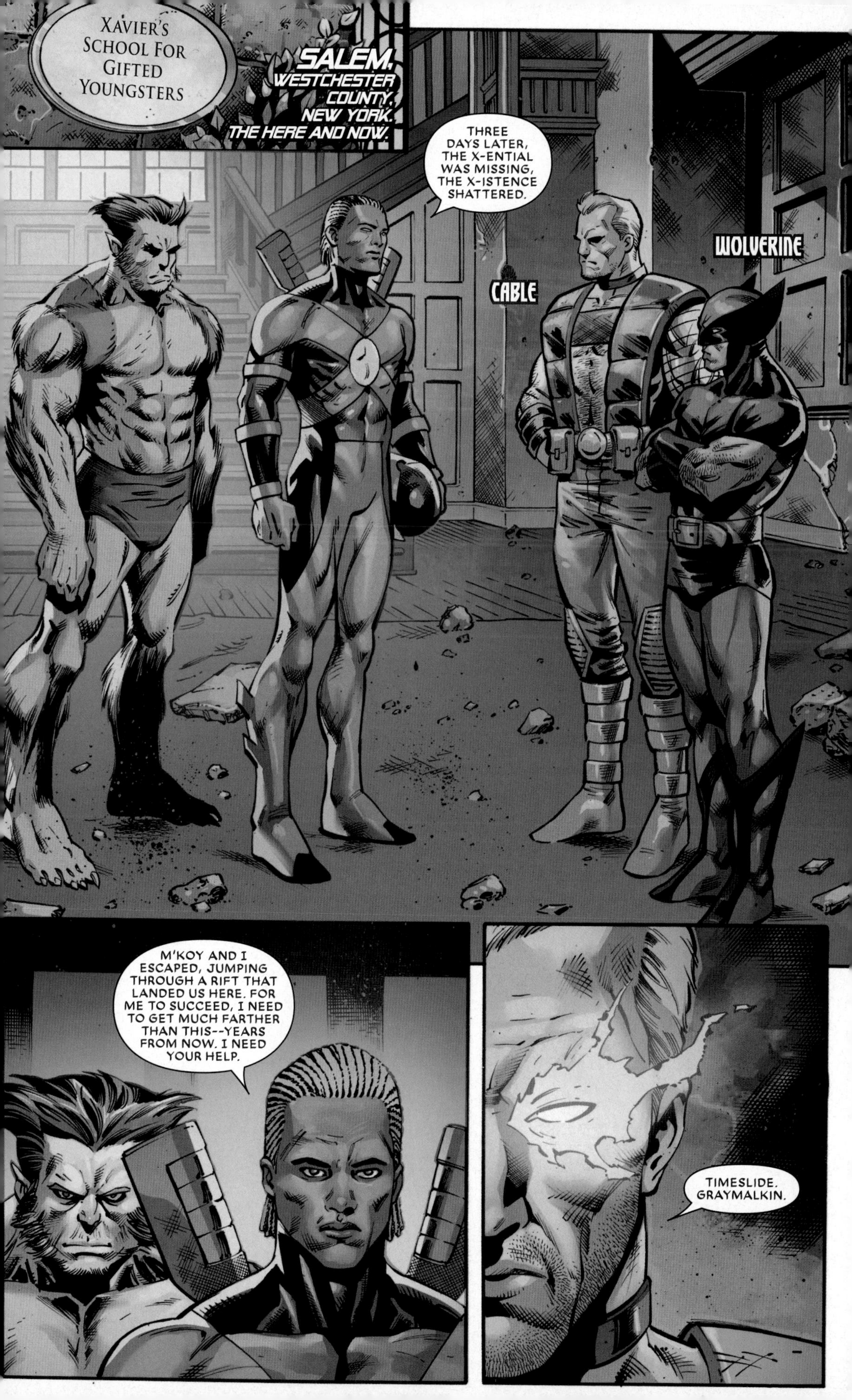
XAVIER'S SCHOOL FOR GIFTED YOUNGSTERS
SALEM, WESTCHESTER COUNTY, NEW YORK. THE HERE AND NOW.
THREE DAYS LATER, THE X-ENTIAL WAS MISSING, THE X-ISTENCE SHATTERED.
CABLE
WOLVERINE
M'KOY AND I ESCAPED, JUMPING THROUGH A RIFT THAT LANDED US HERE. FOR ME TO SUCCEED, I NEED TO GET MUCH FARTHER THAN THIS--YEARS FROM NOW. I NEED YOUR HELP.
TIMESLIDE. GRAYMALKIN.

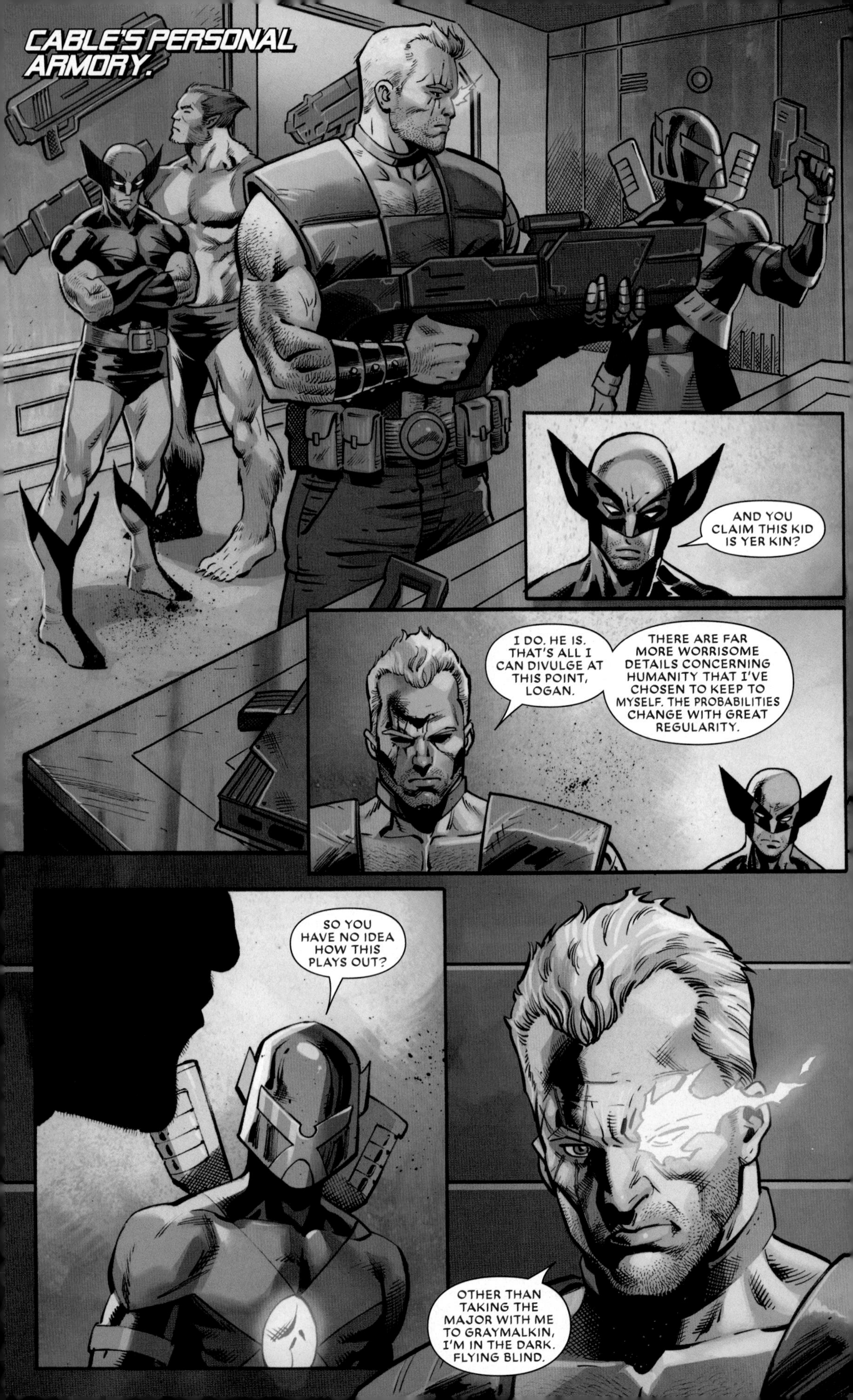
CABLE'S PERSONAL ARMORY.
AND YOU CLAIM THIS KID IS YER KIN?
I DO. HE IS. THAT'S ALL I CAN DIVULGE AT THIS POINT, LOGAN.
THERE ARE FAR MORE WORRISOME DETAILS CONCERNING HUMANITY THAT I'VE CHOSEN TO KEEP TO MYSELF. THE PROBABILITIES CHANGE WITH GREAT REGULARITY.
SO YOU HAVE NO IDEA HOW THIS PLAYS OUT?
OTHER THAN TAKING THE MAJOR WITH ME TO GRAYMALKIN, I'M IN THE DARK. FLYING BLIND.

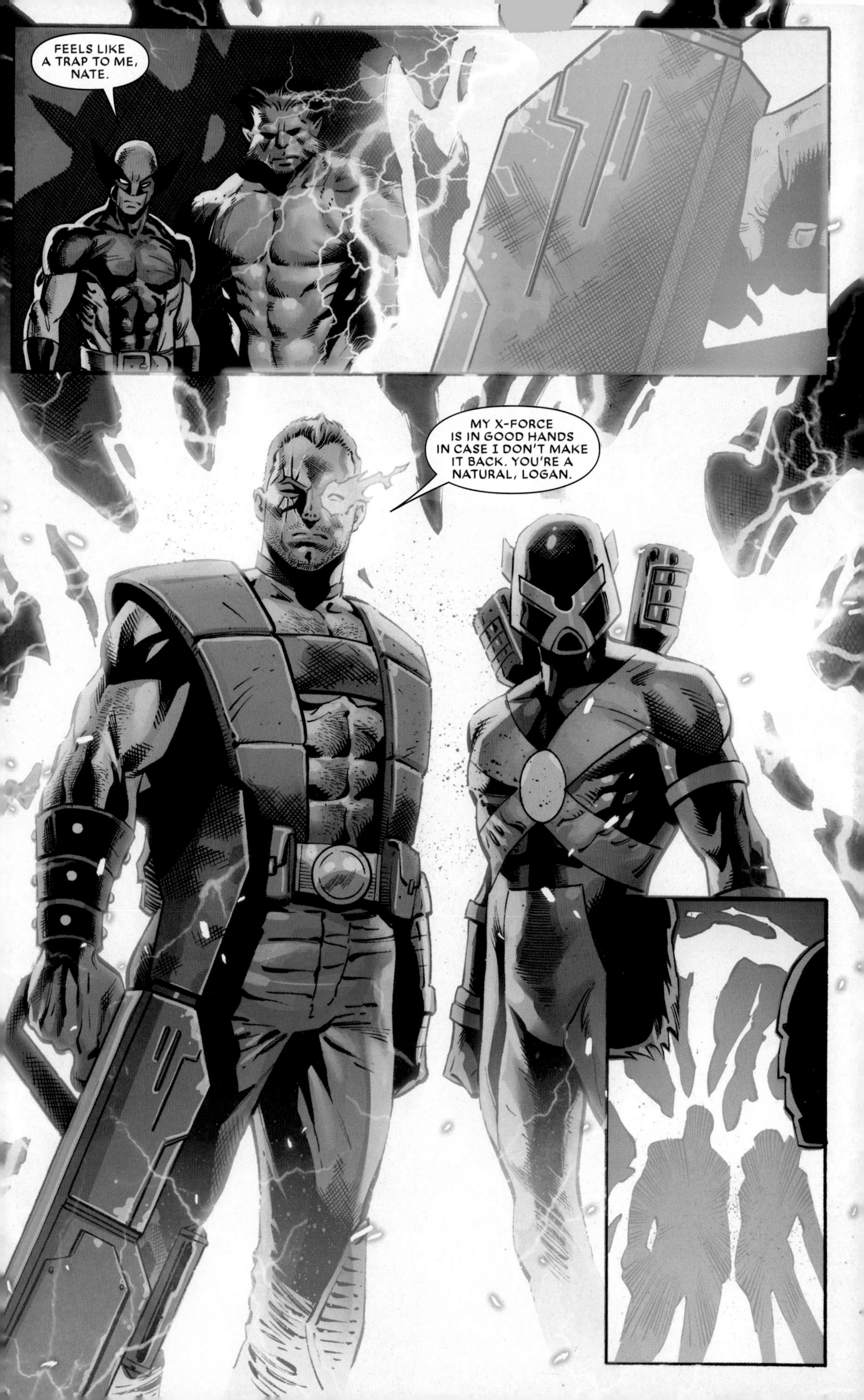
FEELS LIKE A TRAP TO ME, NATE.
MY X-FORCE IS IN GOOD HANDS IN CASE I DON'T MAKE IT BACK. YOU'RE A NATURAL, LOGAN.

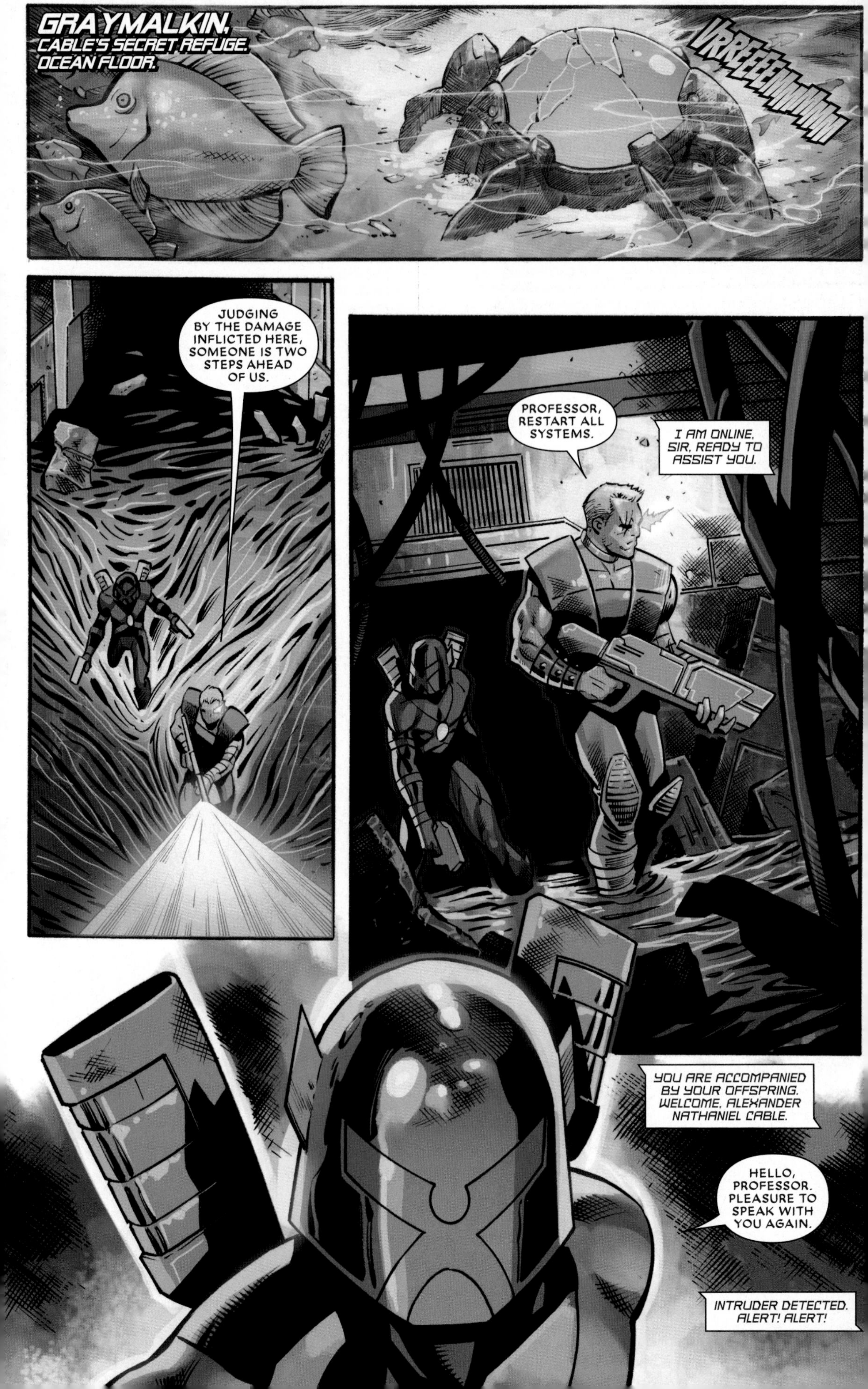
GRAYMALKIN, CABLE'S SECRET REFUGE. OCEAN FLOOR.
VRREEEMMMMM
JUDGING BY THE DAMAGE INFLICTED HERE, SOMEONE IS TWO STEPS AHEAD OF US.
PROFESSOR, RESTART ALL SYSTEMS.
I AM ONLINE, SIR, READY TO ASSIST YOU.
YOU ARE ACCOMPANIED BY YOUR OFFSPRING. WELCOME, ALEXANDER NATHANIEL CABLE.
HELLO, PROFESSOR. PLEASURE TO SPEAK WITH YOU AGAIN.
INTRUDER DETECTED. ALERT! ALERT!

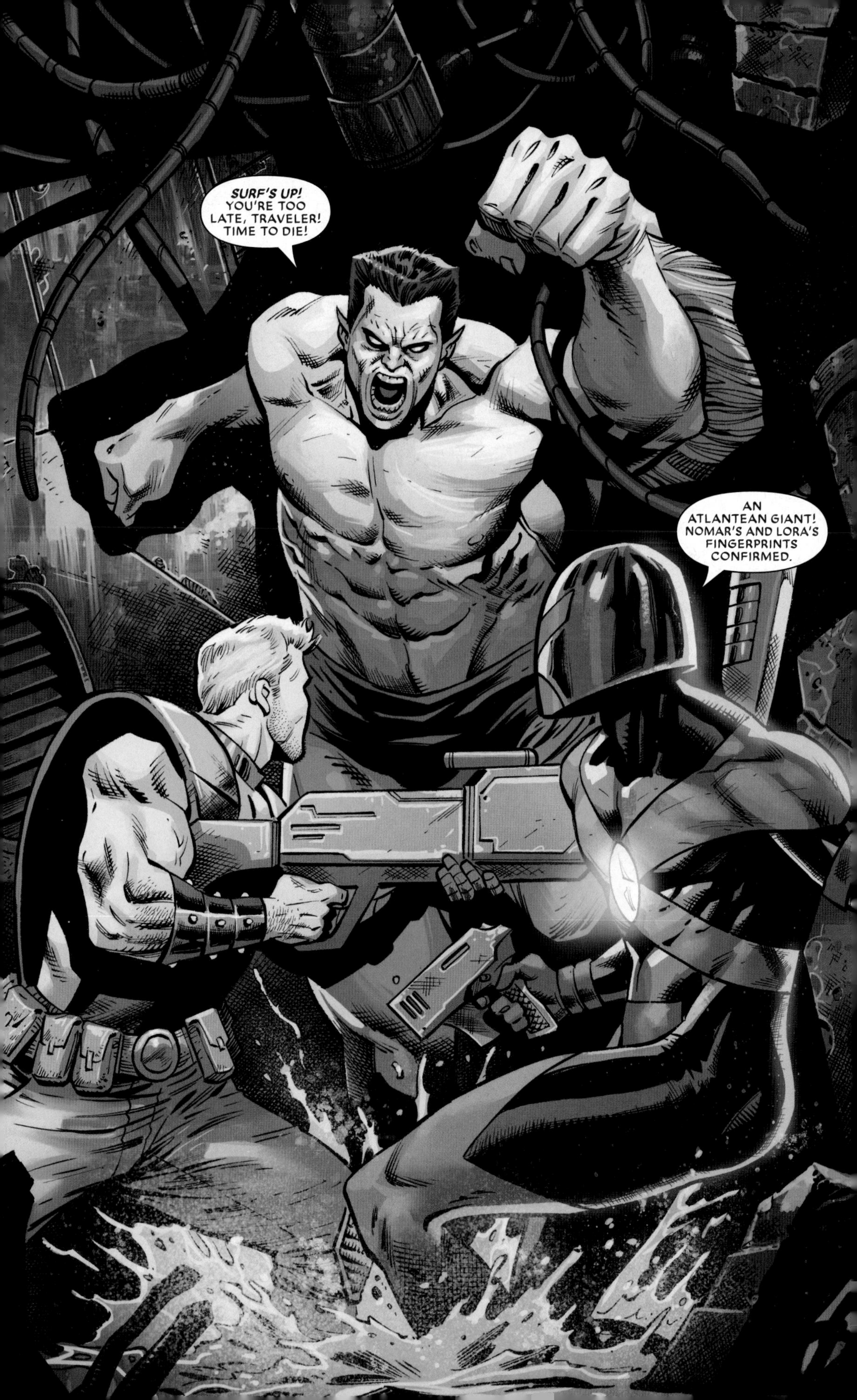
SURF'S UP! YOU'RE TOO LATE, TRAVELER! TIME TO DIE!
AN ATLANTEAN GIANT! NOMAR'S AND LORA'S FINGERPRINTS CONFIRMED.

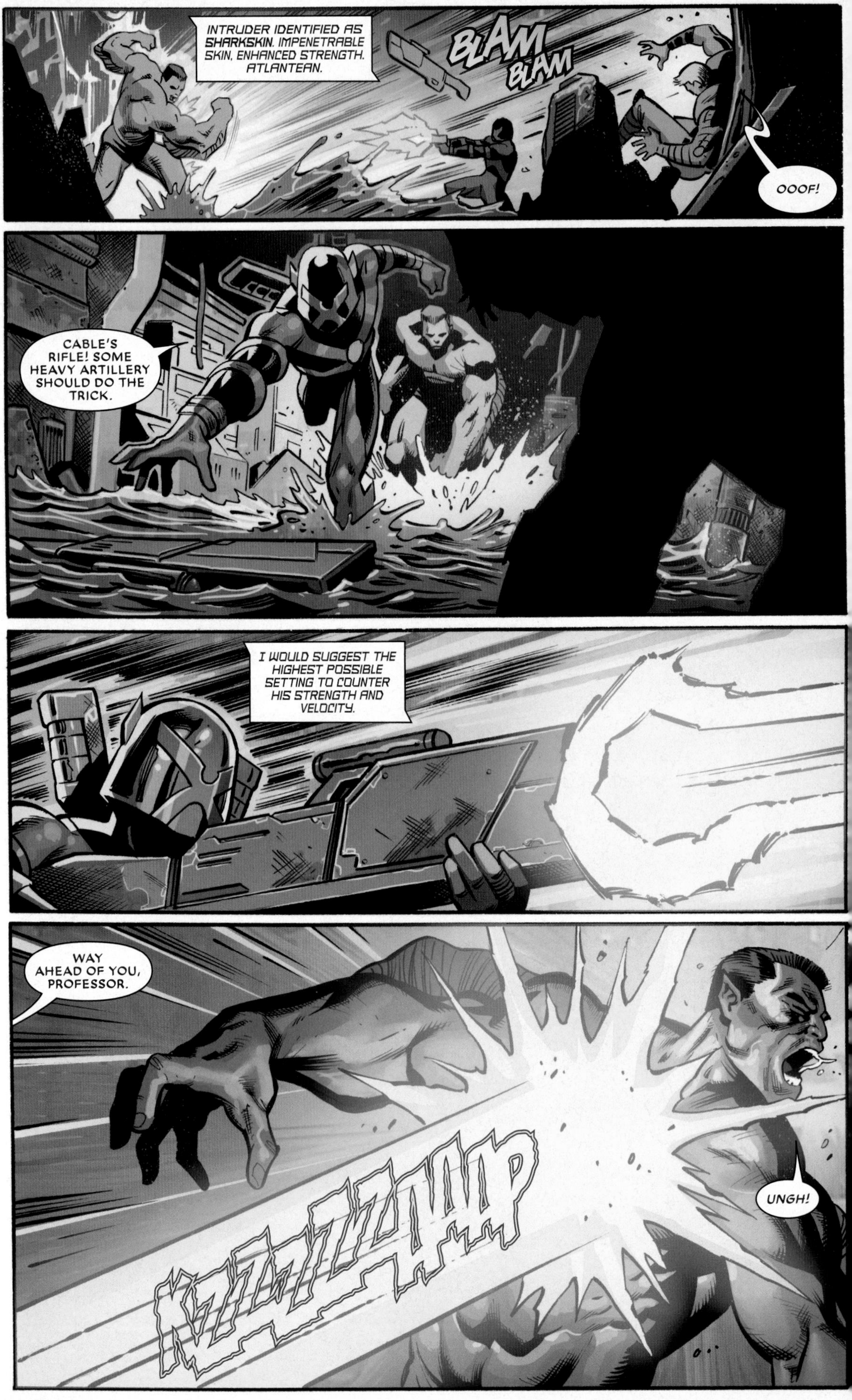

INTRUDER IDENTIFIED AS SHARKSKIN. IMPENETRABLE SKIN, ENHANCED STRENGTH. ATLANTEAN.
BLAM
BLAM
OOOF!
CABLE'S RIFLE! SOME HEAVY ARTILLERY SHOULD DO THE TRICK.
I WOULD SUGGEST THE HIGHEST POSSIBLE SETTING TO COUNTER HIS STRENGTH AND VELOCITY.
WAY AHEAD OF YOU, PROFESSOR.
UNGH!

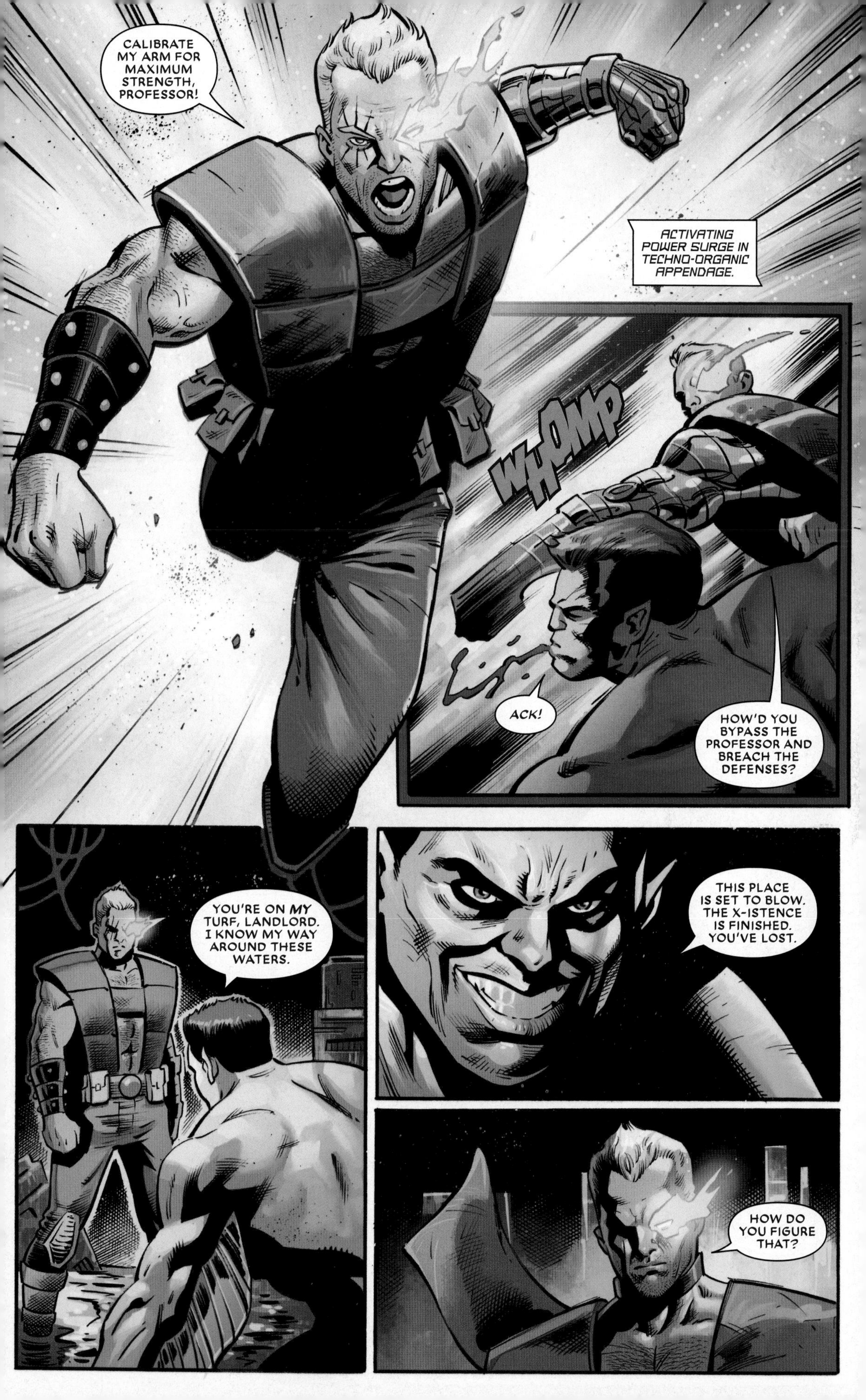
CALIBRATE MY ARM FOR MAXIMUM STRENGTH, PROFESSOR!
ACTIVATING POWER SURGE IN TECHNO-ORGANIC APPENDAGE.
WHOMP
ACK!
HOW'D YOU BYPASS THE PROFESSOR AND BREACH THE DEFENSES?
YOU'RE ON MY TURF, LANDLORD. I KNOW MY WAY AROUND THESE WATERS.
THIS PLACE IS SET TO BLOW. THE X-ISTENCE IS FINISHED. YOU'VE LOST.
HOW DO YOU FIGURE THAT?

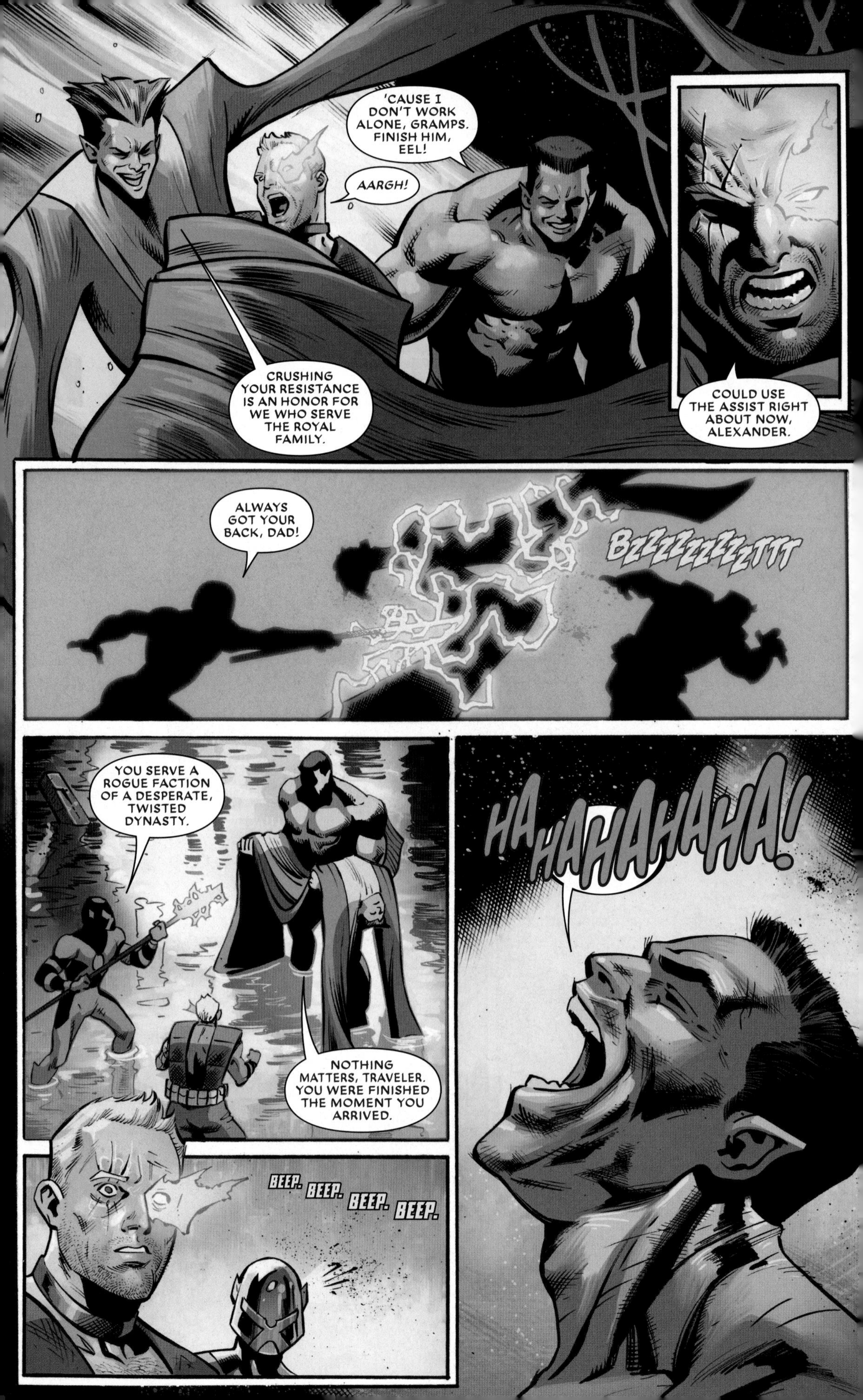
'CAUSE I DON'T WORK ALONE, GRAMPS. FINISH HIM, EEL!
AARGH!
CRUSHING YOUR RESISTANCE IS AN HONOR FOR WE WHO SERVE THE ROYAL FAMILY.
COULD USE THE ASSIST RIGHT ABOUT NOW, ALEXANDER.
ALWAYS GOT YOUR BACK, DAD!
BZZZZZZZZZZTTT
YOU SERVE A ROGUE FACTION OF A DESPERATE, TWISTED DYNASTY.
NOTHING MATTERS, TRAVELER. YOU WERE FINISHED THE MOMENT YOU ARRIVED.
HAHAHAHAHAHA!
BEEP. BEEP. BEEP. BEEP.

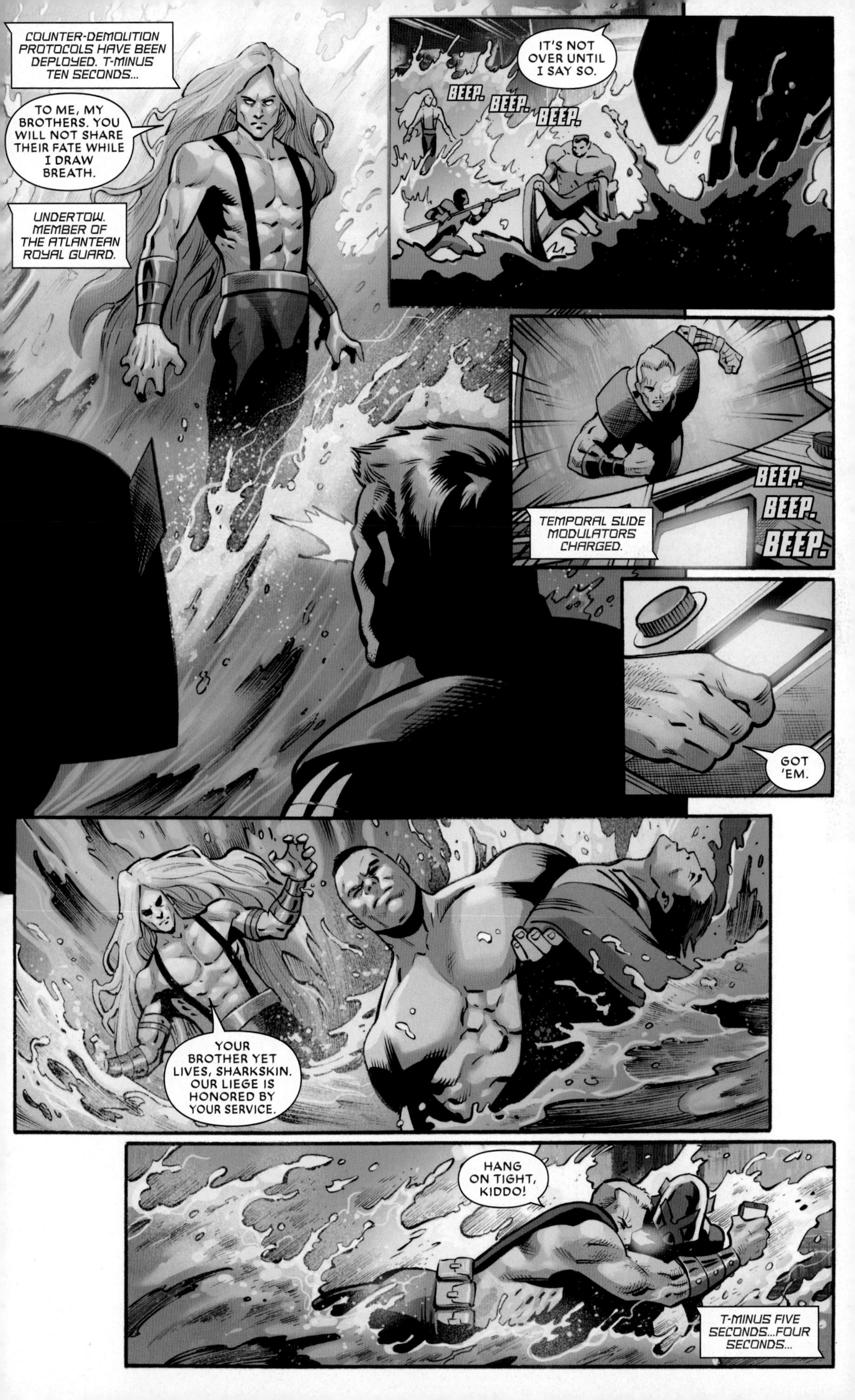
COUNTER-DEMOLITION PROTOCOLS HAVE BEEN DEPLOYED. T-MINUS TEN SECONDS...
TO ME, MY BROTHERS. YOU WILL NOT SHARE THEIR FATE WHILE I DRAW BREATH.
UNDERTOW. MEMBER OF THE ATLANTEAN ROYAL GUARD.
IT'S NOT OVER UNTIL I SAY SO.
BEEP. BEEP. BEEP.
TEMPORAL SLIDE MODULATORS CHARGED.
BEEP. BEEP. BEEP.
GOT 'EM.
YOUR BROTHER YET LIVES, SHARKSKIN. OUR LIEGE IS HONORED BY YOUR SERVICE.
HANG ON TIGHT, KIDDO!
T-MINUS FIVE SECONDS...FOUR SECONDS...

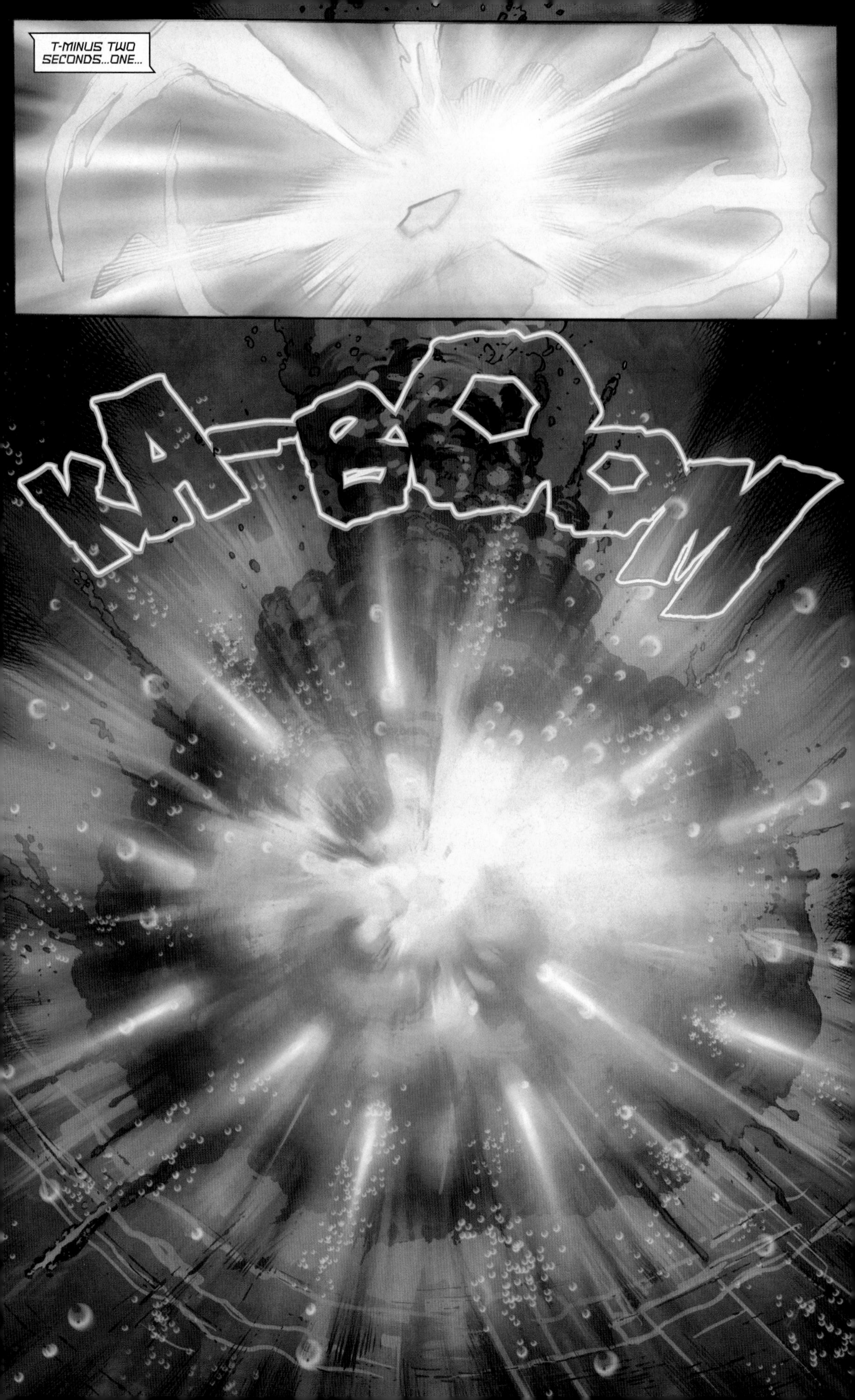
T-MINUS TWO SECONDS...ONE...
KA-BOOM

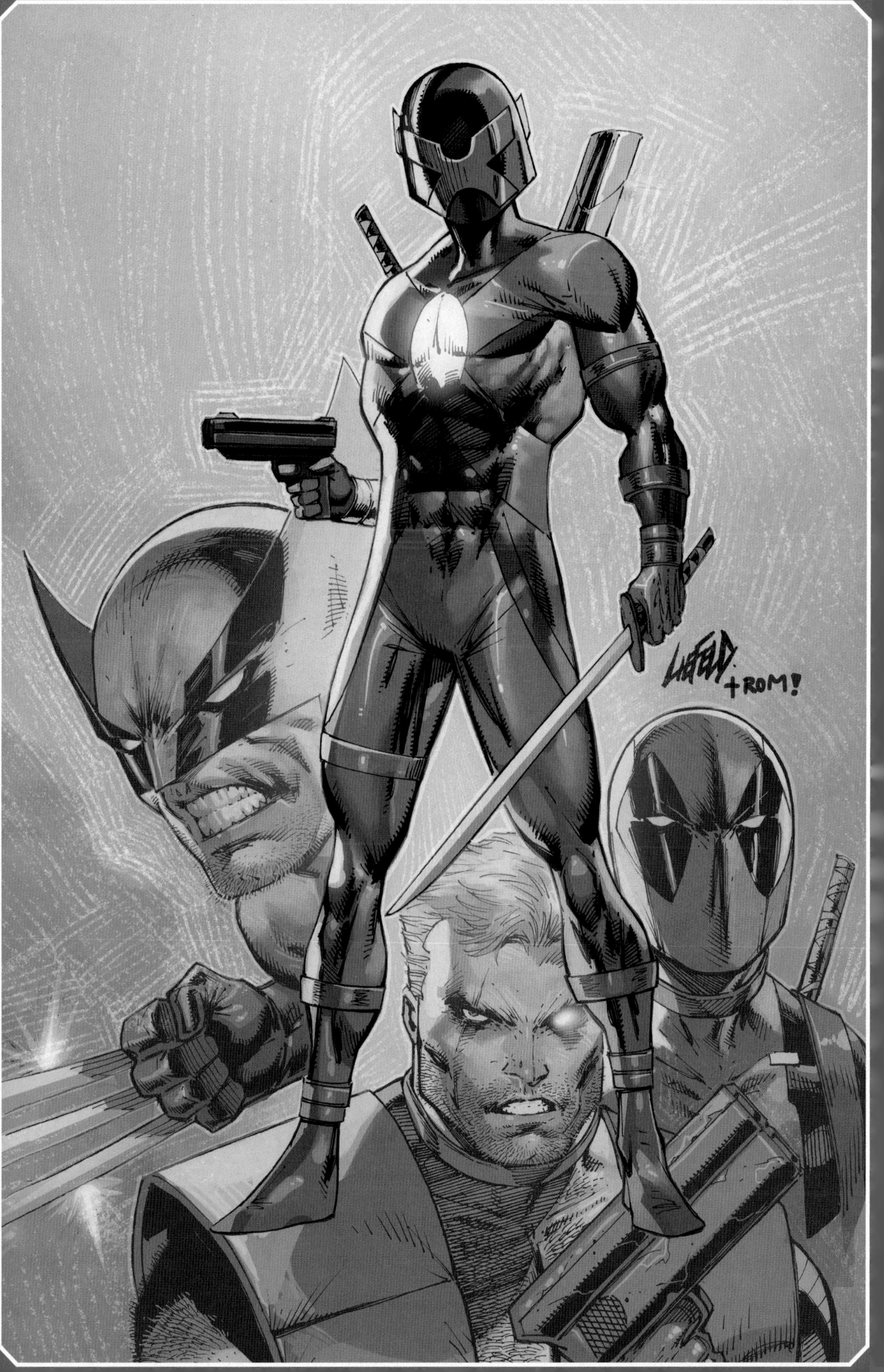
LIEFELD.
+ROM!

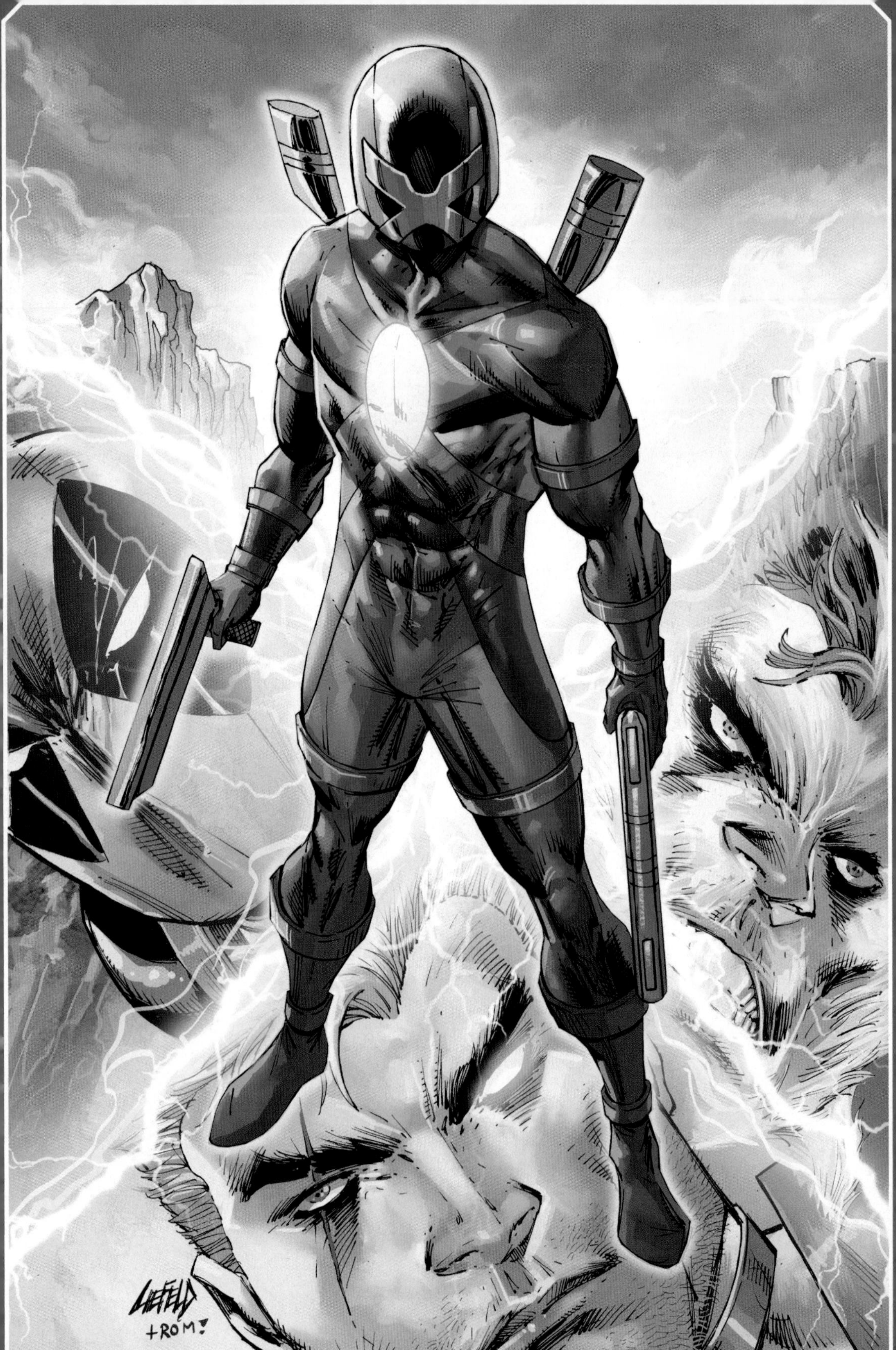
LIEFELD
+ROM!

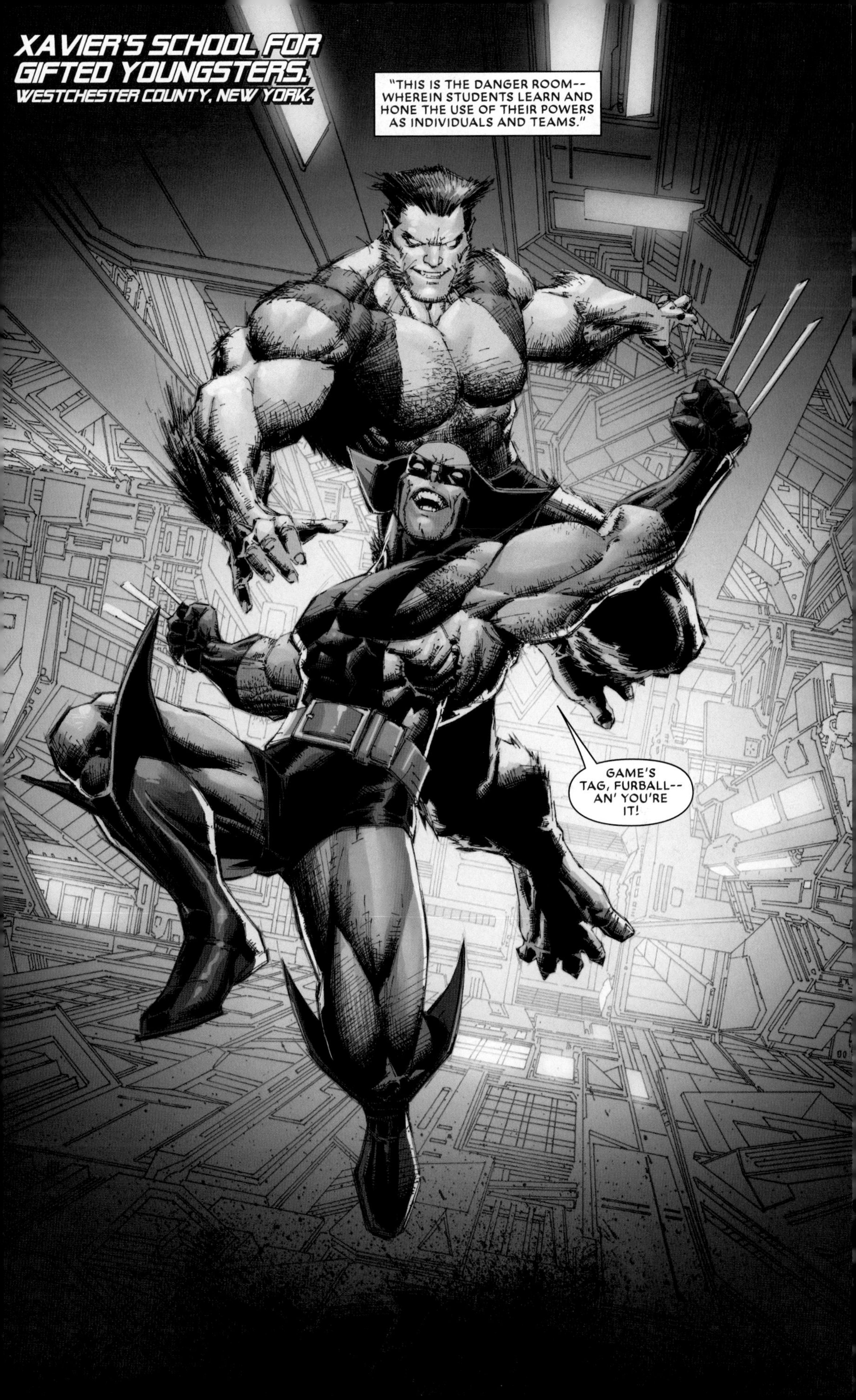
XAVIER'S SCHOOL FOR GIFTED YOUNGSTERS. WESTCHESTER COUNTY, NEW YORK.
"THIS IS THE DANGER ROOM-- WHEREIN STUDENTS LEARN AND HONE THE USE OF THEIR POWERS AS INDIVIDUALS AND TEAMS."
GAME'S TAG, FURBALL-- AN' YOU'RE IT!

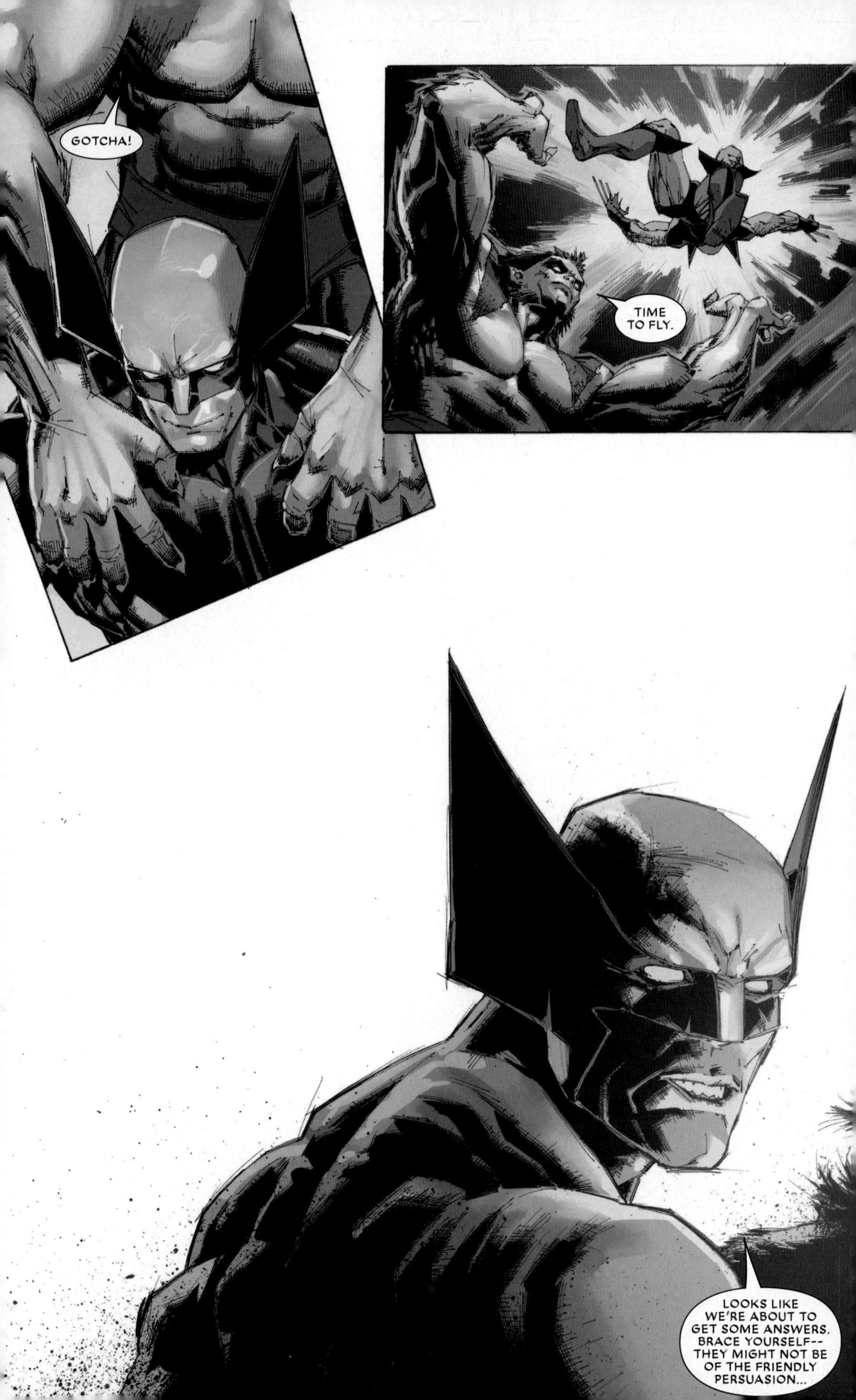
GOTCHA!
TIME TO FLY.
LOOKS LIKE WE'RE ABOUT TO GET SOME ANSWERS. BRACE YOURSELF-- THEY MIGHT NOT BE OF THE FRIENDLY PERSUASION...

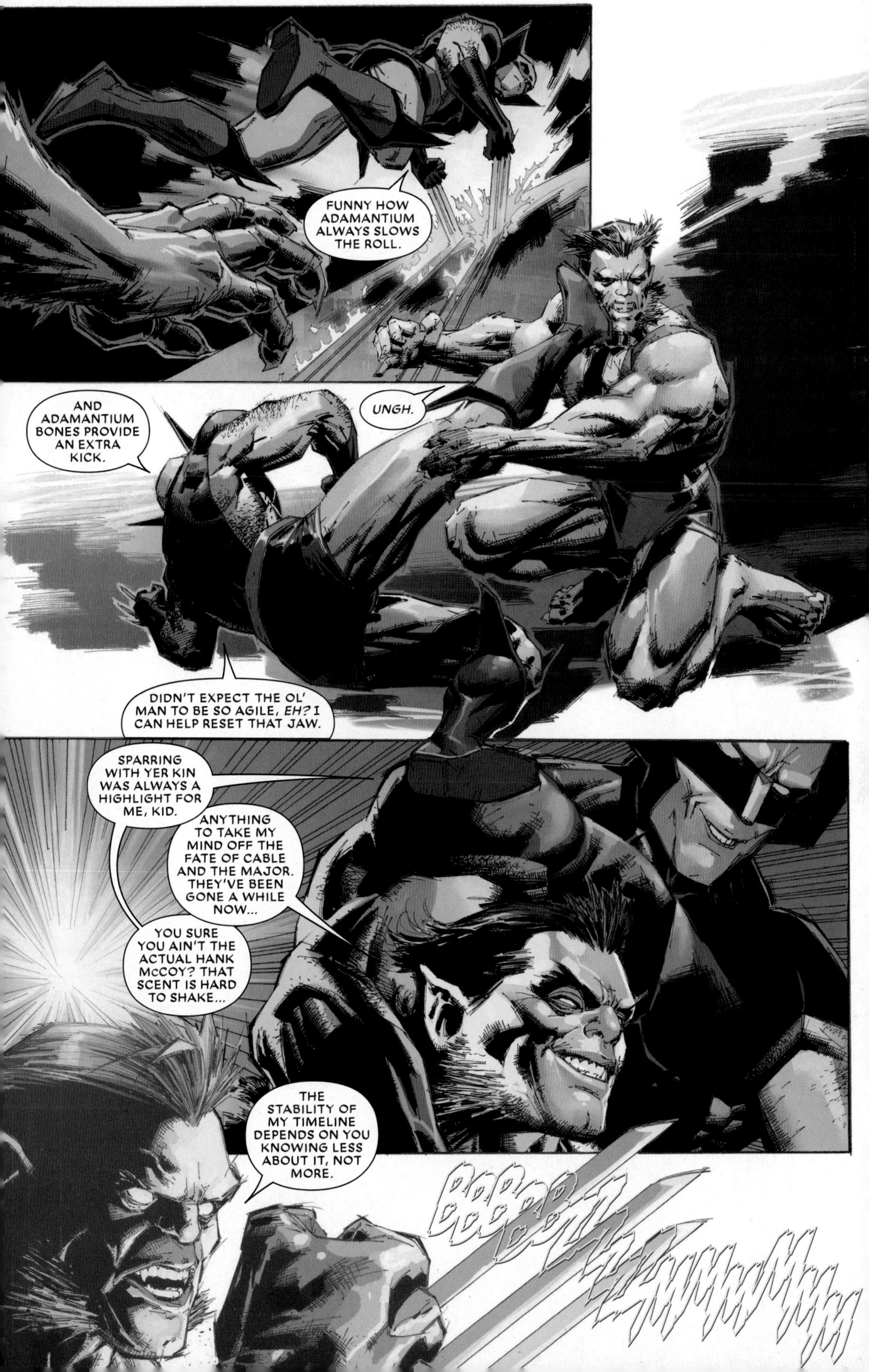
FUNNY HOW ADAMANTIUM ALWAYS SLOWS THE ROLL.
AND ADAMANTIUM BONES PROVIDE AN EXTRA KICK.
UNGH.
DIDN'T EXPECT THE OL' MAN TO BE SO AGILE, *EH?* I CAN HELP RESET THAT JAW.
SPARRING WITH YER KIN WAS ALWAYS A HIGHLIGHT FOR ME, KID.
ANYTHING TO TAKE MY MIND OFF THE FATE OF CABLE AND THE MAJOR. THEY'VE BEEN GONE A WHILE NOW...
YOU SURE YOU AIN'T THE ACTUAL HANK McCOY? THAT SCENT IS HARD TO SHAKE...
THE STABILITY OF MY TIMELINE DEPENDS ON YOU KNOWING LESS ABOUT IT, NOT MORE.

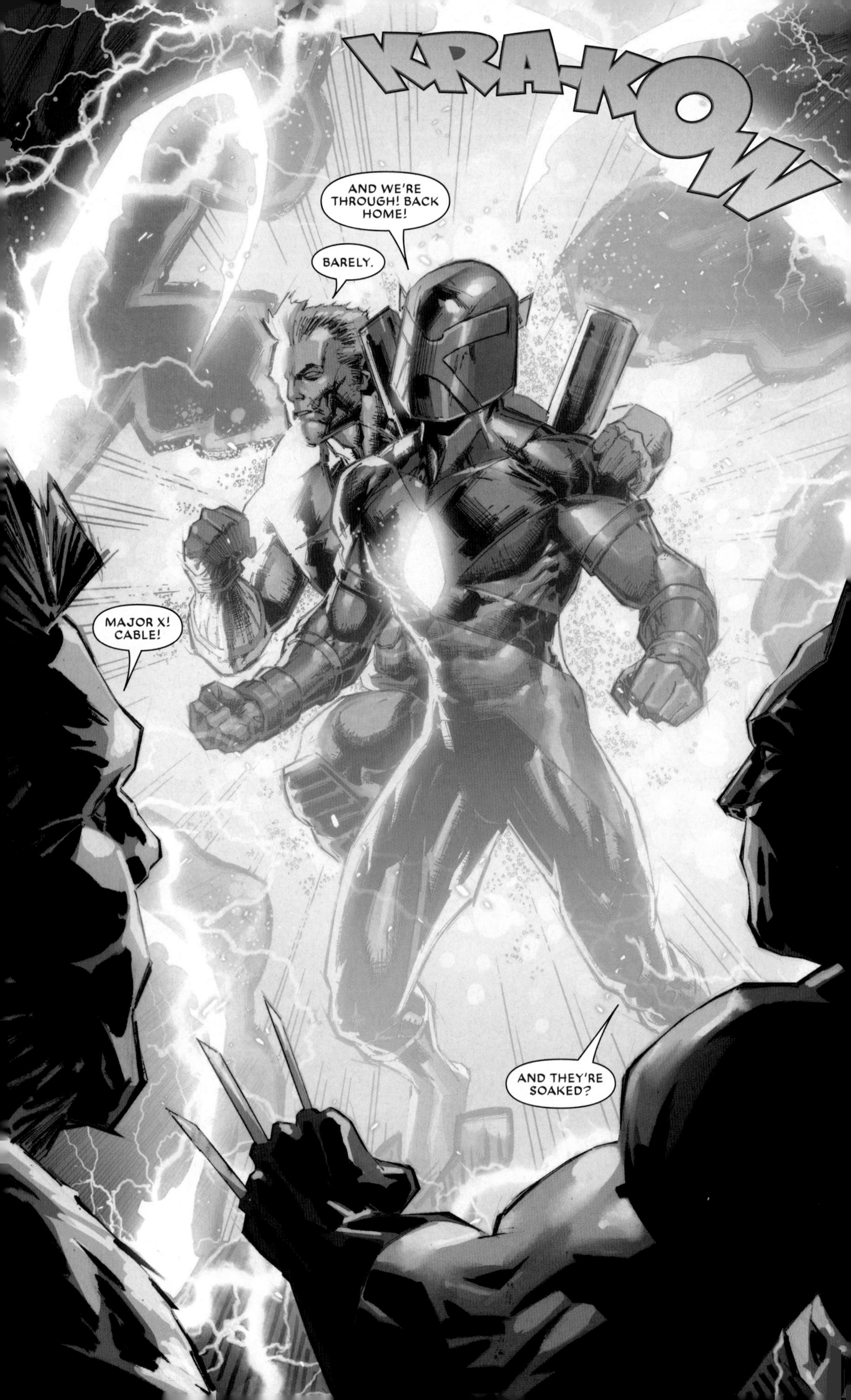
KRA-KOW
AND WE'RE THROUGH! BACK HOME!
BARELY.
MAJOR X! CABLE!
AND THEY'RE SOAKED?

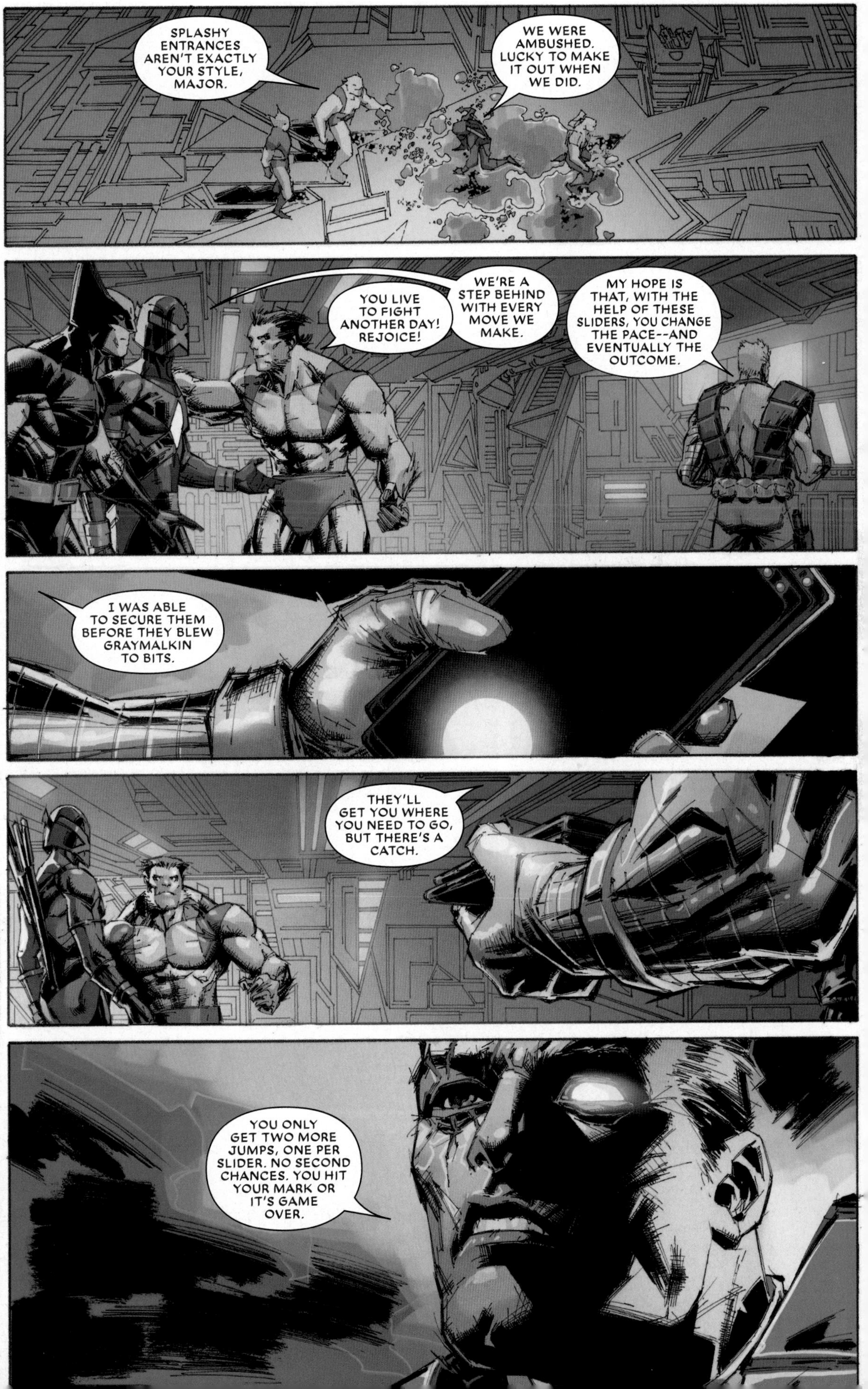
SPLASHY ENTRANCES AREN'T EXACTLY YOUR STYLE, MAJOR.
WE WERE AMBUSHED. LUCKY TO MAKE IT OUT WHEN WE DID.
YOU LIVE TO FIGHT ANOTHER DAY! REJOICE!
WE'RE A STEP BEHIND WITH EVERY MOVE WE MAKE.
MY HOPE IS THAT, WITH THE HELP OF THESE SLIDERS, YOU CHANGE THE PACE--AND EVENTUALLY THE OUTCOME.
I WAS ABLE TO SECURE THEM BEFORE THEY BLEW GRAYMALKIN TO BITS.
THEY'LL GET YOU WHERE YOU NEED TO GO, BUT THERE'S A CATCH.
YOU ONLY GET TWO MORE JUMPS, ONE PER SLIDER. NO SECOND CHANCES. YOU HIT YOUR MARK OR IT'S GAME OVER.

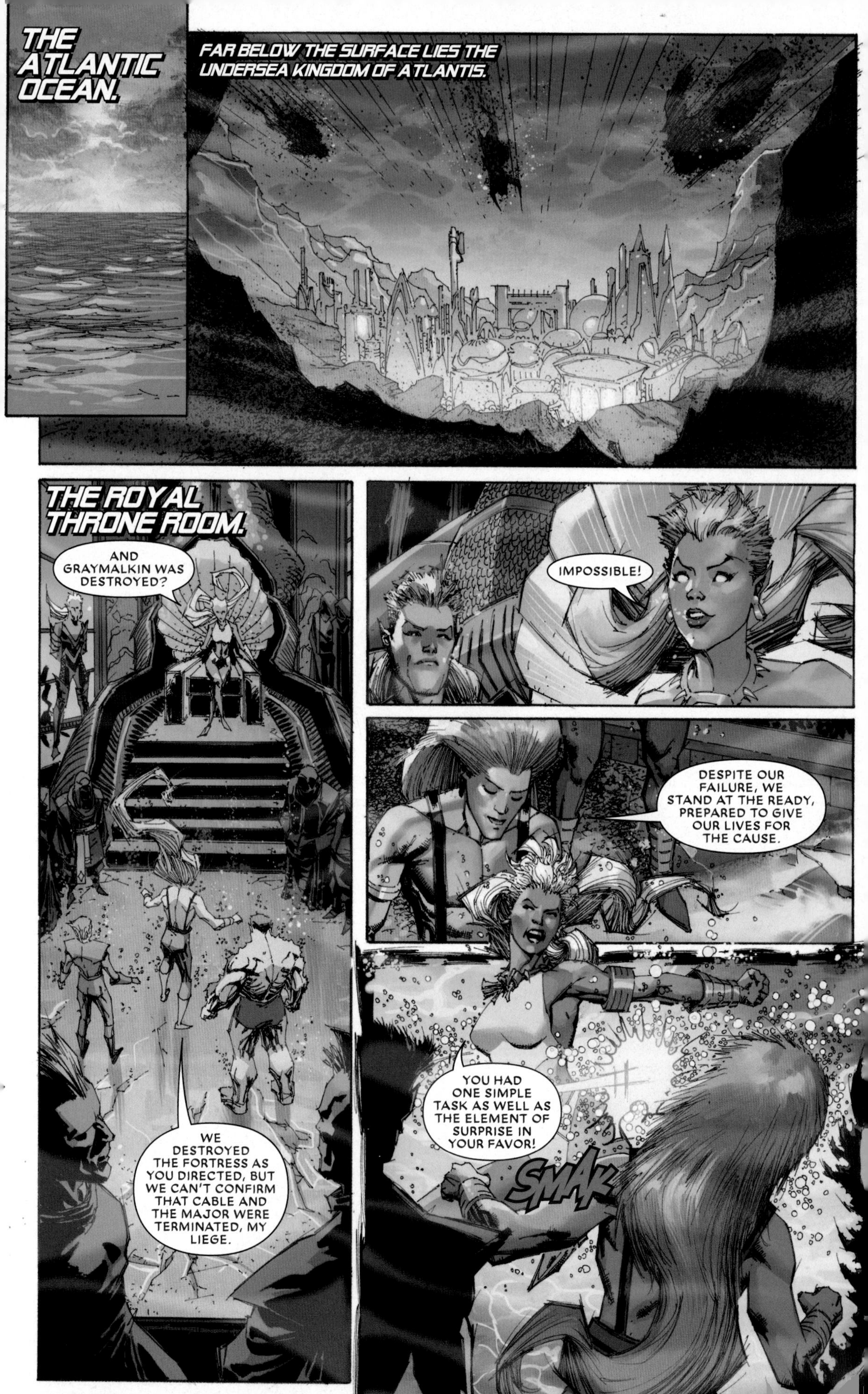
THE ATLANTIC OCEAN.
FAR BELOW THE SURFACE LIES THE UNDERSEA KINGDOM OF ATLANTIS.
THE ROYAL THRONE ROOM.
AND GRAYMALKIN WAS DESTROYED?
WE DESTROYED THE FORTRESS AS YOU DIRECTED, BUT WE CAN'T CONFIRM THAT CABLE AND THE MAJOR WERE TERMINATED, MY LIEGE.
IMPOSSIBLE!
DESPITE OUR FAILURE, WE STAND AT THE READY, PREPARED TO GIVE OUR LIVES FOR THE CAUSE.
YOU HAD ONE SIMPLE TASK AS WELL AS THE ELEMENT OF SURPRISE IN YOUR FAVOR!
SMAK

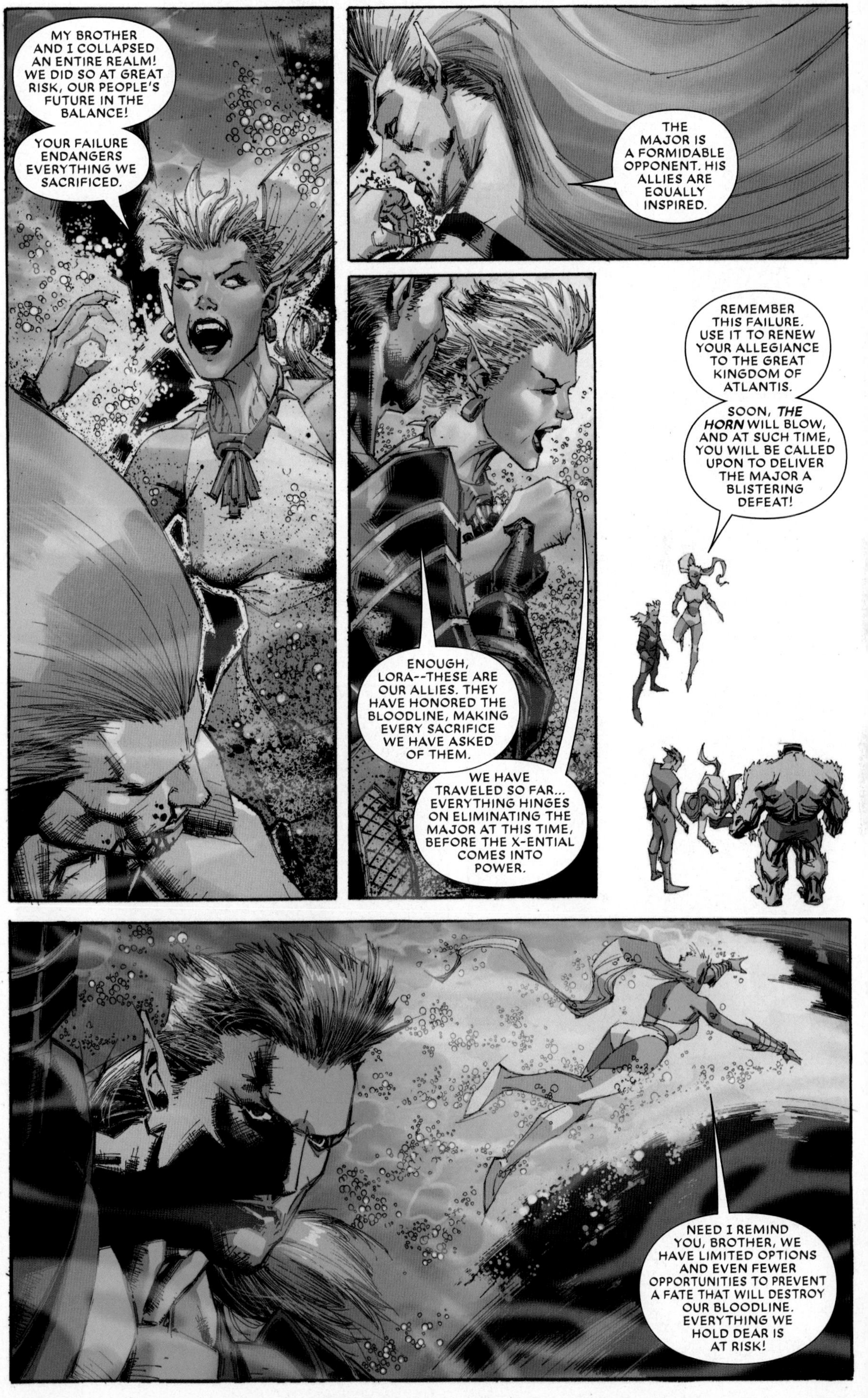
MY BROTHER AND I COLLAPSED AN ENTIRE REALM! WE DID SO AT GREAT RISK, OUR PEOPLE'S FUTURE IN THE BALANCE!
YOUR FAILURE ENDANGERS EVERYTHING WE SACRIFICED.
THE MAJOR IS A FORMIDABLE OPPONENT. HIS ALLIES ARE EQUALLY INSPIRED.
ENOUGH, LORA--THESE ARE OUR ALLIES. THEY HAVE HONORED THE BLOODLINE, MAKING EVERY SACRIFICE WE HAVE ASKED OF THEM.
WE HAVE TRAVELED SO FAR... EVERYTHING HINGES ON ELIMINATING THE MAJOR AT THIS TIME, BEFORE THE X-ENTIAL COMES INTO POWER.
REMEMBER THIS FAILURE. USE IT TO RENEW YOUR ALLEGIANCE TO THE GREAT KINGDOM OF ATLANTIS.
SOON, *THE HORN* WILL BLOW, AND AT SUCH TIME, YOU WILL BE CALLED UPON TO DELIVER THE MAJOR A BLISTERING DEFEAT!
NEED I REMIND YOU, BROTHER, WE HAVE LIMITED OPTIONS AND EVEN FEWER OPPORTUNITIES TO PREVENT A FATE THAT WILL DESTROY OUR BLOODLINE. EVERYTHING WE HOLD DEAR IS AT RISK!

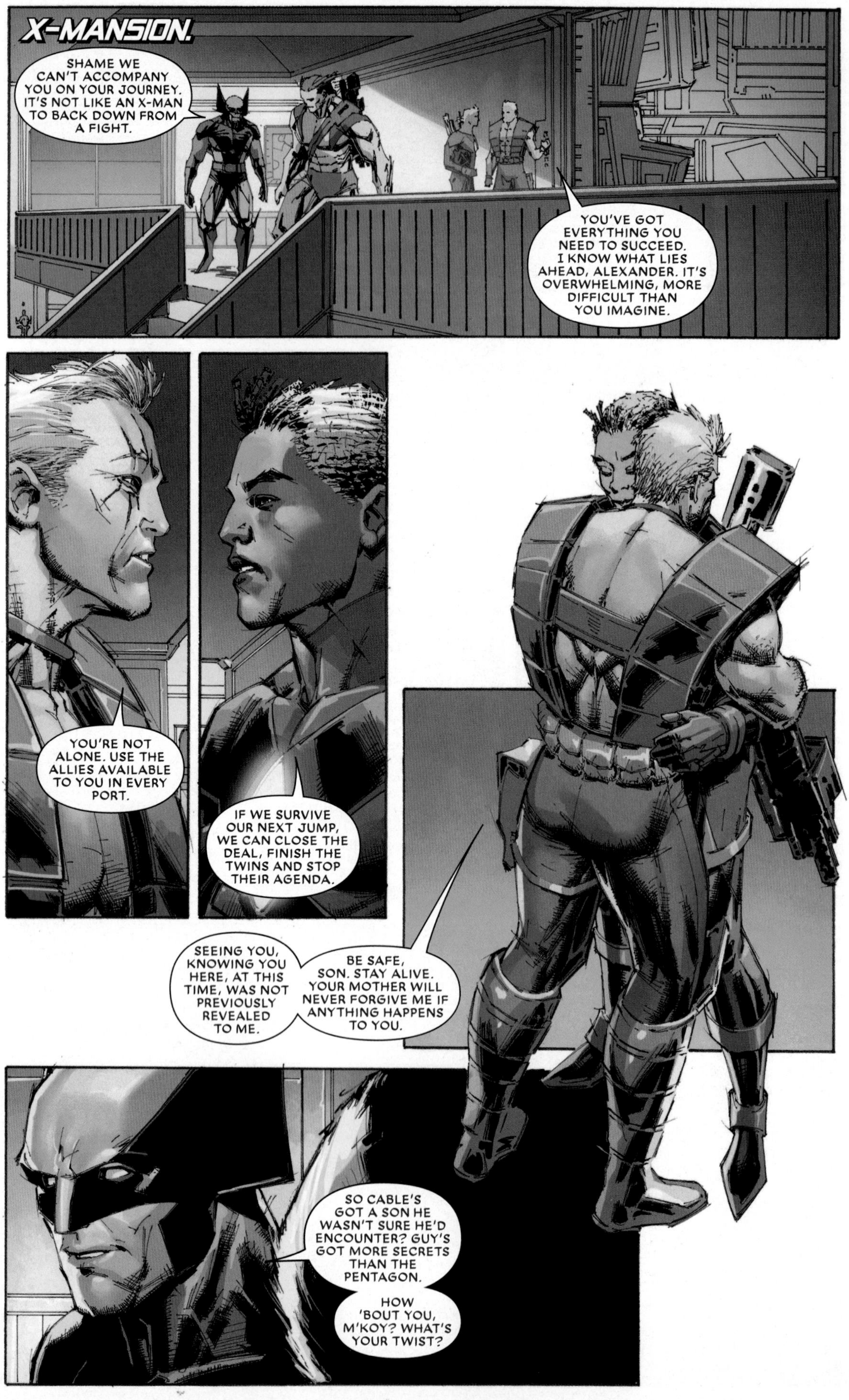
X-MANSION.
SHAME WE CAN'T ACCOMPANY YOU ON YOUR JOURNEY. IT'S NOT LIKE AN X-MAN TO BACK DOWN FROM A FIGHT.
YOU'VE GOT EVERYTHING YOU NEED TO SUCCEED. I KNOW WHAT LIES AHEAD, ALEXANDER. IT'S OVERWHELMING, MORE DIFFICULT THAN YOU IMAGINE.
YOU'RE NOT ALONE. USE THE ALLIES AVAILABLE TO YOU IN EVERY PORT.
IF WE SURVIVE OUR NEXT JUMP, WE CAN CLOSE THE DEAL, FINISH THE TWINS AND STOP THEIR AGENDA.
SEEING YOU, KNOWING YOU HERE, AT THIS TIME, WAS NOT PREVIOUSLY REVEALED TO ME.
BE SAFE, SON. STAY ALIVE. YOUR MOTHER WILL NEVER FORGIVE ME IF ANYTHING HAPPENS TO YOU.
SO CABLE'S GOT A SON HE WASN'T SURE HE'D ENCOUNTER? GUY'S GOT MORE SECRETS THAN THE PENTAGON.
HOW 'BOUT YOU, M'KOY? WHAT'S YOUR TWIST?

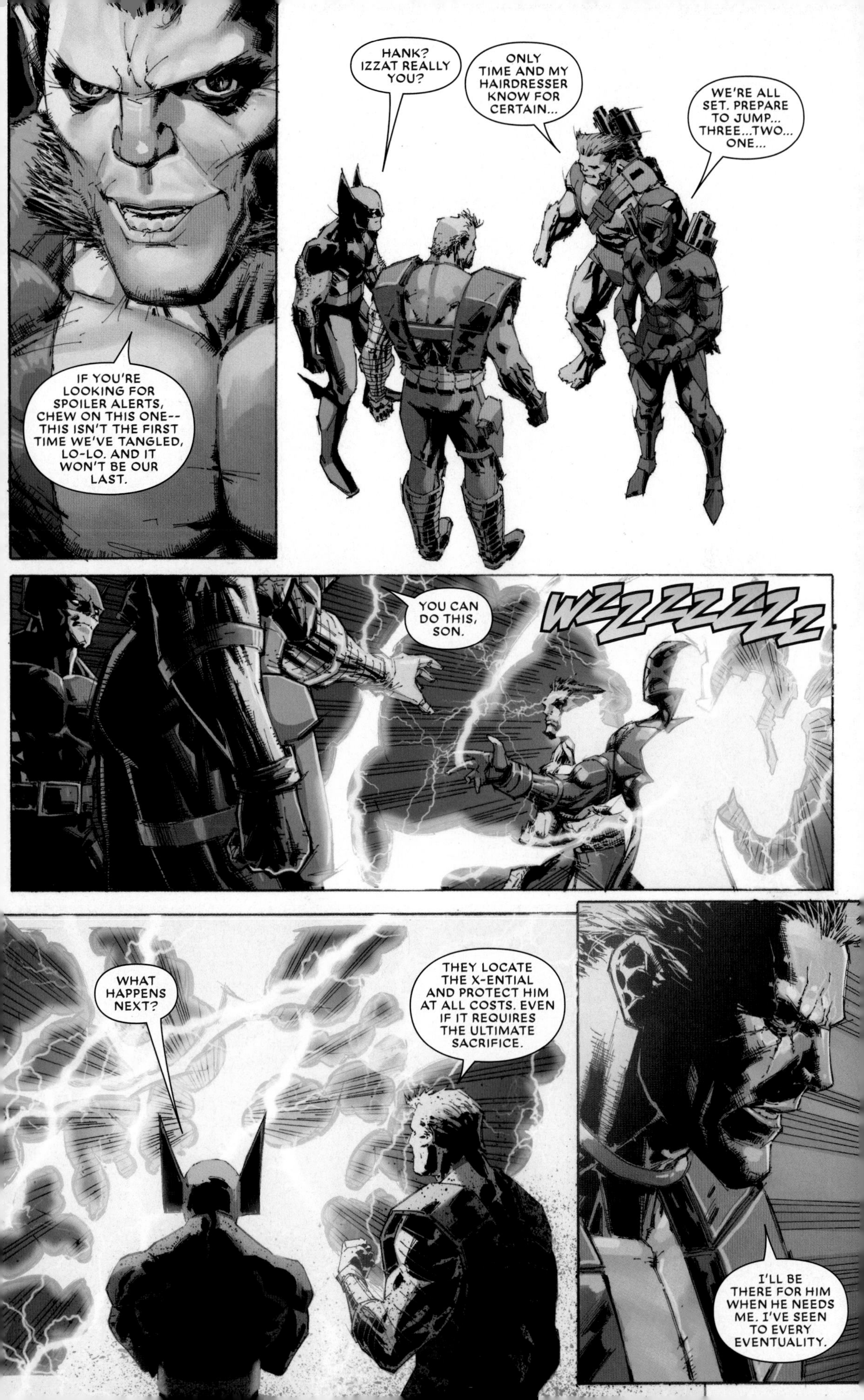
IF YOU'RE LOOKING FOR SPOILER ALERTS, CHEW ON THIS ONE-- THIS ISN'T THE FIRST TIME WE'VE TANGLED, LO-LO. AND IT WON'T BE OUR LAST.
HANK? IZZAT REALLY YOU?
ONLY TIME AND MY HAIRDRESSER KNOW FOR CERTAIN...
WE'RE ALL SET. PREPARE TO JUMP... THREE...TWO... ONE...
YOU CAN DO THIS, SON.
WZZZZZZZZ
WHAT HAPPENS NEXT?
THEY LOCATE THE X-ENTIAL AND PROTECT HIM AT ALL COSTS. EVEN IF IT REQUIRES THE ULTIMATE SACRIFICE.
I'LL BE THERE FOR HIM WHEN HE NEEDS ME. I'VE SEEN TO EVERY EVENTUALITY.

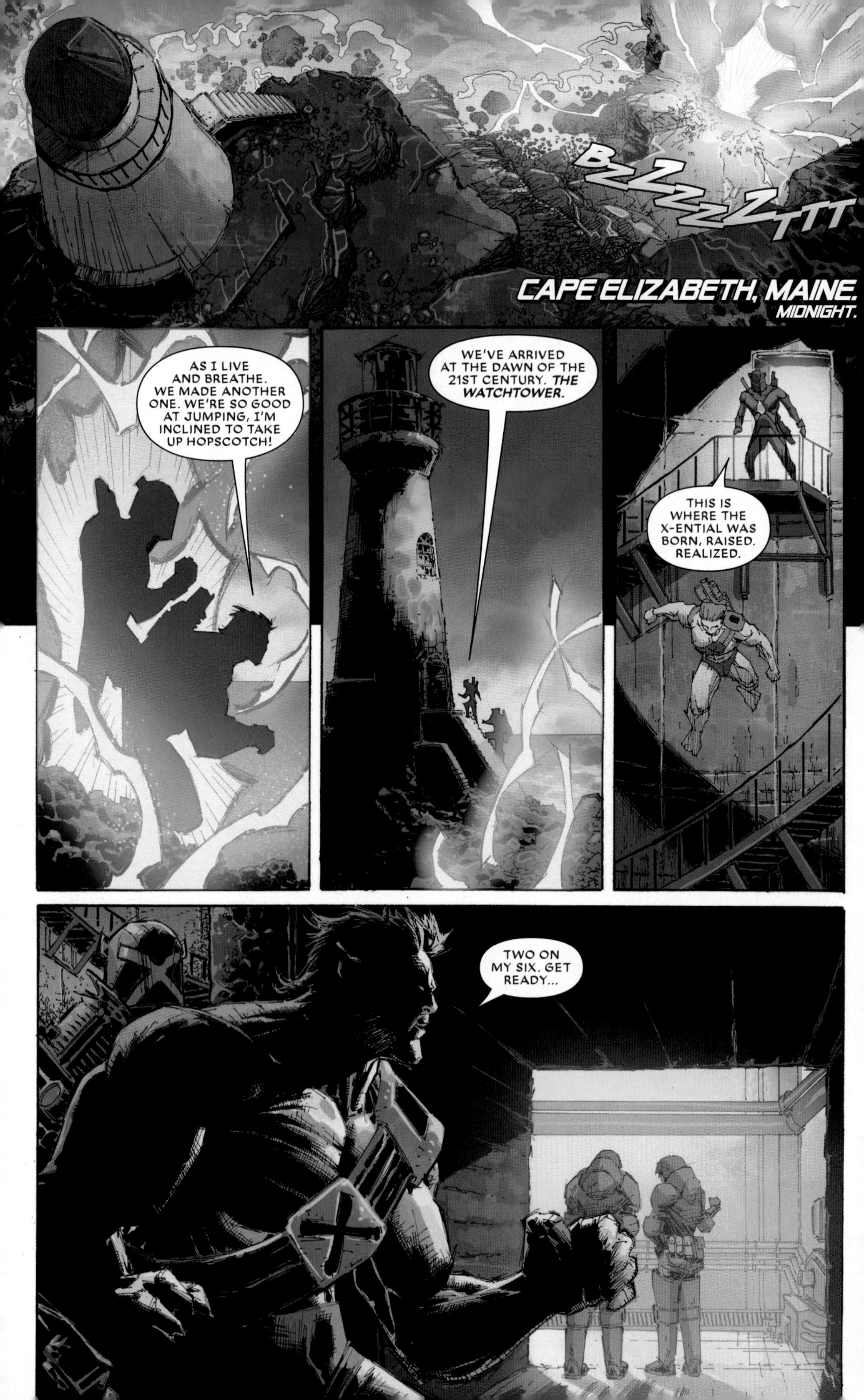
BZZZZZZTTT
CAPE ELIZABETH, MAINE.
MIDNIGHT.
AS I LIVE AND BREATHE. WE MADE ANOTHER ONE. WE'RE SO GOOD AT JUMPING, I'M INCLINED TO TAKE UP HOPSCOTCH!
WE'VE ARRIVED AT THE DAWN OF THE 21ST CENTURY. THE WATCHTOWER.
THIS IS WHERE THE X-ENTIAL WAS BORN, RAISED. REALIZED.
TWO ON MY SIX. GET READY...

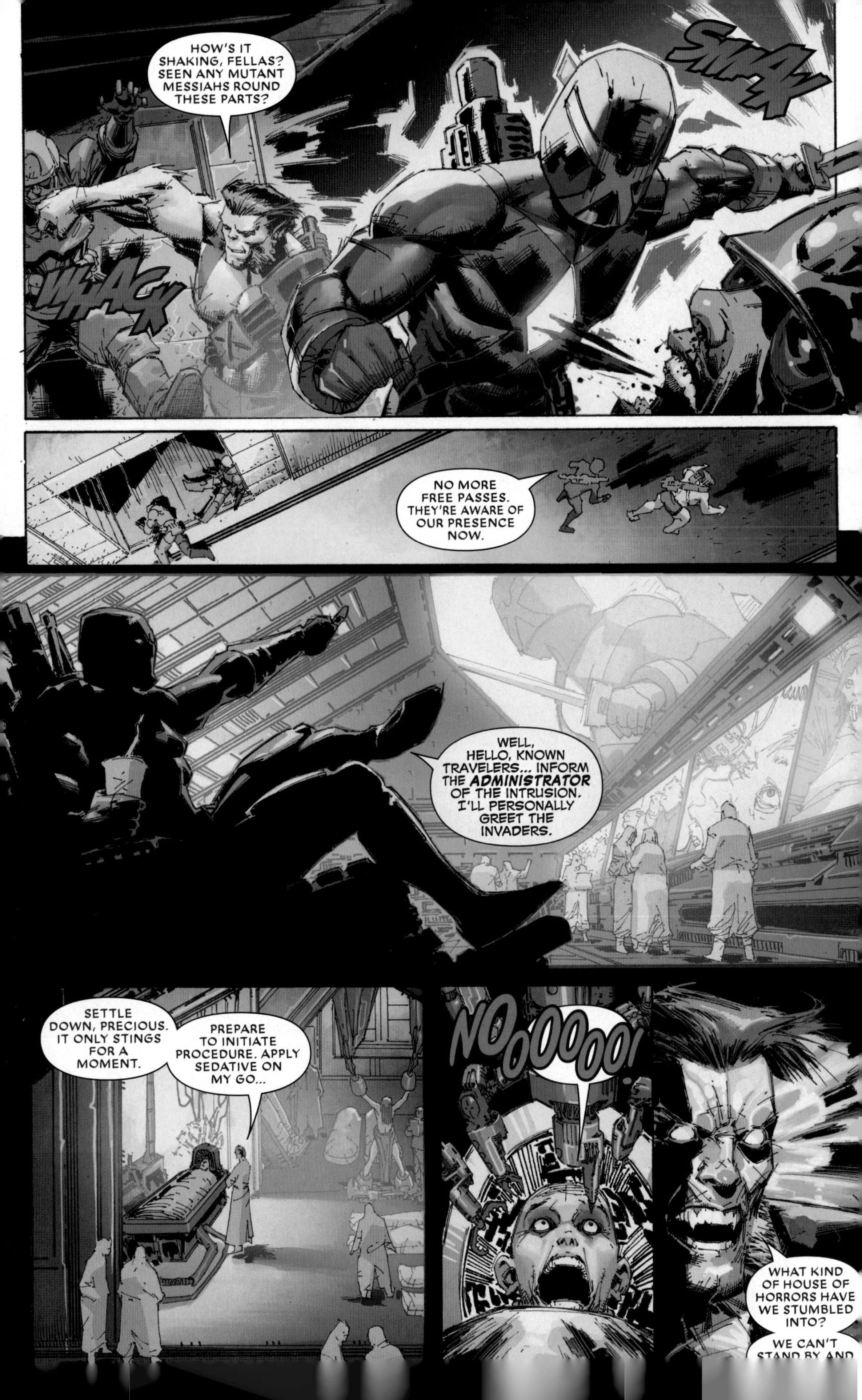
HOW'S IT SHAKING, FELLAS? SEEN ANY MUTANT MESSIAHS ROUND THESE PARTS?
SNAK
WHACK
NO MORE FREE PASSES. THEY'RE AWARE OF OUR PRESENCE NOW.
WELL, HELLO, KNOWN TRAVELERS... INFORM THE ADMINISTRATOR OF THE INTRUSION. I'LL PERSONALLY GREET THE INVADERS.
SETTLE DOWN, PRECIOUS. IT ONLY STINGS FOR A MOMENT.
PREPARE TO INITIATE PROCEDURE. APPLY SEDATIVE ON MY GO...
NOOOOOOO!
WHAT KIND OF HOUSE OF HORRORS HAVE WE STUMBLED INTO?
WE CAN'T STAND BY AND

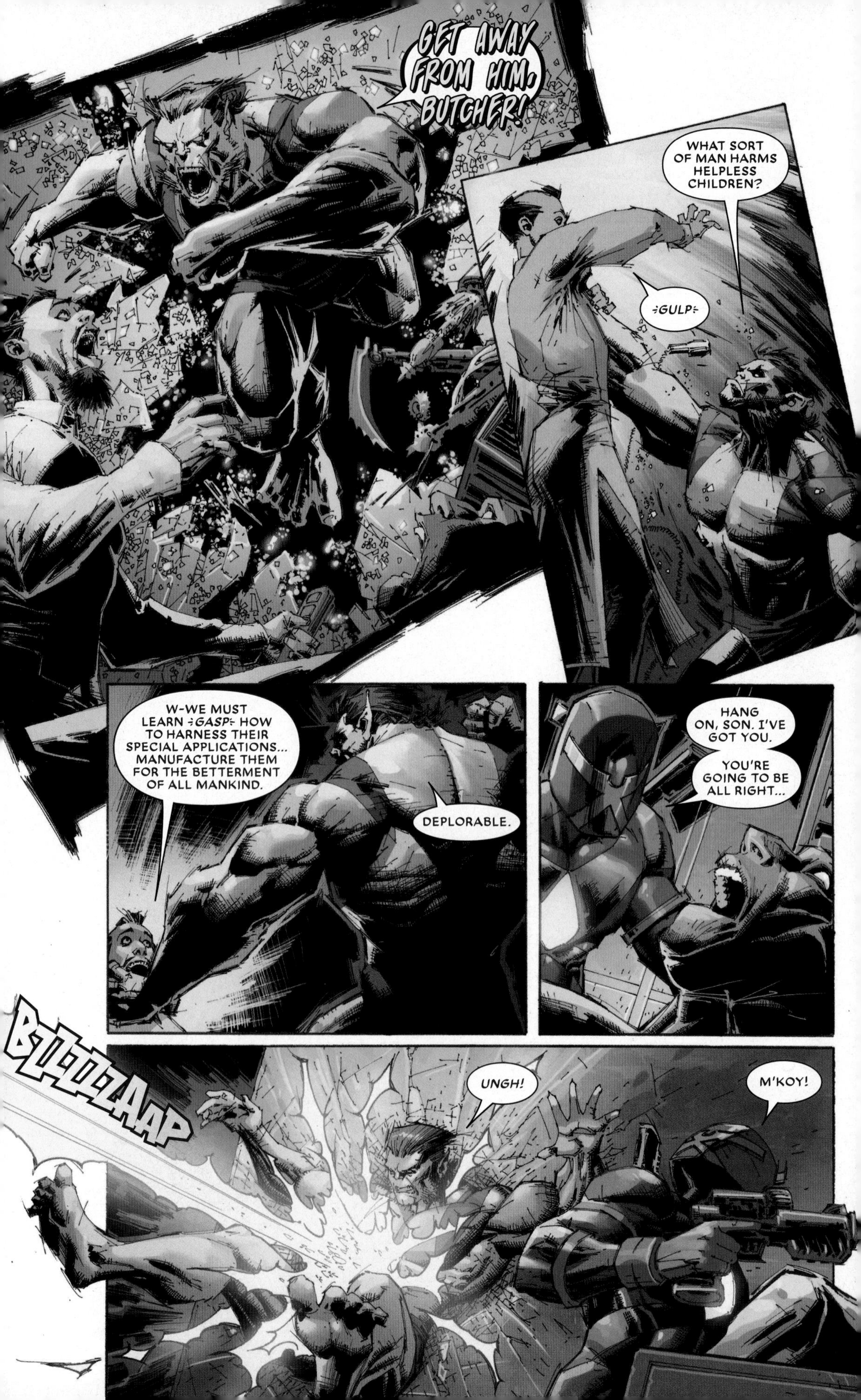
GET AWAY FROM HIM, BUTCHER!
WHAT SORT OF MAN HARMS HELPLESS CHILDREN?
=GULP=
W-WE MUST LEARN =GASP= HOW TO HARNESS THEIR SPECIAL APPLICATIONS... MANUFACTURE THEM FOR THE BETTERMENT OF ALL MANKIND.
DEPLORABLE.
HANG ON, SON. I'VE GOT YOU.
YOU'RE GOING TO BE ALL RIGHT...
BZZZZAAP
UNGH!
M'KOY!

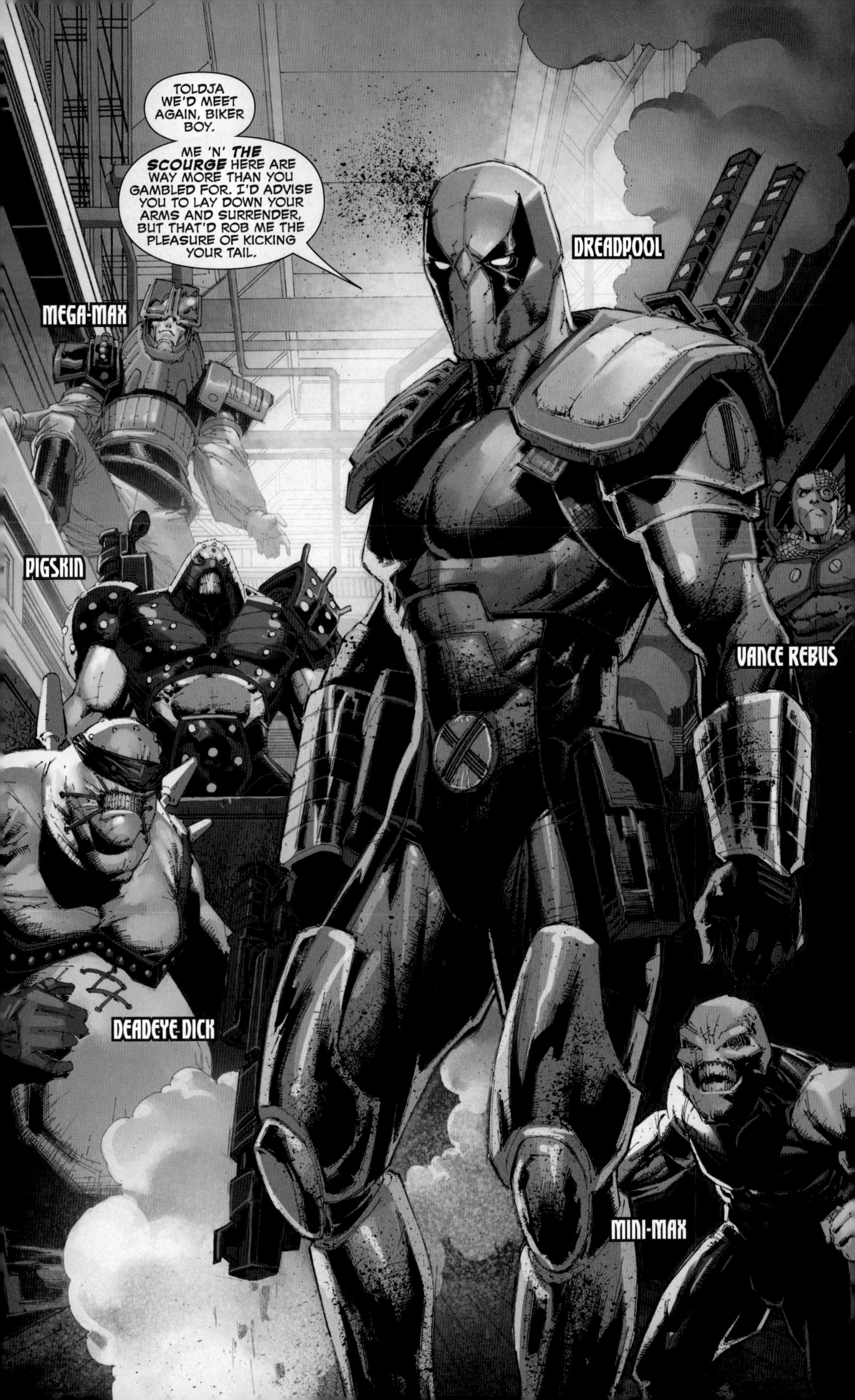
TOLDJA WE'D MEET AGAIN, BIKER BOY.
ME 'N' THE SCOURGE HERE ARE WAY MORE THAN YOU GAMBLED FOR. I'D ADVISE YOU TO LAY DOWN YOUR ARMS AND SURRENDER, BUT THAT'D ROB ME THE PLEASURE OF KICKING YOUR TAIL.
DREADPOOL
MEGA-MAX
PIGSKIN
VANCE REBUS
DEADEYE DICK
MINI-MAX

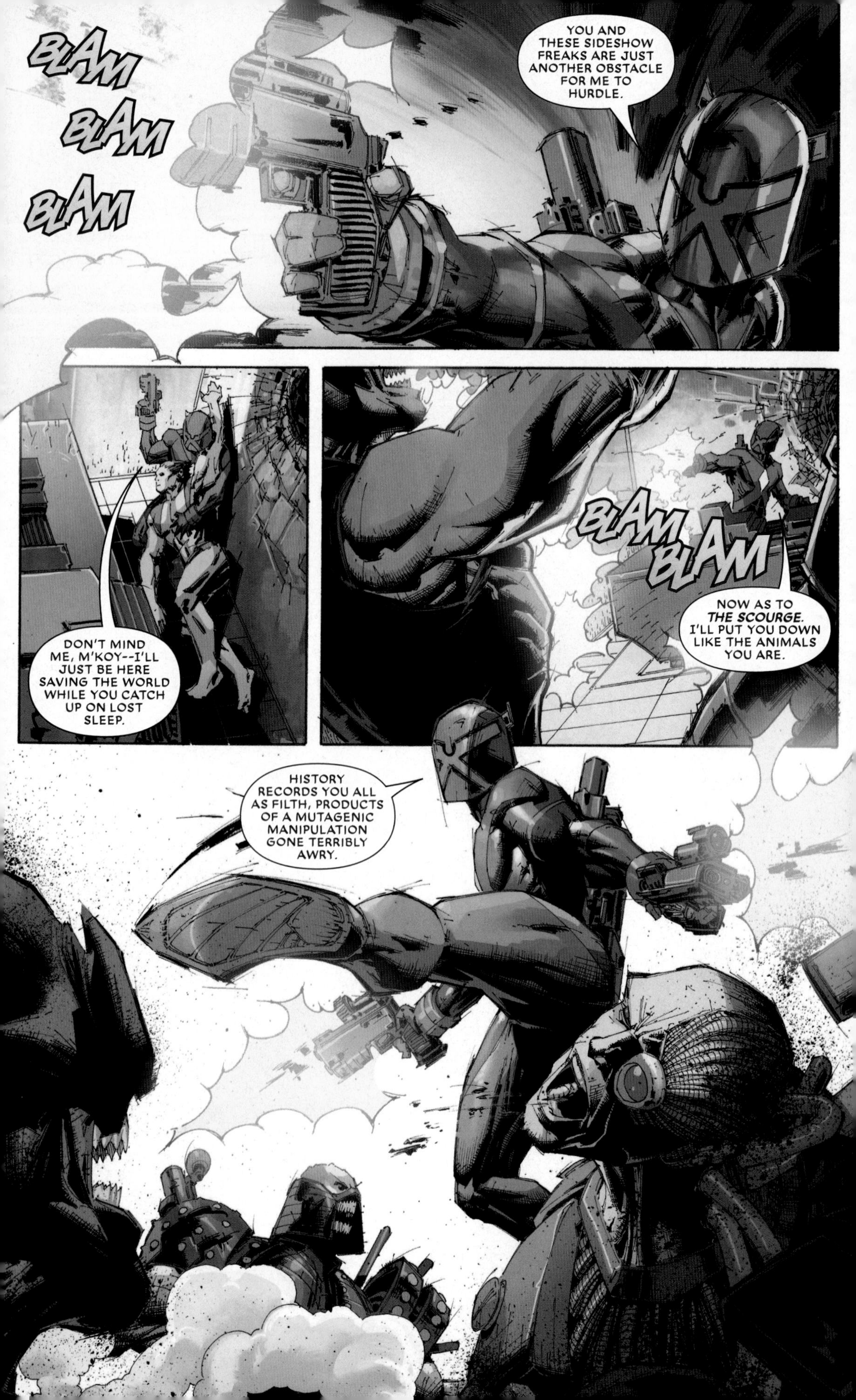
BLAM
BLAM
BLAM
YOU AND THESE SIDESHOW FREAKS ARE JUST ANOTHER OBSTACLE FOR ME TO HURDLE.
DON'T MIND ME, M'KOY--I'LL JUST BE HERE SAVING THE WORLD WHILE YOU CATCH UP ON LOST SLEEP.
BLAM BLAM
NOW AS TO *THE SCOURGE.* I'LL PUT YOU DOWN LIKE THE ANIMALS YOU ARE.
HISTORY RECORDS YOU ALL AS FILTH, PRODUCTS OF A MUTAGENIC MANIPULATION GONE TERRIBLY AWRY.

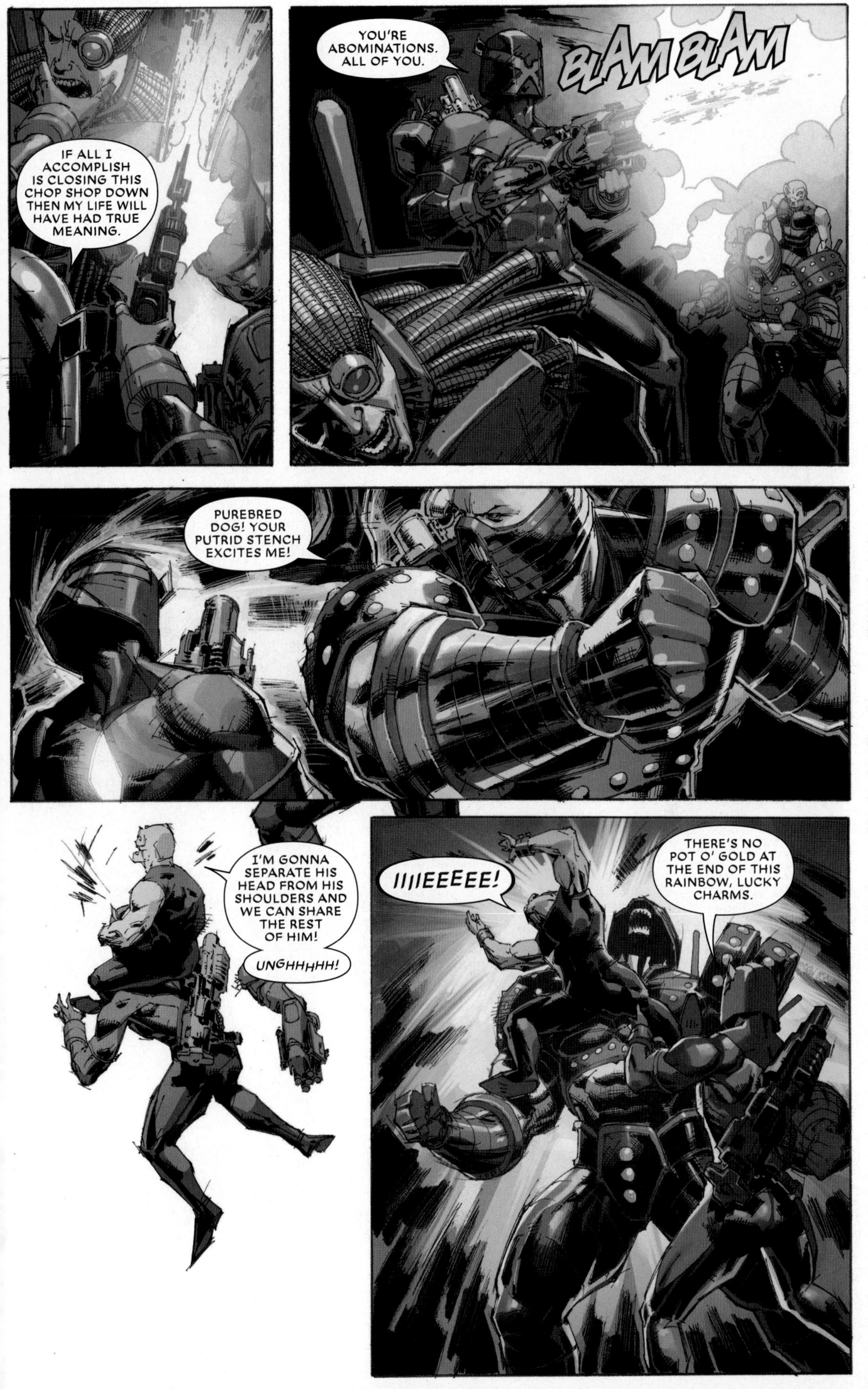
IF ALL I ACCOMPLISH IS CLOSING THIS CHOP SHOP DOWN THEN MY LIFE WILL HAVE HAD TRUE MEANING.
YOU'RE ABOMINATIONS. ALL OF YOU.
BLAM BLAM
PUREBRED DOG! YOUR PUTRID STENCH EXCITES ME!
I'M GONNA SEPARATE HIS HEAD FROM HIS SHOULDERS AND WE CAN SHARE THE REST OF HIM!
UNGHHHHH!
IIIIEEEEE!
THERE'S NO POT O' GOLD AT THE END OF THIS RAINBOW, LUCKY CHARMS.

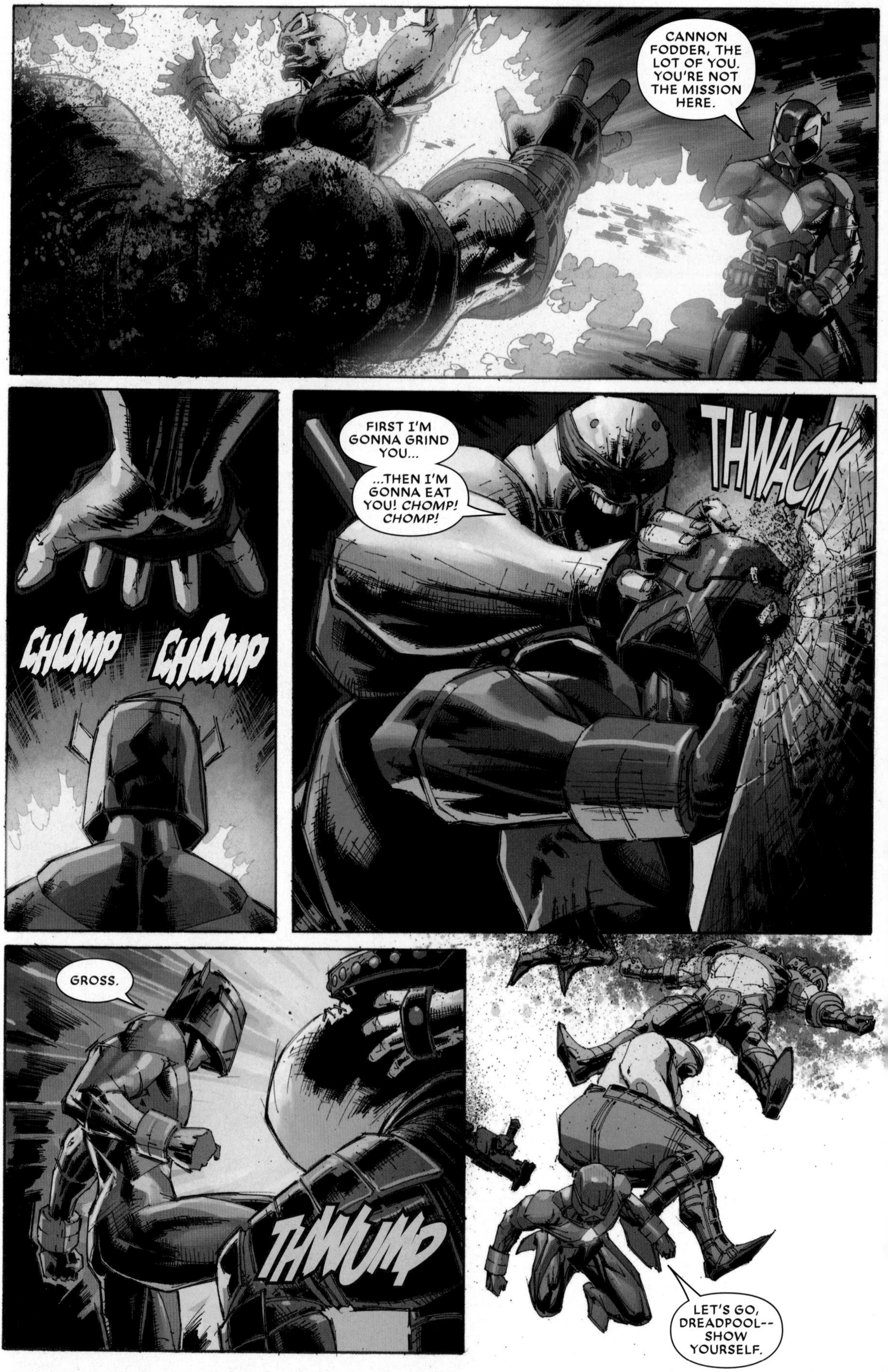
CANNON FODDER, THE LOT OF YOU. YOU'RE NOT THE MISSION HERE.
CHOMP CHOMP
FIRST I'M GONNA GRIND YOU...
...THEN I'M GONNA EAT YOU! *CHOMP! CHOMP!*
THWACK
GROSS.
THWUMP
LET'S GO, DREADPOOL-- SHOW YOURSELF.

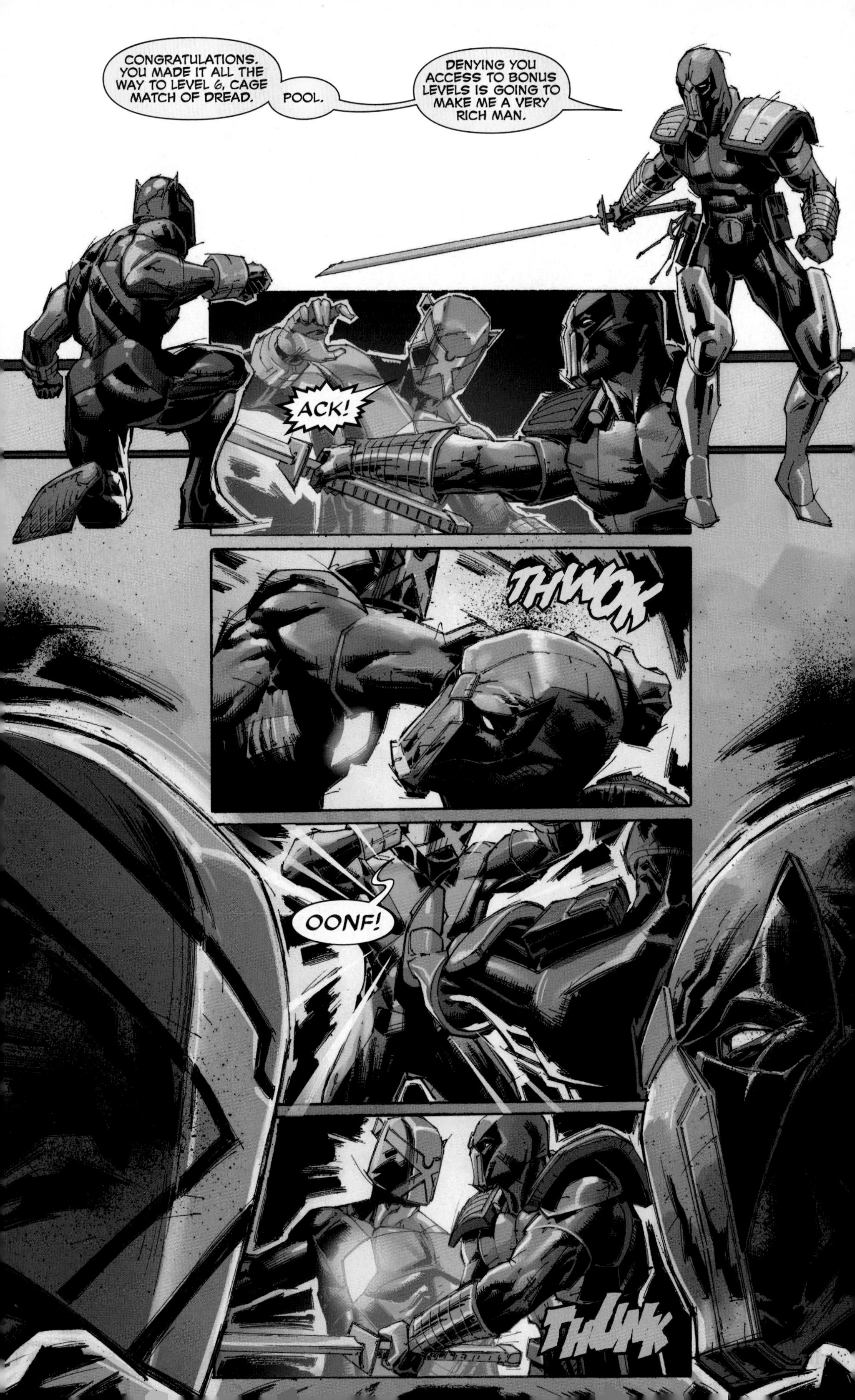
CONGRATULATIONS. YOU MADE IT ALL THE WAY TO LEVEL 6, CAGE MATCH OF DREAD.
POOL.
DENYING YOU ACCESS TO BONUS LEVELS IS GOING TO MAKE ME A VERY RICH MAN.
ACK!
THWOK
OONF!
THUNK

CLOK

GAME OVER, MAJOR.

NO.

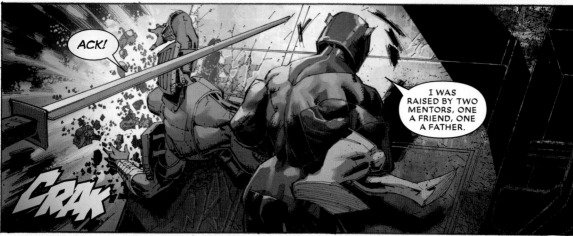

ACK!

CRAK

I WAS RAISED BY TWO MENTORS, ONE A FRIEND, ONE A FATHER.

BOTH STRESSED TENACITY. DETERMINATION. RESILIENCE.

THIS DOESN'T END UNTIL THE X-ENTIAL IS SAFE IN MY CARE AND YOUR BENEFACTORS ARE DESTROYED.

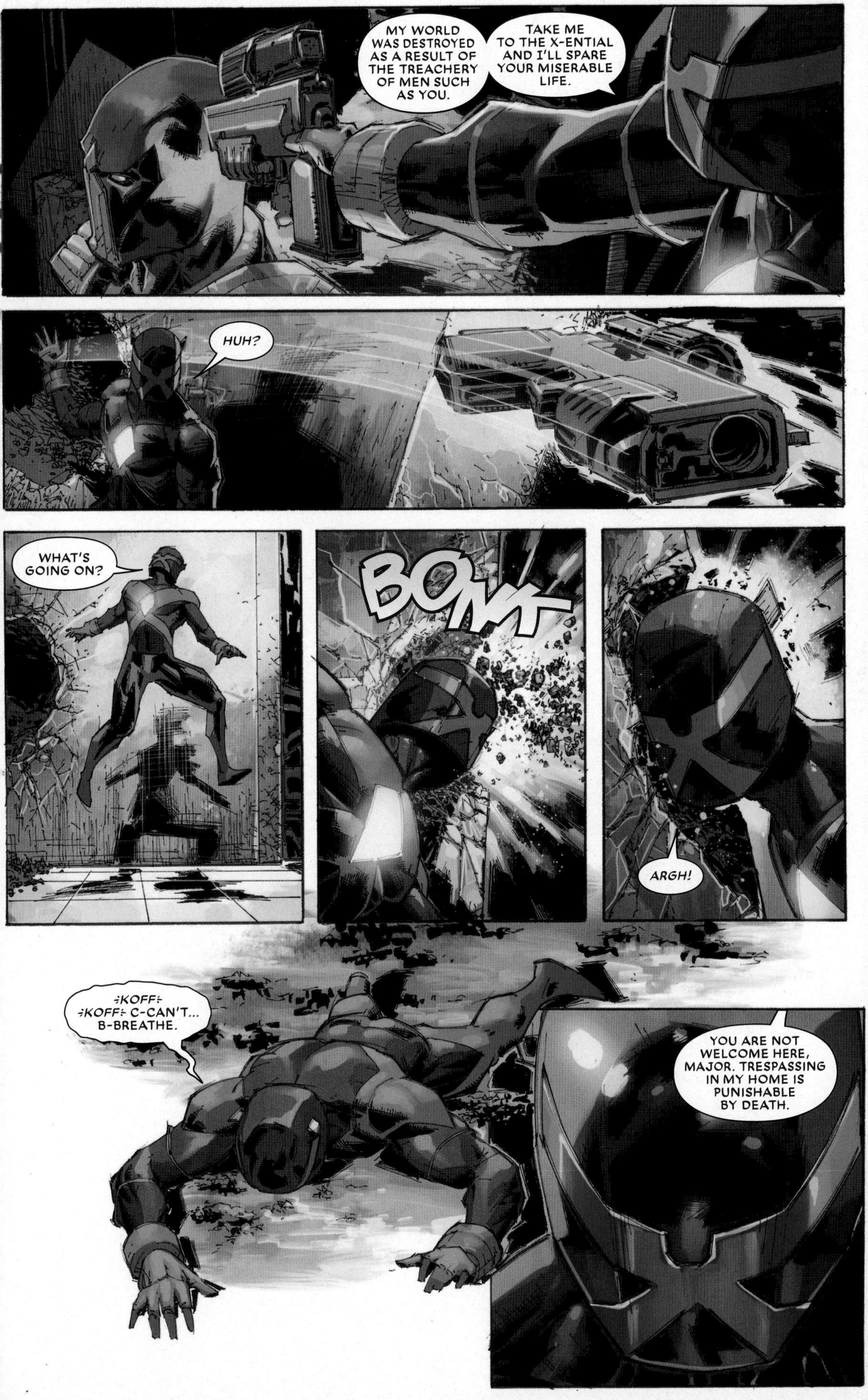
MY WORLD WAS DESTROYED AS A RESULT OF THE TREACHERY OF MEN SUCH AS YOU.
TAKE ME TO THE X-ENTIAL AND I'LL SPARE YOUR MISERABLE LIFE.
HUH?
WHAT'S GOING ON?
BONK
ARGH!
=KOFF= =KOFF= C-CAN'T... B-BREATHE.
YOU ARE NOT WELCOME HERE, MAJOR. TRESPASSING IN MY HOME IS PUNISHABLE BY DEATH.

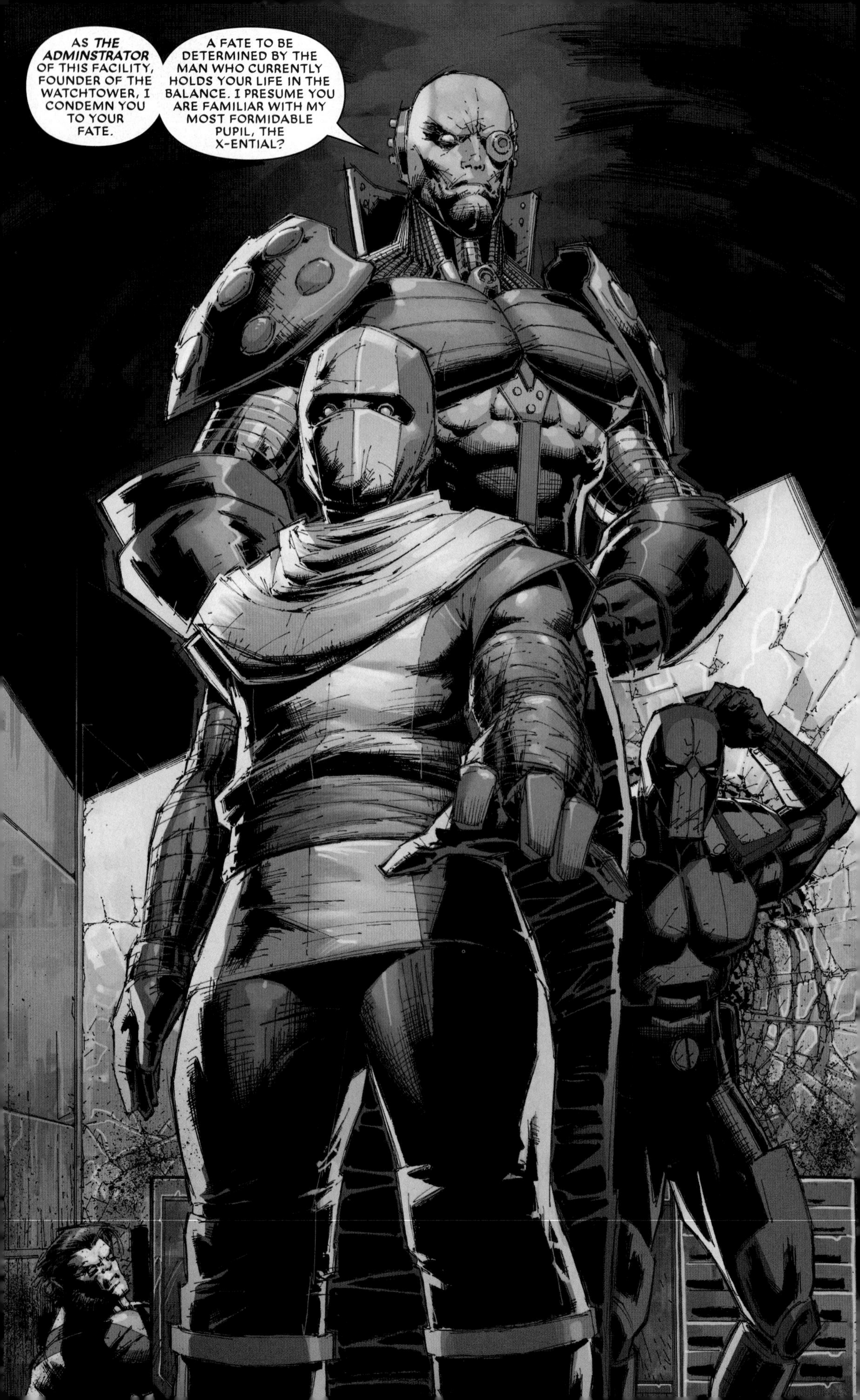
AS *THE ADMINSTRATOR* OF THIS FACILITY, FOUNDER OF THE WATCHTOWER, I CONDEMN YOU TO YOUR FATE.
A FATE TO BE DETERMINED BY THE MAN WHO CURRENTLY HOLDS YOUR LIFE IN THE BALANCE. I PRESUME YOU ARE FAMILIAR WITH MY MOST FORMIDABLE PUPIL, THE X-ENTIAL?

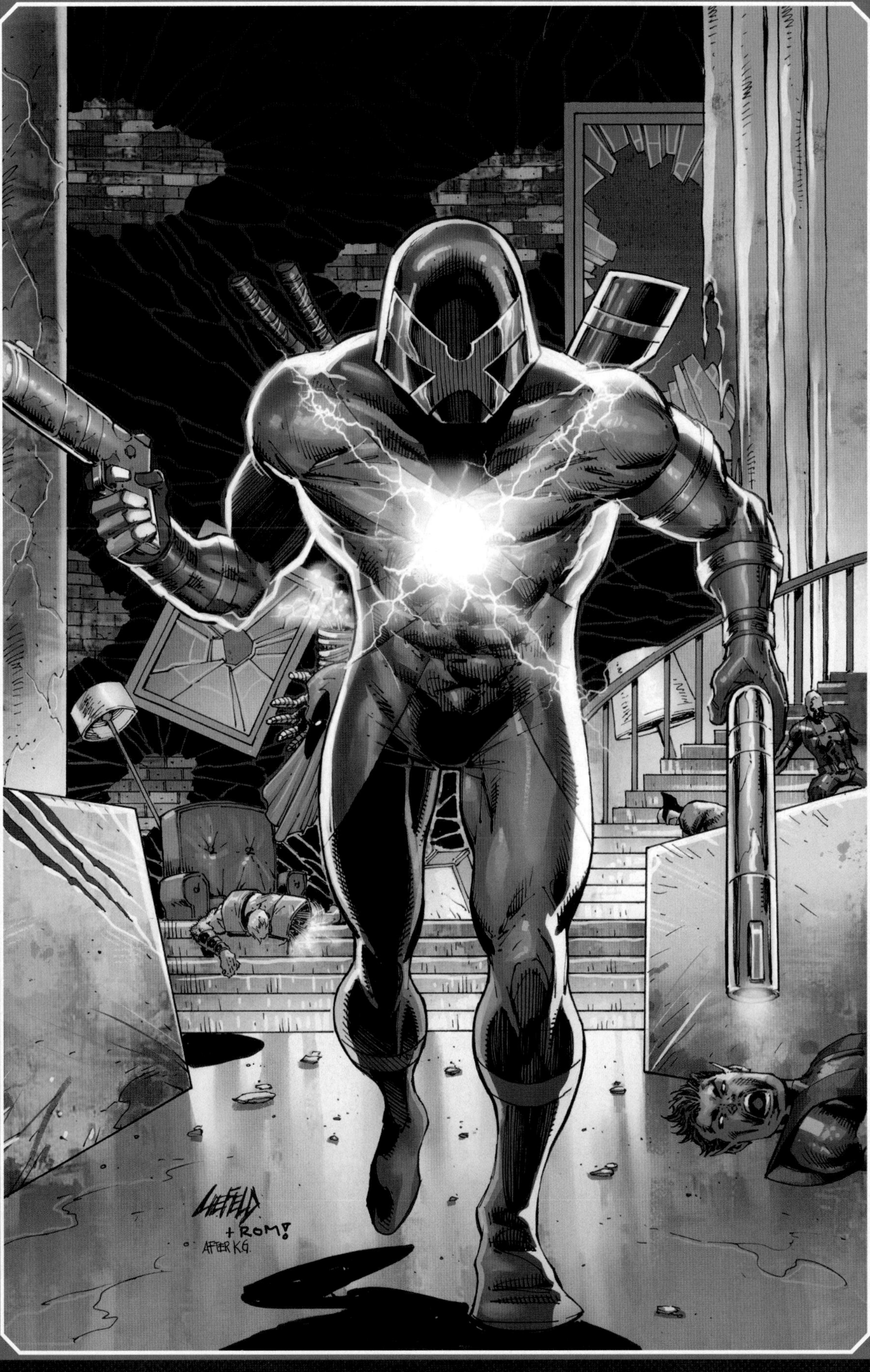
LIEFELD
+ROM!
AFTER K.G.

ROB LIEFELD & ROMULO FAJARDO JR.

#2 SECOND PRINTING COVER

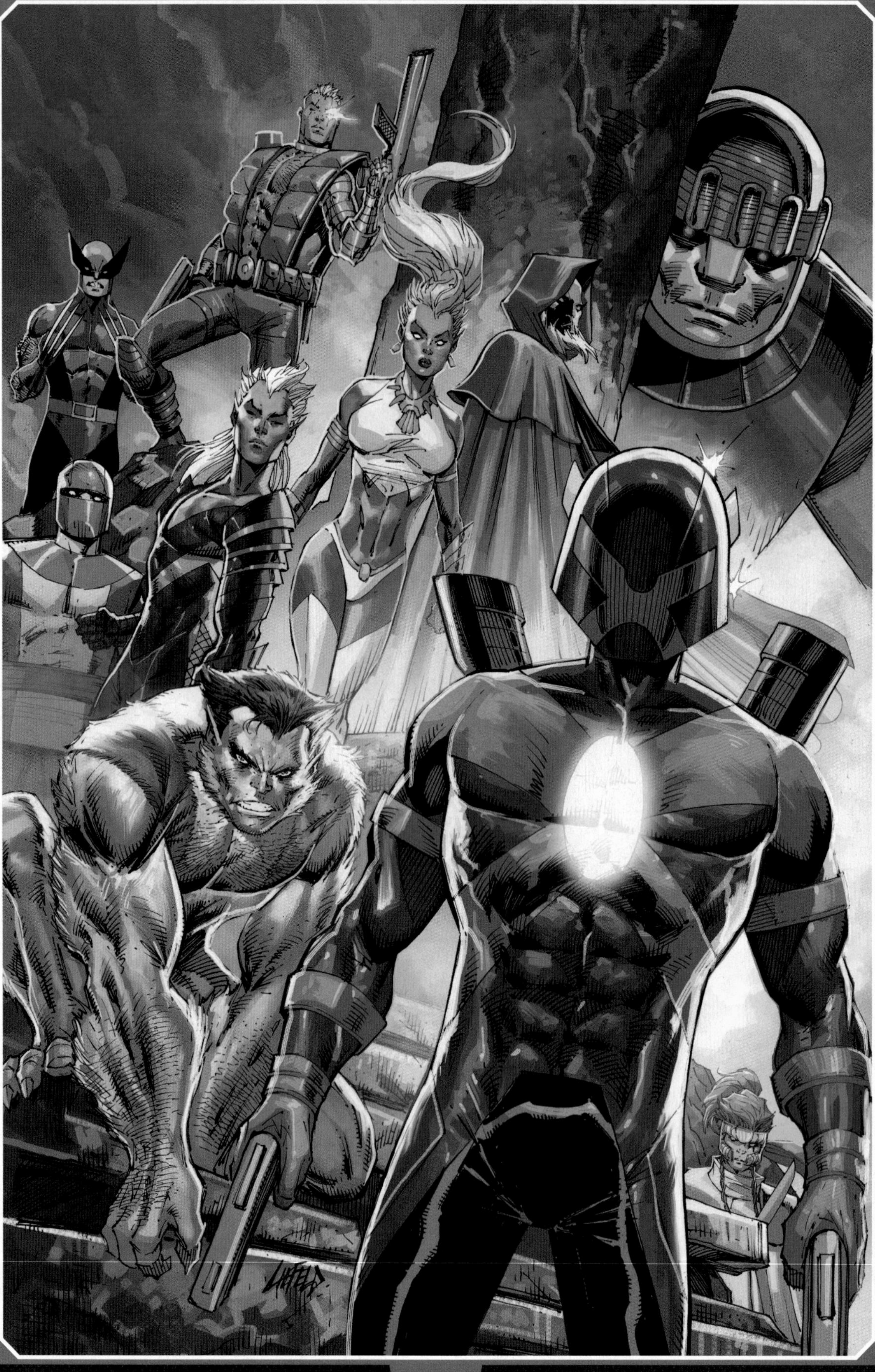

4

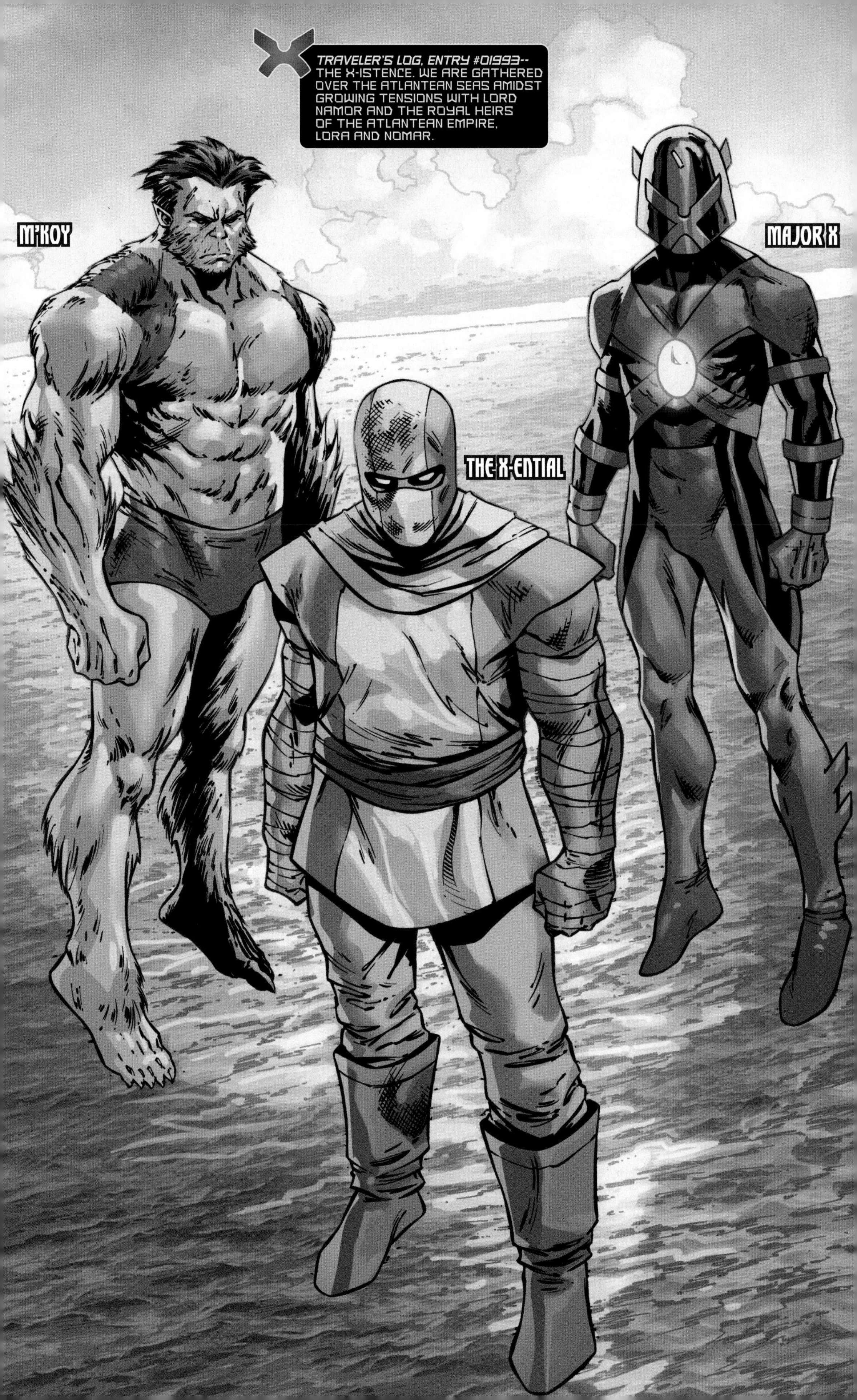
TRAVELER'S LOG, ENTRY #01993-- THE X-ISTENCE. WE ARE GATHERED OVER THE ATLANTEAN SEAS AMIDST GROWING TENSIONS WITH LORD NAMOR AND THE ROYAL HEIRS OF THE ATLANTEAN EMPIRE, LORA AND NOMAR.
M'KOY
MAJOR X
THE X-ENTIAL

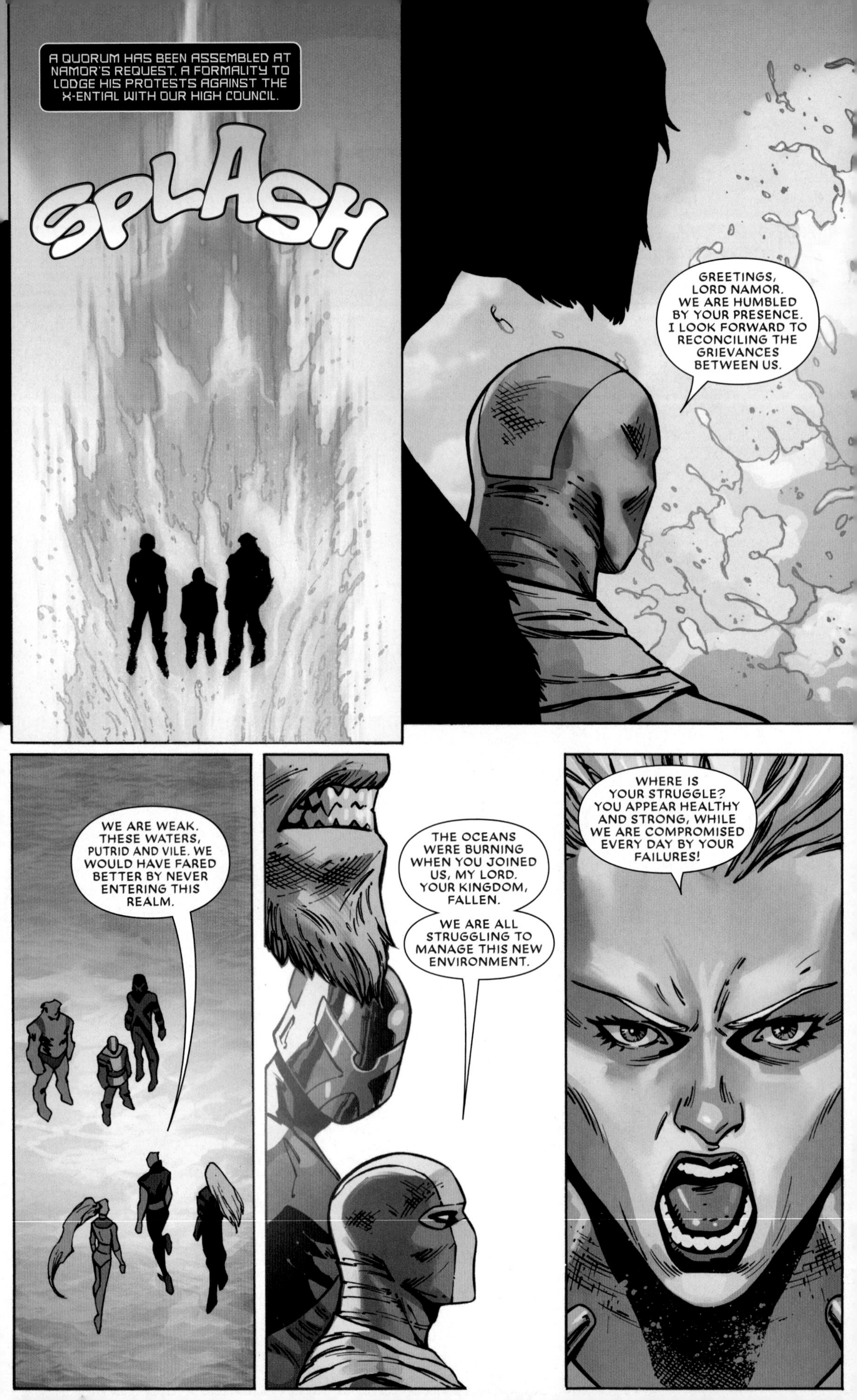
A QUORUM HAS BEEN ASSEMBLED AT NAMOR'S REQUEST, A FORMALITY TO LODGE HIS PROTESTS AGAINST THE X-ENTIAL WITH OUR HIGH COUNCIL.
SPLASH
GREETINGS, LORD NAMOR. WE ARE HUMBLED BY YOUR PRESENCE. I LOOK FORWARD TO RECONCILING THE GRIEVANCES BETWEEN US.
WE ARE WEAK. THESE WATERS, PUTRID AND VILE. WE WOULD HAVE FARED BETTER BY NEVER ENTERING THIS REALM.
THE OCEANS WERE BURNING WHEN YOU JOINED US, MY LORD. YOUR KINGDOM, FALLEN.
WE ARE ALL STRUGGLING TO MANAGE THIS NEW ENVIRONMENT.
WHERE IS YOUR STRUGGLE? YOU APPEAR HEALTHY AND STRONG, WHILE WE ARE COMPROMISED EVERY DAY BY YOUR FAILURES!

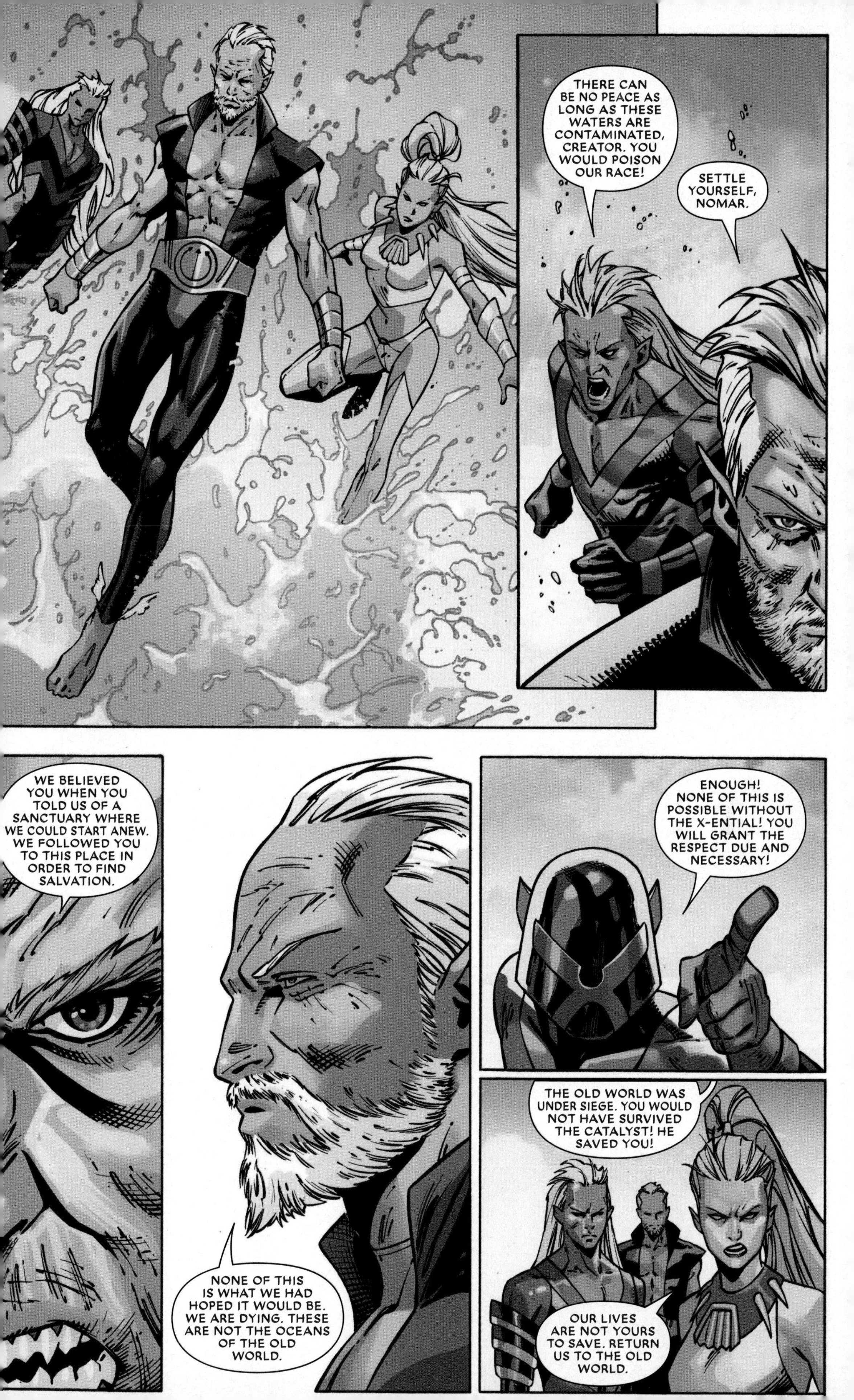
THERE CAN BE NO PEACE AS LONG AS THESE WATERS ARE CONTAMINATED, CREATOR. YOU WOULD POISON OUR RACE!
SETTLE YOURSELF, NOMAR.
WE BELIEVED YOU WHEN YOU TOLD US OF A SANCTUARY WHERE WE COULD START ANEW. WE FOLLOWED YOU TO THIS PLACE IN ORDER TO FIND SALVATION.
NONE OF THIS IS WHAT WE HAD HOPED IT WOULD BE. WE ARE DYING. THESE ARE NOT THE OCEANS OF THE OLD WORLD.
ENOUGH! NONE OF THIS IS POSSIBLE WITHOUT THE X-ENTIAL! YOU WILL GRANT THE RESPECT DUE AND NECESSARY!
THE OLD WORLD WAS UNDER SIEGE. YOU WOULD NOT HAVE SURVIVED THE CATALYST! HE SAVED YOU!
OUR LIVES ARE NOT YOURS TO SAVE. RETURN US TO THE OLD WORLD.

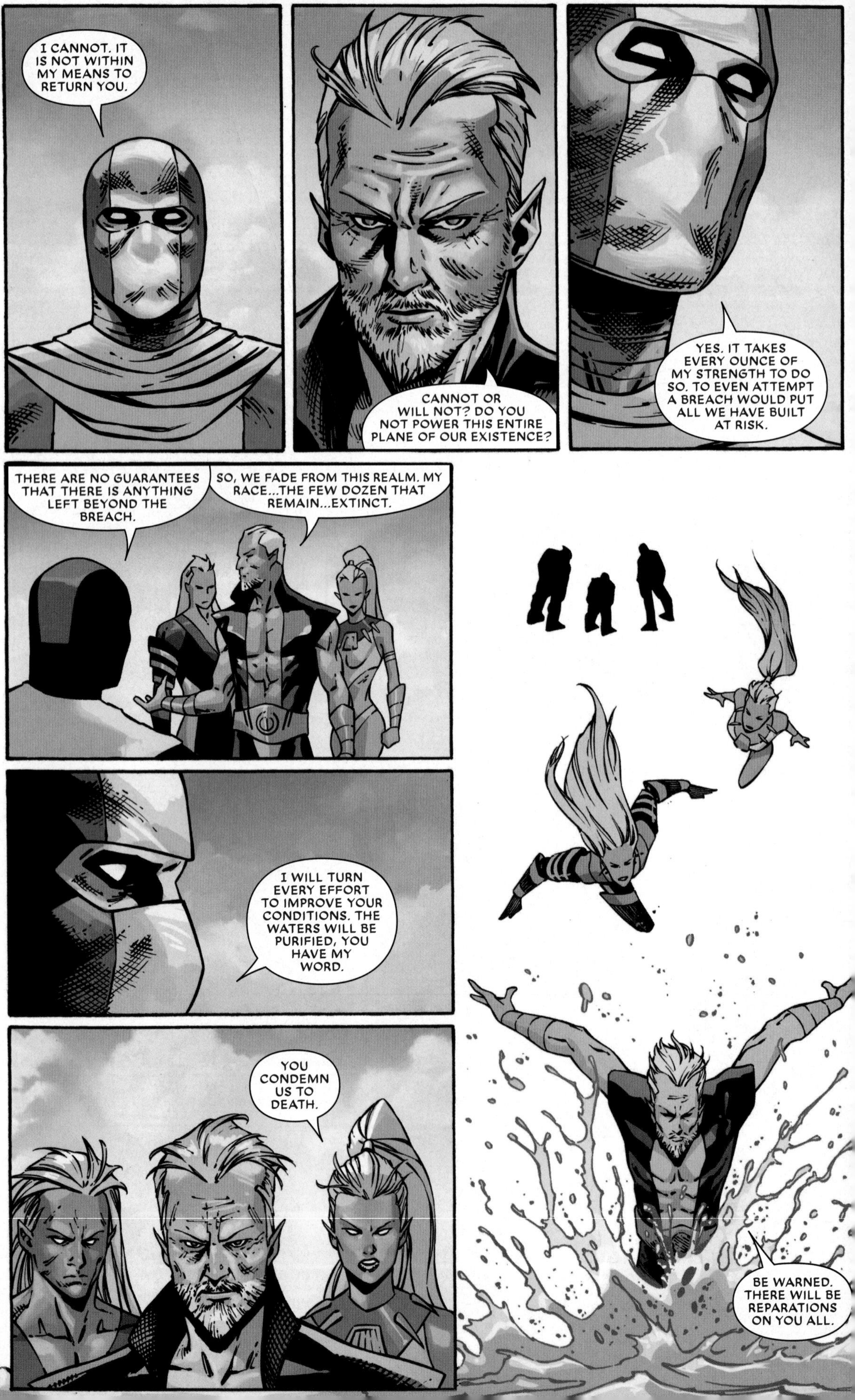
I CANNOT. IT IS NOT WITHIN MY MEANS TO RETURN YOU.
CANNOT OR WILL NOT? DO YOU NOT POWER THIS ENTIRE PLANE OF OUR EXISTENCE?
YES. IT TAKES EVERY OUNCE OF MY STRENGTH TO DO SO. TO EVEN ATTEMPT A BREACH WOULD PUT ALL WE HAVE BUILT AT RISK.
THERE ARE NO GUARANTEES THAT THERE IS ANYTHING LEFT BEYOND THE BREACH.
SO, WE FADE FROM THIS REALM. MY RACE...THE FEW DOZEN THAT REMAIN...EXTINCT.
I WILL TURN EVERY EFFORT TO IMPROVE YOUR CONDITIONS. THE WATERS WILL BE PURIFIED, YOU HAVE MY WORD.
YOU CONDEMN US TO DEATH.
BE WARNED. THERE WILL BE REPARATIONS ON YOU ALL.

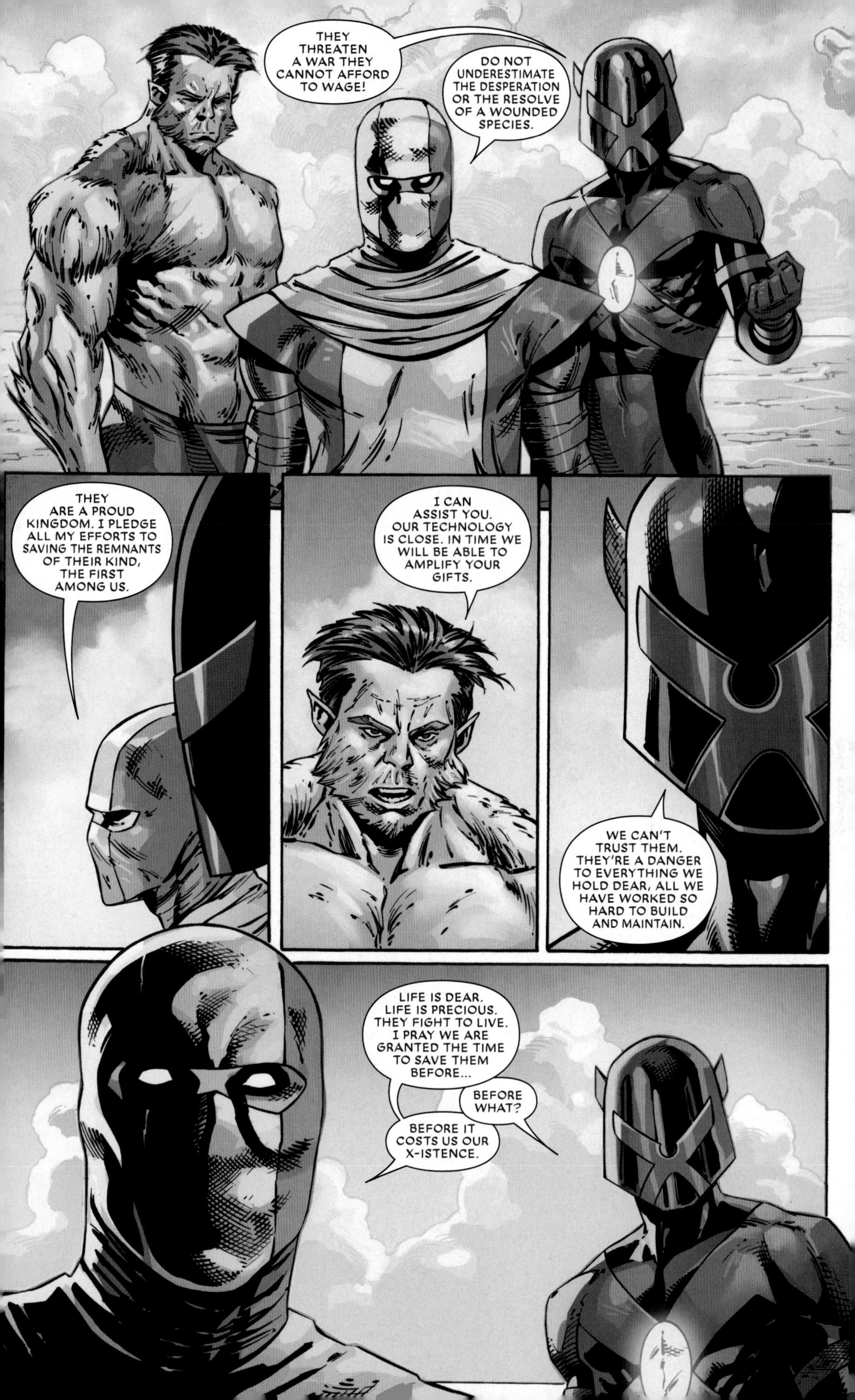
THEY THREATEN A WAR THEY CANNOT AFFORD TO WAGE!
DO NOT UNDERESTIMATE THE DESPERATION OR THE RESOLVE OF A WOUNDED SPECIES.
THEY ARE A PROUD KINGDOM. I PLEDGE ALL MY EFFORTS TO SAVING THE REMNANTS OF THEIR KIND, THE FIRST AMONG US.
I CAN ASSIST YOU. OUR TECHNOLOGY IS CLOSE. IN TIME WE WILL BE ABLE TO AMPLIFY YOUR GIFTS.
WE CAN'T TRUST THEM. THEY'RE A DANGER TO EVERYTHING WE HOLD DEAR, ALL WE HAVE WORKED SO HARD TO BUILD AND MAINTAIN.
LIFE IS DEAR. LIFE IS PRECIOUS. THEY FIGHT TO LIVE. I PRAY WE ARE GRANTED THE TIME TO SAVE THEM BEFORE...
BEFORE WHAT?
BEFORE IT COSTS US OUR X-ISTENCE.

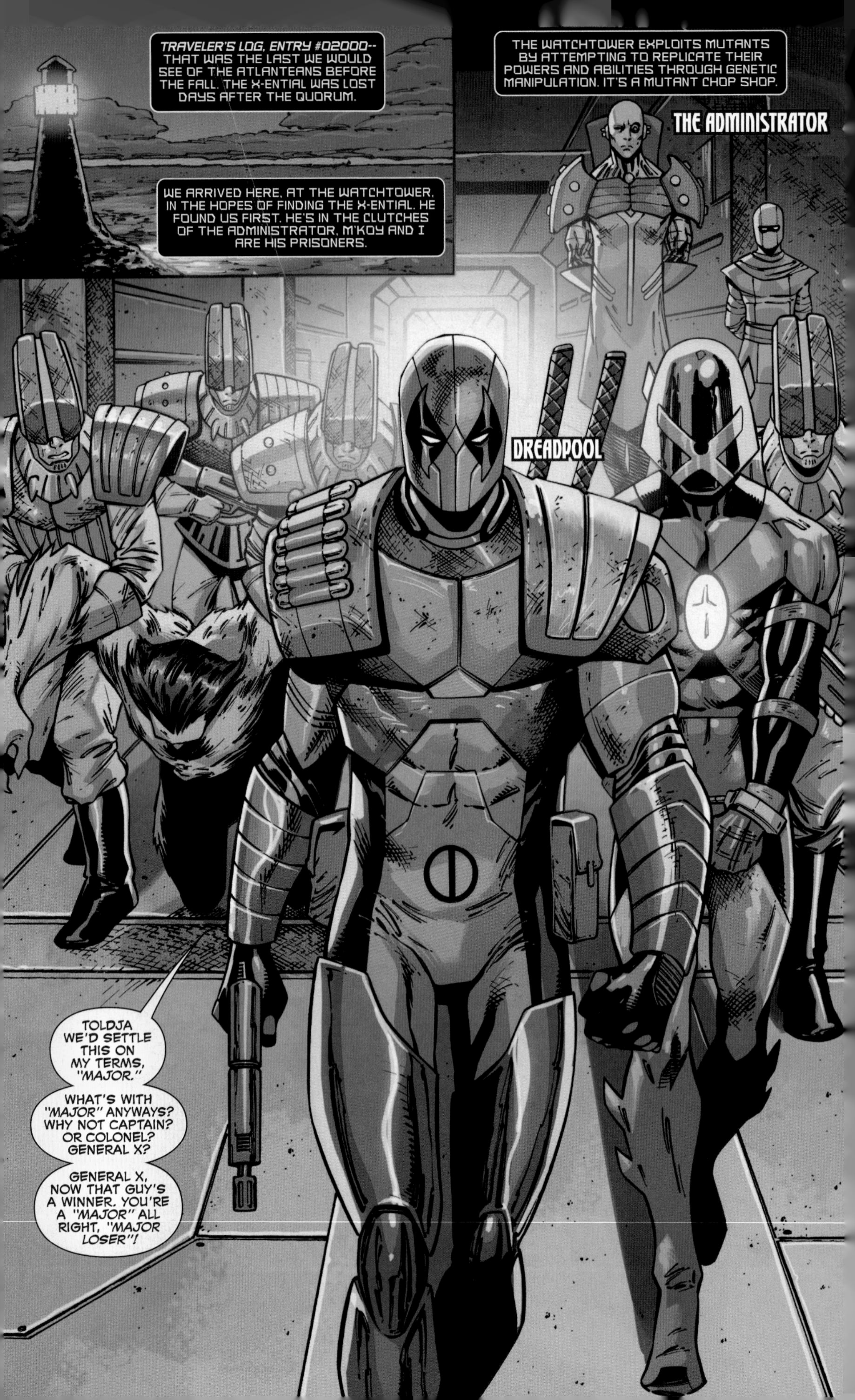
TRAVELER'S LOG, ENTRY #02000-- THAT WAS THE LAST WE WOULD SEE OF THE ATLANTEANS BEFORE THE FALL. THE X-ENTIAL WAS LOST DAYS AFTER THE QUORUM.
WE ARRIVED HERE, AT THE WATCHTOWER, IN THE HOPES OF FINDING THE X-ENTIAL. HE FOUND US FIRST. HE'S IN THE CLUTCHES OF THE ADMINISTRATOR, M'KOY AND I ARE HIS PRISONERS.
THE WATCHTOWER EXPLOITS MUTANTS BY ATTEMPTING TO REPLICATE THEIR POWERS AND ABILITIES THROUGH GENETIC MANIPULATION. IT'S A MUTANT CHOP SHOP.
THE ADMINISTRATOR
DREADPOOL
TOLDJA WE'D SETTLE THIS ON MY TERMS, "MAJOR."
WHAT'S WITH "MAJOR" ANYWAYS? WHY NOT CAPTAIN? OR COLONEL? GENERAL X?
GENERAL X, NOW THAT GUY'S A WINNER. YOU'RE A "MAJOR" ALL RIGHT, "MAJOR LOSER"!

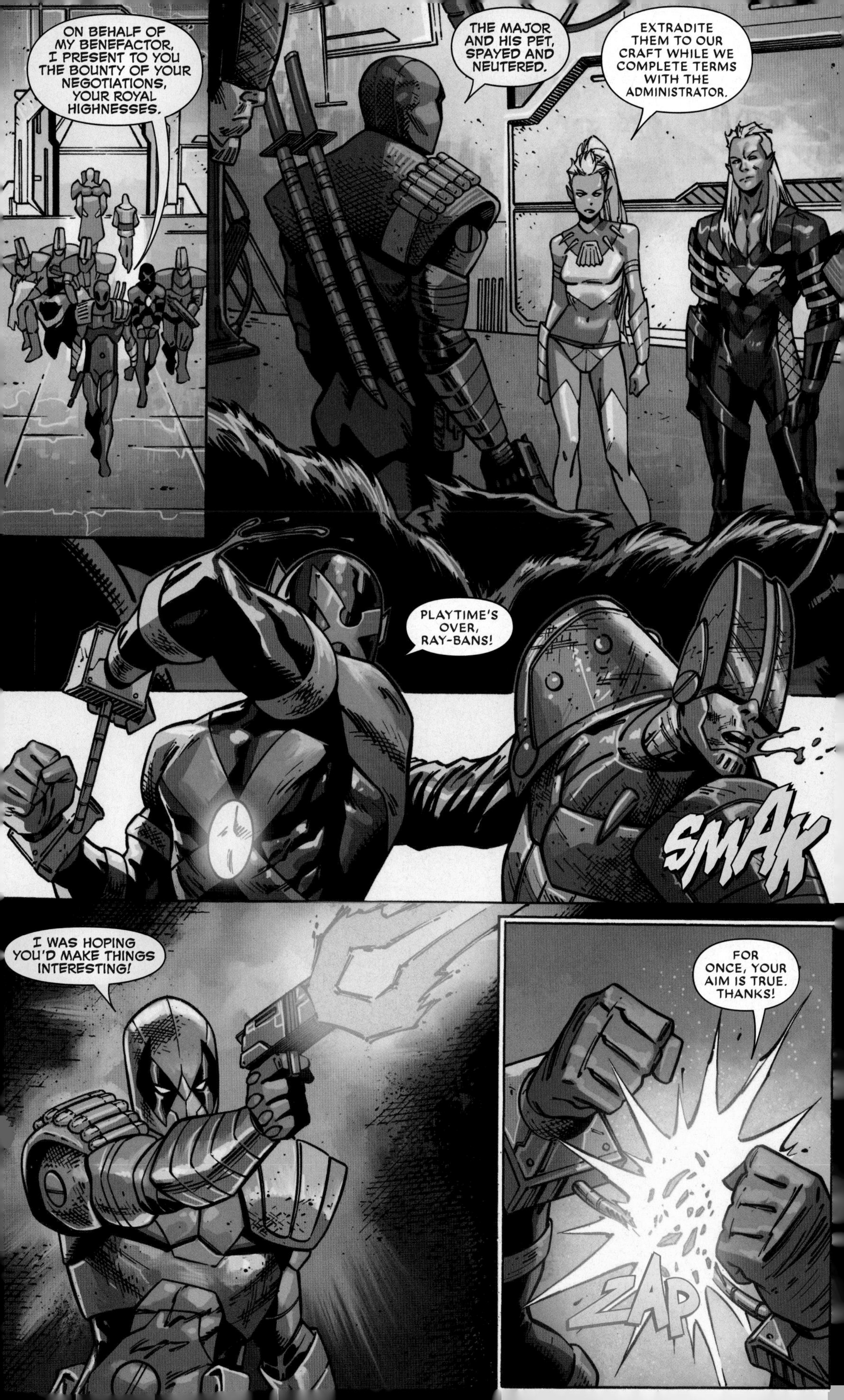
ON BEHALF OF MY BENEFACTOR, I PRESENT TO YOU THE BOUNTY OF YOUR NEGOTIATIONS, YOUR ROYAL HIGHNESSES.
THE MAJOR AND HIS PET, SPAYED AND NEUTERED.
EXTRADITE THEM TO OUR CRAFT WHILE WE COMPLETE TERMS WITH THE ADMINISTRATOR.
PLAYTIME'S OVER, RAY-BANS!
SMAK
I WAS HOPING YOU'D MAKE THINGS INTERESTING!
FOR ONCE, YOUR AIM IS TRUE. THANKS!
ZAP

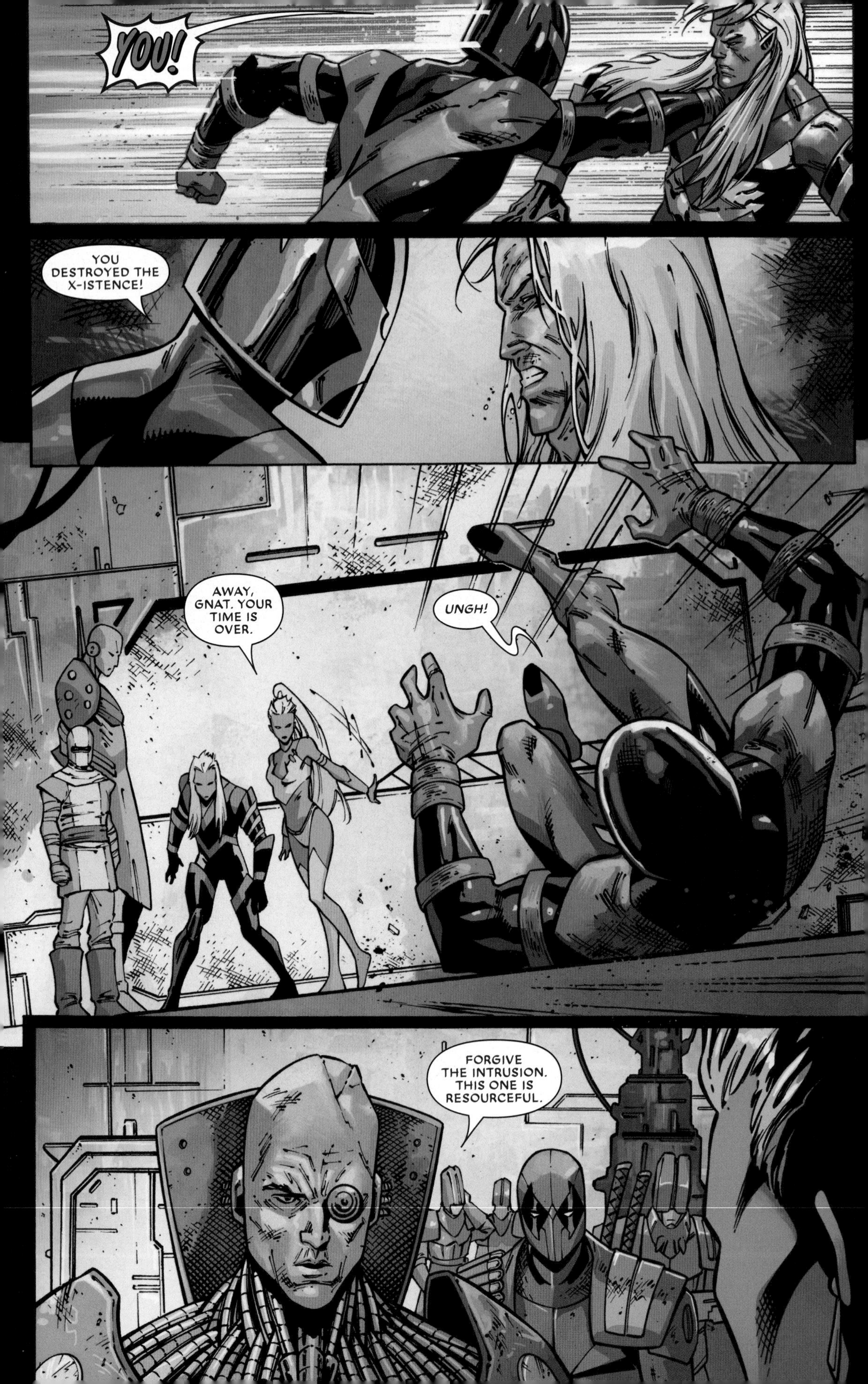
YOU!
YOU DESTROYED THE X-ISTENCE!
AWAY, GNAT. YOUR TIME IS OVER.
UNGH!
FORGIVE THE INTRUSION. THIS ONE IS RESOURCEFUL.

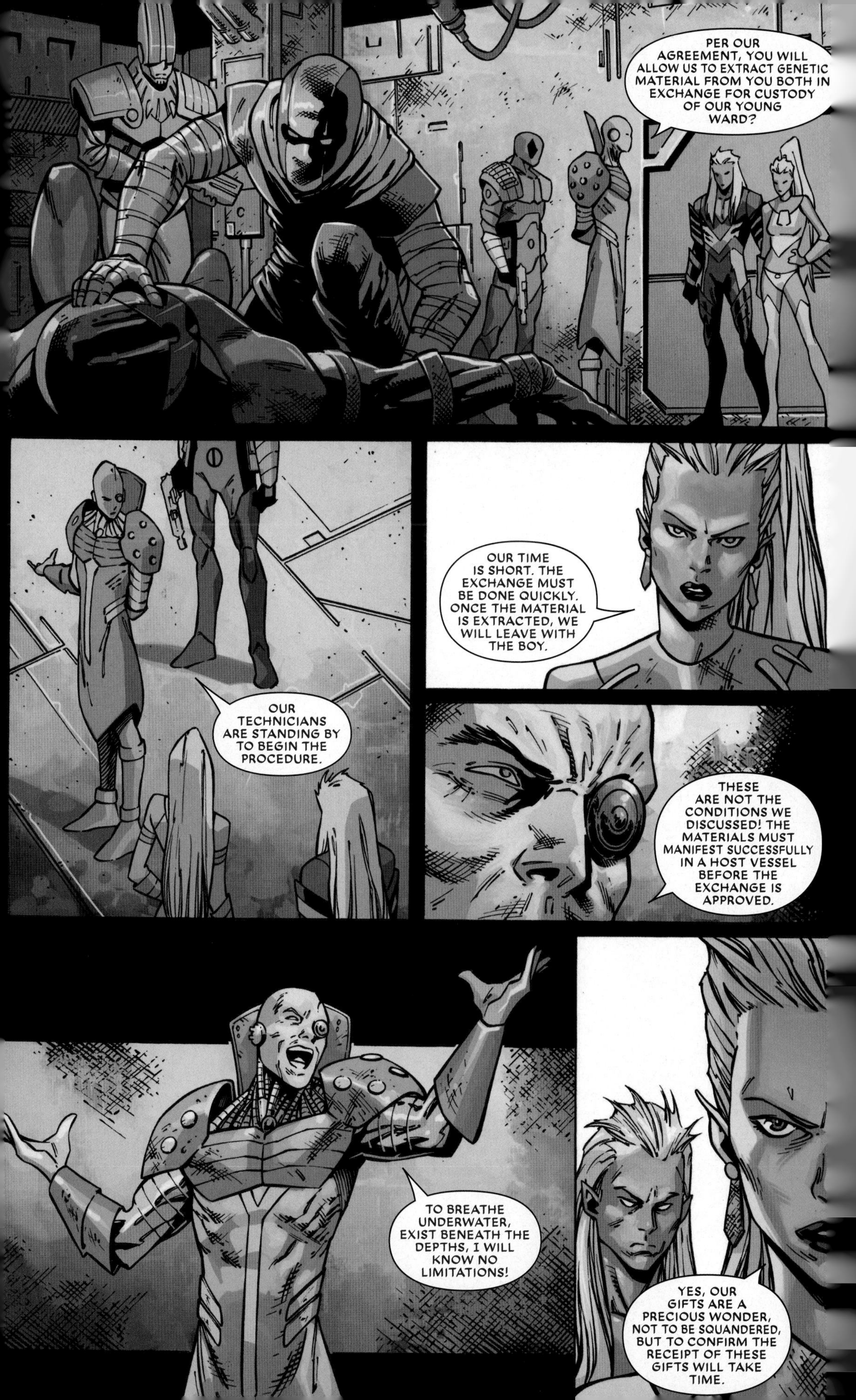
PER OUR AGREEMENT, YOU WILL ALLOW US TO EXTRACT GENETIC MATERIAL FROM YOU BOTH IN EXCHANGE FOR CUSTODY OF OUR YOUNG WARD?
OUR TECHNICIANS ARE STANDING BY TO BEGIN THE PROCEDURE.
OUR TIME IS SHORT. THE EXCHANGE MUST BE DONE QUICKLY. ONCE THE MATERIAL IS EXTRACTED, WE WILL LEAVE WITH THE BOY.
THESE ARE NOT THE CONDITIONS WE DISCUSSED! THE MATERIALS MUST MANIFEST SUCCESSFULLY IN A HOST VESSEL BEFORE THE EXCHANGE IS APPROVED.
TO BREATHE UNDERWATER, EXIST BENEATH THE DEPTHS, I WILL KNOW NO LIMITATIONS!
YES, OUR GIFTS ARE A PRECIOUS WONDER, NOT TO BE SQUANDERED, BUT TO CONFIRM THE RECEIPT OF THESE GIFTS WILL TAKE TIME.

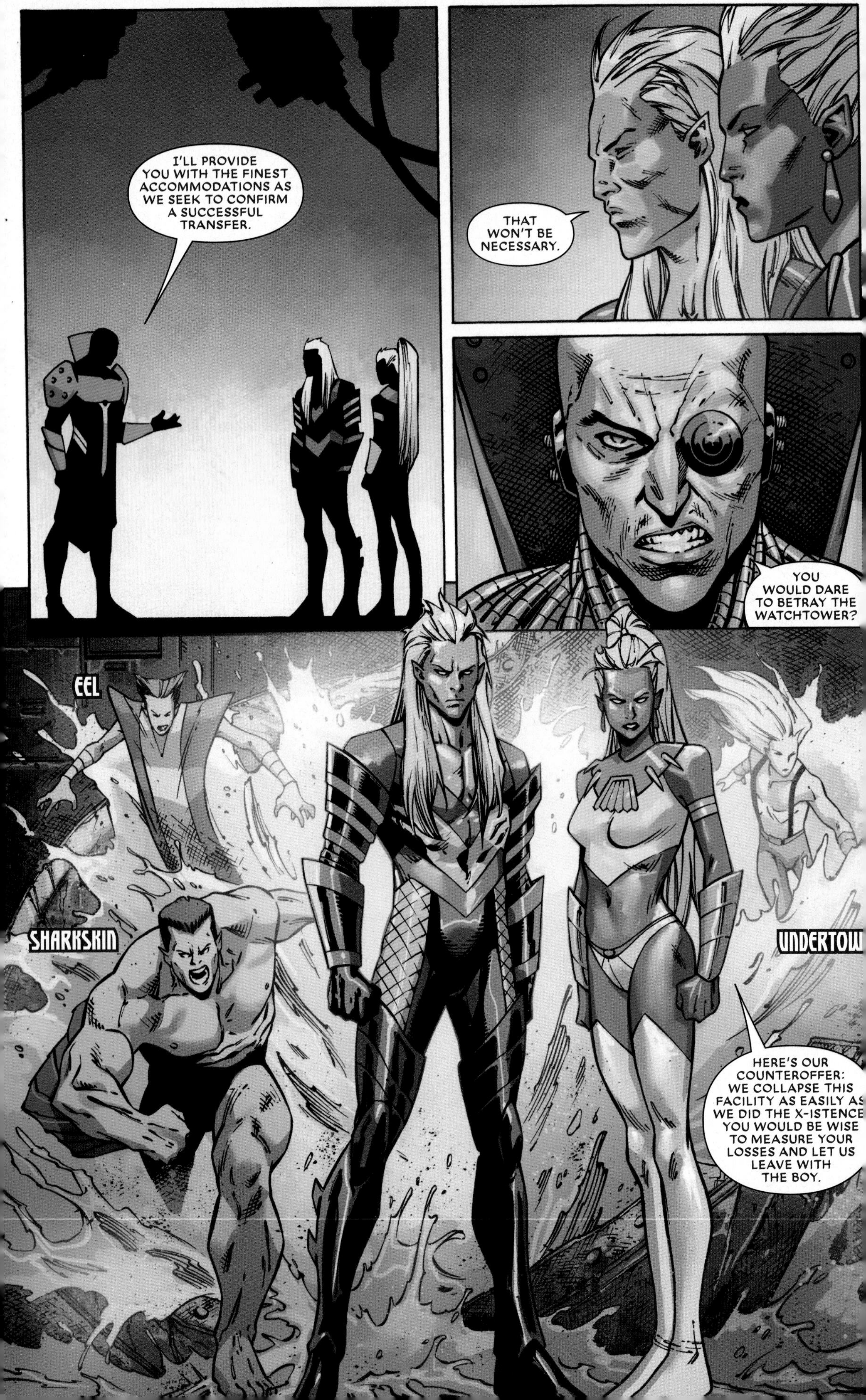
I'LL PROVIDE YOU WITH THE FINEST ACCOMMODATIONS AS WE SEEK TO CONFIRM A SUCCESSFUL TRANSFER.
THAT WON'T BE NECESSARY.
YOU WOULD DARE TO BETRAY THE WATCHTOWER?
EEL
SHARKSKIN
UNDERTOW
HERE'S OUR COUNTEROFFER: WE COLLAPSE THIS FACILITY AS EASILY AS WE DID THE X-ISTENCE. YOU WOULD BE WISE TO MEASURE YOUR LOSSES AND LET US LEAVE WITH THE BOY.

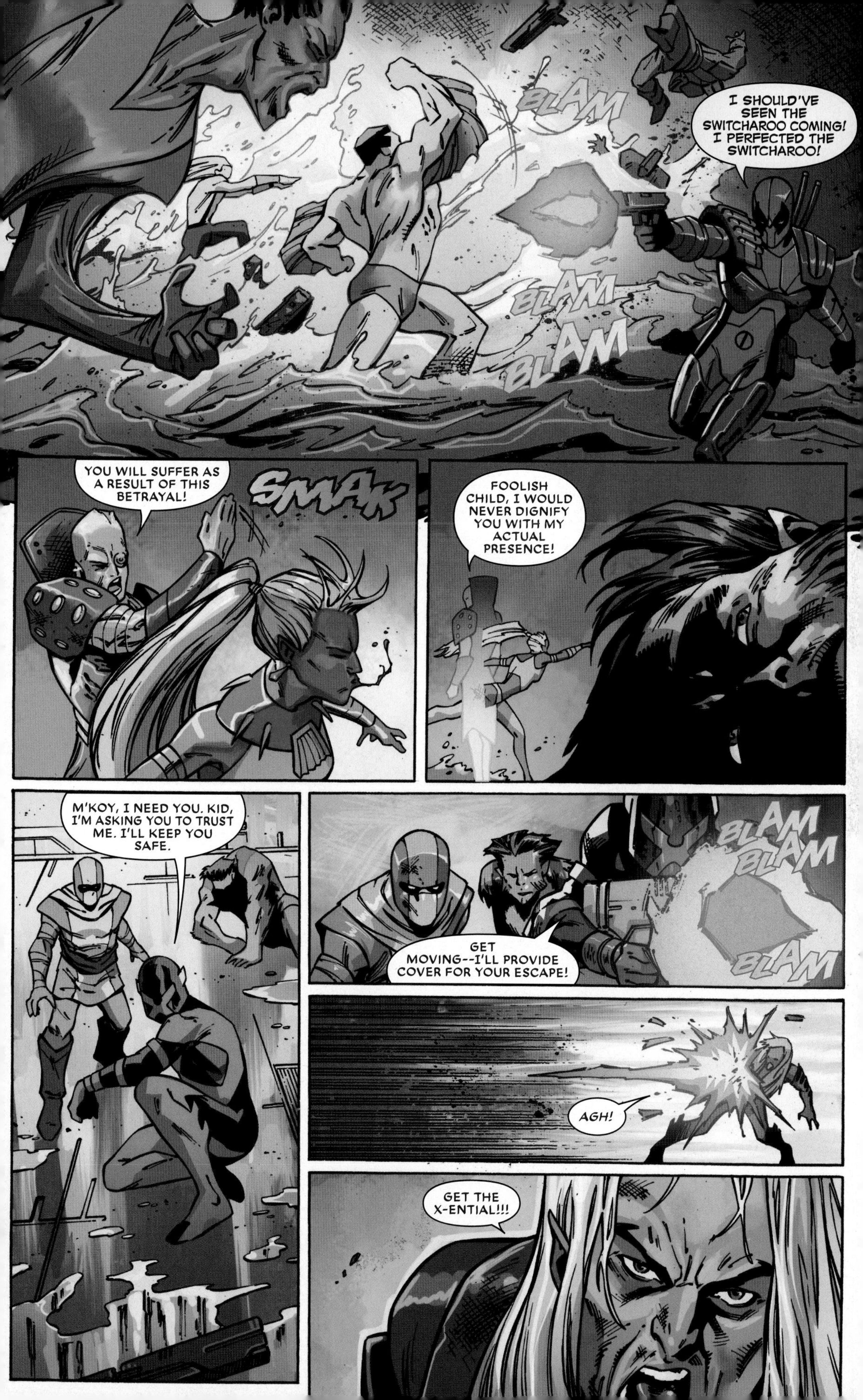
BLAM
I SHOULD'VE SEEN THE SWITCHAROO COMING! I PERFECTED THE SWITCHAROO!
BLAM
BLAM
BLAM
YOU WILL SUFFER AS A RESULT OF THIS BETRAYAL!
SMAK
FOOLISH CHILD, I WOULD NEVER DIGNIFY YOU WITH MY ACTUAL PRESENCE!
M'KOY, I NEED YOU. KID, I'M ASKING YOU TO TRUST ME. I'LL KEEP YOU SAFE.
BLAM
BLAM
GET MOVING--I'LL PROVIDE COVER FOR YOUR ESCAPE!
BLAM
AGH!
GET THE X-ENTIAL!!!

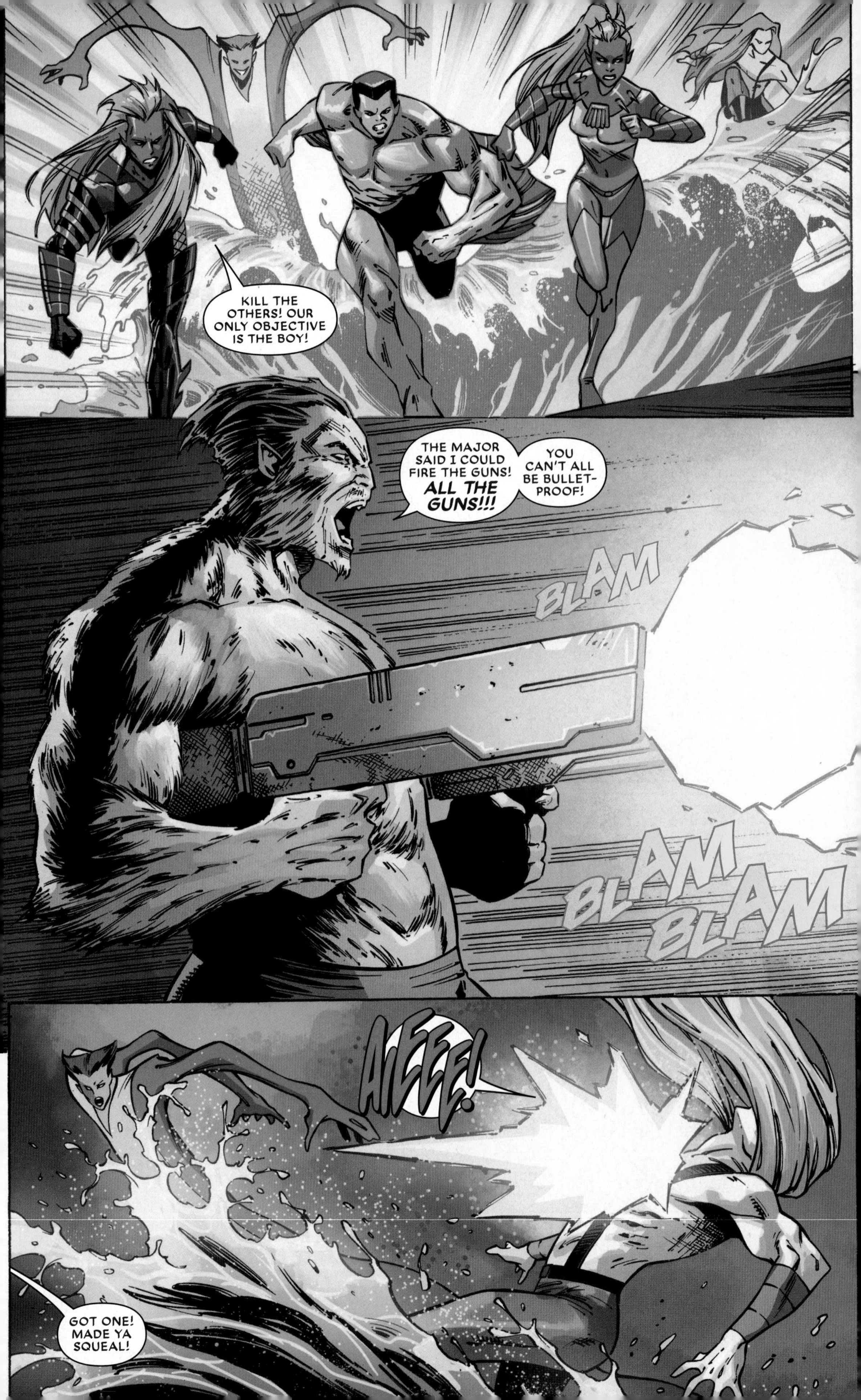
KILL THE OTHERS! OUR ONLY OBJECTIVE IS THE BOY!
THE MAJOR SAID I COULD FIRE THE GUNS! ALL THE GUNS!!!
YOU CAN'T ALL BE BULLET-PROOF!
BLAM
BLAM
BLAM
AIEEE!
GOT ONE! MADE YA SQUEAL!

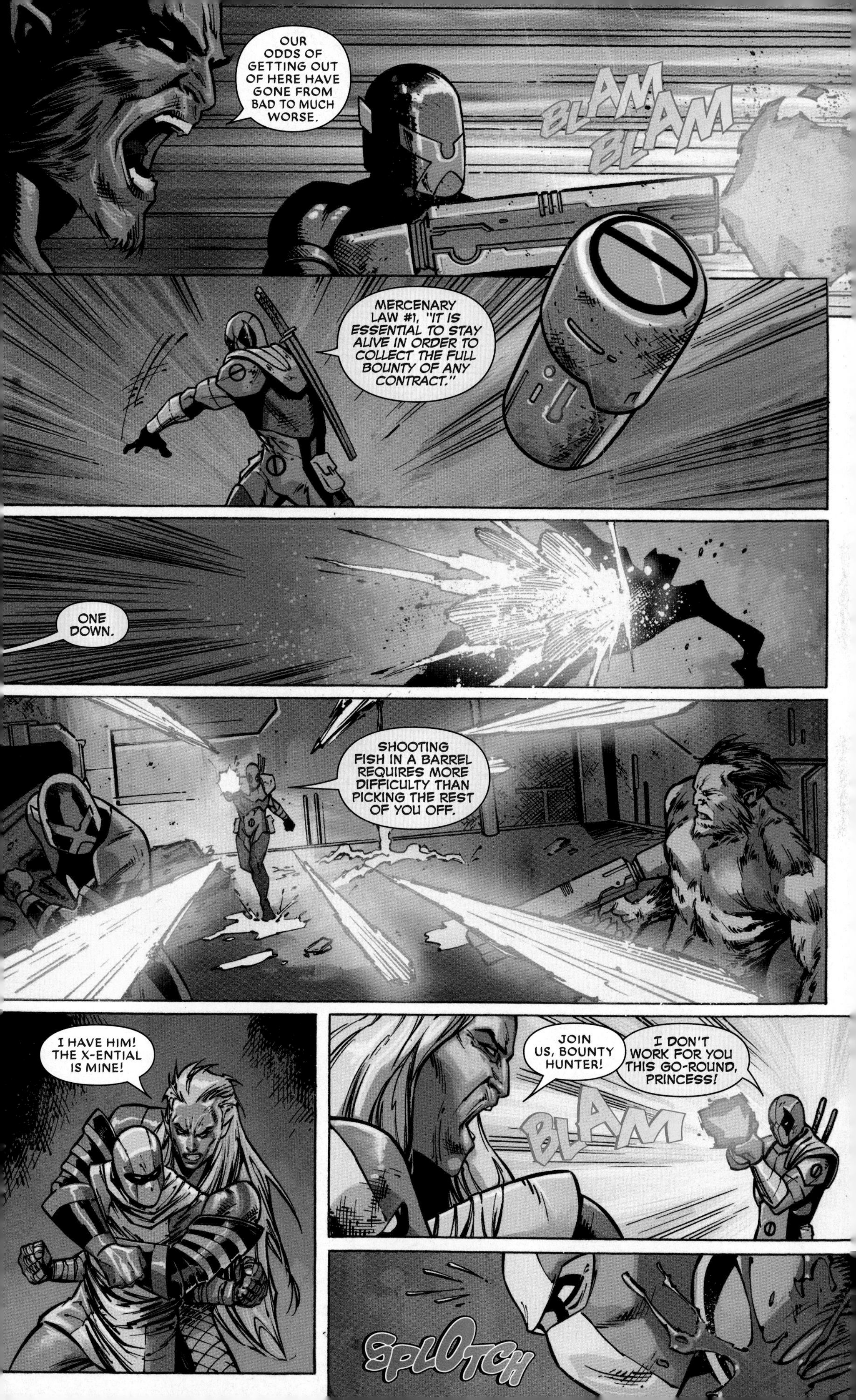
OUR ODDS OF GETTING OUT OF HERE HAVE GONE FROM BAD TO MUCH WORSE.
BLAM BLAM
MERCENARY LAW #1, "IT IS ESSENTIAL TO STAY ALIVE IN ORDER TO COLLECT THE FULL BOUNTY OF ANY CONTRACT."
ONE DOWN.
SHOOTING FISH IN A BARREL REQUIRES MORE DIFFICULTY THAN PICKING THE REST OF YOU OFF.
I HAVE HIM! THE X-ENTIAL IS MINE!
JOIN US, BOUNTY HUNTER!
I DON'T WORK FOR YOU THIS GO-ROUND, PRINCESS!
BLAM
SPLOTCH

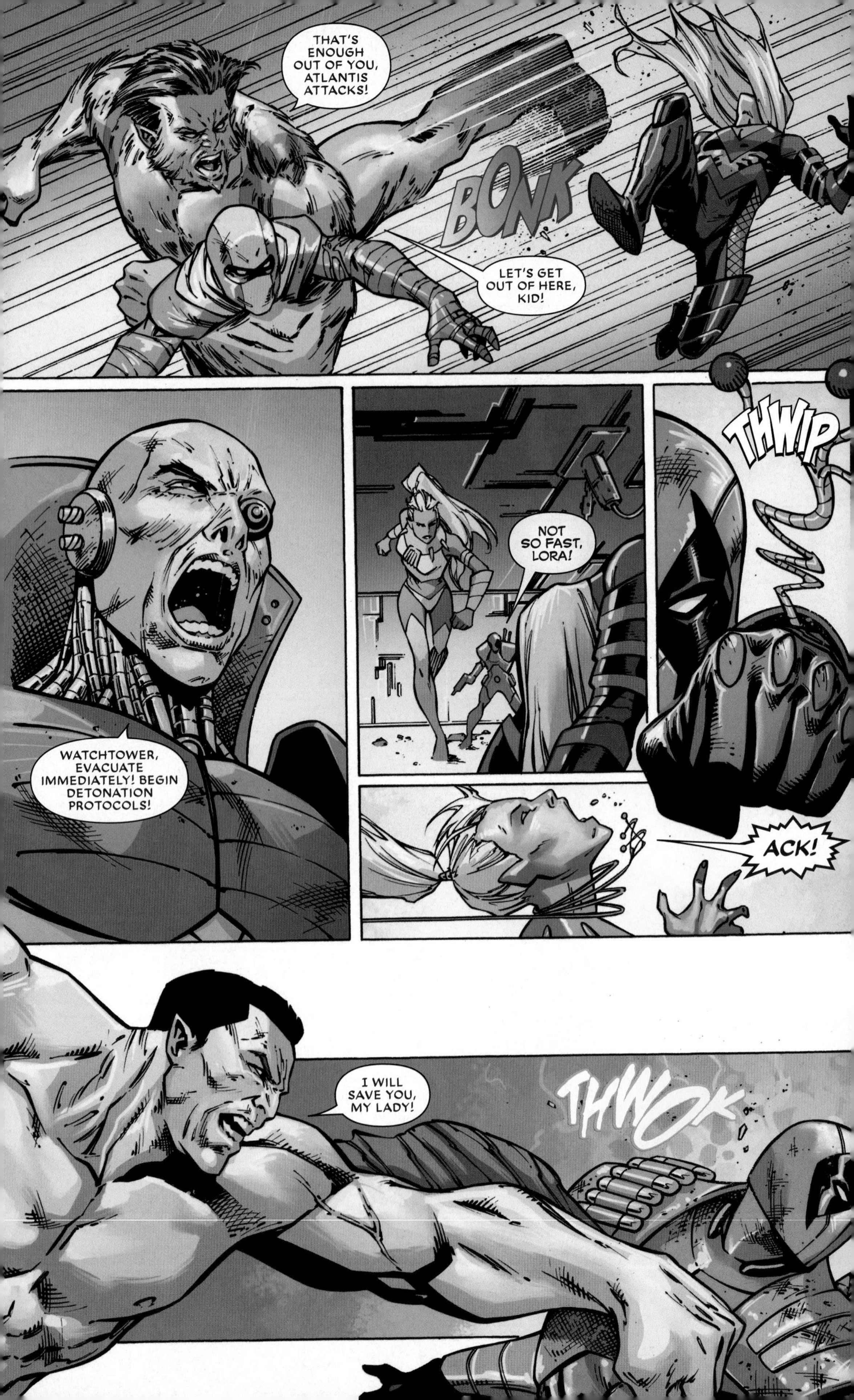
THAT'S ENOUGH OUT OF YOU, ATLANTIS ATTACKS!
BONK
LET'S GET OUT OF HERE, KID!
WATCHTOWER, EVACUATE IMMEDIATELY! BEGIN DETONATION PROTOCOLS!
NOT SO FAST, LORA!
THWIP
ACK!
I WILL SAVE YOU, MY LADY!
THWOK

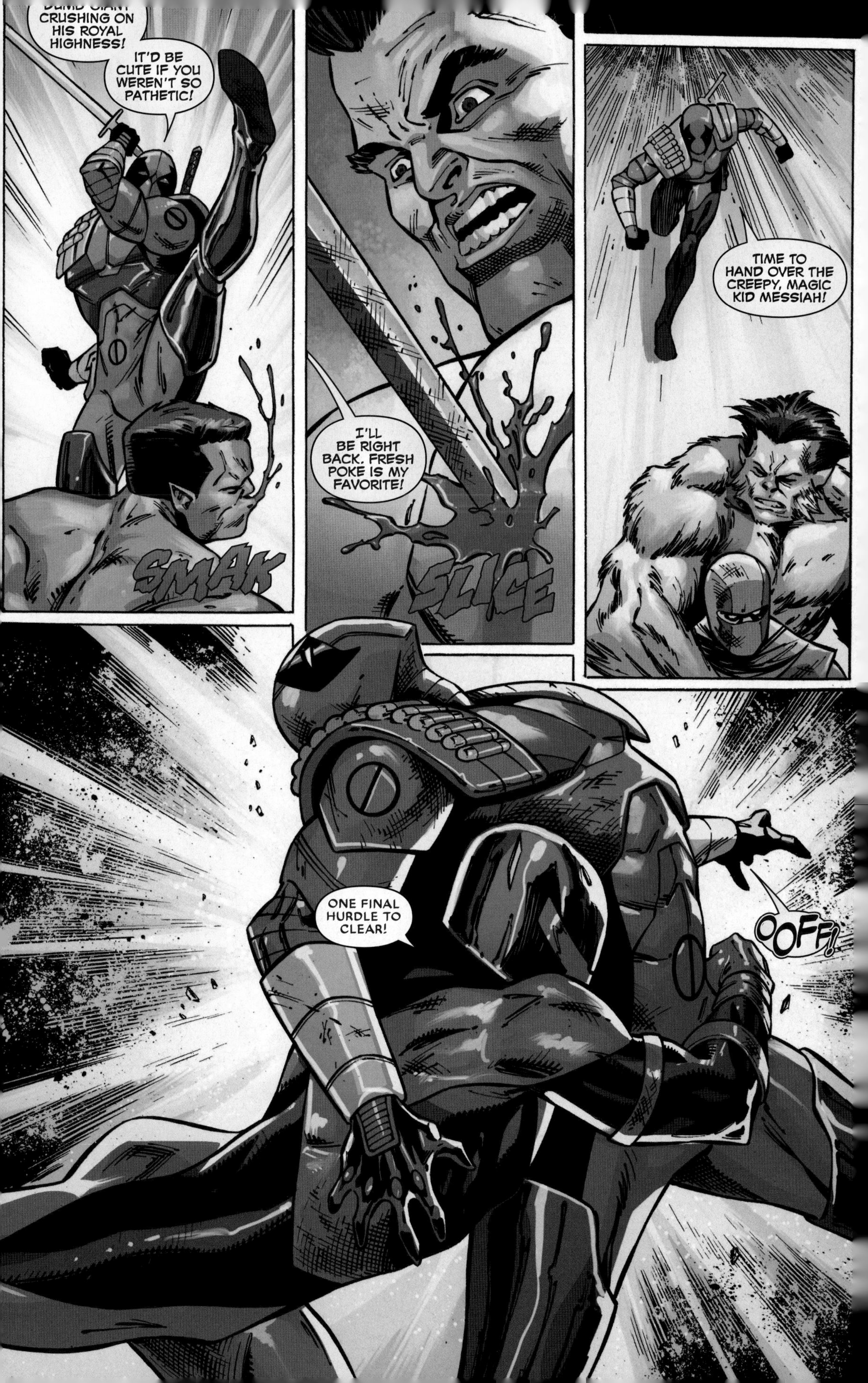
CRUSHING ON HIS ROYAL HIGHNESS!
IT'D BE CUTE IF YOU WEREN'T SO PATHETIC!
SMAK
I'LL BE RIGHT BACK. FRESH POKE IS MY FAVORITE!
SLICE
TIME TO HAND OVER THE CREEPY, MAGIC KID MESSIAH!
ONE FINAL HURDLE TO CLEAR!
OOFF!

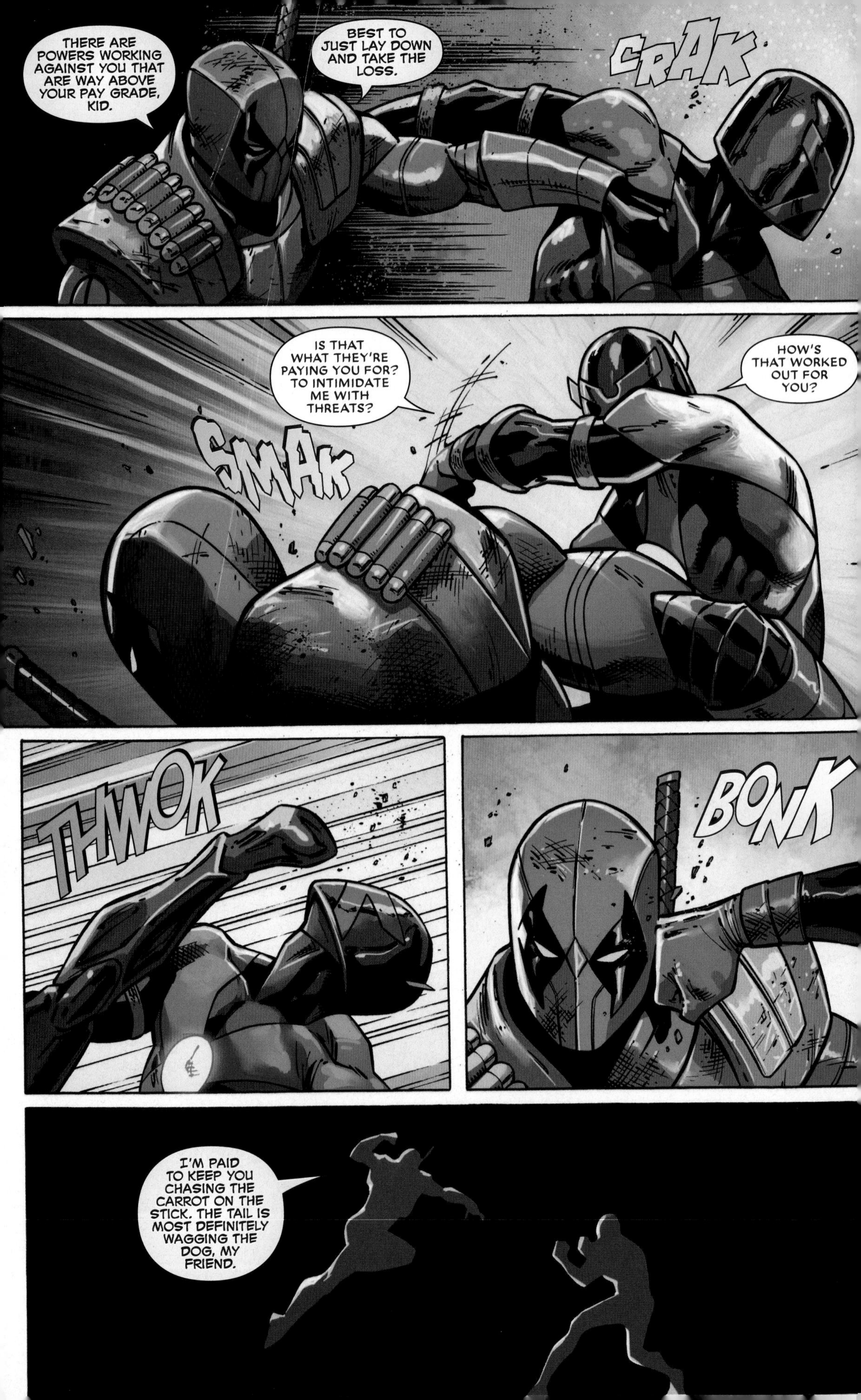
THERE ARE POWERS WORKING AGAINST YOU THAT ARE WAY ABOVE YOUR PAY GRADE, KID.
BEST TO JUST LAY DOWN AND TAKE THE LOSS.
CRAK
IS THAT WHAT THEY'RE PAYING YOU FOR? TO INTIMIDATE ME WITH THREATS?
HOW'S THAT WORKED OUT FOR YOU?
SMAK
THWOK
BONK
I'M PAID TO KEEP YOU CHASING THE CARROT ON THE STICK. THE TAIL IS MOST DEFINITELY WAGGING THE DOG, MY FRIEND.

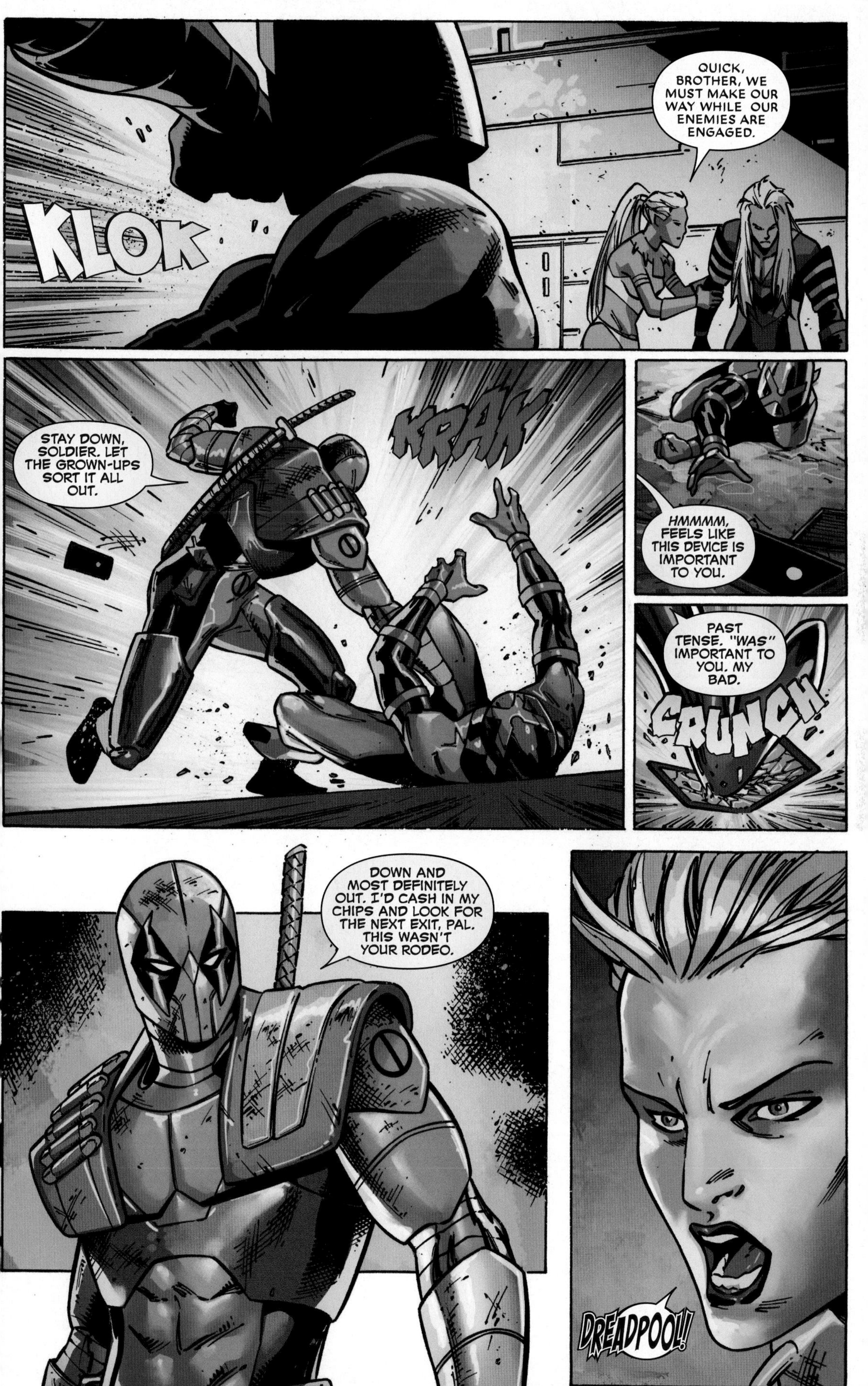
KLOK
QUICK, BROTHER, WE MUST MAKE OUR WAY WHILE OUR ENEMIES ARE ENGAGED.
STAY DOWN, SOLDIER. LET THE GROWN-UPS SORT IT ALL OUT.
KRAK
HMMMM, FEELS LIKE THIS DEVICE IS IMPORTANT TO YOU.
PAST TENSE. "WAS" IMPORTANT TO YOU. MY BAD.
CRUNCH
DOWN AND MOST DEFINITELY OUT. I'D CASH IN MY CHIPS AND LOOK FOR THE NEXT EXIT, PAL. THIS WASN'T YOUR RODEO.
DREADPOOL!

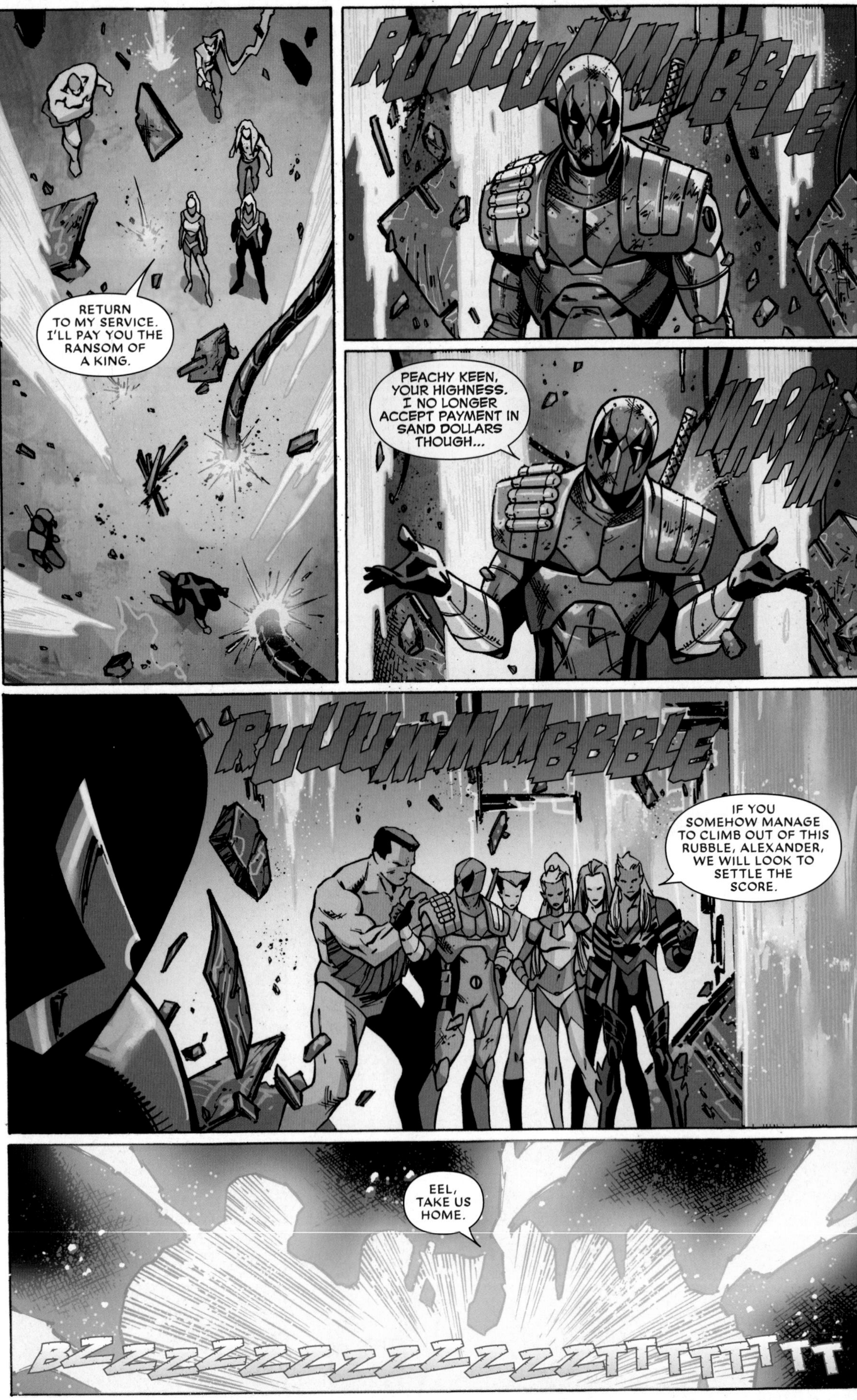
RETURN TO MY SERVICE. I'LL PAY YOU THE RANSOM OF A KING.
RUUUUMMMBBLE
PEACHY KEEN, YOUR HIGHNESS. I NO LONGER ACCEPT PAYMENT IN SAND DOLLARS THOUGH...
WHRAM
RUUUMMMBBBLE
IF YOU SOMEHOW MANAGE TO CLIMB OUT OF THIS RUBBLE, ALEXANDER, WE WILL LOOK TO SETTLE THE SCORE.
EEL, TAKE US HOME.
BZZZZZZZZZZZZZZTTTTTTTTT

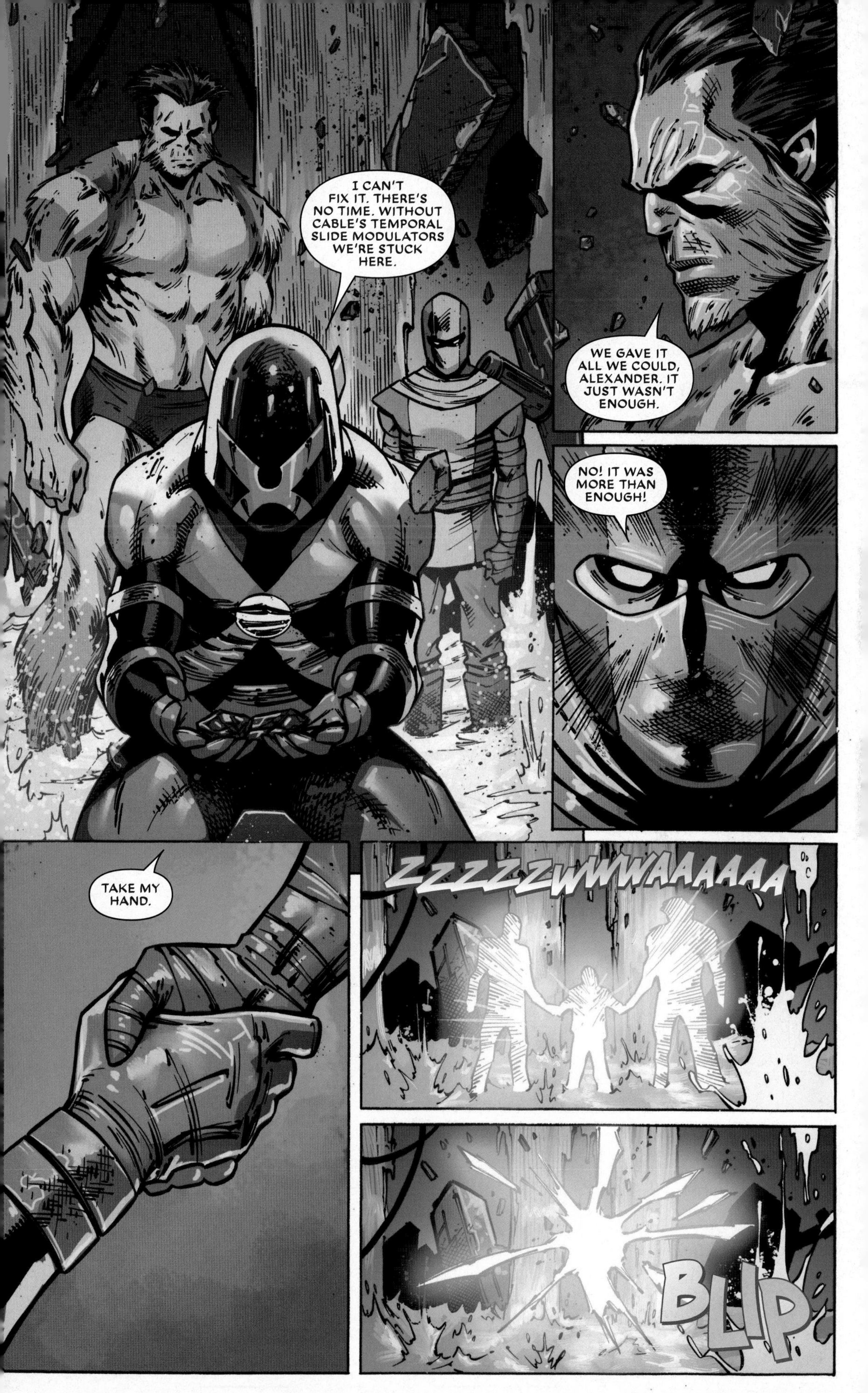
I CAN'T FIX IT. THERE'S NO TIME. WITHOUT CABLE'S TEMPORAL SLIDE MODULATORS WE'RE STUCK HERE.
WE GAVE IT ALL WE COULD, ALEXANDER. IT JUST WASN'T ENOUGH.
NO! IT WAS MORE THAN ENOUGH!
TAKE MY HAND.
ZZZZZWWWAAAAAA
BLIP

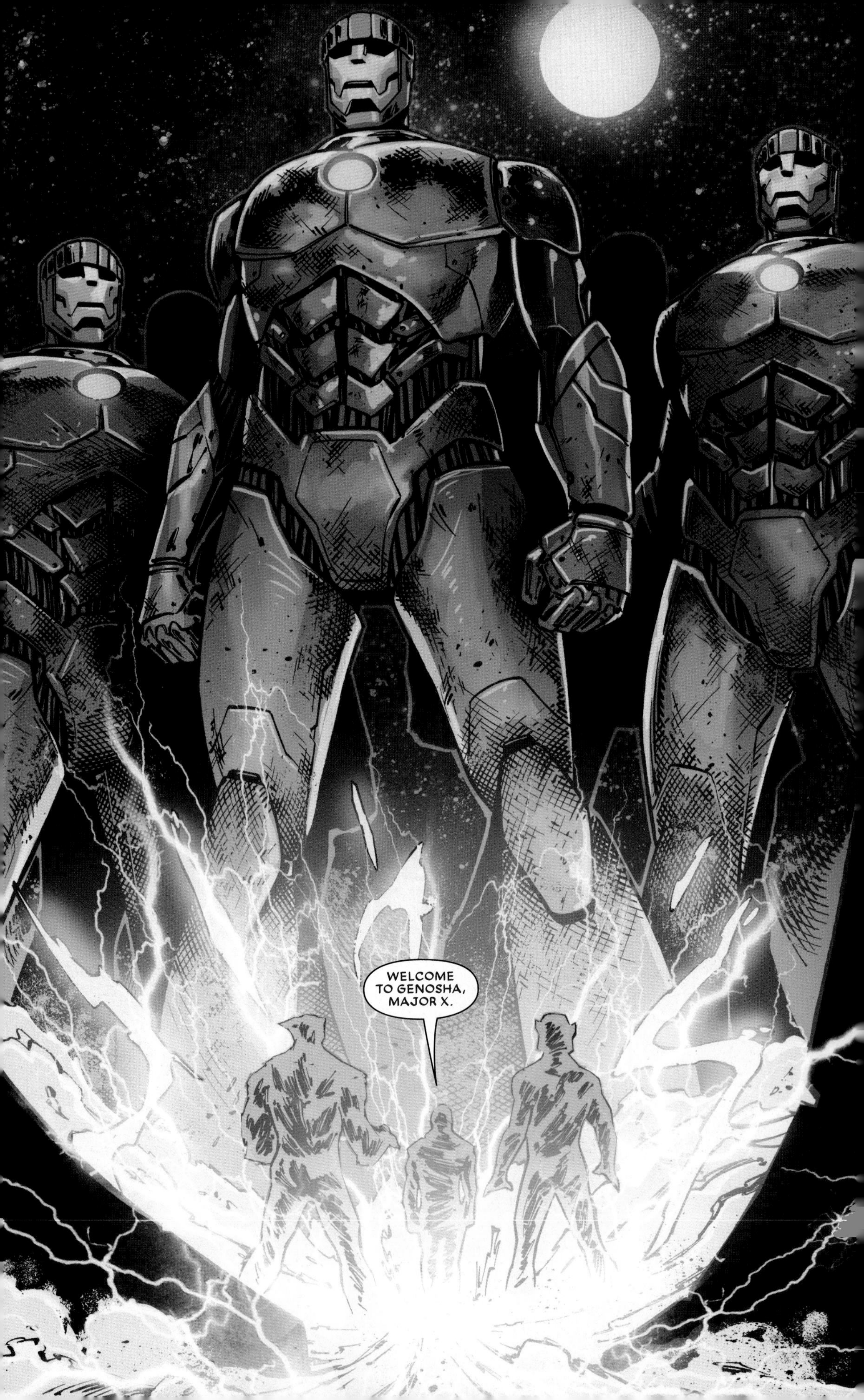
WELCOME TO GENOSHA, MAJOR X.

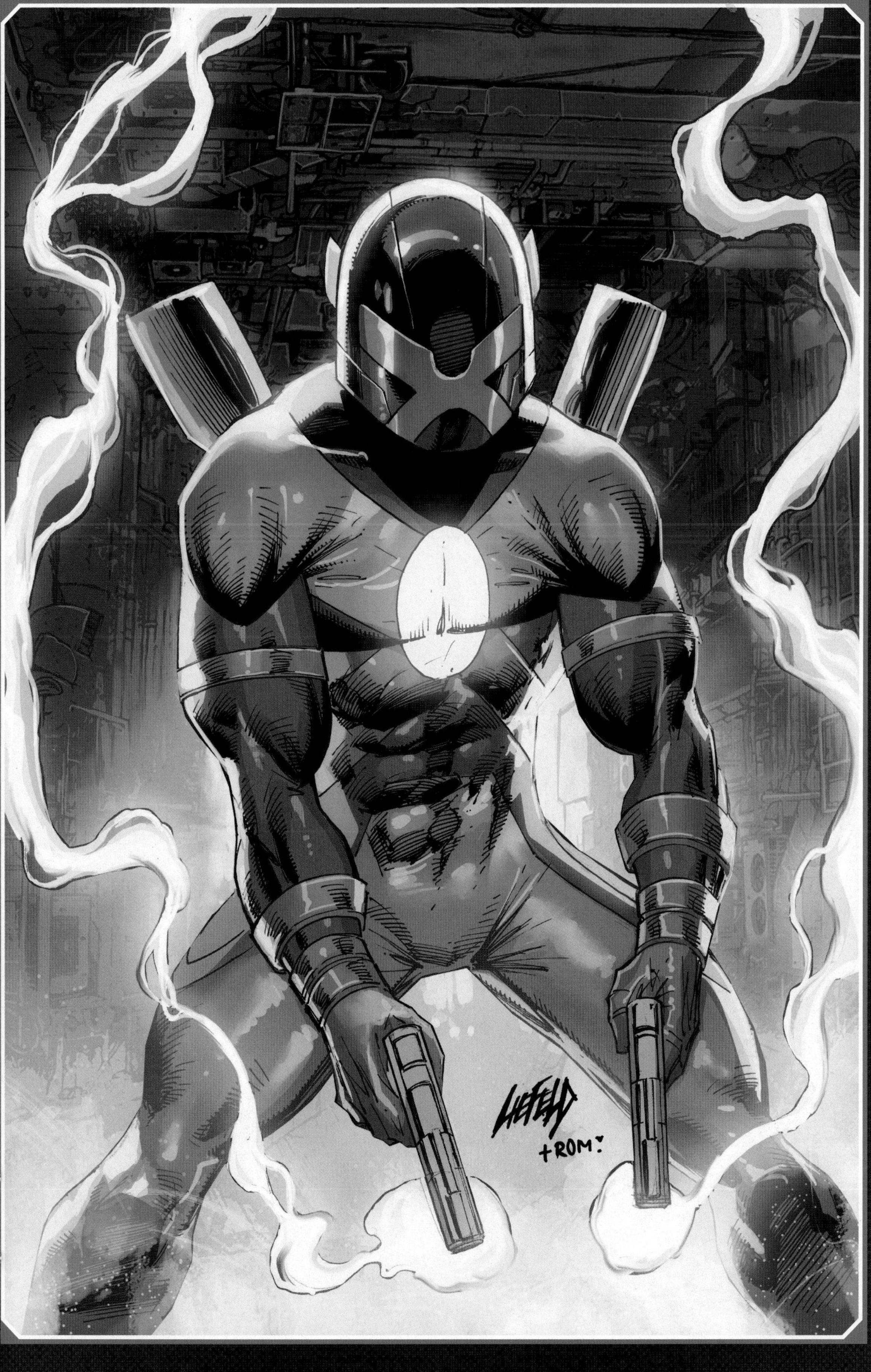
LIEFELD
+ROM

ROB LIEFELD & ROMULO FAJARDO JR.

#3 SECOND PRINTING COVER

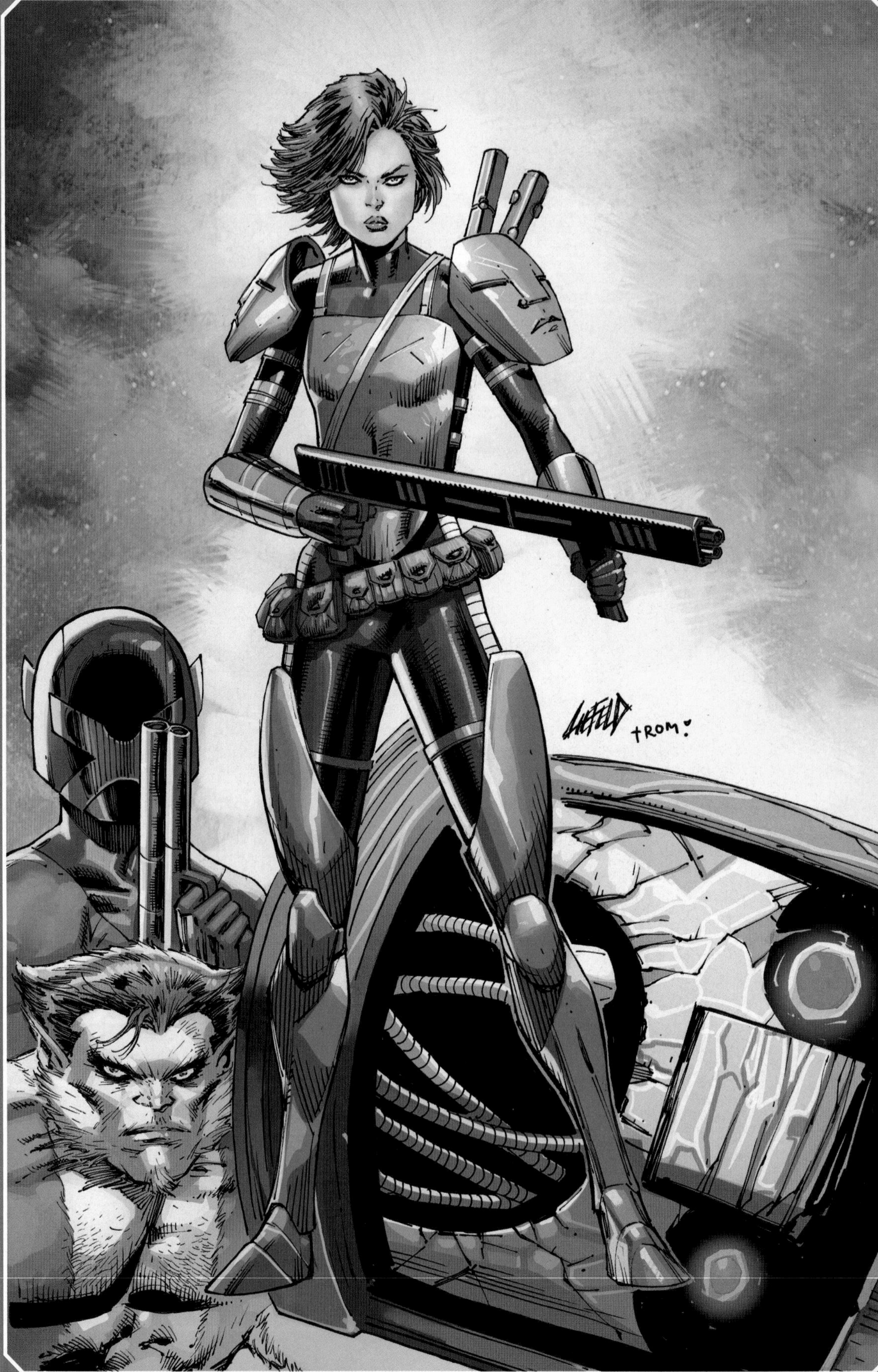

5

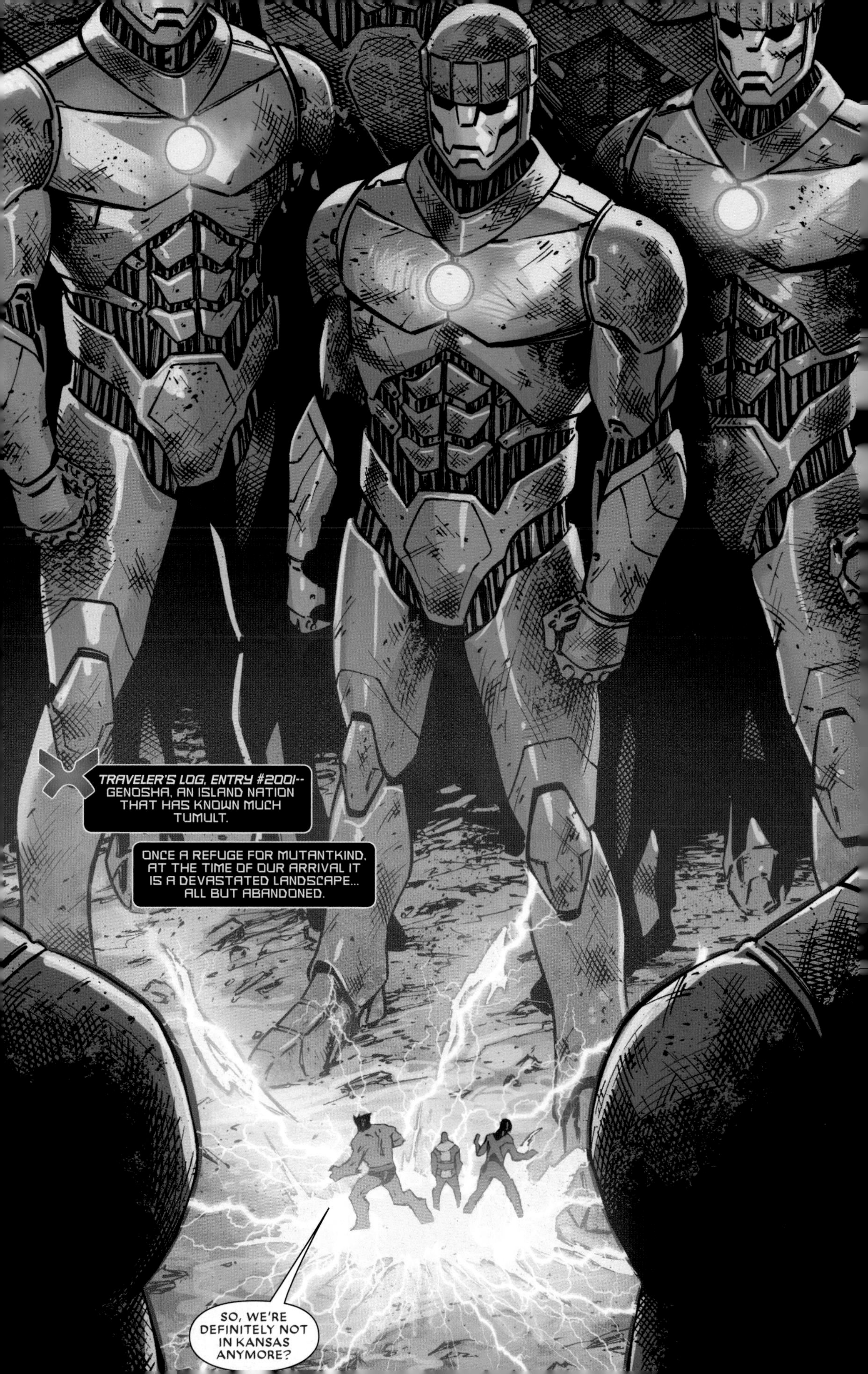
TRAVELER'S LOG, ENTRY #2001-- GENOSHA, AN ISLAND NATION THAT HAS KNOWN MUCH TUMULT.
ONCE A REFUGE FOR MUTANTKIND, AT THE TIME OF OUR ARRIVAL IT IS A DEVASTATED LANDSCAPE... ALL BUT ABANDONED.
SO, WE'RE DEFINITELY NOT IN KANSAS ANYMORE?

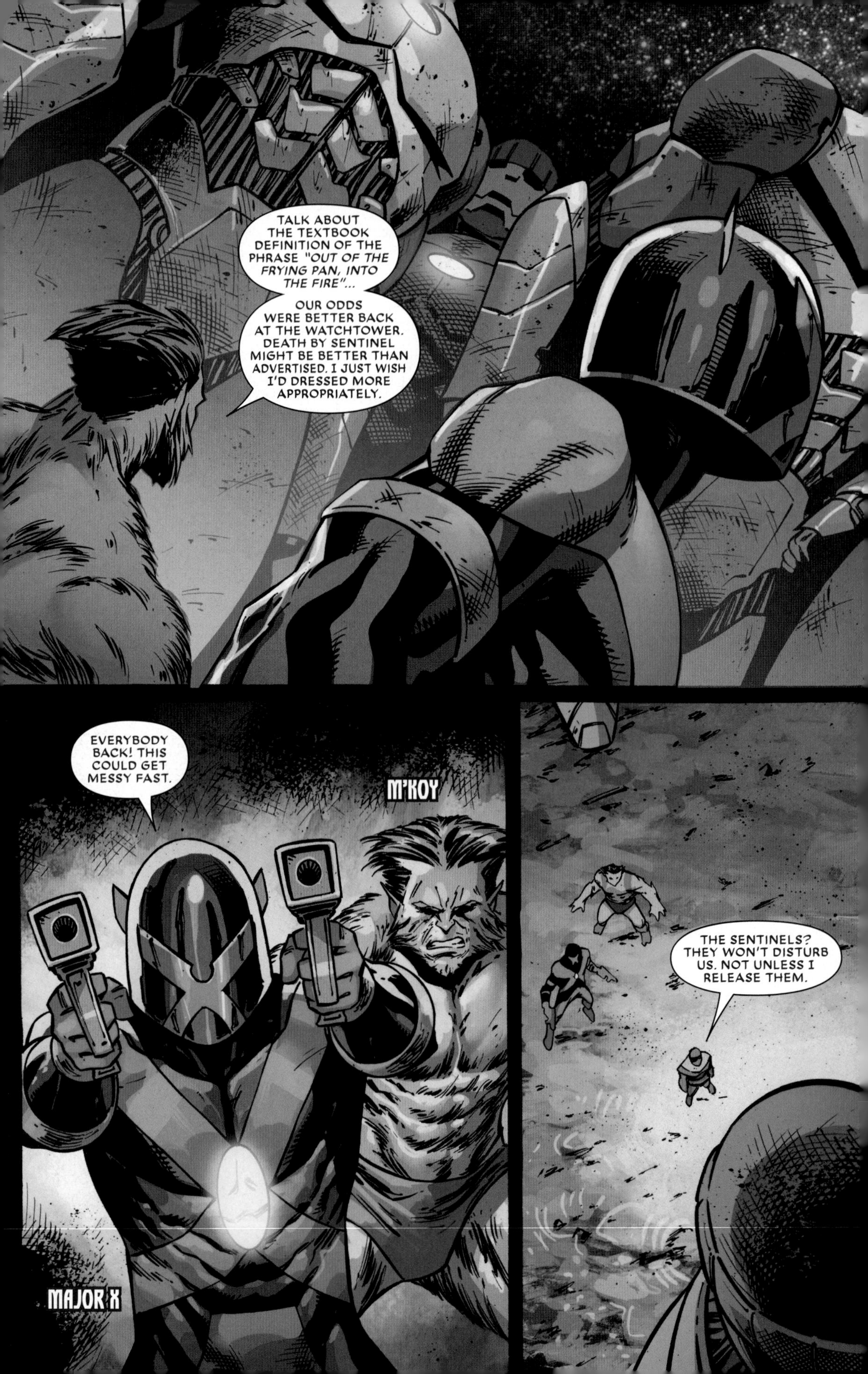
TALK ABOUT THE TEXTBOOK DEFINITION OF THE PHRASE "OUT OF THE FRYING PAN, INTO THE FIRE"...
OUR ODDS WERE BETTER BACK AT THE WATCHTOWER. DEATH BY SENTINEL MIGHT BE BETTER THAN ADVERTISED. I JUST WISH I'D DRESSED MORE APPROPRIATELY.
EVERYBODY BACK! THIS COULD GET MESSY FAST.
M'KOY
MAJOR X
THE SENTINELS? THEY WON'T DISTURB US. NOT UNLESS I RELEASE THEM.

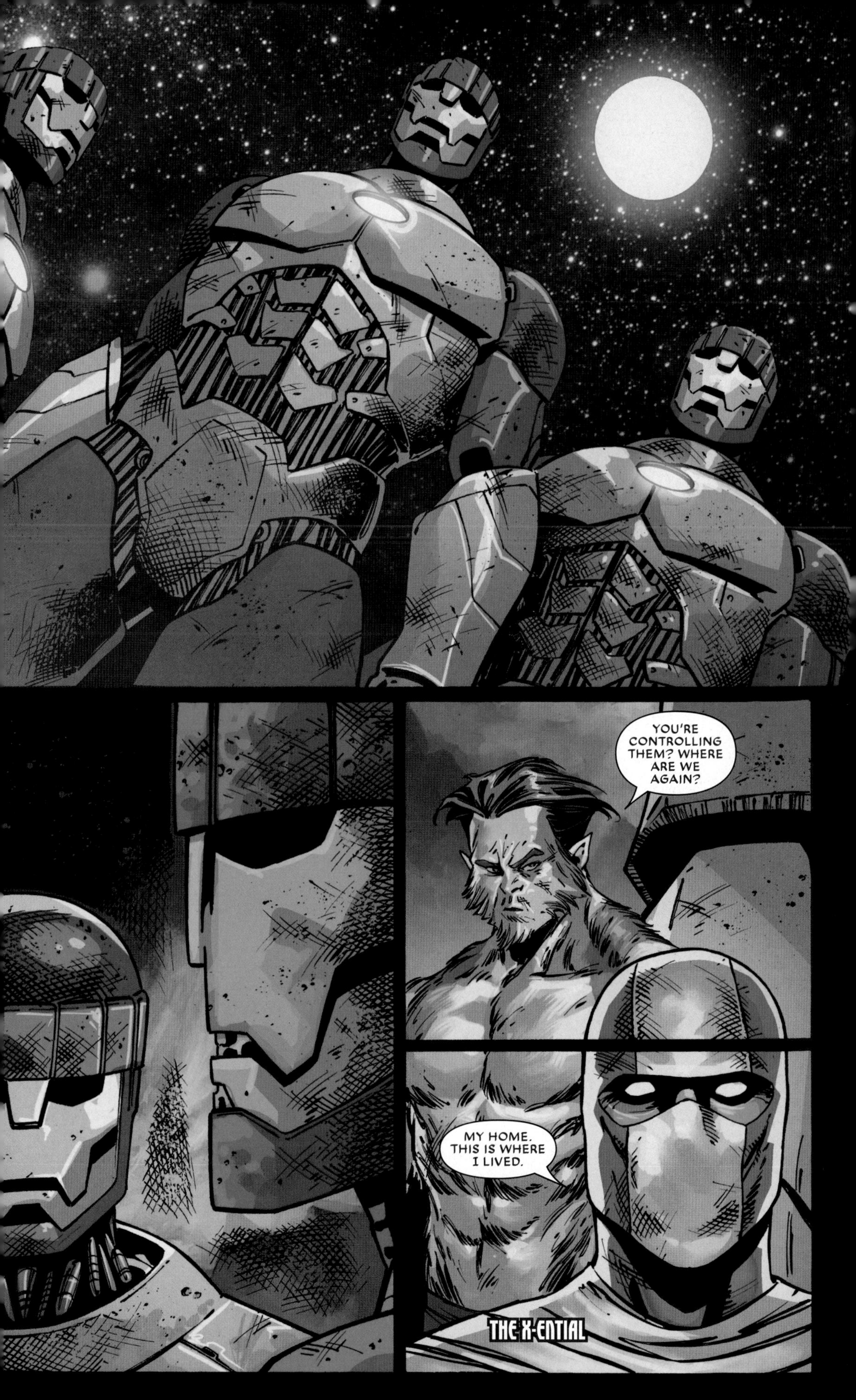
YOU'RE CONTROLLING THEM? WHERE ARE WE AGAIN?
MY HOME. THIS IS WHERE I LIVED.
THE X-ENTIAL

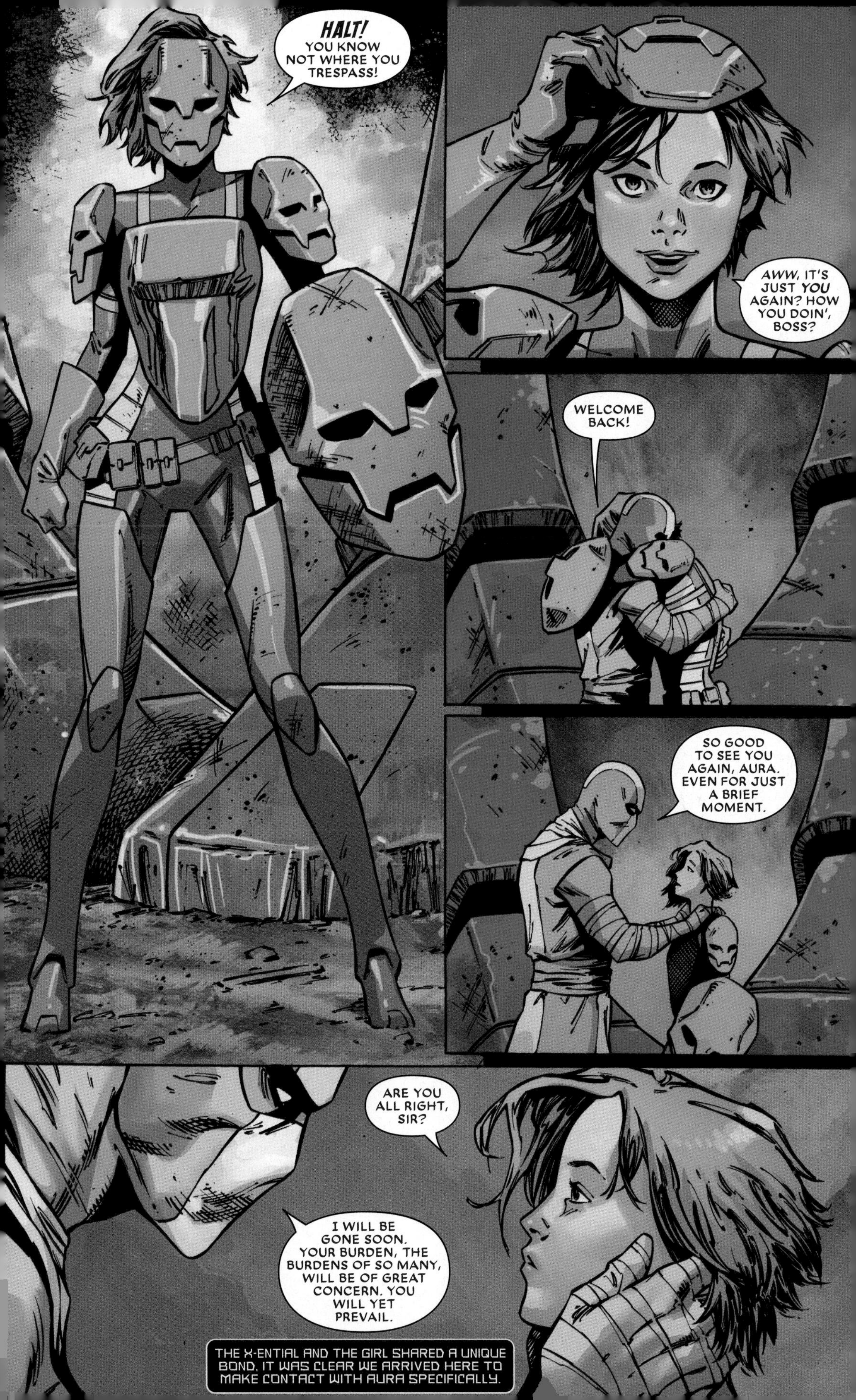
HALT! YOU KNOW NOT WHERE YOU TRESPASS!
AWW, IT'S JUST YOU AGAIN? HOW YOU DOIN', BOSS?
WELCOME BACK!
SO GOOD TO SEE YOU AGAIN, AURA. EVEN FOR JUST A BRIEF MOMENT.
ARE YOU ALL RIGHT, SIR?
I WILL BE GONE SOON. YOUR BURDEN, THE BURDENS OF SO MANY, WILL BE OF GREAT CONCERN. YOU WILL YET PREVAIL.
THE X-ENTIAL AND THE GIRL SHARED A UNIQUE BOND. IT WAS CLEAR WE ARRIVED HERE TO MAKE CONTACT WITH AURA SPECIFICALLY.

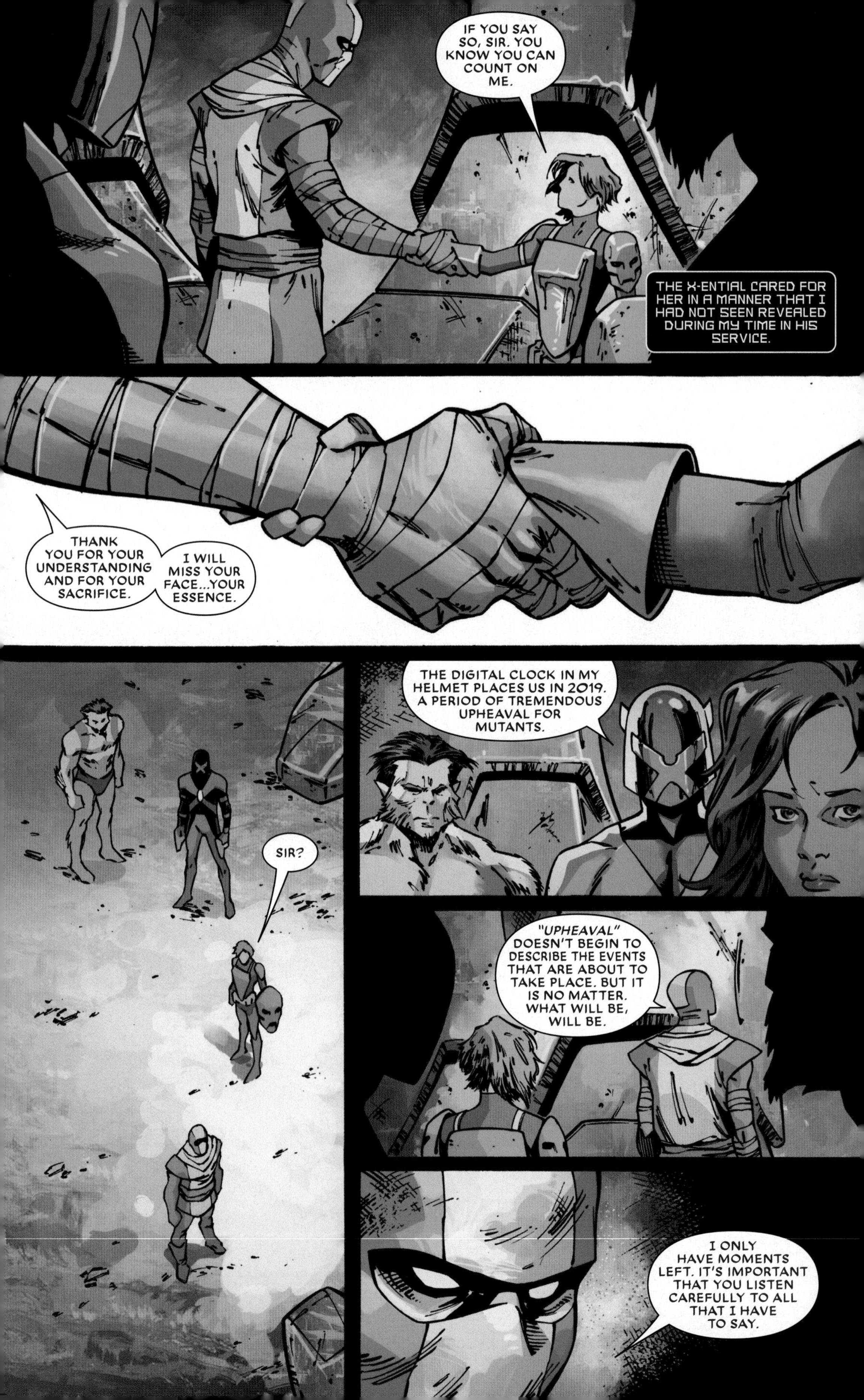
IF YOU SAY SO, SIR. YOU KNOW YOU CAN COUNT ON ME.
THE X-ENTIAL CARED FOR HER IN A MANNER THAT I HAD NOT SEEN REVEALED DURING MY TIME IN HIS SERVICE.
THANK YOU FOR YOUR UNDERSTANDING AND FOR YOUR SACRIFICE.
I WILL MISS YOUR FACE...YOUR ESSENCE.
SIR?
THE DIGITAL CLOCK IN MY HELMET PLACES US IN 2019. A PERIOD OF TREMENDOUS UPHEAVAL FOR MUTANTS.
"UPHEAVAL" DOESN'T BEGIN TO DESCRIBE THE EVENTS THAT ARE ABOUT TO TAKE PLACE. BUT IT IS NO MATTER. WHAT WILL BE, WILL BE.
I ONLY HAVE MOMENTS LEFT. IT'S IMPORTANT THAT YOU LISTEN CAREFULLY TO ALL THAT I HAVE TO SAY.

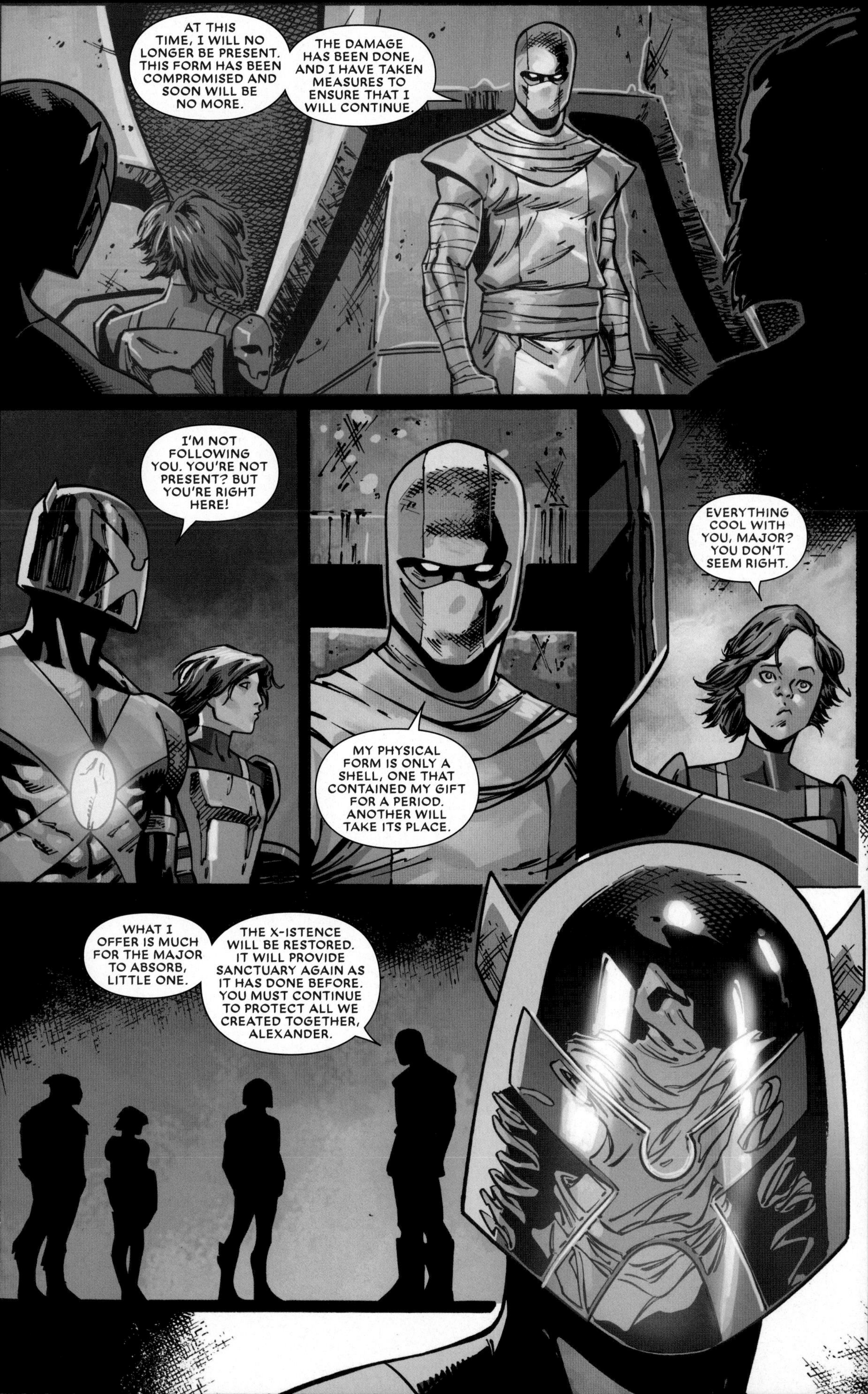
AT THIS TIME, I WILL NO LONGER BE PRESENT. THIS FORM HAS BEEN COMPROMISED AND SOON WILL BE NO MORE.
THE DAMAGE HAS BEEN DONE, AND I HAVE TAKEN MEASURES TO ENSURE THAT I WILL CONTINUE.
I'M NOT FOLLOWING YOU. YOU'RE NOT PRESENT? BUT YOU'RE RIGHT HERE!
MY PHYSICAL FORM IS ONLY A SHELL, ONE THAT CONTAINED MY GIFT FOR A PERIOD. ANOTHER WILL TAKE ITS PLACE.
EVERYTHING COOL WITH YOU, MAJOR? YOU DON'T SEEM RIGHT.
WHAT I OFFER IS MUCH FOR THE MAJOR TO ABSORB, LITTLE ONE.
THE X-ISTENCE WILL BE RESTORED. IT WILL PROVIDE SANCTUARY AGAIN AS IT HAS DONE BEFORE. YOU MUST CONTINUE TO PROTECT ALL WE CREATED TOGETHER, ALEXANDER.

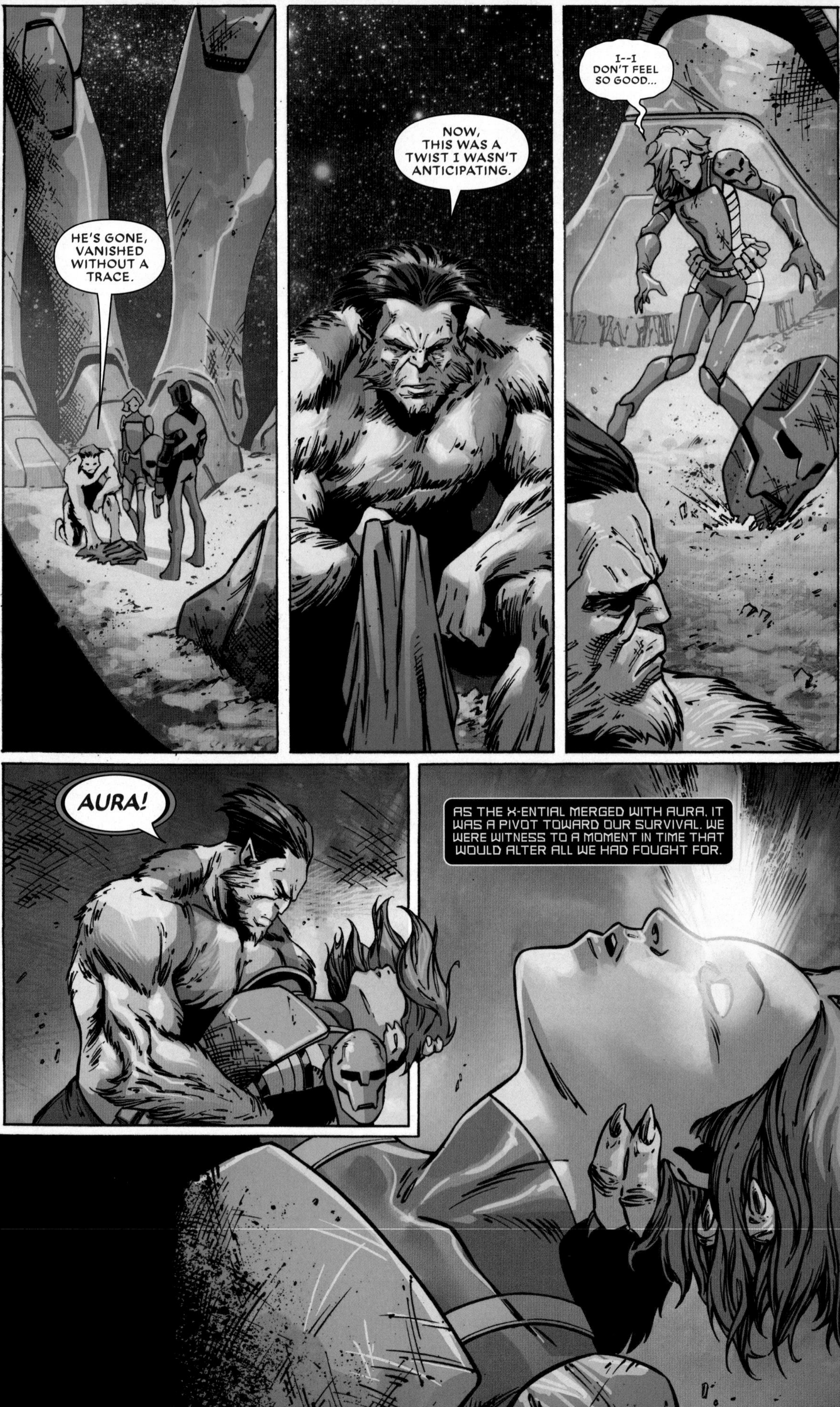
HE'S GONE, VANISHED WITHOUT A TRACE.
NOW, THIS WAS A TWIST I WASN'T ANTICIPATING.
I--I DON'T FEEL SO GOOD...
AURA!
AS THE X-ENTIAL MERGED WITH AURA, IT WAS A PIVOT TOWARD OUR SURVIVAL. WE WERE WITNESS TO A MOMENT IN TIME THAT WOULD ALTER ALL WE HAD FOUGHT FOR.

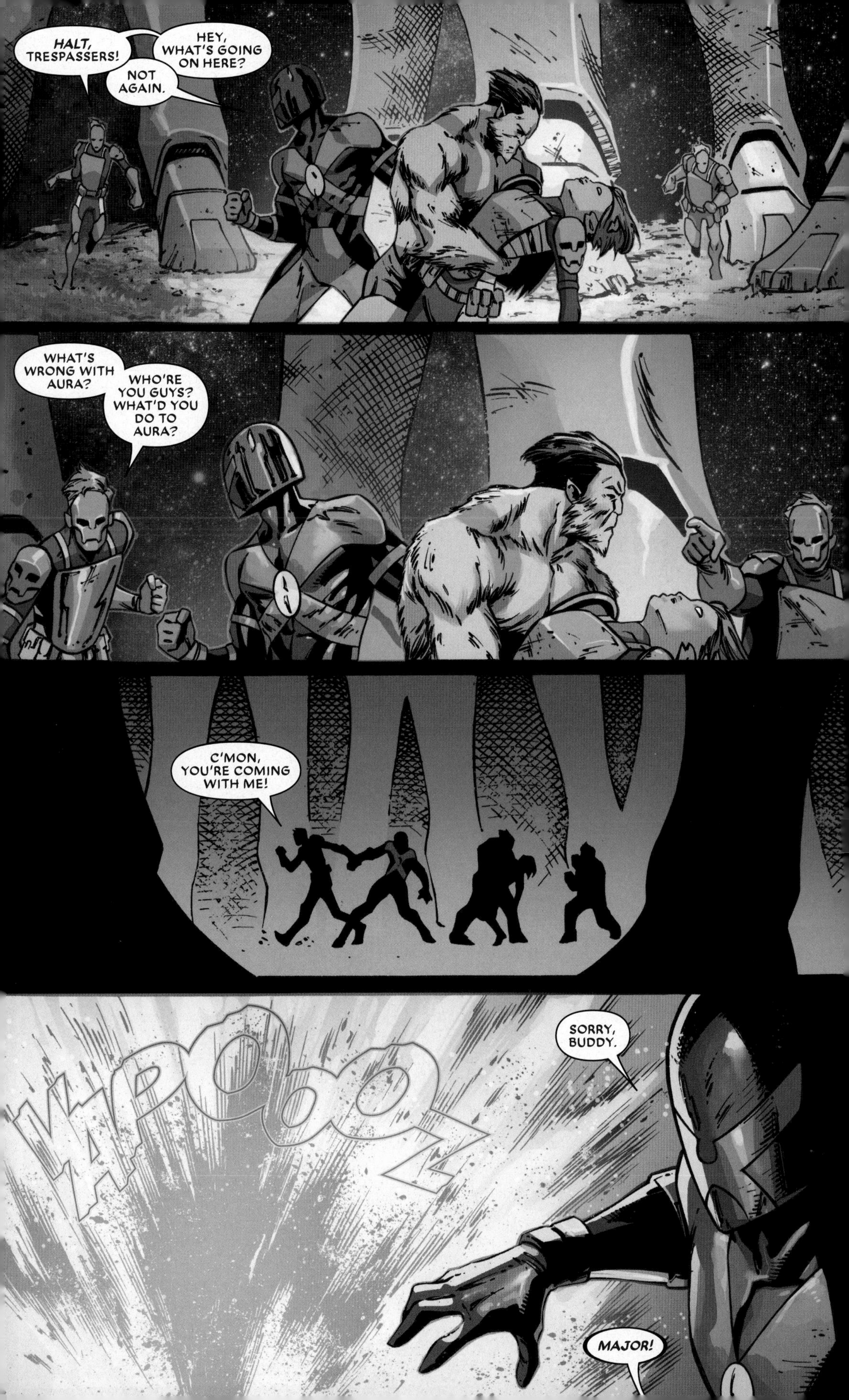
HALT, TRESPASSERS!
HEY, WHAT'S GOING ON HERE?
NOT AGAIN.
WHAT'S WRONG WITH AURA?
WHO'RE YOU GUYS? WHAT'D YOU DO TO AURA?
C'MON, YOU'RE COMING WITH ME!
SORRY, BUDDY.
WHOOOM
MAJOR!

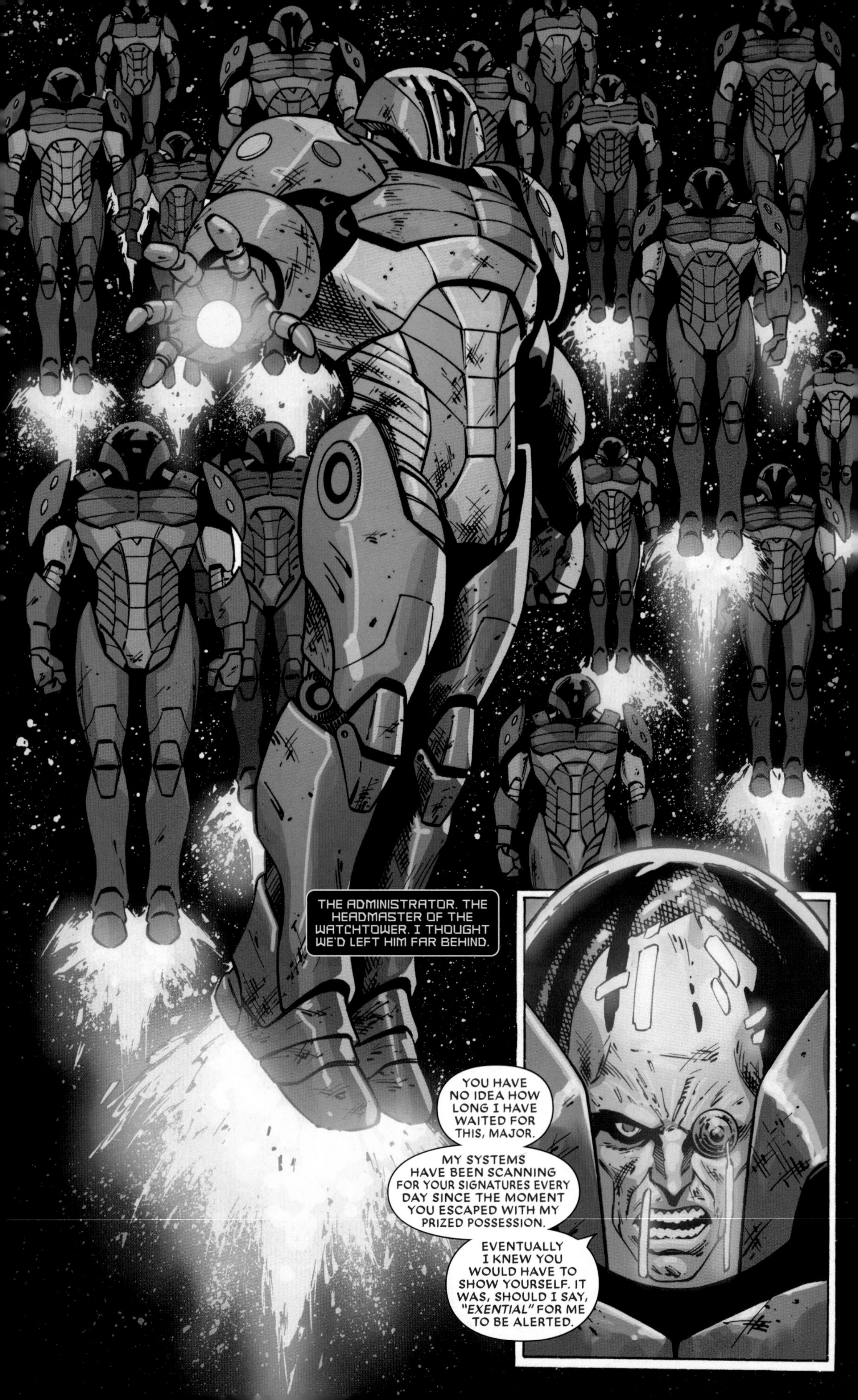
THE ADMINISTRATOR. THE HEADMASTER OF THE WATCHTOWER. I THOUGHT WE'D LEFT HIM FAR BEHIND.
YOU HAVE NO IDEA HOW LONG I HAVE WAITED FOR THIS, MAJOR.
MY SYSTEMS HAVE BEEN SCANNING FOR YOUR SIGNATURES EVERY DAY SINCE THE MOMENT YOU ESCAPED WITH MY PRIZED POSSESSION.
EVENTUALLY I KNEW YOU WOULD HAVE TO SHOW YOURSELF. IT WAS, SHOULD I SAY, "EXENTIAL" FOR ME TO BE ALERTED.

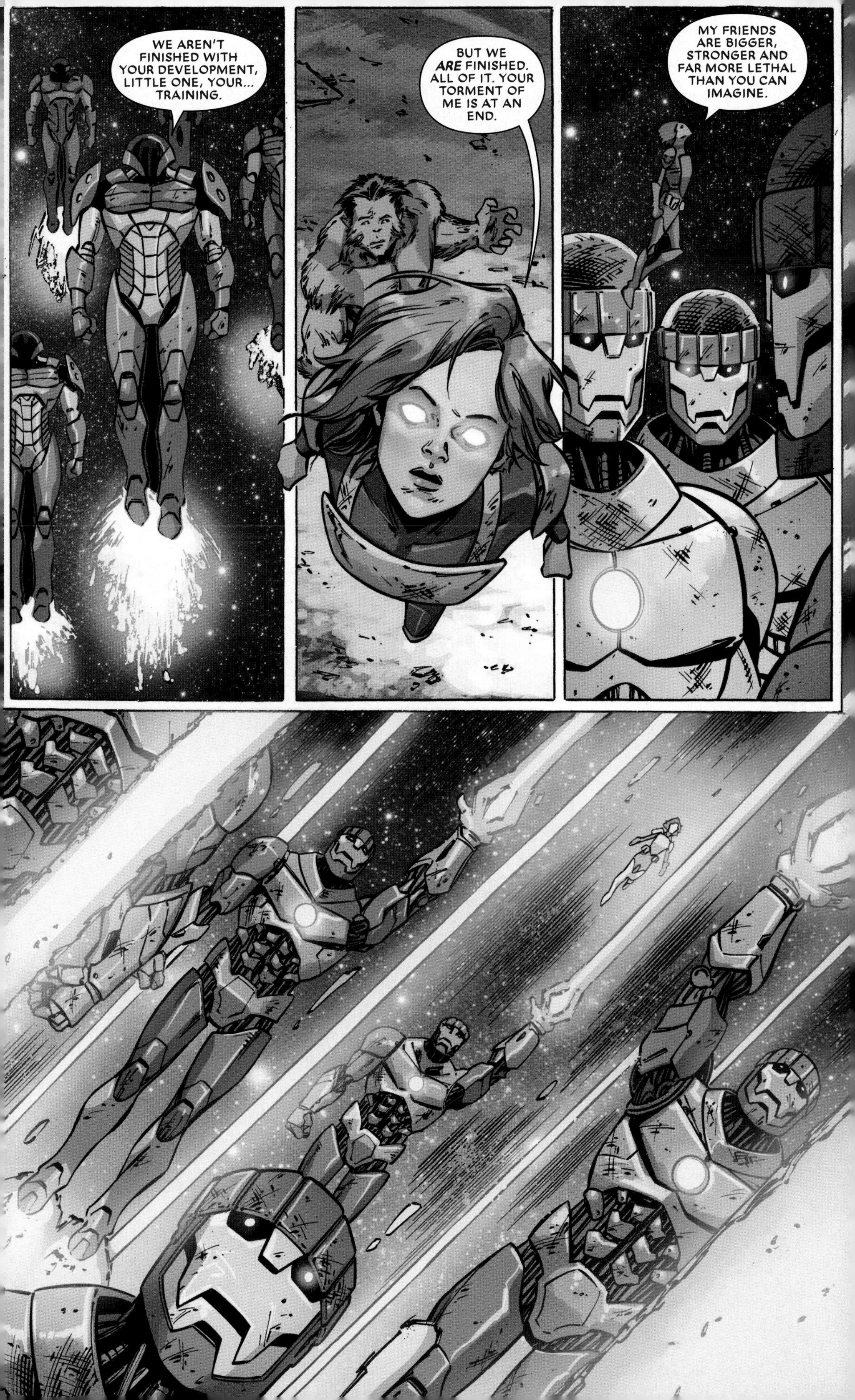
WE AREN'T FINISHED WITH YOUR DEVELOPMENT, LITTLE ONE, YOUR... TRAINING.
BUT WE *ARE* FINISHED. ALL OF IT. YOUR TORMENT OF ME IS AT AN END.
MY FRIENDS ARE BIGGER, STRONGER AND FAR MORE LETHAL THAN YOU CAN IMAGINE.

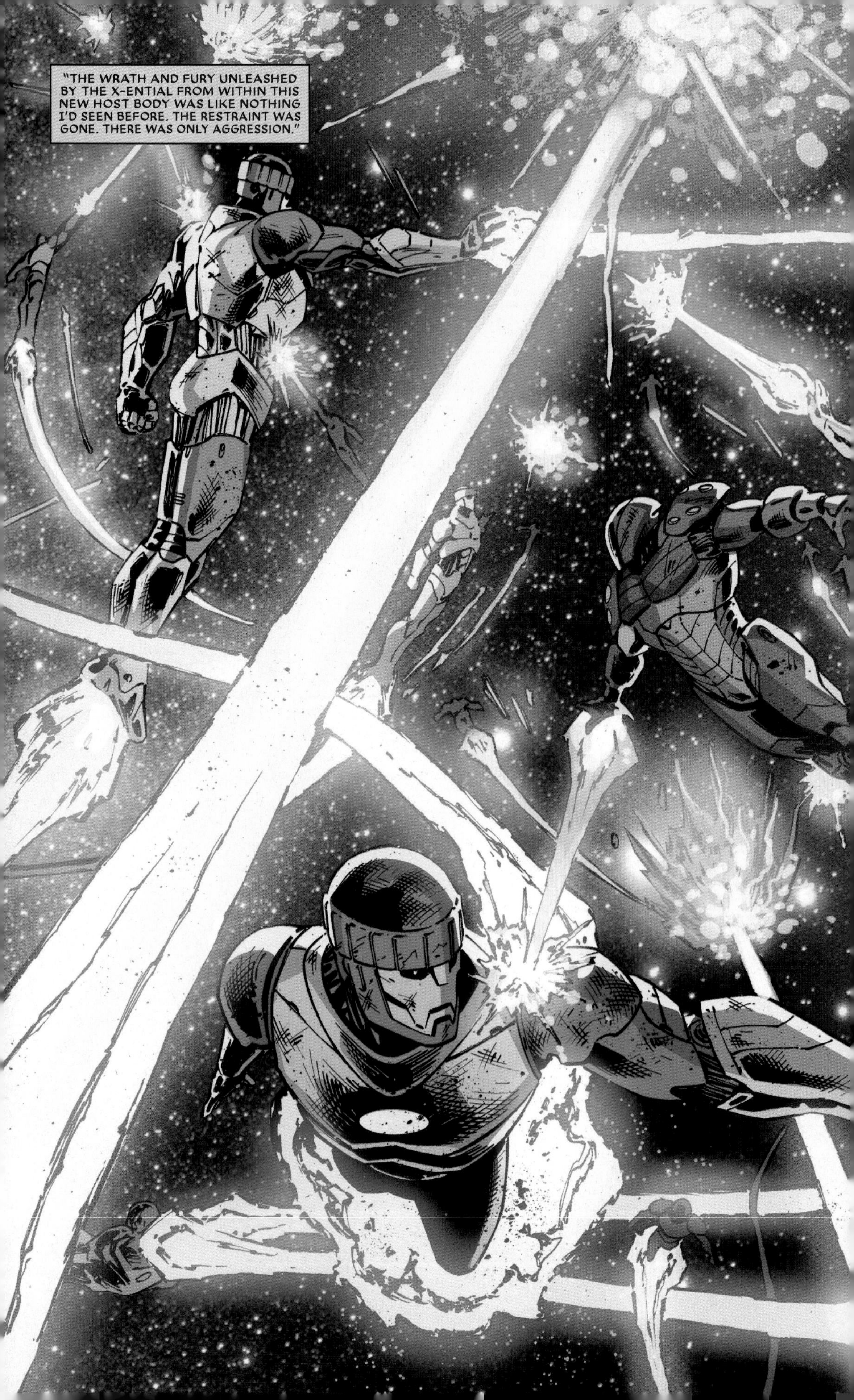
"THE WRATH AND FURY UNLEASHED BY THE X-ENTIAL FROM WITHIN THIS NEW HOST BODY WAS LIKE NOTHING I'D SEEN BEFORE. THE RESTRAINT WAS GONE. THERE WAS ONLY AGGRESSION."

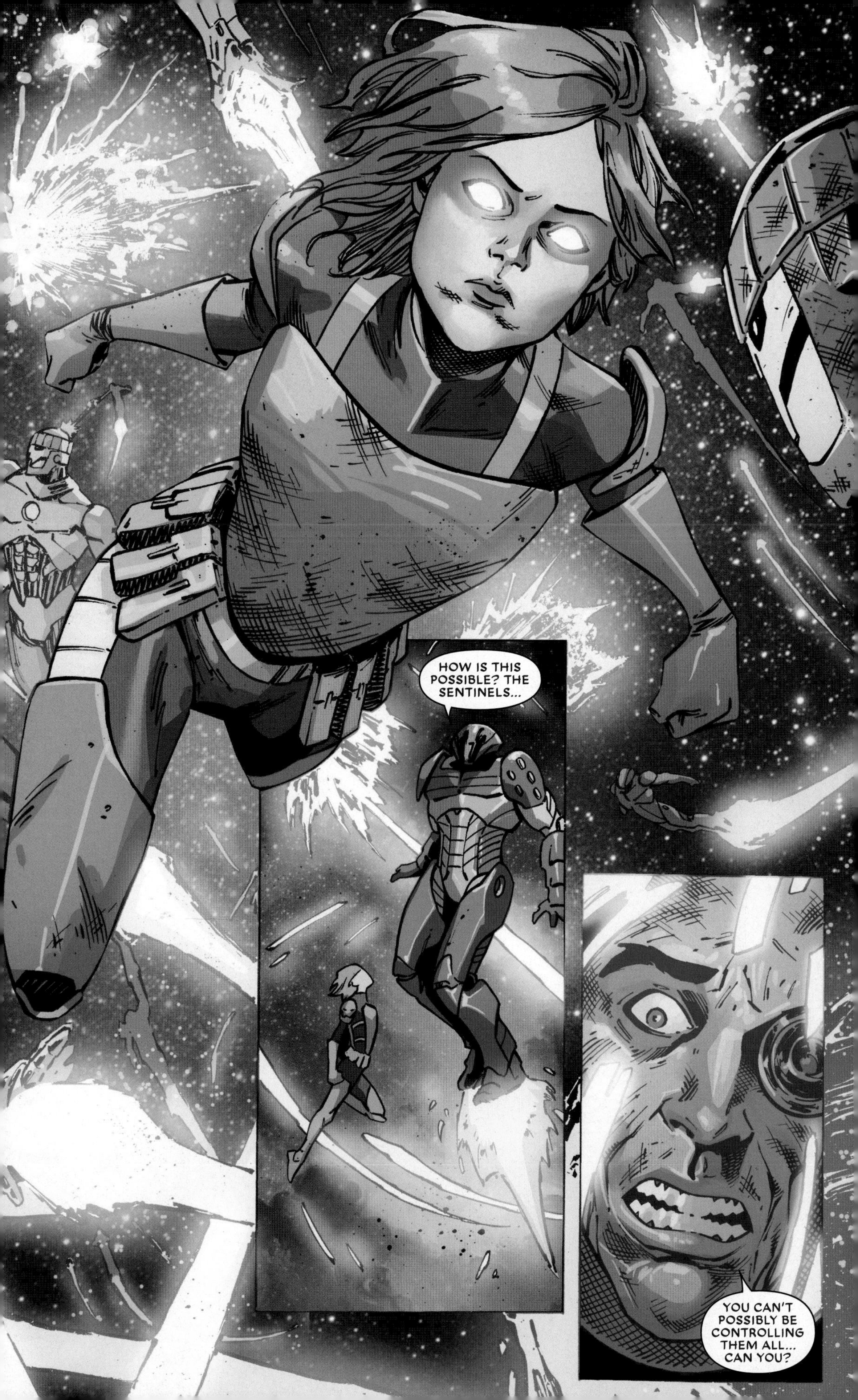
HOW IS THIS POSSIBLE? THE SENTINELS...
YOU CAN'T POSSIBLY BE CONTROLLING THEM ALL... CAN YOU?

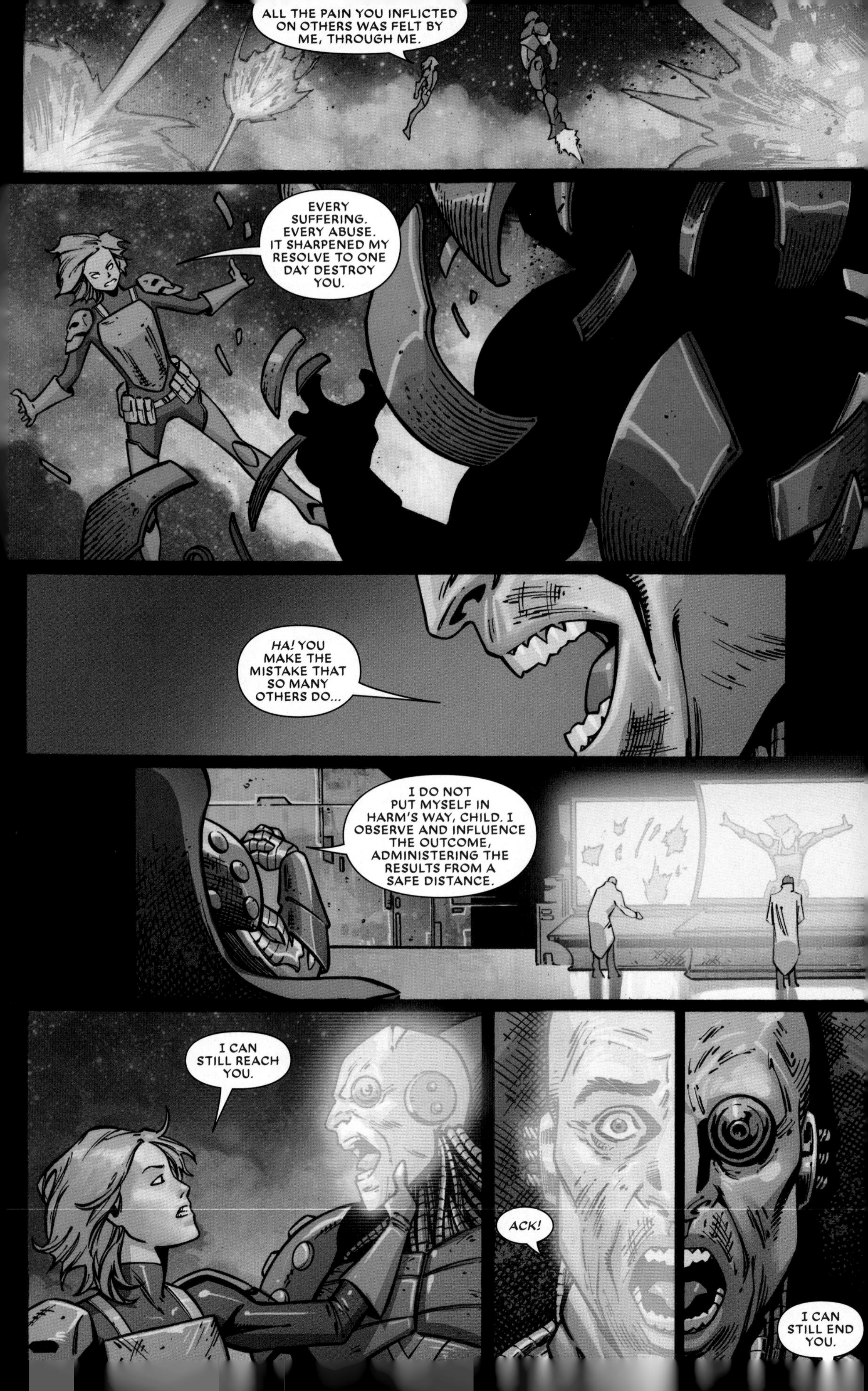
ALL THE PAIN YOU INFLICTED ON OTHERS WAS FELT BY ME, THROUGH ME.
EVERY SUFFERING. EVERY ABUSE. IT SHARPENED MY RESOLVE TO ONE DAY DESTROY YOU.
HA! YOU MAKE THE MISTAKE THAT SO MANY OTHERS DO...
I DO NOT PUT MYSELF IN HARM'S WAY, CHILD. I OBSERVE AND INFLUENCE THE OUTCOME, ADMINISTERING THE RESULTS FROM A SAFE DISTANCE.
I CAN STILL REACH YOU.
ACK!
I CAN STILL END YOU.

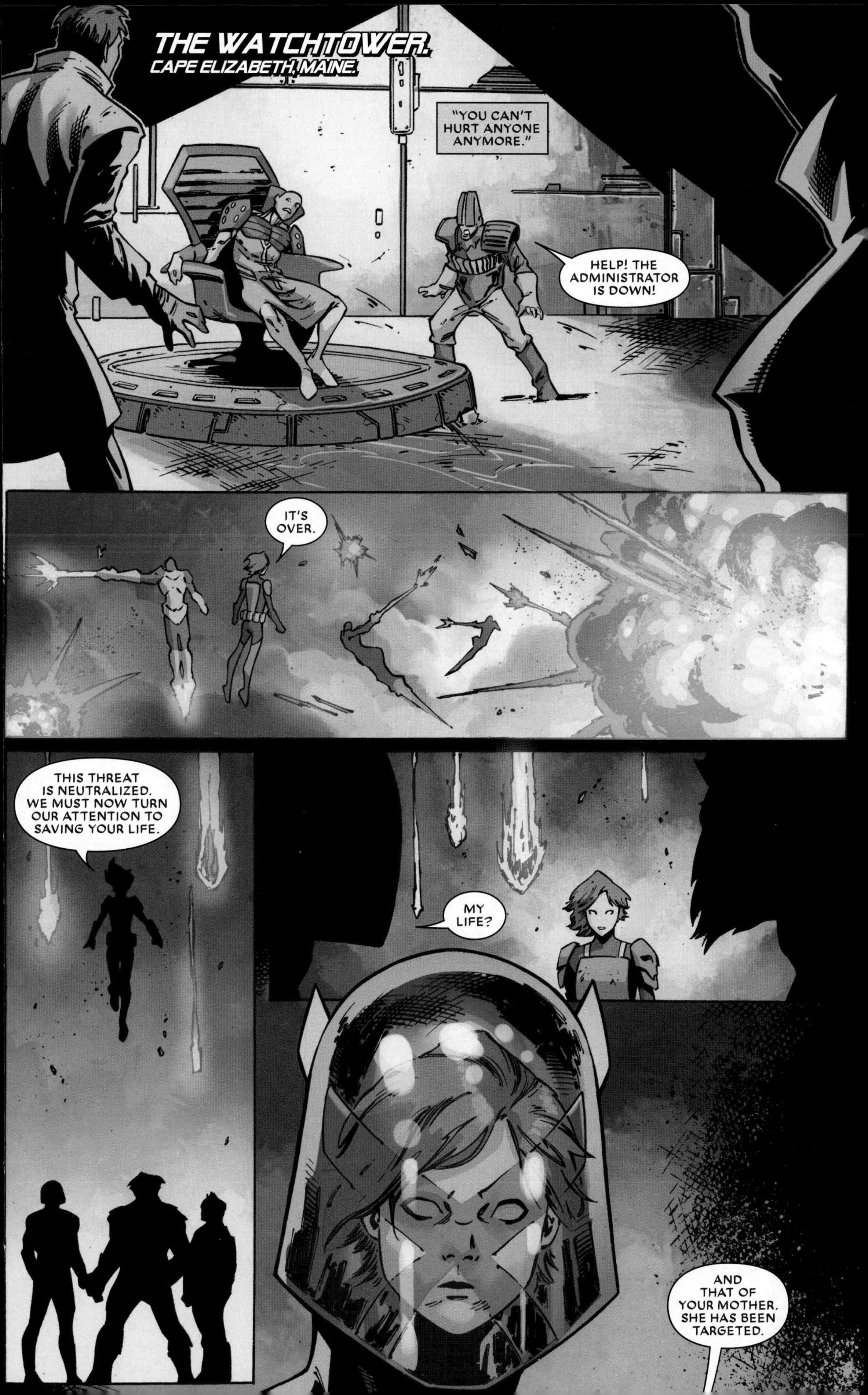
THE WATCHTOWER.
CAPE ELIZABETH, MAINE.
"YOU CAN'T HURT ANYONE ANYMORE."
HELP! THE ADMINISTRATOR IS DOWN!
IT'S OVER.
THIS THREAT IS NEUTRALIZED. WE MUST NOW TURN OUR ATTENTION TO SAVING YOUR LIFE.
MY LIFE?
AND THAT OF YOUR MOTHER. SHE HAS BEEN TARGETED.

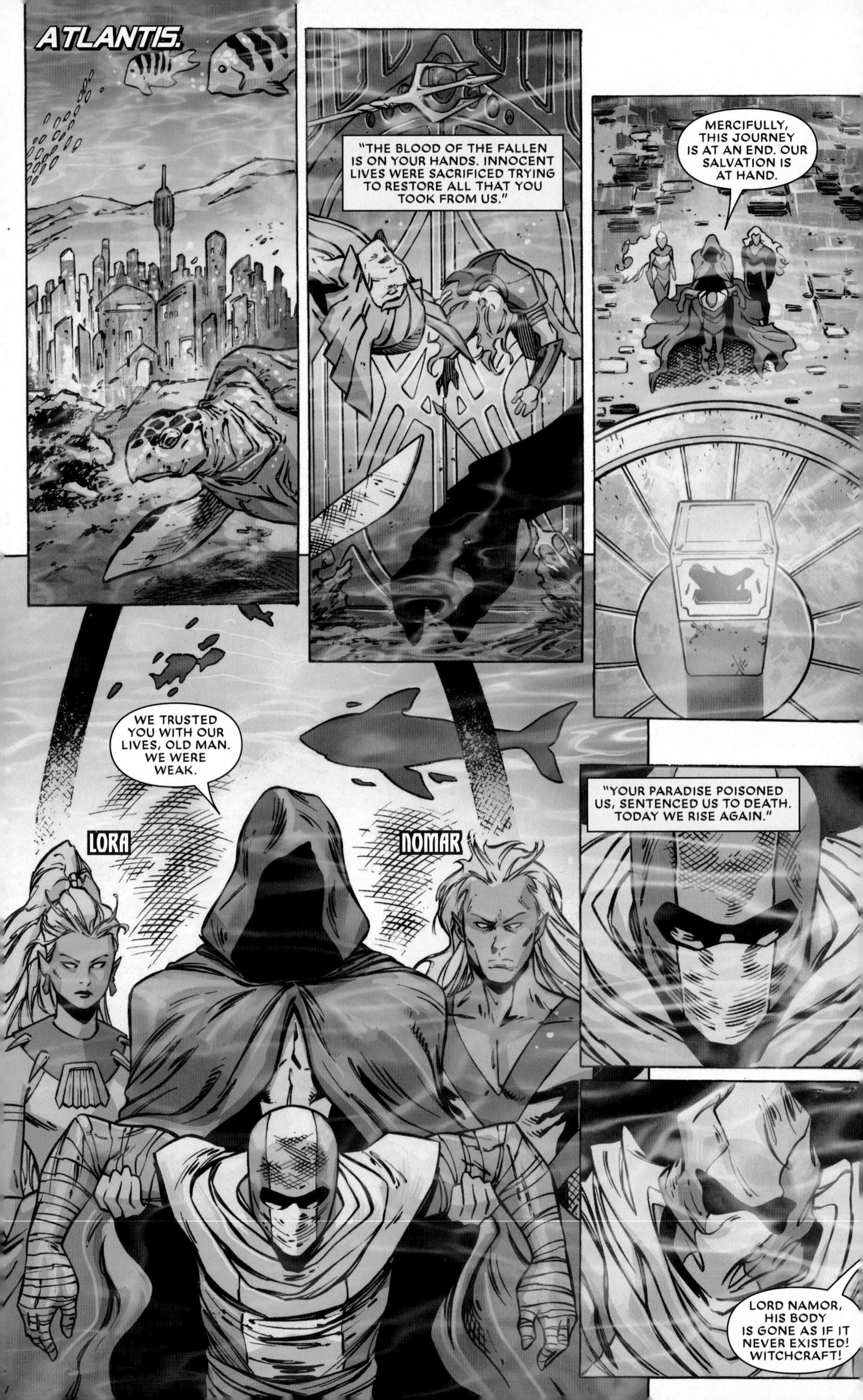
ATLANTIS.
"THE BLOOD OF THE FALLEN IS ON YOUR HANDS. INNOCENT LIVES WERE SACRIFICED TRYING TO RESTORE ALL THAT YOU TOOK FROM US."
MERCIFULLY, THIS JOURNEY IS AT AN END. OUR SALVATION IS AT HAND.
WE TRUSTED YOU WITH OUR LIVES, OLD MAN. WE WERE WEAK.
LORA
NOMAR
"YOUR PARADISE POISONED US, SENTENCED US TO DEATH. TODAY WE RISE AGAIN."
LORD NAMOR, HIS BODY IS GONE AS IF IT NEVER EXISTED! WITCHCRAFT!

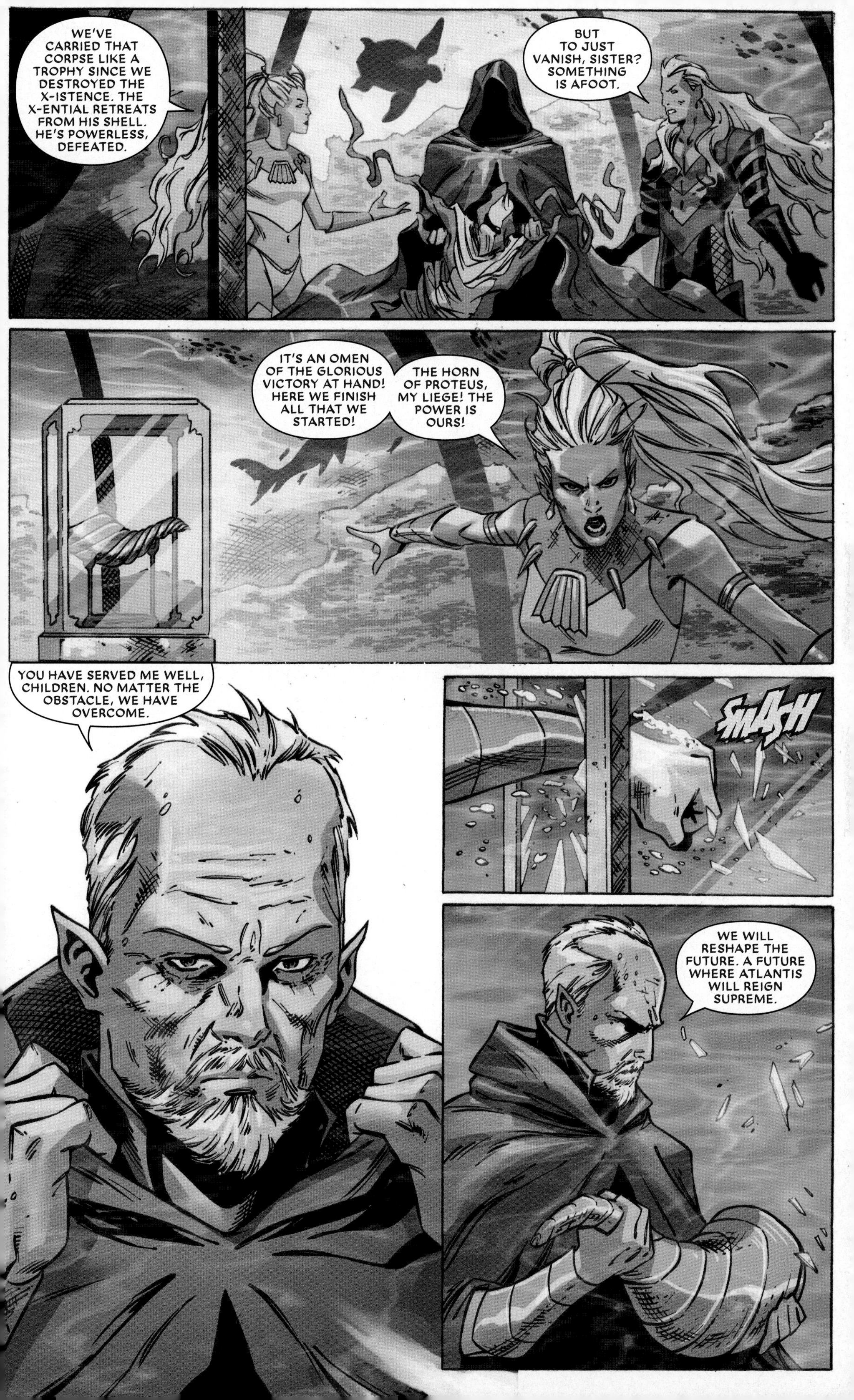
WE'VE CARRIED THAT CORPSE LIKE A TROPHY SINCE WE DESTROYED THE X-ISTENCE. THE X-ENTIAL RETREATS FROM HIS SHELL. HE'S POWERLESS, DEFEATED.
BUT TO JUST VANISH, SISTER? SOMETHING IS AFOOT.
IT'S AN OMEN OF THE GLORIOUS VICTORY AT HAND! HERE WE FINISH ALL THAT WE STARTED!
THE HORN OF PROTEUS, MY LIEGE! THE POWER IS OURS!
YOU HAVE SERVED ME WELL, CHILDREN. NO MATTER THE OBSTACLE, WE HAVE OVERCOME.
SMASH
WE WILL RESHAPE THE FUTURE. A FUTURE WHERE ATLANTIS WILL REIGN SUPREME.

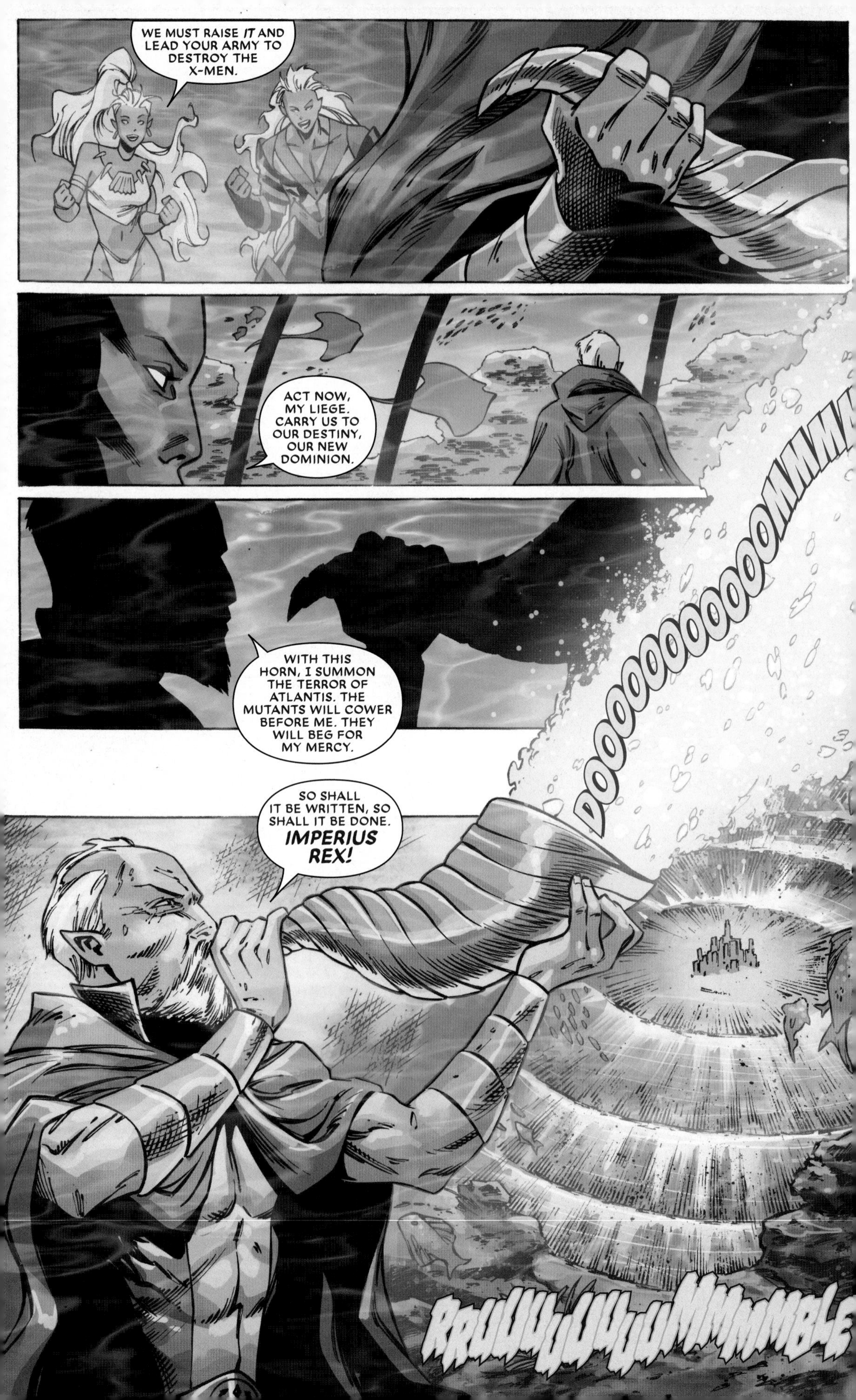
WE MUST RAISE IT AND LEAD YOUR ARMY TO DESTROY THE X-MEN.
ACT NOW, MY LIEGE. CARRY US TO OUR DESTINY, OUR NEW DOMINION.
WITH THIS HORN, I SUMMON THE TERROR OF ATLANTIS. THE MUTANTS WILL COWER BEFORE ME. THEY WILL BEG FOR MY MERCY.
DOOOOOOOOOOOMMMM
SO SHALL IT BE WRITTEN, SO SHALL IT BE DONE. IMPERIUS REX!
RRUUUUUUUUMMMMBLE

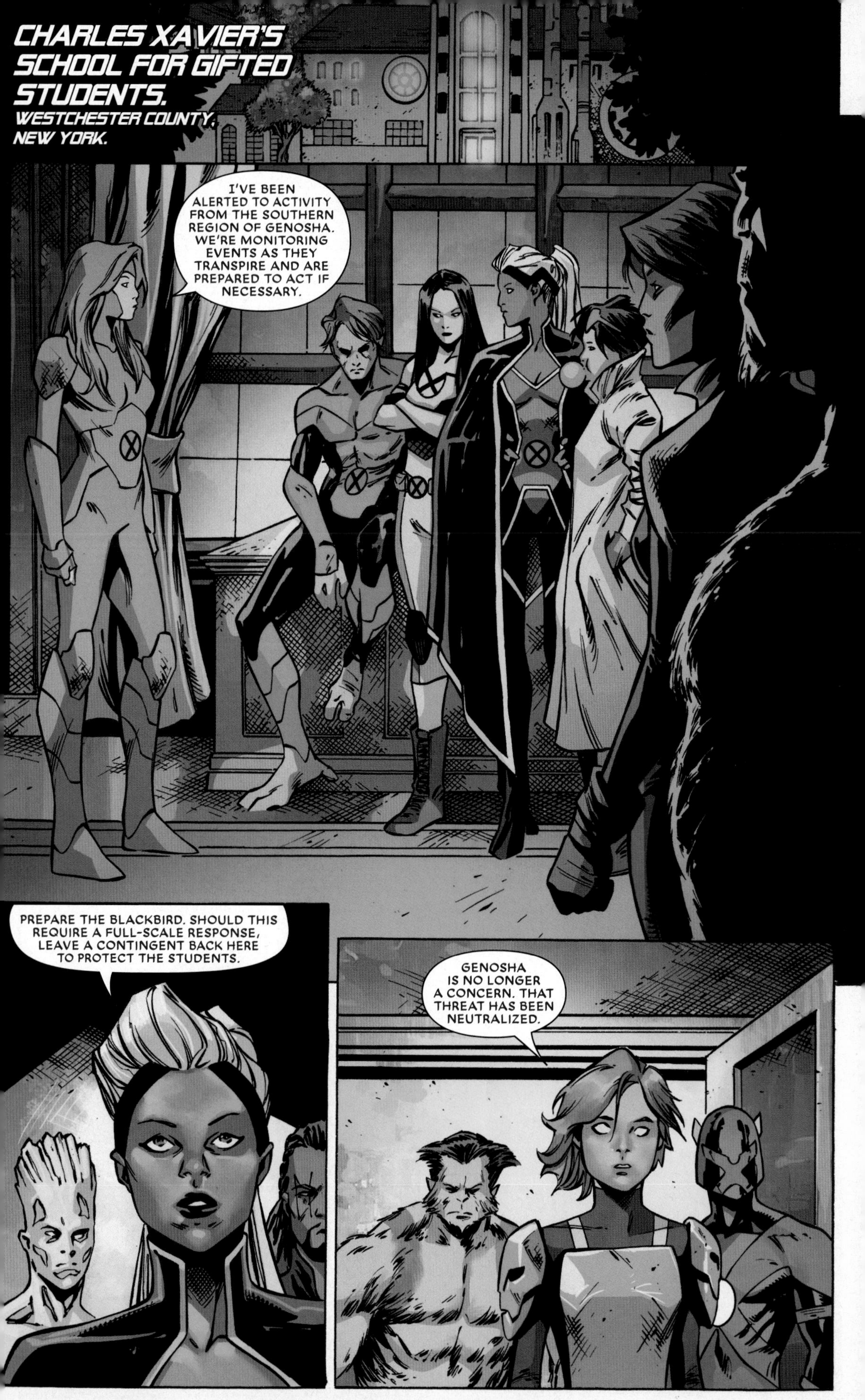

CHARLES XAVIER'S SCHOOL FOR GIFTED STUDENTS.
WESTCHESTER COUNTY, NEW YORK.
I'VE BEEN ALERTED TO ACTIVITY FROM THE SOUTHERN REGION OF GENOSHA. WE'RE MONITORING EVENTS AS THEY TRANSPIRE AND ARE PREPARED TO ACT IF NECESSARY.
PREPARE THE BLACKBIRD. SHOULD THIS REQUIRE A FULL-SCALE RESPONSE, LEAVE A CONTINGENT BACK HERE TO PROTECT THE STUDENTS.
GENOSHA IS NO LONGER A CONCERN. THAT THREAT HAS BEEN NEUTRALIZED.

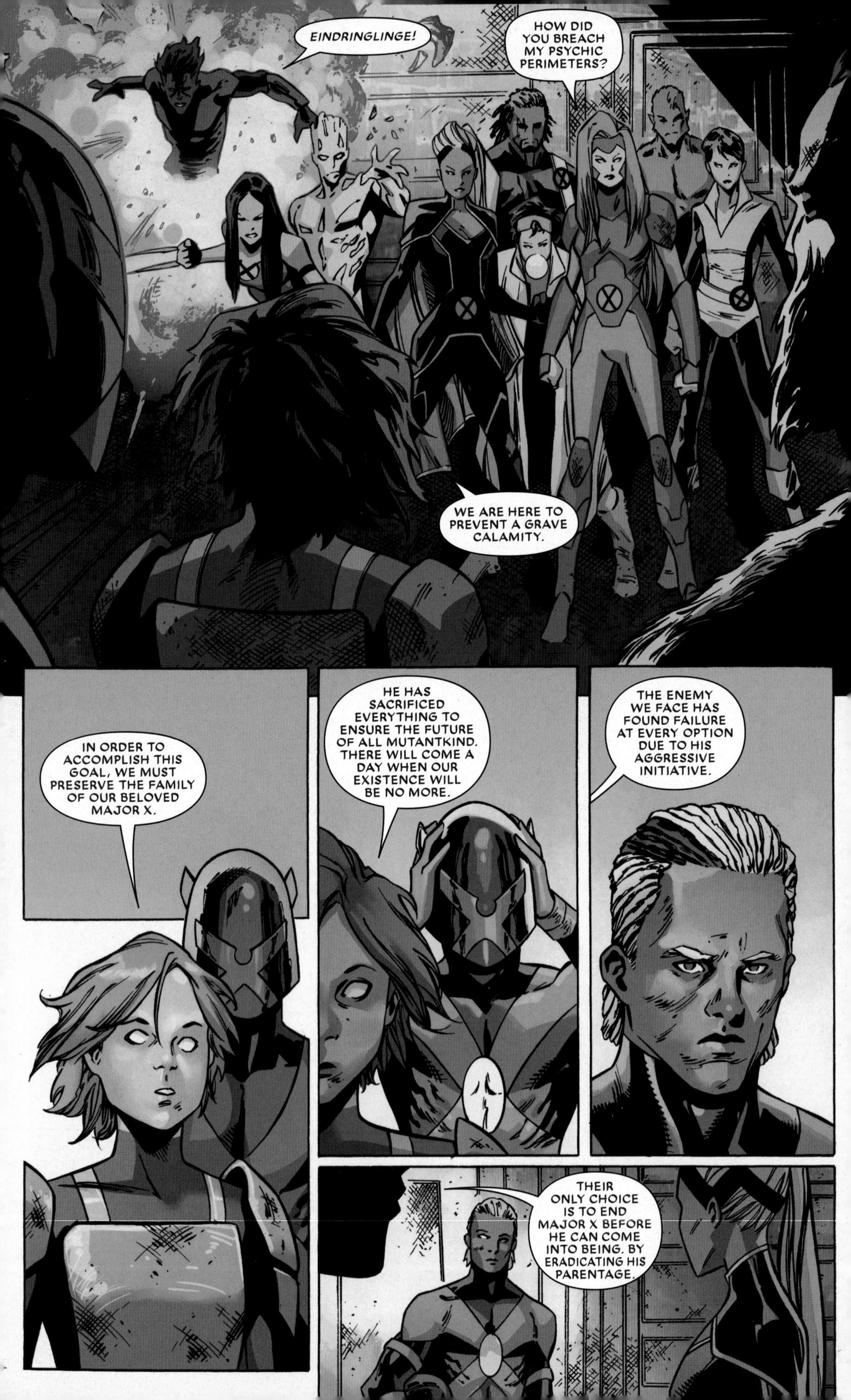
EINDRINGLINGE!
HOW DID YOU BREACH MY PSYCHIC PERIMETERS?
WE ARE HERE TO PREVENT A GRAVE CALAMITY.
IN ORDER TO ACCOMPLISH THIS GOAL, WE MUST PRESERVE THE FAMILY OF OUR BELOVED MAJOR X.
HE HAS SACRIFICED EVERYTHING TO ENSURE THE FUTURE OF ALL MUTANTKIND. THERE WILL COME A DAY WHEN OUR EXISTENCE WILL BE NO MORE.
THE ENEMY WE FACE HAS FOUND FAILURE AT EVERY OPTION DUE TO HIS AGGRESSIVE INITIATIVE.
THEIR ONLY CHOICE IS TO END MAJOR X BEFORE HE CAN COME INTO BEING. BY ERADICATING HIS PARENTAGE.

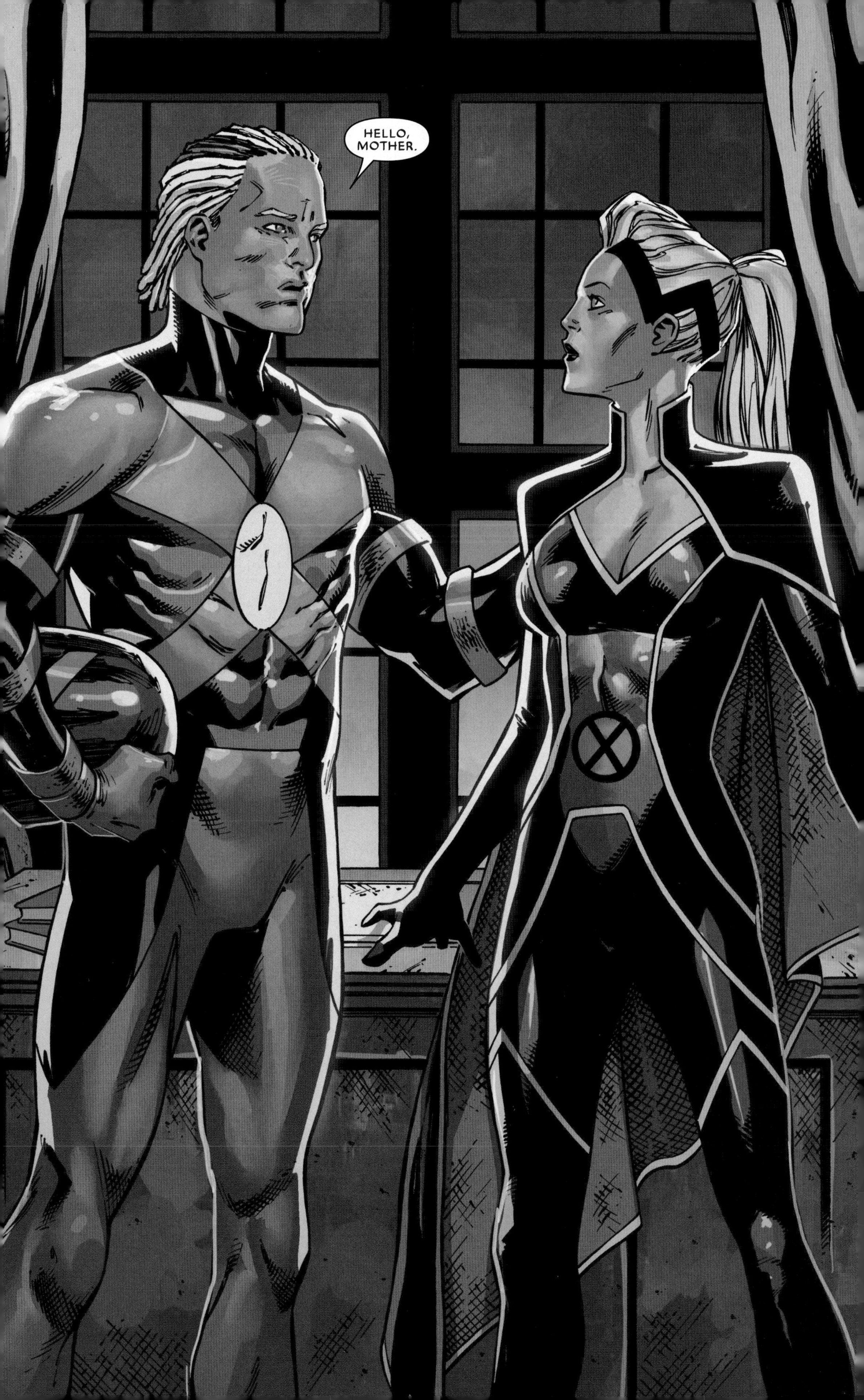
HELLO, MOTHER.

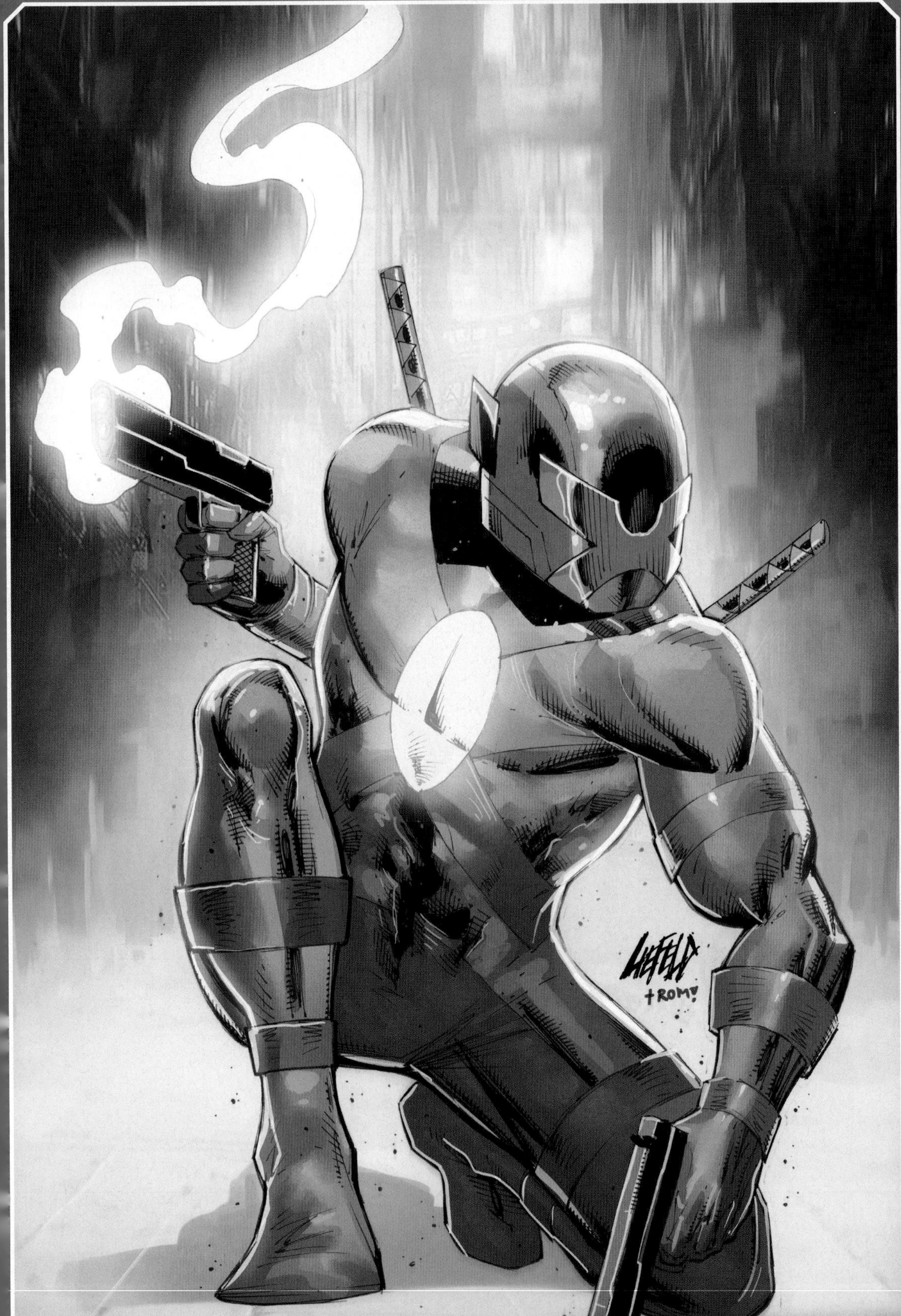

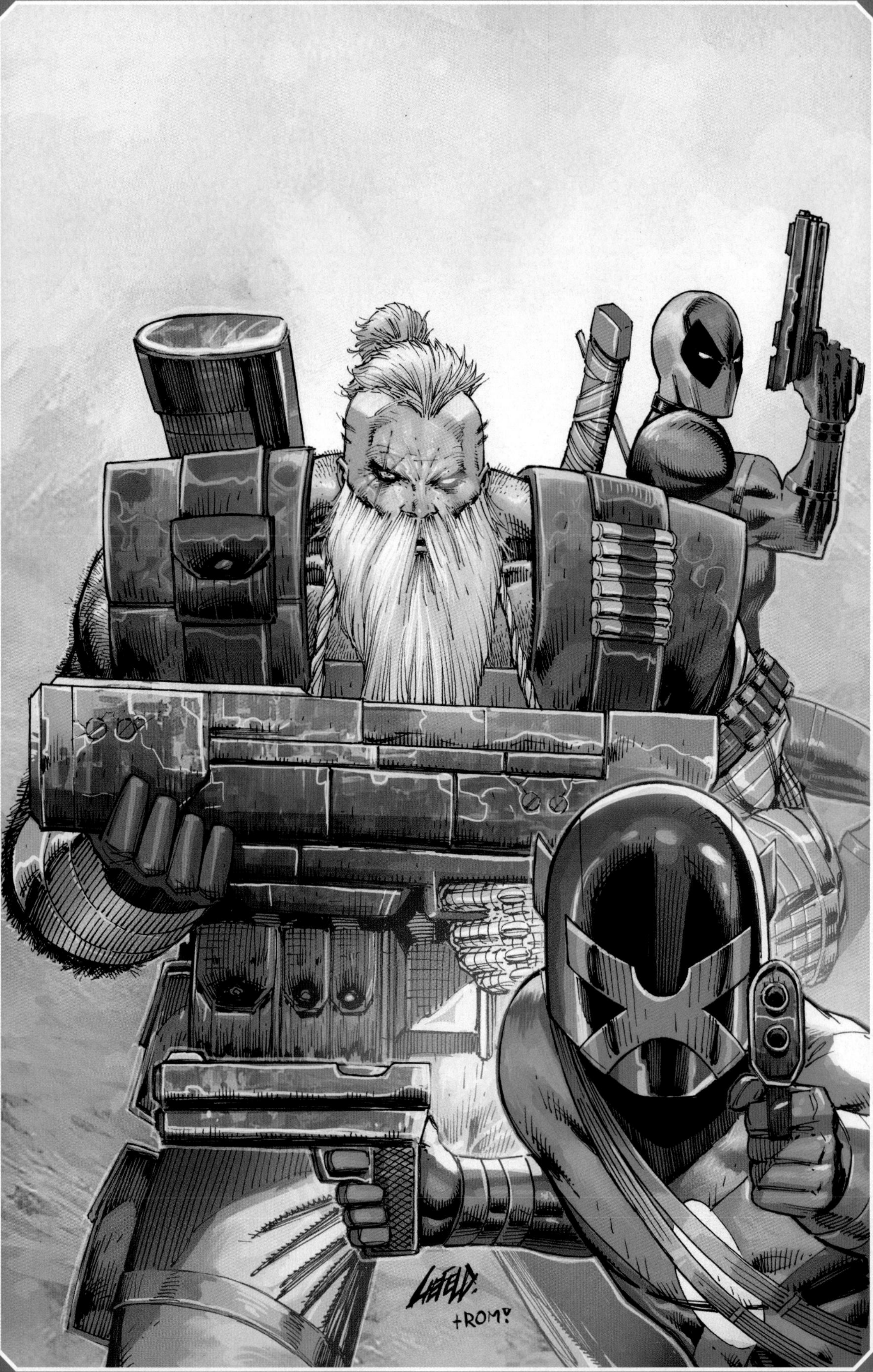

6

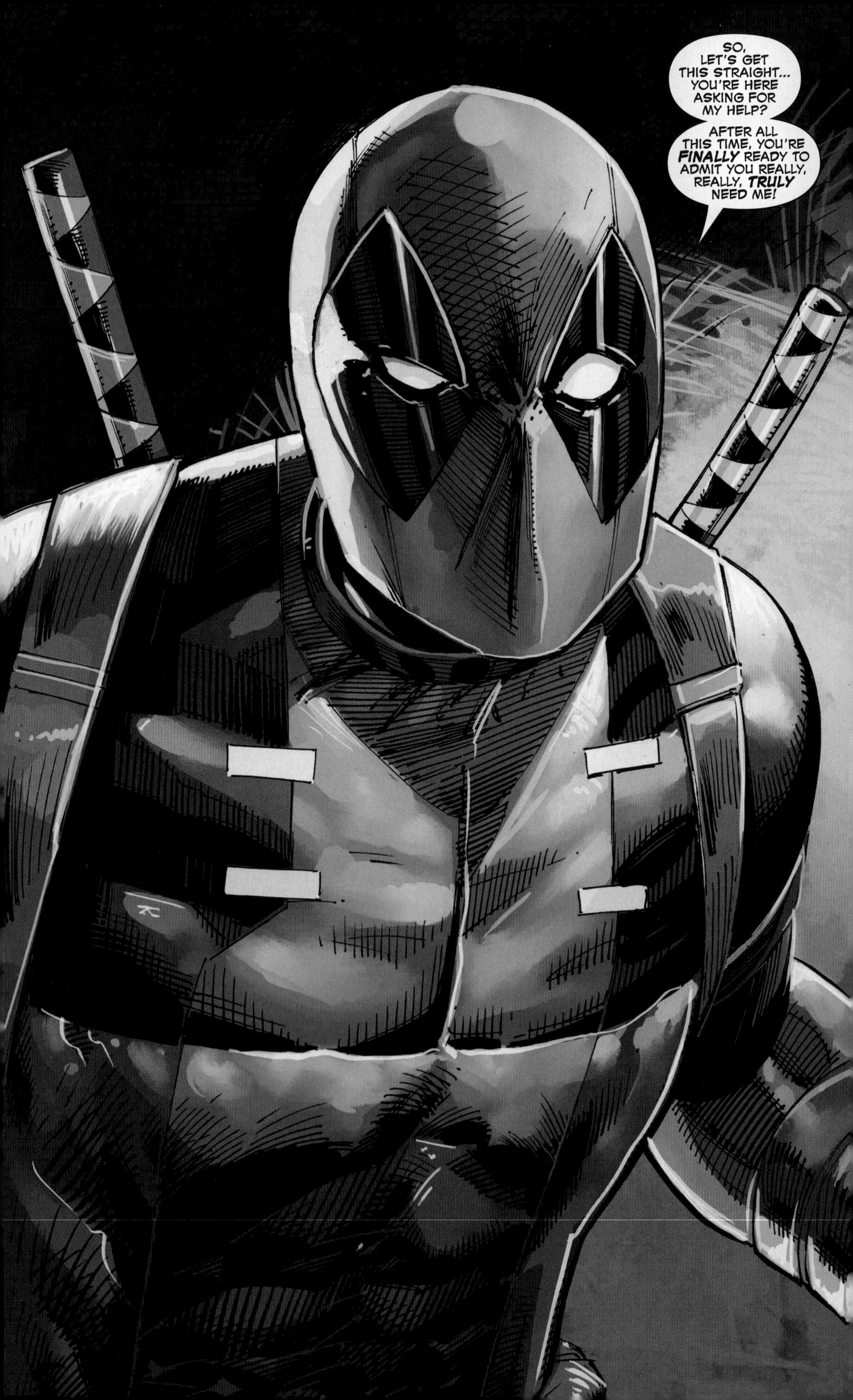
SO, LET'S GET THIS STRAIGHT... YOU'RE HERE ASKING FOR MY HELP?
AFTER ALL THIS TIME, YOU'RE ***FINALLY*** READY TO ADMIT YOU REALLY, REALLY, ***TRULY*** NEED ME!

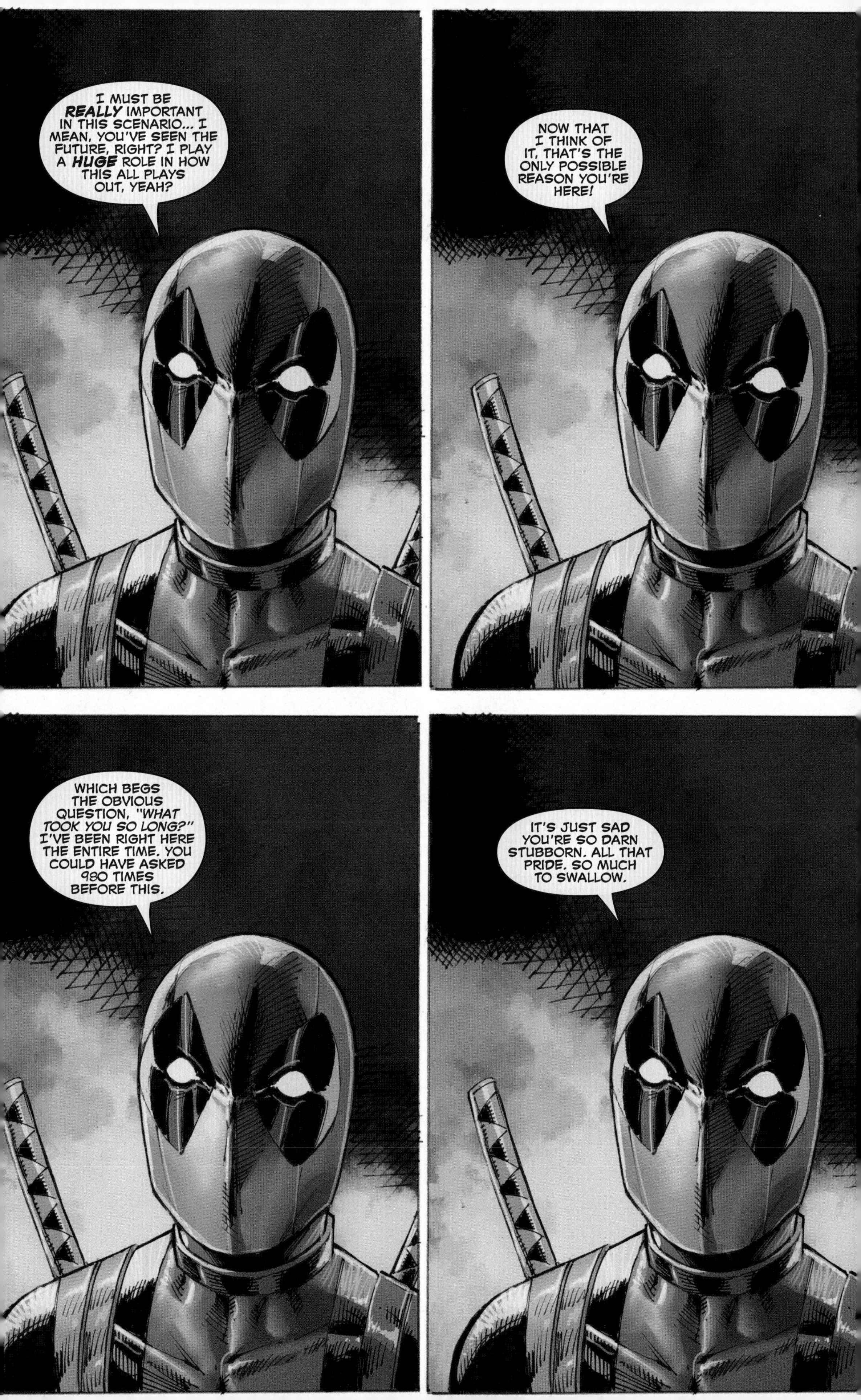
I MUST BE REALLY IMPORTANT IN THIS SCENARIO... I MEAN, YOU'VE SEEN THE FUTURE, RIGHT? I PLAY A HUGE ROLE IN HOW THIS ALL PLAYS OUT, YEAH?
NOW THAT I THINK OF IT, THAT'S THE ONLY POSSIBLE REASON YOU'RE HERE!
WHICH BEGS THE OBVIOUS QUESTION, "WHAT TOOK YOU SO LONG?" I'VE BEEN RIGHT HERE THE ENTIRE TIME. YOU COULD HAVE ASKED 980 TIMES BEFORE THIS.
IT'S JUST SAD YOU'RE SO DARN STUBBORN. ALL THAT PRIDE. SO MUCH TO SWALLOW.

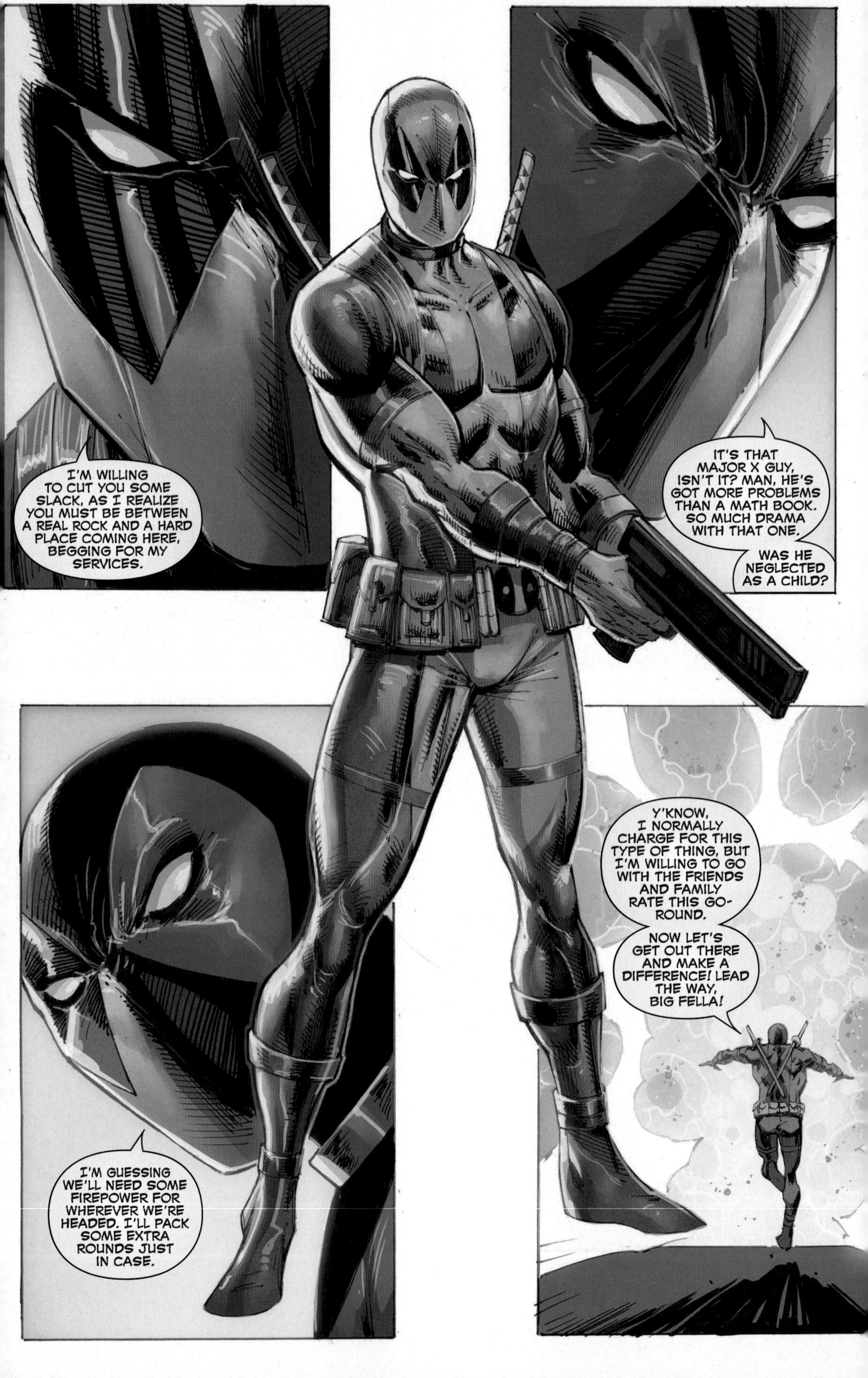
I'M WILLING TO CUT YOU SOME SLACK, AS I REALIZE YOU MUST BE BETWEEN A REAL ROCK AND A HARD PLACE COMING HERE, BEGGING FOR MY SERVICES.
IT'S THAT MAJOR X GUY, ISN'T IT? MAN, HE'S GOT MORE PROBLEMS THAN A MATH BOOK. SO MUCH DRAMA WITH THAT ONE.
WAS HE NEGLECTED AS A CHILD?
I'M GUESSING WE'LL NEED SOME FIREPOWER FOR WHEREVER WE'RE HEADED. I'LL PACK SOME EXTRA ROUNDS JUST IN CASE.
Y'KNOW, I NORMALLY CHARGE FOR THIS TYPE OF THING, BUT I'M WILLING TO GO WITH THE FRIENDS AND FAMILY RATE THIS GO-ROUND.
NOW LET'S GET OUT THERE AND MAKE A DIFFERENCE! LEAD THE WAY, BIG FELLA!

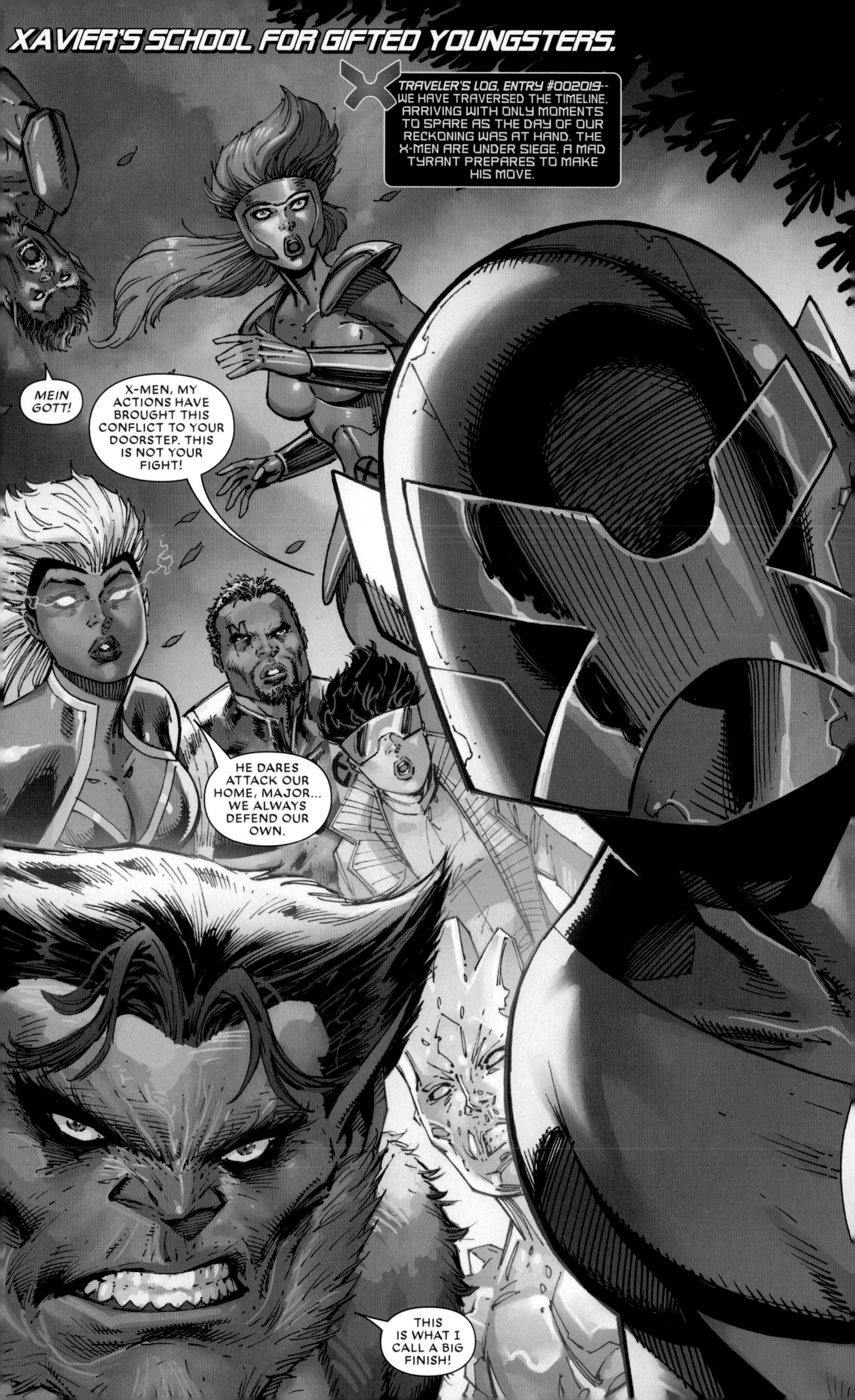
XAVIER'S SCHOOL FOR GIFTED YOUNGSTERS.
TRAVELER'S LOG, ENTRY #002019-- WE HAVE TRAVERSED THE TIMELINE, ARRIVING WITH ONLY MOMENTS TO SPARE AS THE DAY OF OUR RECKONING WAS AT HAND. THE X-MEN ARE UNDER SIEGE. A MAD TYRANT PREPARES TO MAKE HIS MOVE.
MEIN GOTT!
X-MEN, MY ACTIONS HAVE BROUGHT THIS CONFLICT TO YOUR DOORSTEP. THIS IS NOT YOUR FIGHT!
HE DARES ATTACK OUR HOME, MAJOR... WE ALWAYS DEFEND OUR OWN.
THIS IS WHAT I CALL A BIG FINISH!

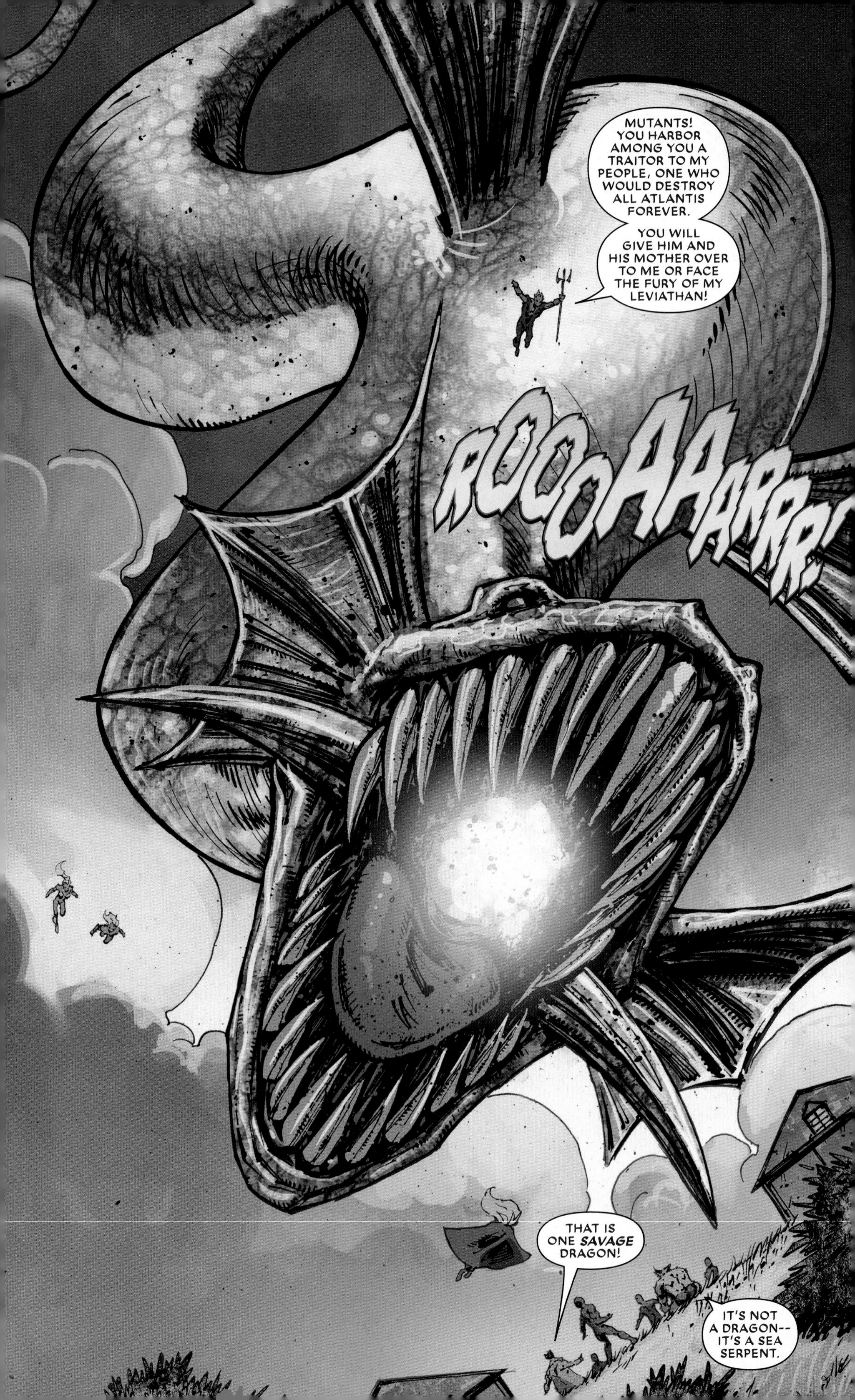
MUTANTS! YOU HARBOR AMONG YOU A TRAITOR TO MY PEOPLE, ONE WHO WOULD DESTROY ALL ATLANTIS FOREVER.
YOU WILL GIVE HIM AND HIS MOTHER OVER TO ME OR FACE THE FURY OF MY LEVIATHAN!
ROOOAAARRR!
THAT IS ONE *SAVAGE* DRAGON!
IT'S NOT A DRAGON-- IT'S A SEA SERPENT.

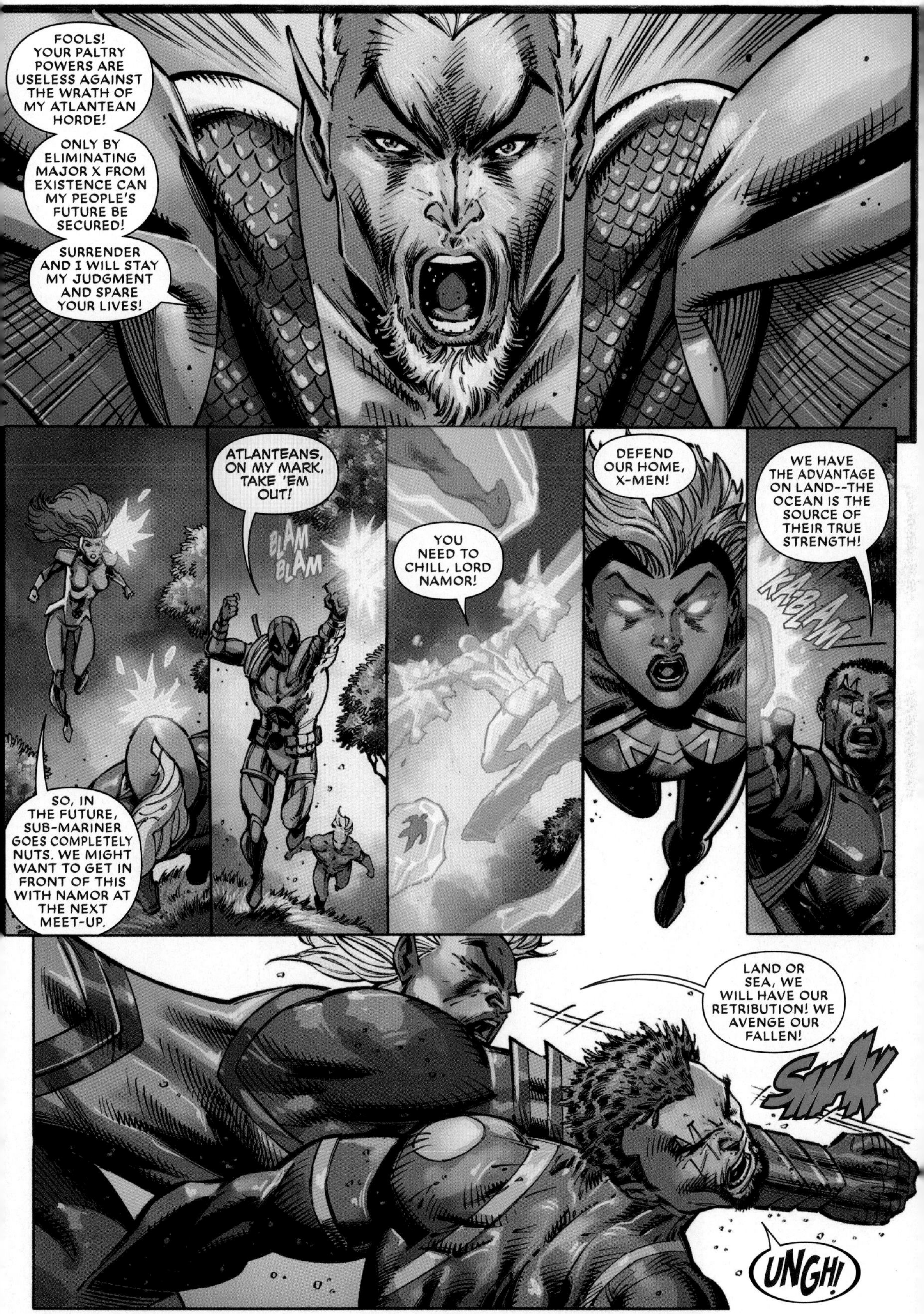
FOOLS! YOUR PALTRY POWERS ARE USELESS AGAINST THE WRATH OF MY ATLANTEAN HORDE!
ONLY BY ELIMINATING MAJOR X FROM EXISTENCE CAN MY PEOPLE'S FUTURE BE SECURED!
SURRENDER AND I WILL STAY MY JUDGMENT AND SPARE YOUR LIVES!
SO, IN THE FUTURE, SUB-MARINER GOES COMPLETELY NUTS. WE MIGHT WANT TO GET IN FRONT OF THIS WITH NAMOR AT THE NEXT MEET-UP.
ATLANTEANS, ON MY MARK, TAKE 'EM OUT!
BLAM BLAM
YOU NEED TO CHILL, LORD NAMOR!
DEFEND OUR HOME, X-MEN!
WE HAVE THE ADVANTAGE ON LAND--THE OCEAN IS THE SOURCE OF THEIR TRUE STRENGTH!
KABLAM
LAND OR SEA, WE WILL HAVE OUR RETRIBUTION! WE AVENGE OUR FALLEN!
SMAK
UNGH!

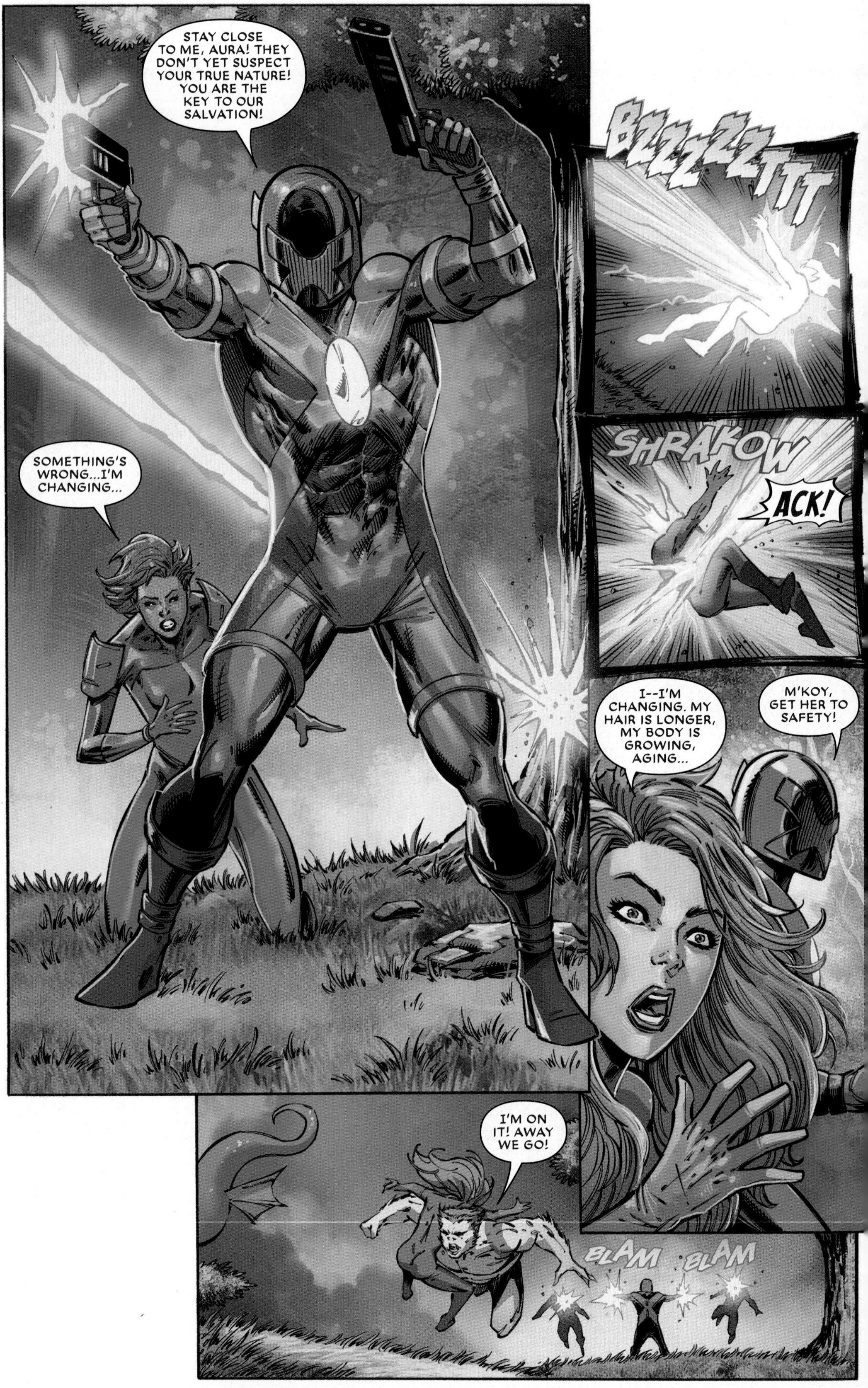
STAY CLOSE TO ME, AURA! THEY DON'T YET SUSPECT YOUR TRUE NATURE! YOU ARE THE KEY TO OUR SALVATION!
SOMETHING'S WRONG...I'M CHANGING...
BZZZZZTTT
SHRAKOW
ACK!
I--I'M CHANGING. MY HAIR IS LONGER, MY BODY IS GROWING, AGING...
M'KOY, GET HER TO SAFETY!
I'M ON IT! AWAY WE GO!
BLAM
BLAM

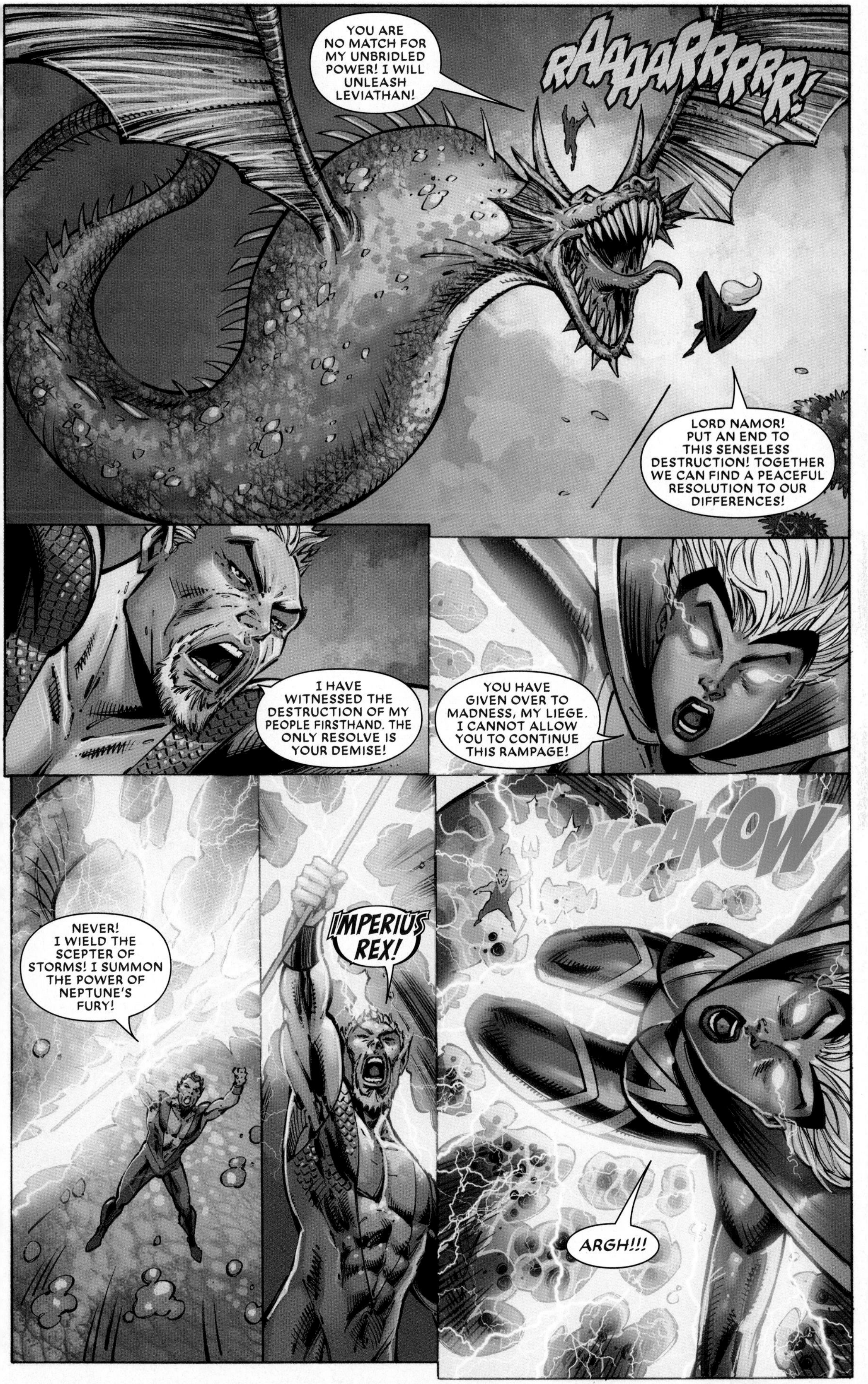
YOU ARE NO MATCH FOR MY UNBRIDLED POWER! I WILL UNLEASH LEVIATHAN!
RAAAARRRRR!
LORD NAMOR! PUT AN END TO THIS SENSELESS DESTRUCTION! TOGETHER WE CAN FIND A PEACEFUL RESOLUTION TO OUR DIFFERENCES!
I HAVE WITNESSED THE DESTRUCTION OF MY PEOPLE FIRSTHAND. THE ONLY RESOLVE IS YOUR DEMISE!
YOU HAVE GIVEN OVER TO MADNESS, MY LIEGE. I CANNOT ALLOW YOU TO CONTINUE THIS RAMPAGE!
NEVER! I WIELD THE SCEPTER OF STORMS! I SUMMON THE POWER OF NEPTUNE'S FURY!
IMPERIUS REX!
KRAKOW
ARGH!!!

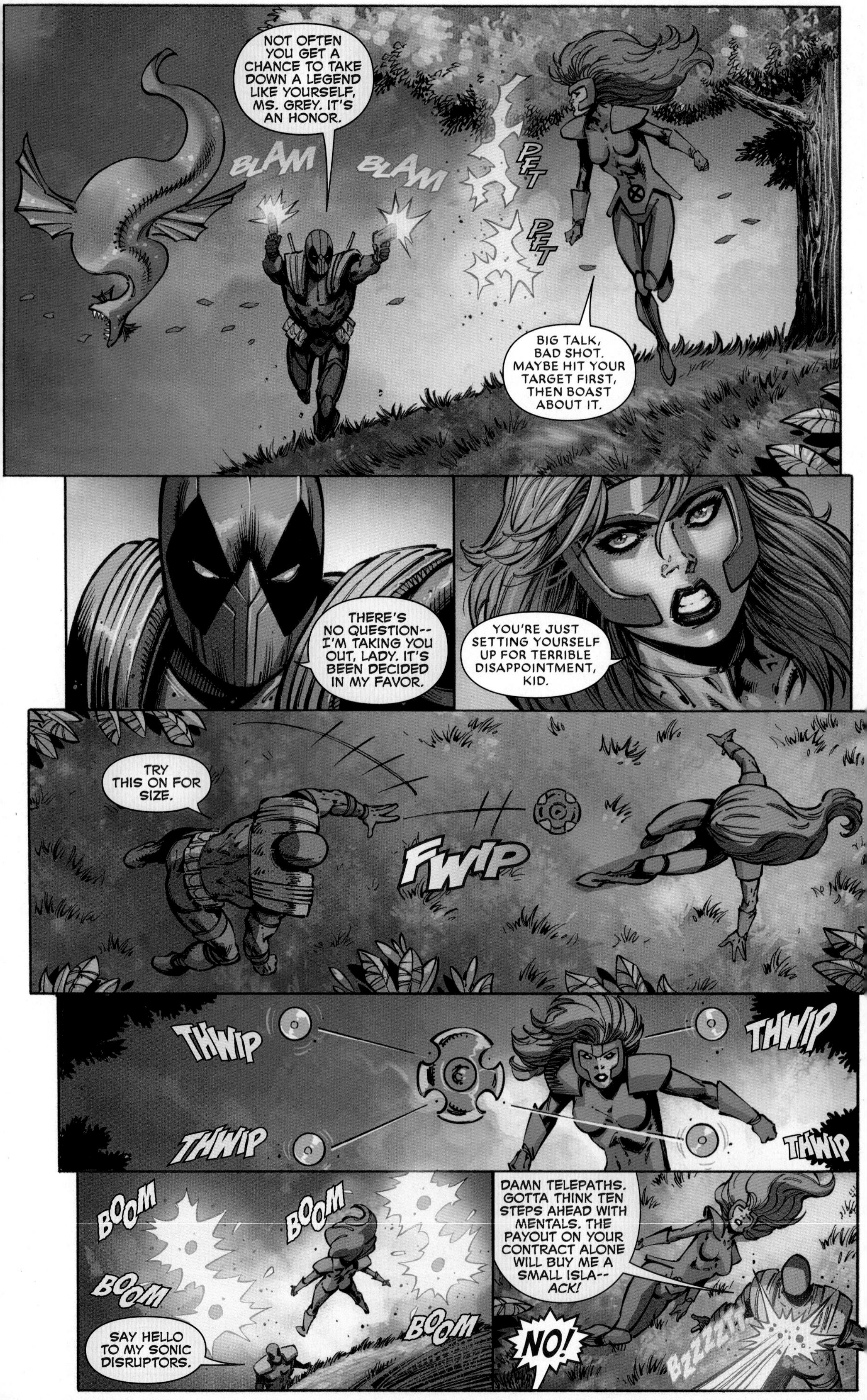
NOT OFTEN YOU GET A CHANCE TO TAKE DOWN A LEGEND LIKE YOURSELF, MS. GREY. IT'S AN HONOR.
BLAM
BLAM
PFT
PFT
BIG TALK, BAD SHOT. MAYBE HIT YOUR TARGET FIRST, THEN BOAST ABOUT IT.
THERE'S NO QUESTION-- I'M TAKING YOU OUT, LADY. IT'S BEEN DECIDED IN MY FAVOR.
YOU'RE JUST SETTING YOURSELF UP FOR TERRIBLE DISAPPOINTMENT, KID.
TRY THIS ON FOR SIZE.
FWIP
THWIP
THWIP
THWIP
THWIP
BOOM
BOOM
BOOM
BOOM
SAY HELLO TO MY SONIC DISRUPTORS.
DAMN TELEPATHS. GOTTA THINK TEN STEPS AHEAD WITH MENTALS. THE PAYOUT ON YOUR CONTRACT ALONE WILL BUY ME A SMALL ISLA-- ACK!
NO!
BZZZZZT

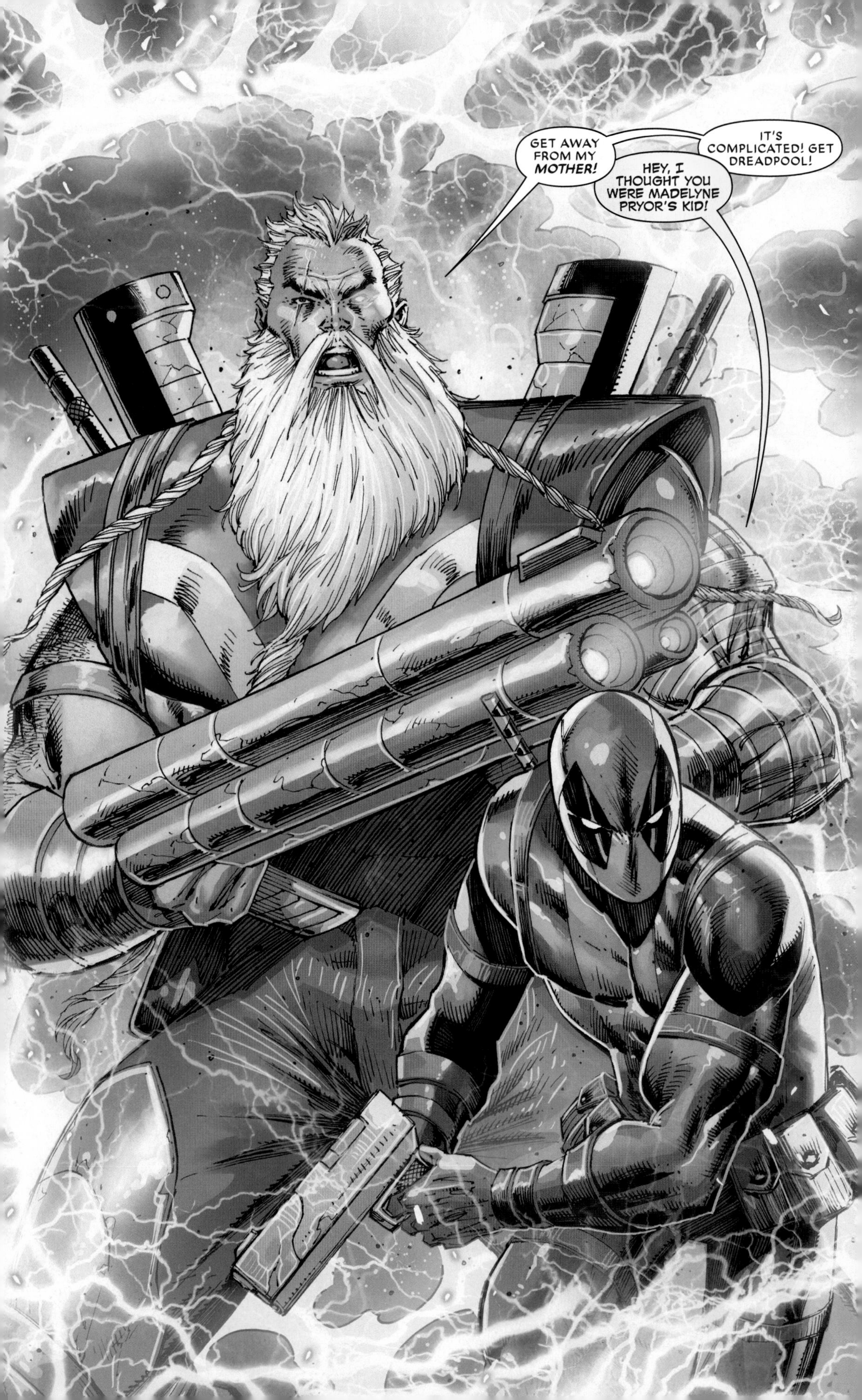
GET AWAY FROM MY *MOTHER!*
IT'S COMPLICATED! GET DREADPOOL!
HEY, I THOUGHT YOU WERE MADELYNE PRYOR'S KID!

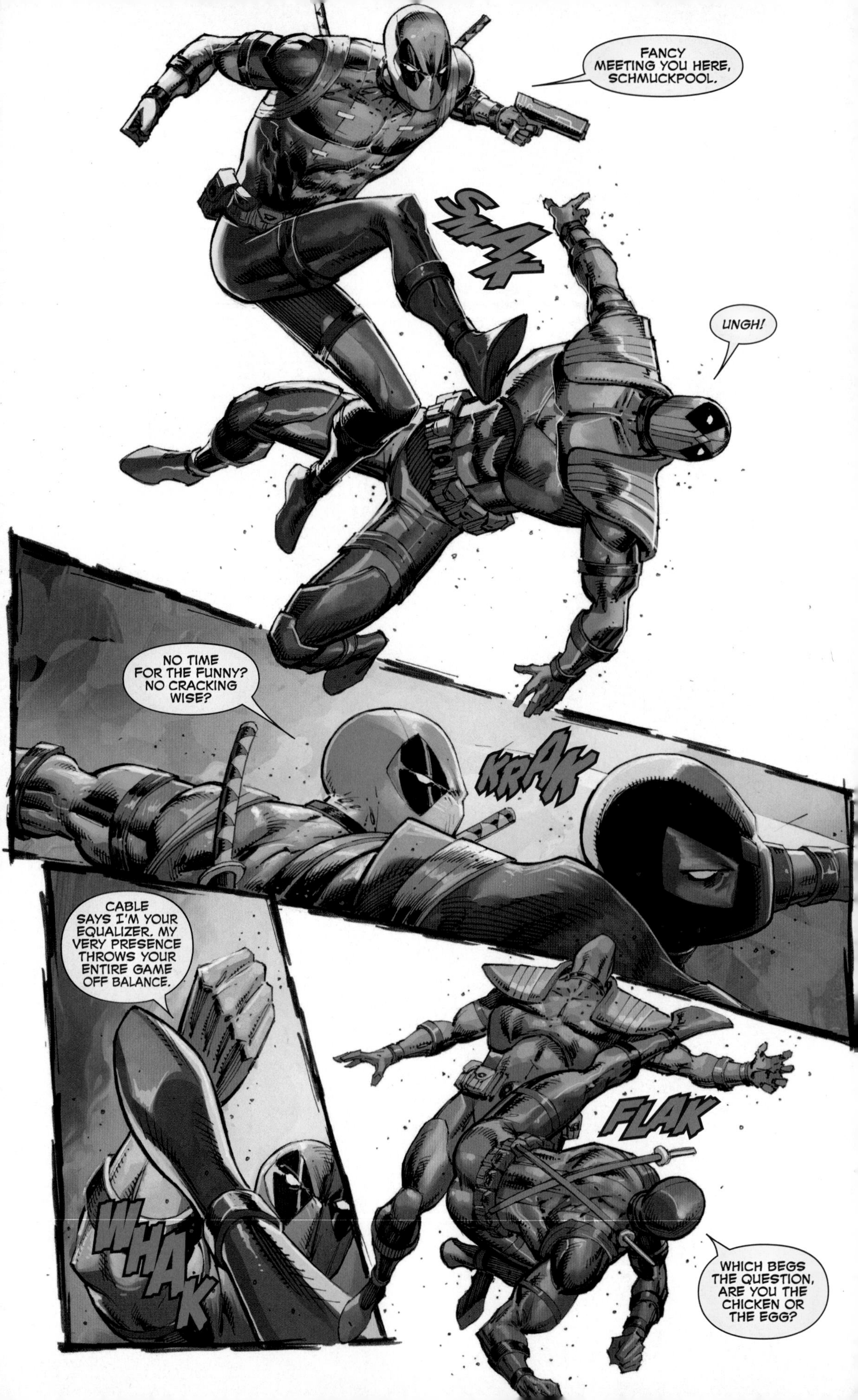
FANCY MEETING YOU HERE, SCHMUCKPOOL.
SNAK
UNGH!
NO TIME FOR THE FUNNY? NO CRACKING WISE?
KRAK
CABLE SAYS I'M YOUR EQUALIZER. MY VERY PRESENCE THROWS YOUR ENTIRE GAME OFF BALANCE.
WHAK
FLAK
WHICH BEGS THE QUESTION, ARE YOU THE CHICKEN OR THE EGG?

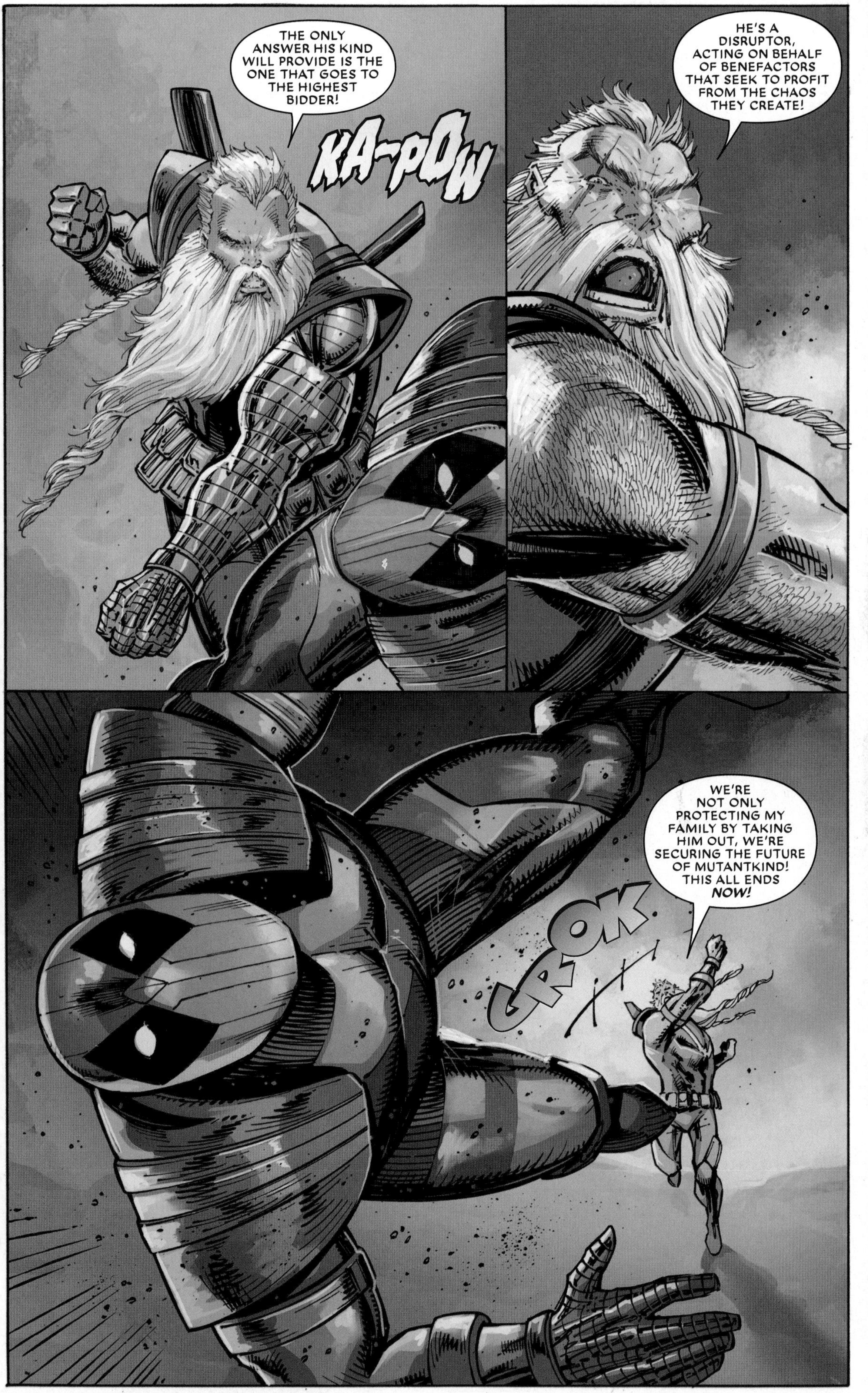
THE ONLY ANSWER HIS KIND WILL PROVIDE IS THE ONE THAT GOES TO THE HIGHEST BIDDER!
KA-POW
HE'S A DISRUPTOR, ACTING ON BEHALF OF BENEFACTORS THAT SEEK TO PROFIT FROM THE CHAOS THEY CREATE!
WE'RE NOT ONLY PROTECTING MY FAMILY BY TAKING HIM OUT, WE'RE SECURING THE FUTURE OF MUTANTKIND! THIS ALL ENDS ***NOW!***
GROK

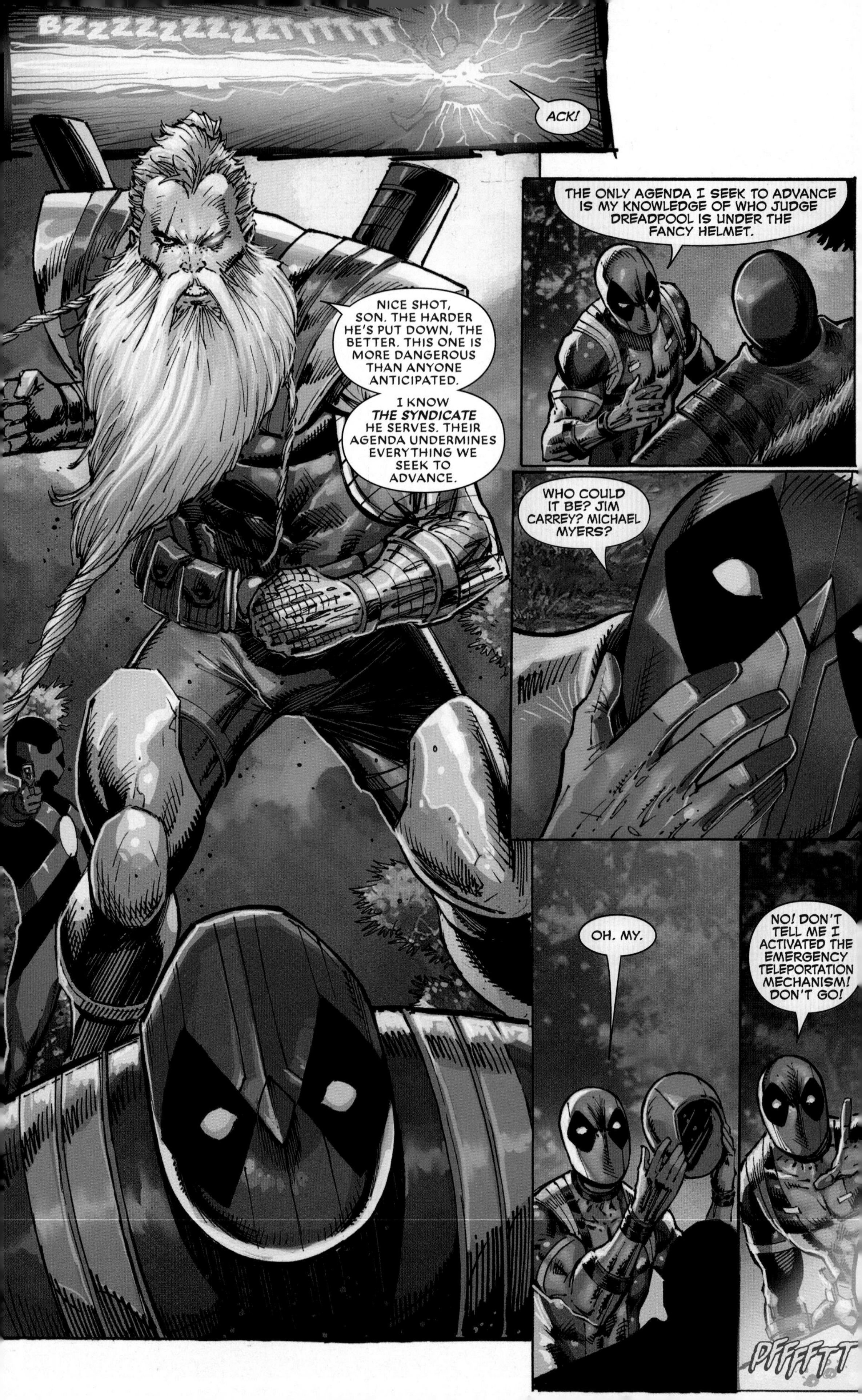
BZZZZZZZZZZTTTTTT
ACK!
NICE SHOT, SON. THE HARDER HE'S PUT DOWN, THE BETTER. THIS ONE IS MORE DANGEROUS THAN ANYONE ANTICIPATED.
I KNOW THE SYNDICATE HE SERVES. THEIR AGENDA UNDERMINES EVERYTHING WE SEEK TO ADVANCE.
THE ONLY AGENDA I SEEK TO ADVANCE IS MY KNOWLEDGE OF WHO JUDGE DREADPOOL IS UNDER THE FANCY HELMET.
WHO COULD IT BE? JIM CARREY? MICHAEL MYERS?
OH. MY.
NO! DON'T TELL ME I ACTIVATED THE EMERGENCY TELEPORTATION MECHANISM! DON'T GO!
PFFFFTT

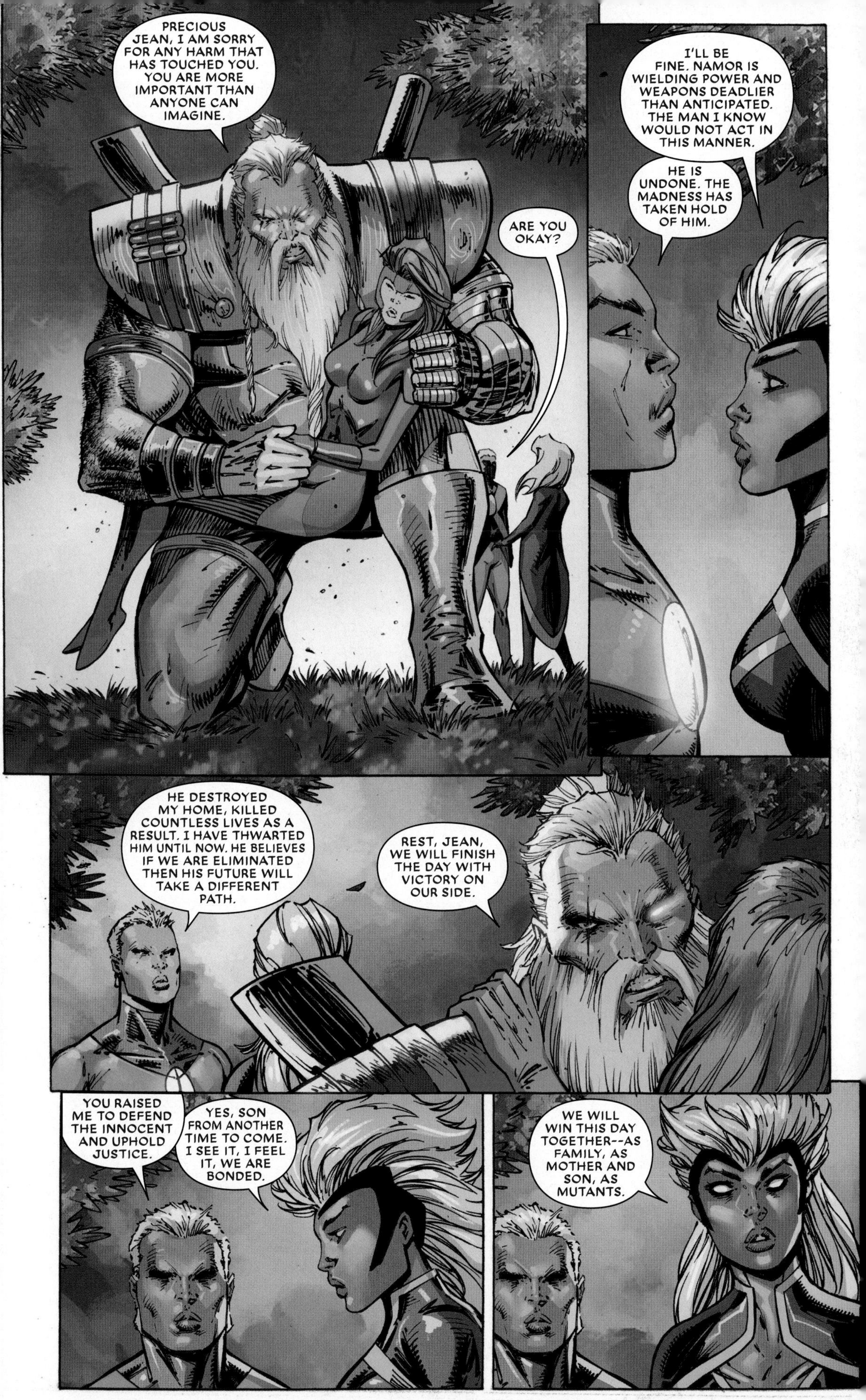
PRECIOUS JEAN, I AM SORRY FOR ANY HARM THAT HAS TOUCHED YOU. YOU ARE MORE IMPORTANT THAN ANYONE CAN IMAGINE.
ARE YOU OKAY?
I'LL BE FINE. NAMOR IS WIELDING POWER AND WEAPONS DEADLIER THAN ANTICIPATED. THE MAN I KNOW WOULD NOT ACT IN THIS MANNER.
HE IS UNDONE. THE MADNESS HAS TAKEN HOLD OF HIM.
HE DESTROYED MY HOME, KILLED COUNTLESS LIVES AS A RESULT. I HAVE THWARTED HIM UNTIL NOW. HE BELIEVES IF WE ARE ELIMINATED THEN HIS FUTURE WILL TAKE A DIFFERENT PATH.
REST, JEAN, WE WILL FINISH THE DAY WITH VICTORY ON OUR SIDE.
YOU RAISED ME TO DEFEND THE INNOCENT AND UPHOLD JUSTICE.
YES, SON FROM ANOTHER TIME TO COME. I SEE IT, I FEEL IT, WE ARE BONDED.
WE WILL WIN THIS DAY TOGETHER--AS FAMILY, AS MOTHER AND SON, AS MUTANTS.

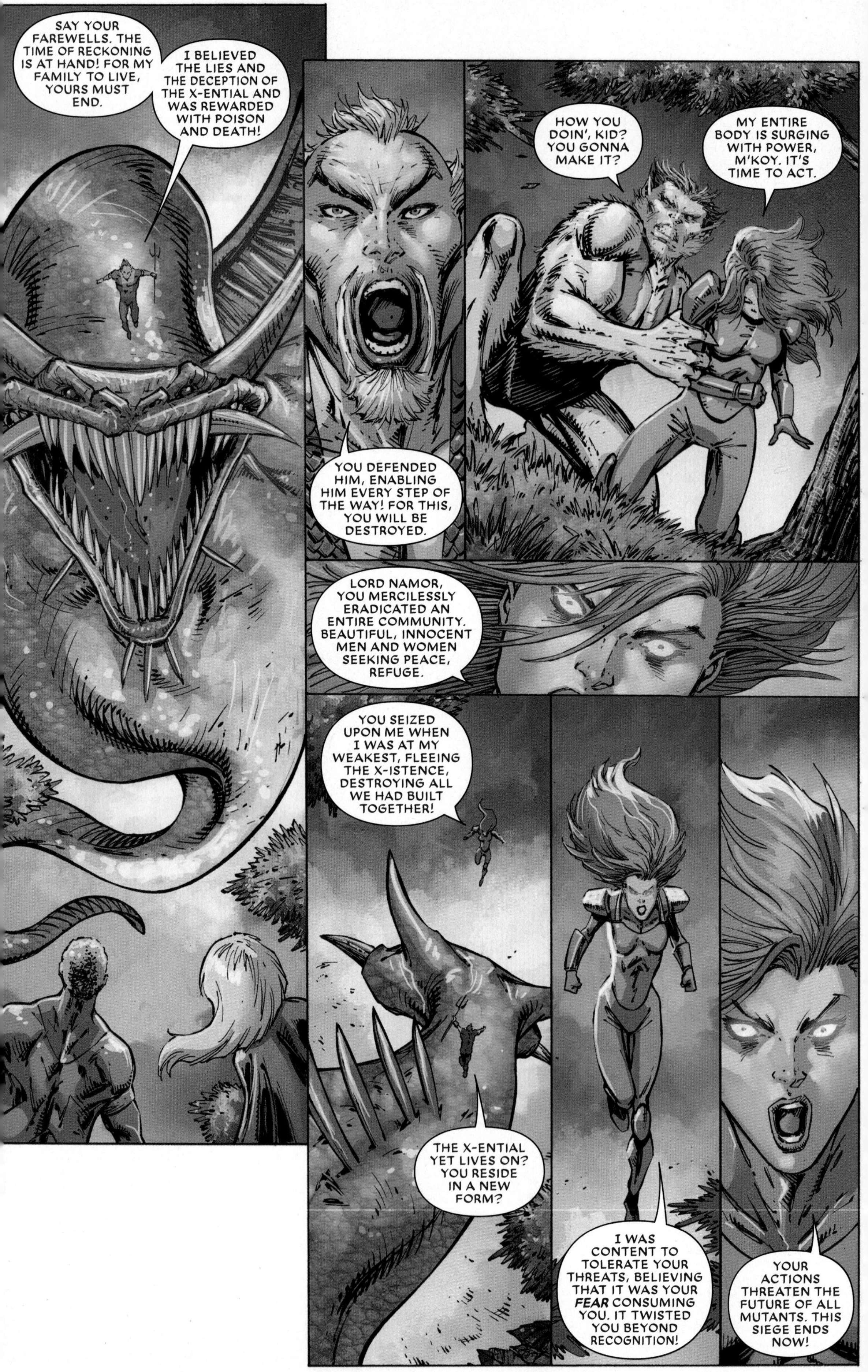
SAY YOUR FAREWELLS. THE TIME OF RECKONING IS AT HAND! FOR MY FAMILY TO LIVE, YOURS MUST END.
I BELIEVED THE LIES AND THE DECEPTION OF THE X-ENTIAL AND WAS REWARDED WITH POISON AND DEATH!
YOU DEFENDED HIM, ENABLING HIM EVERY STEP OF THE WAY! FOR THIS, YOU WILL BE DESTROYED.
HOW YOU DOIN', KID? YOU GONNA MAKE IT?
MY ENTIRE BODY IS SURGING WITH POWER, M'KOY. IT'S TIME TO ACT.
LORD NAMOR, YOU MERCILESSLY ERADICATED AN ENTIRE COMMUNITY. BEAUTIFUL, INNOCENT MEN AND WOMEN SEEKING PEACE, REFUGE.
YOU SEIZED UPON ME WHEN I WAS AT MY WEAKEST, FLEEING THE X-ISTENCE, DESTROYING ALL WE HAD BUILT TOGETHER!
THE X-ENTIAL YET LIVES ON? YOU RESIDE IN A NEW FORM?
I WAS CONTENT TO TOLERATE YOUR THREATS, BELIEVING THAT IT WAS YOUR *FEAR* CONSUMING YOU. IT TWISTED YOU BEYOND RECOGNITION!
YOUR ACTIONS THREATEN THE FUTURE OF ALL MUTANTS. THIS SIEGE ENDS NOW!

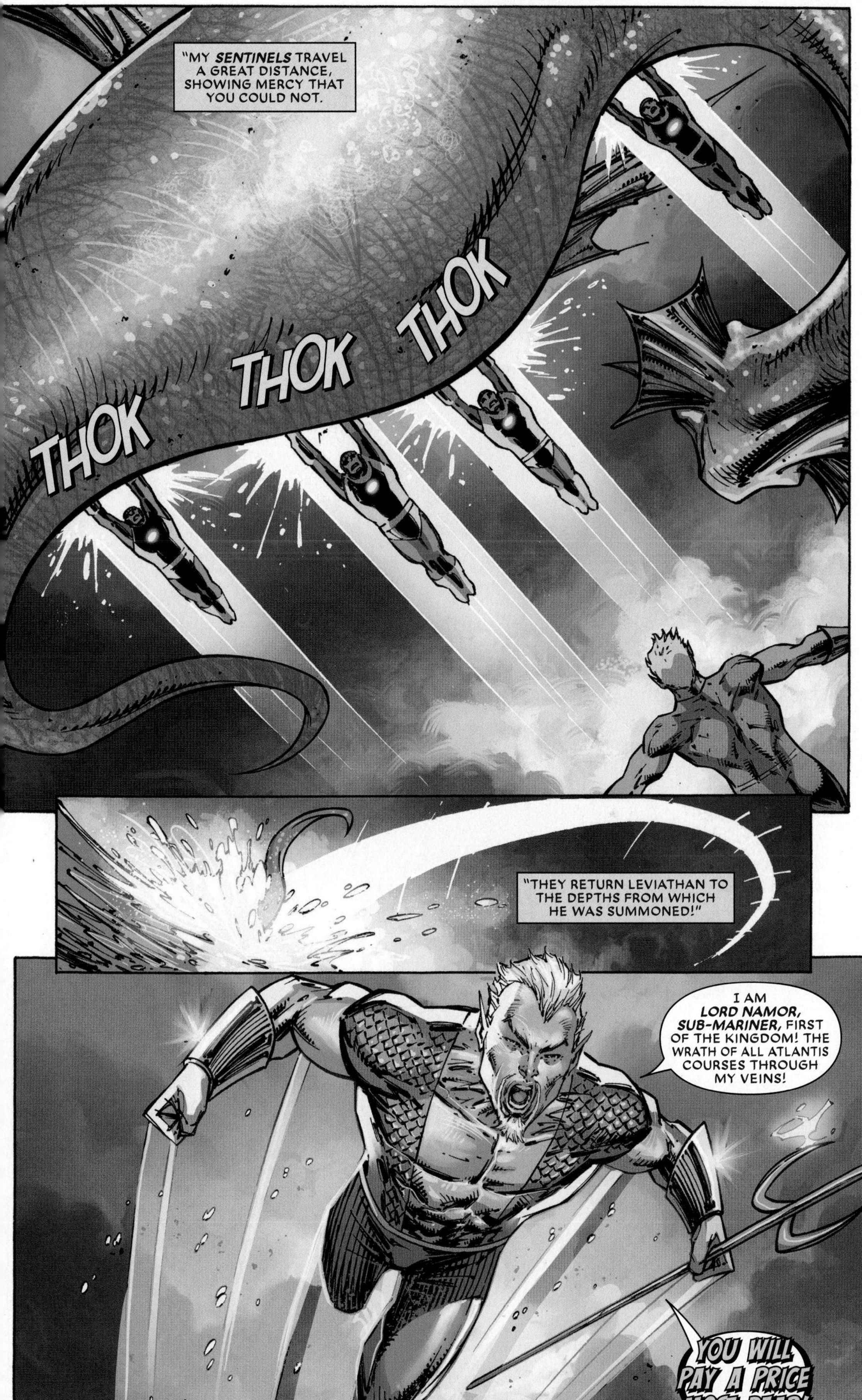

"MY SENTINELS TRAVEL A GREAT DISTANCE, SHOWING MERCY THAT YOU COULD NOT.
THOK
THOK
THOK
"THEY RETURN LEVIATHAN TO THE DEPTHS FROM WHICH HE WAS SUMMONED!"
I AM LORD NAMOR, SUB-MARINER, FIRST OF THE KINGDOM! THE WRATH OF ALL ATLANTIS COURSES THROUGH MY VEINS!
YOU WILL PAY A PRICE MOST DEAR!

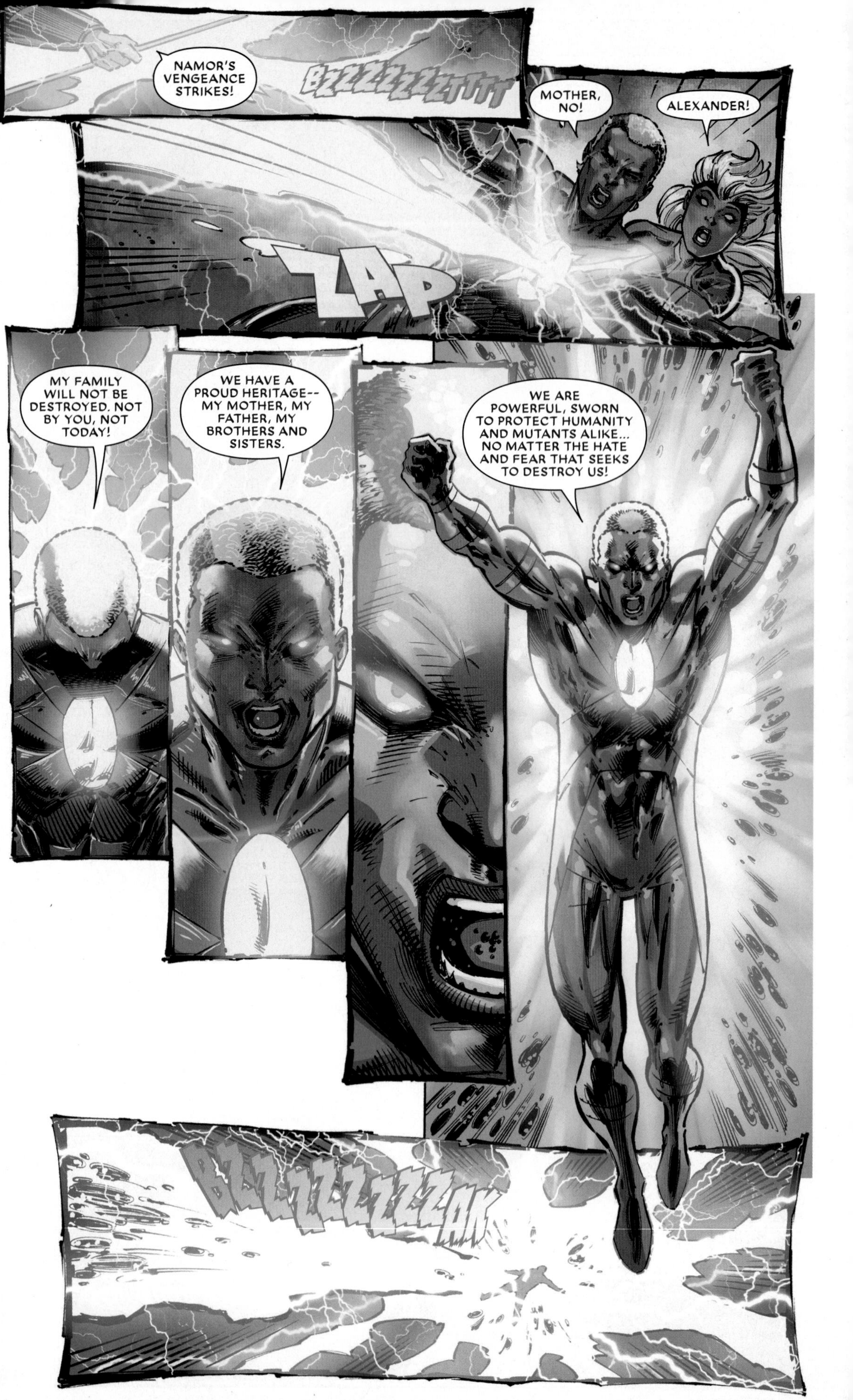
NAMOR'S VENGEANCE STRIKES!
BZZZZZZZZTTTT
MOTHER, NO!
ALEXANDER!
ZAP
MY FAMILY WILL NOT BE DESTROYED. NOT BY YOU, NOT TODAY!
WE HAVE A PROUD HERITAGE-- MY MOTHER, MY FATHER, MY BROTHERS AND SISTERS.
WE ARE POWERFUL, SWORN TO PROTECT HUMANITY AND MUTANTS ALIKE... NO MATTER THE HATE AND FEAR THAT SEEKS TO DESTROY US!
BZZZZZZZZZZAK

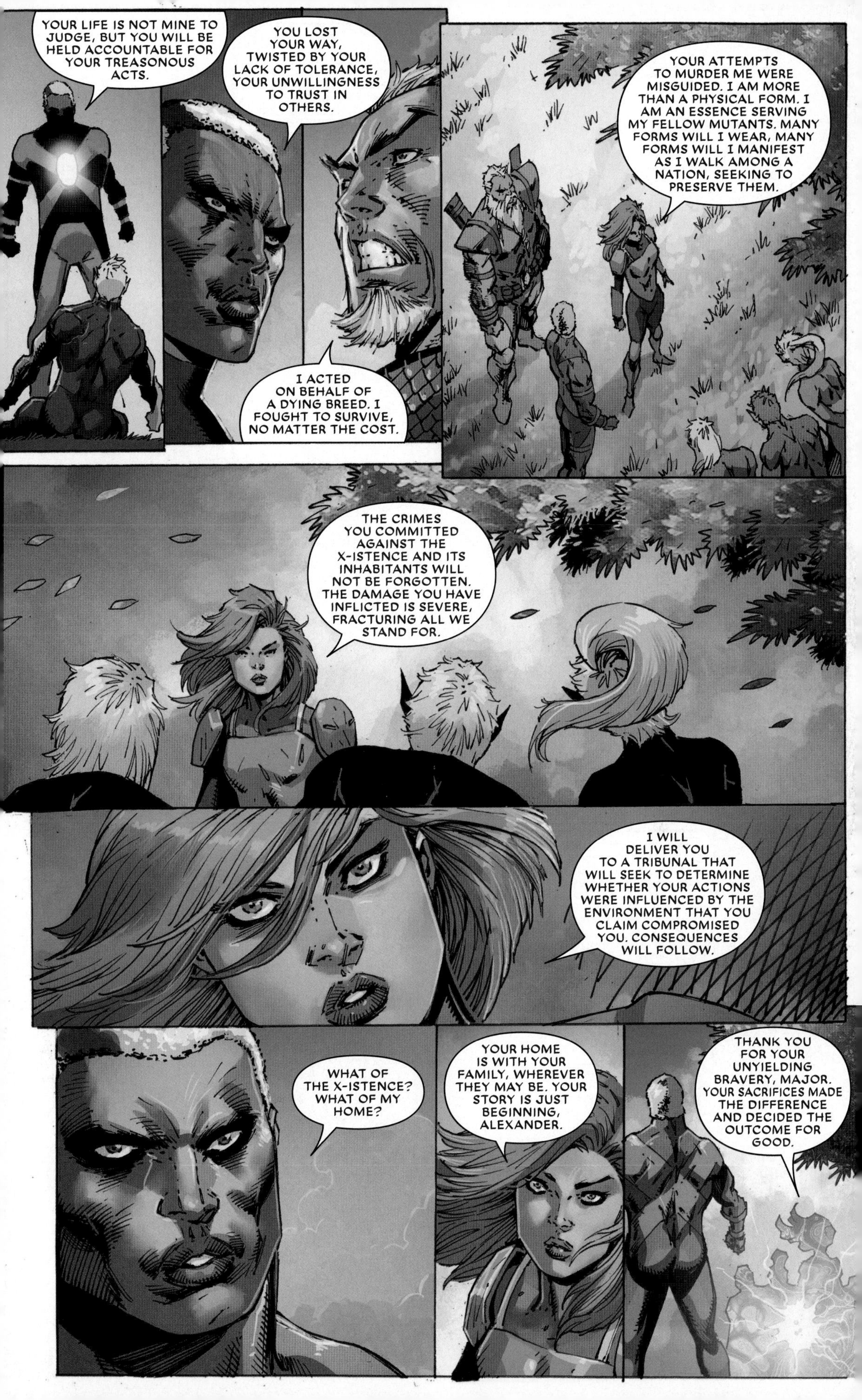
YOUR LIFE IS NOT MINE TO JUDGE, BUT YOU WILL BE HELD ACCOUNTABLE FOR YOUR TREASONOUS ACTS.
YOU LOST YOUR WAY, TWISTED BY YOUR LACK OF TOLERANCE, YOUR UNWILLINGNESS TO TRUST IN OTHERS.
I ACTED ON BEHALF OF A DYING BREED. I FOUGHT TO SURVIVE, NO MATTER THE COST.
YOUR ATTEMPTS TO MURDER ME WERE MISGUIDED. I AM MORE THAN A PHYSICAL FORM. I AM AN ESSENCE SERVING MY FELLOW MUTANTS. MANY FORMS WILL I WEAR, MANY FORMS WILL I MANIFEST AS I WALK AMONG A NATION, SEEKING TO PRESERVE THEM.
THE CRIMES YOU COMMITTED AGAINST THE X-ISTENCE AND ITS INHABITANTS WILL NOT BE FORGOTTEN. THE DAMAGE YOU HAVE INFLICTED IS SEVERE, FRACTURING ALL WE STAND FOR.
I WILL DELIVER YOU TO A TRIBUNAL THAT WILL SEEK TO DETERMINE WHETHER YOUR ACTIONS WERE INFLUENCED BY THE ENVIRONMENT THAT YOU CLAIM COMPROMISED YOU. CONSEQUENCES WILL FOLLOW.
WHAT OF THE X-ISTENCE? WHAT OF MY HOME?
YOUR HOME IS WITH YOUR FAMILY, WHEREVER THEY MAY BE. YOUR STORY IS JUST BEGINNING, ALEXANDER.
THANK YOU FOR YOUR UNYIELDING BRAVERY, MAJOR. YOUR SACRIFICES MADE THE DIFFERENCE AND DECIDED THE OUTCOME FOR GOOD.

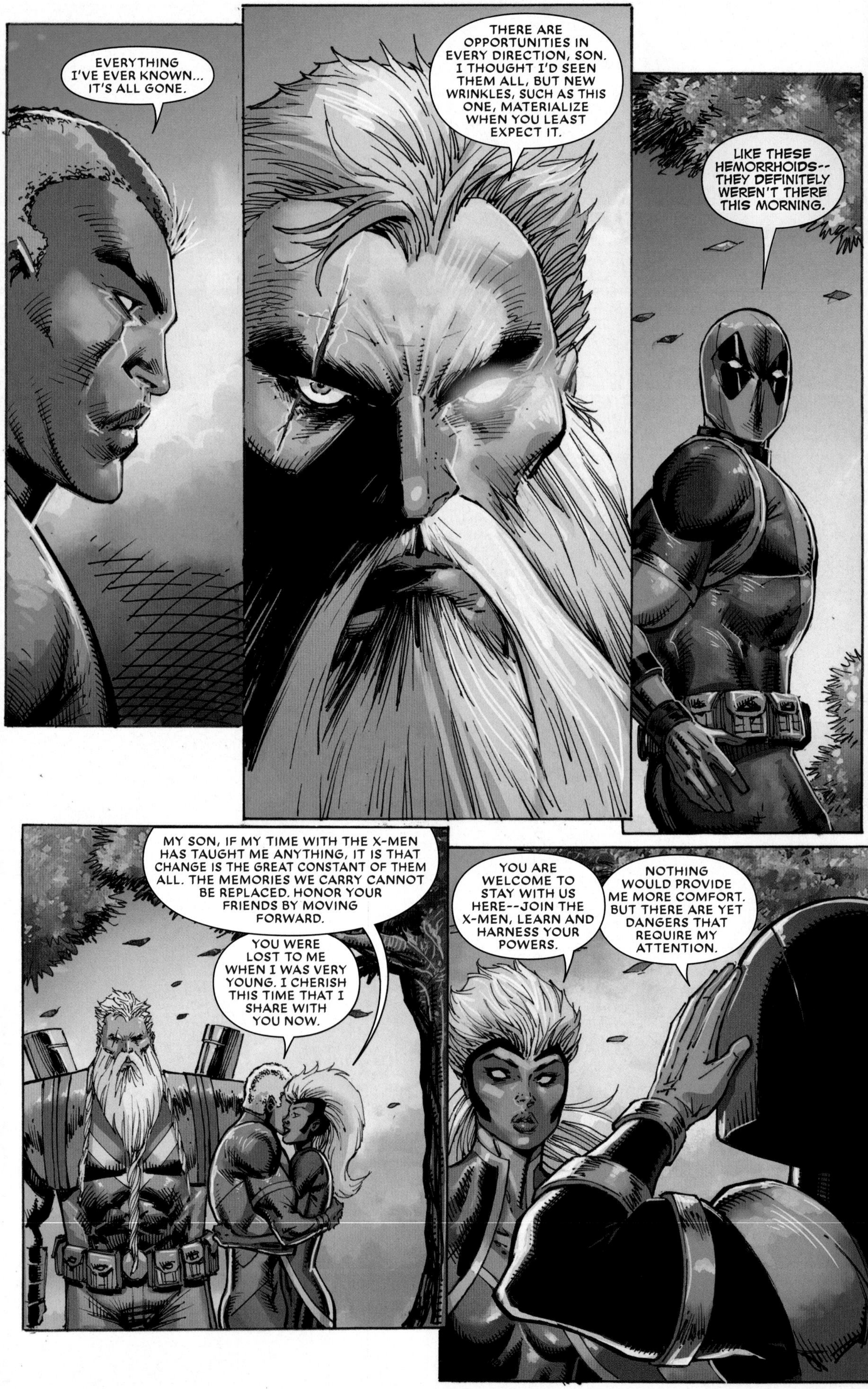
EVERYTHING I'VE EVER KNOWN... IT'S ALL GONE.
THERE ARE OPPORTUNITIES IN EVERY DIRECTION, SON. I THOUGHT I'D SEEN THEM ALL, BUT NEW WRINKLES, SUCH AS THIS ONE, MATERIALIZE WHEN YOU LEAST EXPECT IT.
LIKE THESE HEMORRHOIDS-- THEY DEFINITELY WEREN'T THERE THIS MORNING.
MY SON, IF MY TIME WITH THE X-MEN HAS TAUGHT ME ANYTHING, IT IS THAT CHANGE IS THE GREAT CONSTANT OF THEM ALL. THE MEMORIES WE CARRY CANNOT BE REPLACED. HONOR YOUR FRIENDS BY MOVING FORWARD.
YOU WERE LOST TO ME WHEN I WAS VERY YOUNG. I CHERISH THIS TIME THAT I SHARE WITH YOU NOW.
YOU ARE WELCOME TO STAY WITH US HERE--JOIN THE X-MEN, LEARN AND HARNESS YOUR POWERS.
NOTHING WOULD PROVIDE ME MORE COMFORT. BUT THERE ARE YET DANGERS THAT REQUIRE MY ATTENTION.

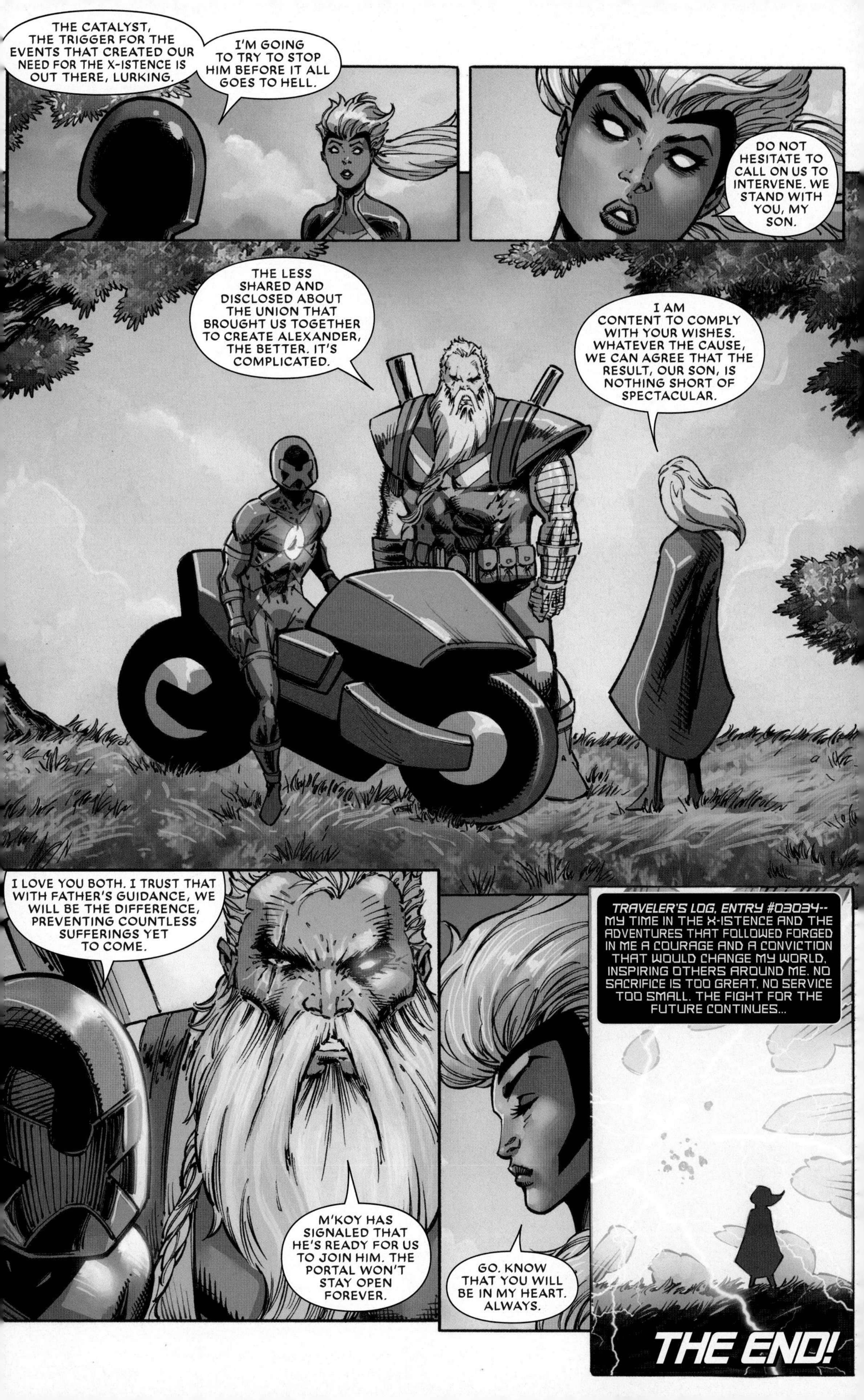
THE CATALYST, THE TRIGGER FOR THE EVENTS THAT CREATED OUR NEED FOR THE X-ISTENCE IS OUT THERE, LURKING.
I'M GOING TO TRY TO STOP HIM BEFORE IT ALL GOES TO HELL.
DO NOT HESITATE TO CALL ON US TO INTERVENE. WE STAND WITH YOU, MY SON.
THE LESS SHARED AND DISCLOSED ABOUT THE UNION THAT BROUGHT US TOGETHER TO CREATE ALEXANDER, THE BETTER. IT'S COMPLICATED.
I AM CONTENT TO COMPLY WITH YOUR WISHES. WHATEVER THE CAUSE, WE CAN AGREE THAT THE RESULT, OUR SON, IS NOTHING SHORT OF SPECTACULAR.
I LOVE YOU BOTH. I TRUST THAT WITH FATHER'S GUIDANCE, WE WILL BE THE DIFFERENCE, PREVENTING COUNTLESS SUFFERINGS YET TO COME.
M'KOY HAS SIGNALED THAT HE'S READY FOR US TO JOIN HIM. THE PORTAL WON'T STAY OPEN FOREVER.
GO. KNOW THAT YOU WILL BE IN MY HEART. ALWAYS.
TRAVELER'S LOG, ENTRY #03034-- MY TIME IN THE X-ISTENCE AND THE ADVENTURES THAT FOLLOWED FORGED IN ME A COURAGE AND A CONVICTION THAT WOULD CHANGE MY WORLD, INSPIRING OTHERS AROUND ME. NO SACRIFICE IS TOO GREAT, NO SERVICE TOO SMALL. THE FIGHT FOR THE FUTURE CONTINUES...
THE END!

MAJOR X #0 REPRINTED **WOLVERINE #154-155** WITH A NEW FRAMING SEQUENCE.

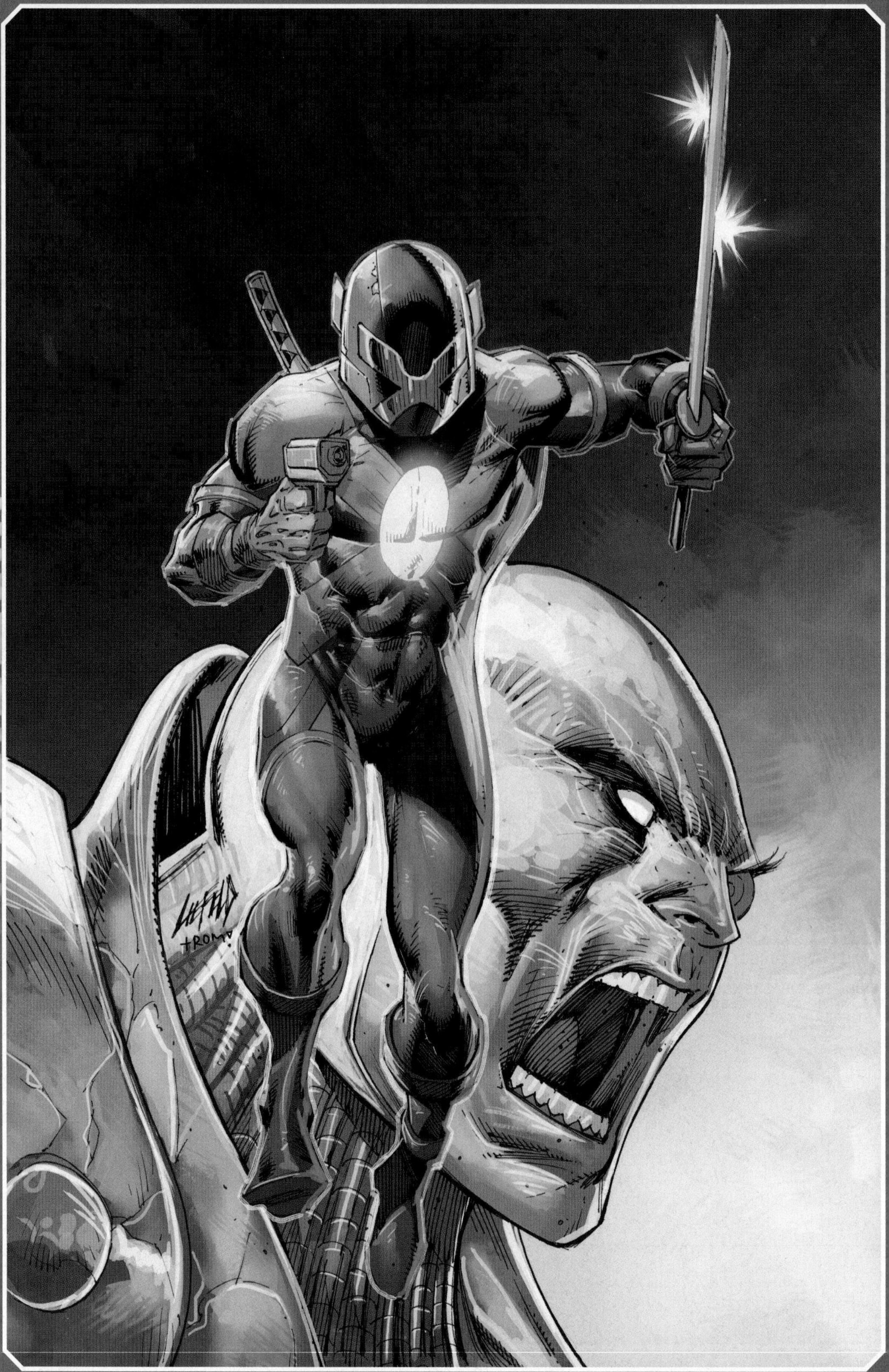

WRITER & PENCILER **ROB LIEFELD**
INKERS **ROB LIEFELD, ADELSO CORONA** & **CORY HAMSCHER**
COLOR ARTIST **ROMULO FAJARDO JR.** • LETTERER **VC's JOE SABINO**
COVER ARTISTS **ROB LIEFELD** & **ROMULO FAJARDO JR.**
ASSISTANT EDITOR **ANNALISE BISSA** • EDITOR **JORDAN D. WHITE**

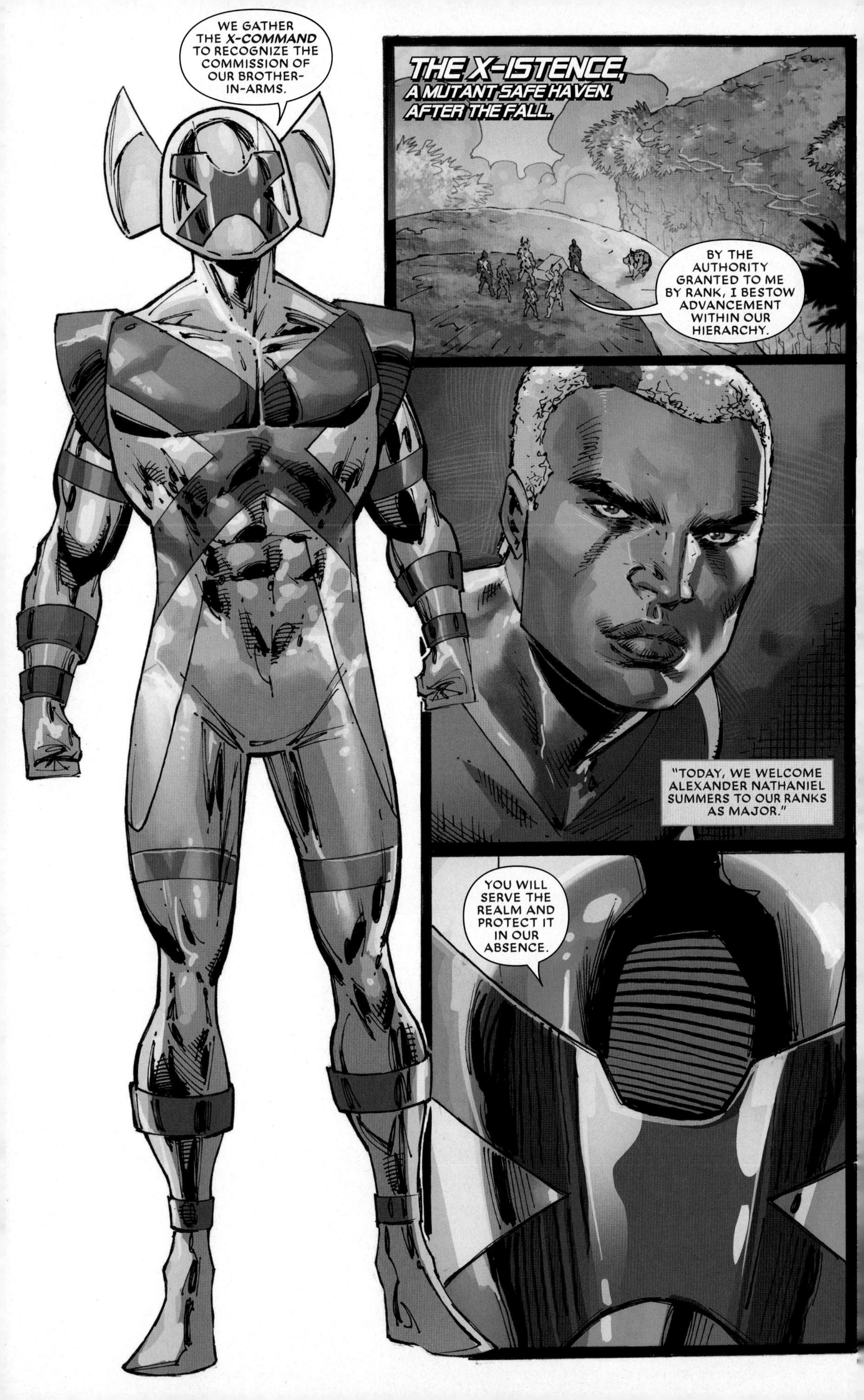
WE GATHER THE X-COMMAND TO RECOGNIZE THE COMMISSION OF OUR BROTHER-IN-ARMS.
THE X-ISTENCE, A MUTANT SAFE HAVEN. AFTER THE FALL.
BY THE AUTHORITY GRANTED TO ME BY RANK, I BESTOW ADVANCEMENT WITHIN OUR HIERARCHY.
"TODAY, WE WELCOME ALEXANDER NATHANIEL SUMMERS TO OUR RANKS AS MAJOR."
YOU WILL SERVE THE REALM AND PROTECT IT IN OUR ABSENCE.

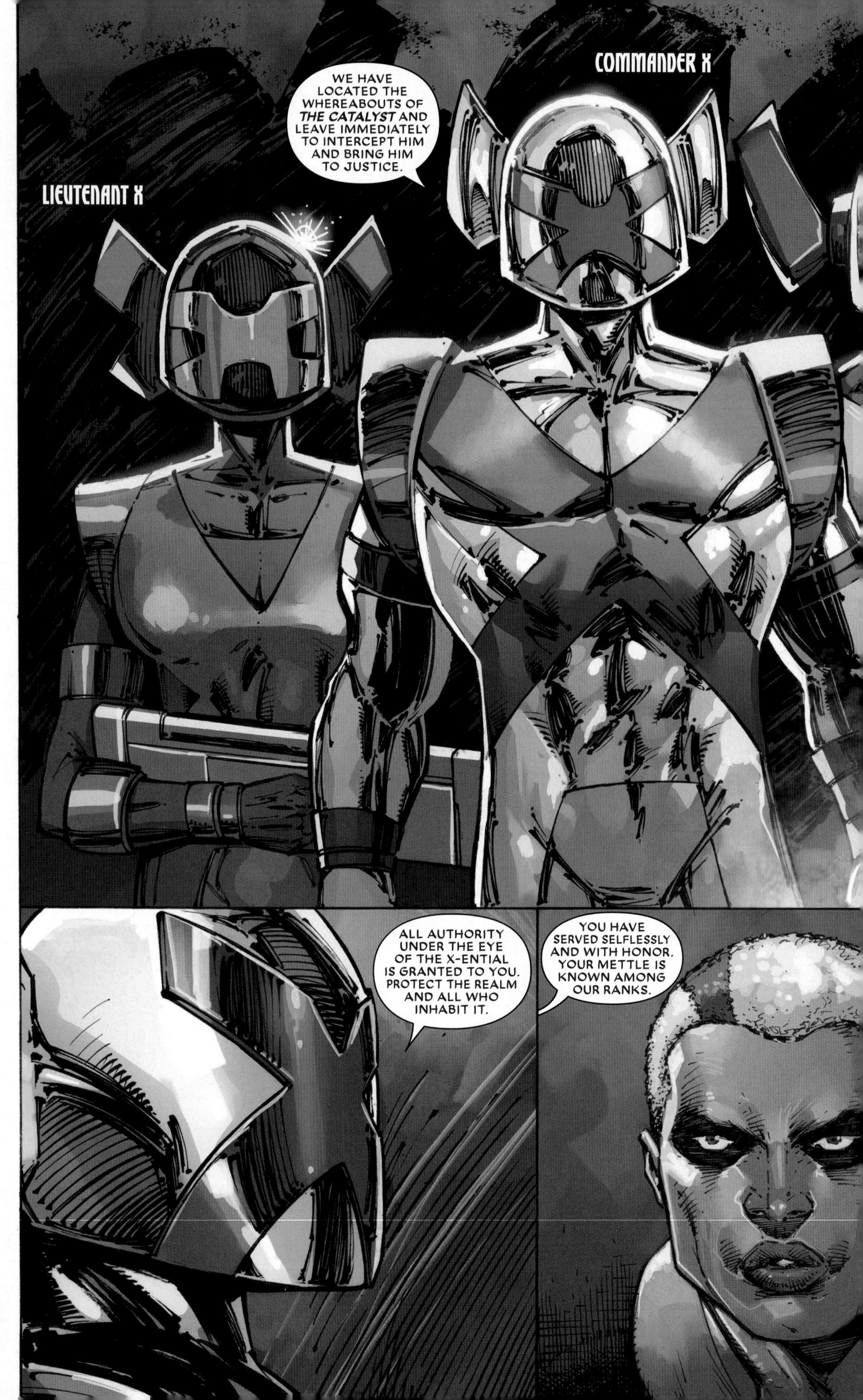
COMMANDER X
WE HAVE LOCATED THE WHEREABOUTS OF THE CATALYST AND LEAVE IMMEDIATELY TO INTERCEPT HIM AND BRING HIM TO JUSTICE.
LIEUTENANT X
ALL AUTHORITY UNDER THE EYE OF THE X-ENTIAL IS GRANTED TO YOU. PROTECT THE REALM AND ALL WHO INHABIT IT.
YOU HAVE SERVED SELFLESSLY AND WITH HONOR. YOUR METTLE IS KNOWN AMONG OUR RANKS.

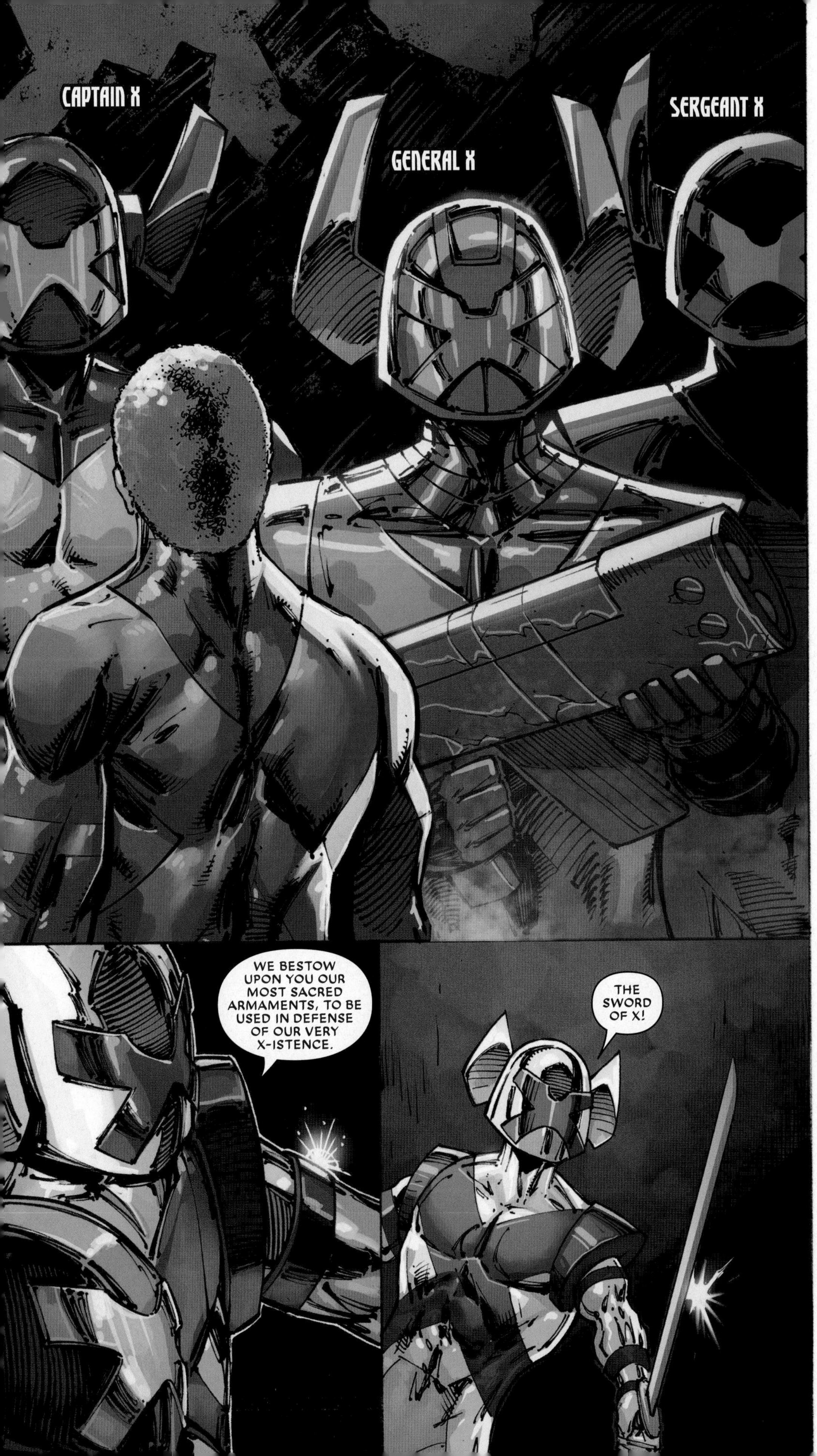
CAPTAIN X
GENERAL X
SERGEANT X
WE BESTOW UPON YOU OUR MOST SACRED ARMAMENTS, TO BE USED IN DEFENSE OF OUR VERY X-ISTENCE.
THE SWORD OF X!

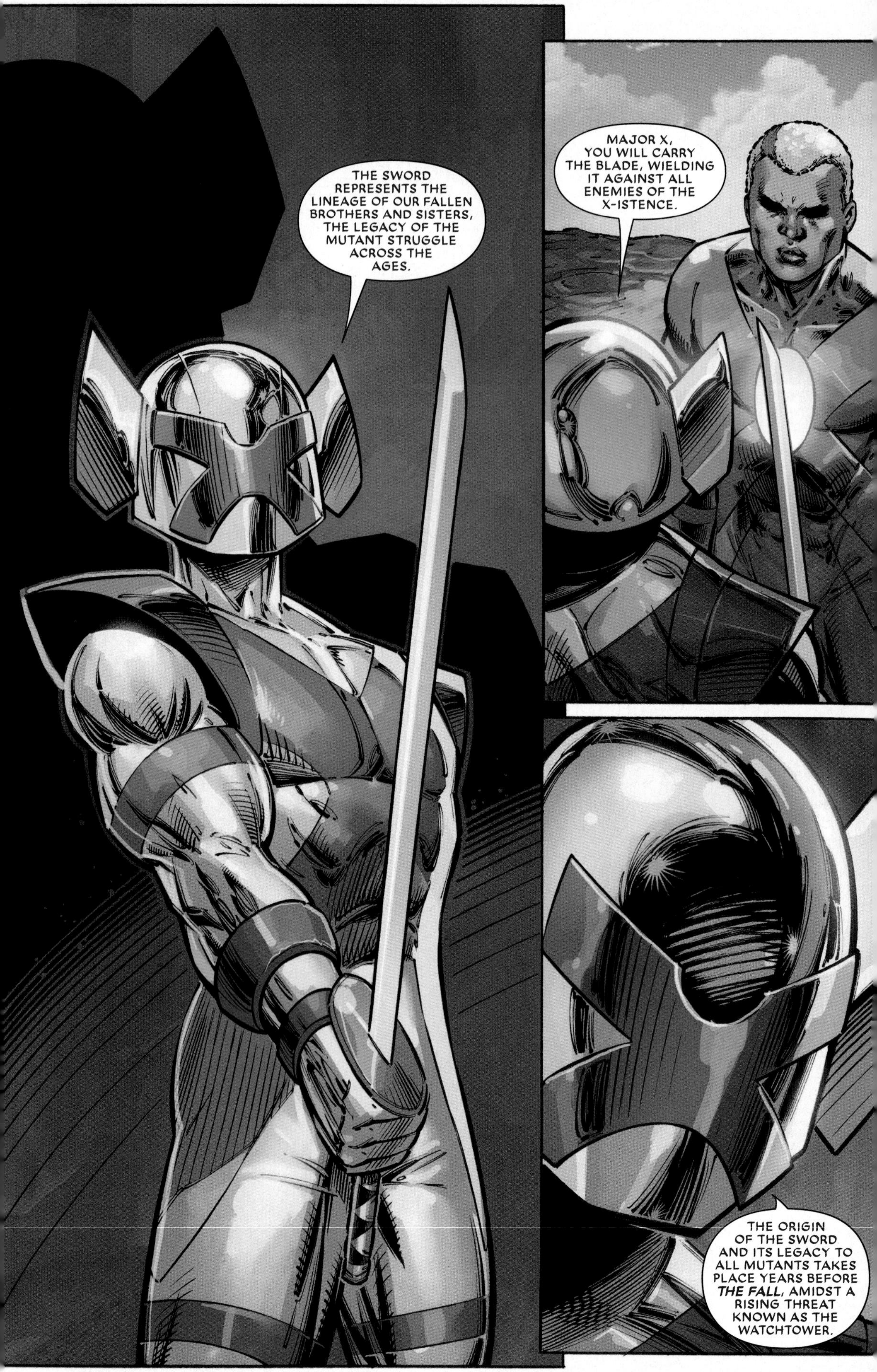
THE SWORD REPRESENTS THE LINEAGE OF OUR FALLEN BROTHERS AND SISTERS, THE LEGACY OF THE MUTANT STRUGGLE ACROSS THE AGES.
MAJOR X, YOU WILL CARRY THE BLADE, WIELDING IT AGAINST ALL ENEMIES OF THE X-ISTENCE.
THE ORIGIN OF THE SWORD AND ITS LEGACY TO ALL MUTANTS TAKES PLACE YEARS BEFORE *THE FALL*, AMIDST A RISING THREAT KNOWN AS THE WATCHTOWER.

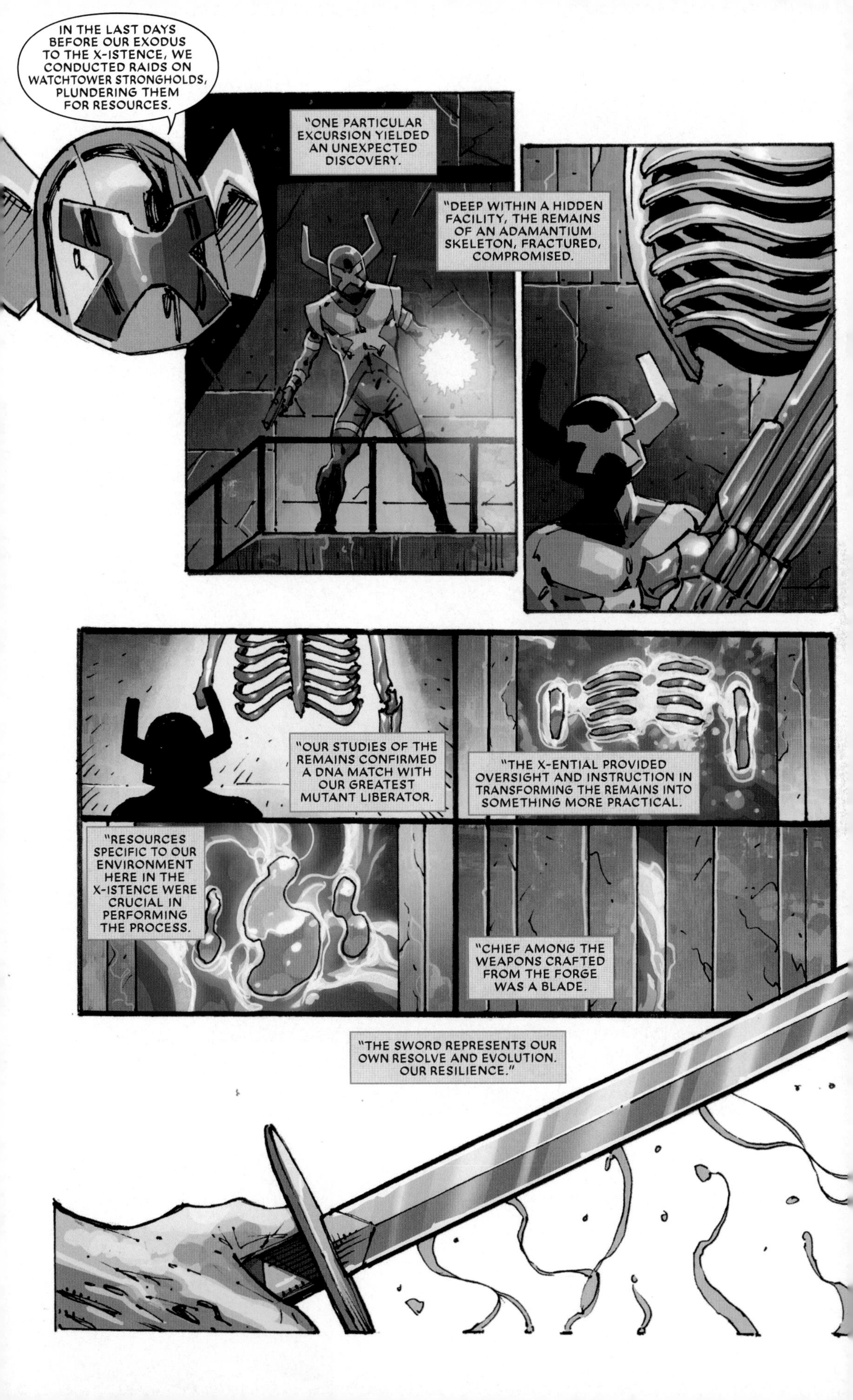

IN THE LAST DAYS BEFORE OUR EXODUS TO THE X-ISTENCE, WE CONDUCTED RAIDS ON WATCHTOWER STRONGHOLDS, PLUNDERING THEM FOR RESOURCES.
"ONE PARTICULAR EXCURSION YIELDED AN UNEXPECTED DISCOVERY.
"DEEP WITHIN A HIDDEN FACILITY, THE REMAINS OF AN ADAMANTIUM SKELETON, FRACTURED, COMPROMISED.
"OUR STUDIES OF THE REMAINS CONFIRMED A DNA MATCH WITH OUR GREATEST MUTANT LIBERATOR.
"THE X-ENTIAL PROVIDED OVERSIGHT AND INSTRUCTION IN TRANSFORMING THE REMAINS INTO SOMETHING MORE PRACTICAL.
"RESOURCES SPECIFIC TO OUR ENVIRONMENT HERE IN THE X-ISTENCE WERE CRUCIAL IN PERFORMING THE PROCESS.
"CHIEF AMONG THE WEAPONS CRAFTED FROM THE FORGE WAS A BLADE.
"THE SWORD REPRESENTS OUR OWN RESOLVE AND EVOLUTION. OUR RESILIENCE."

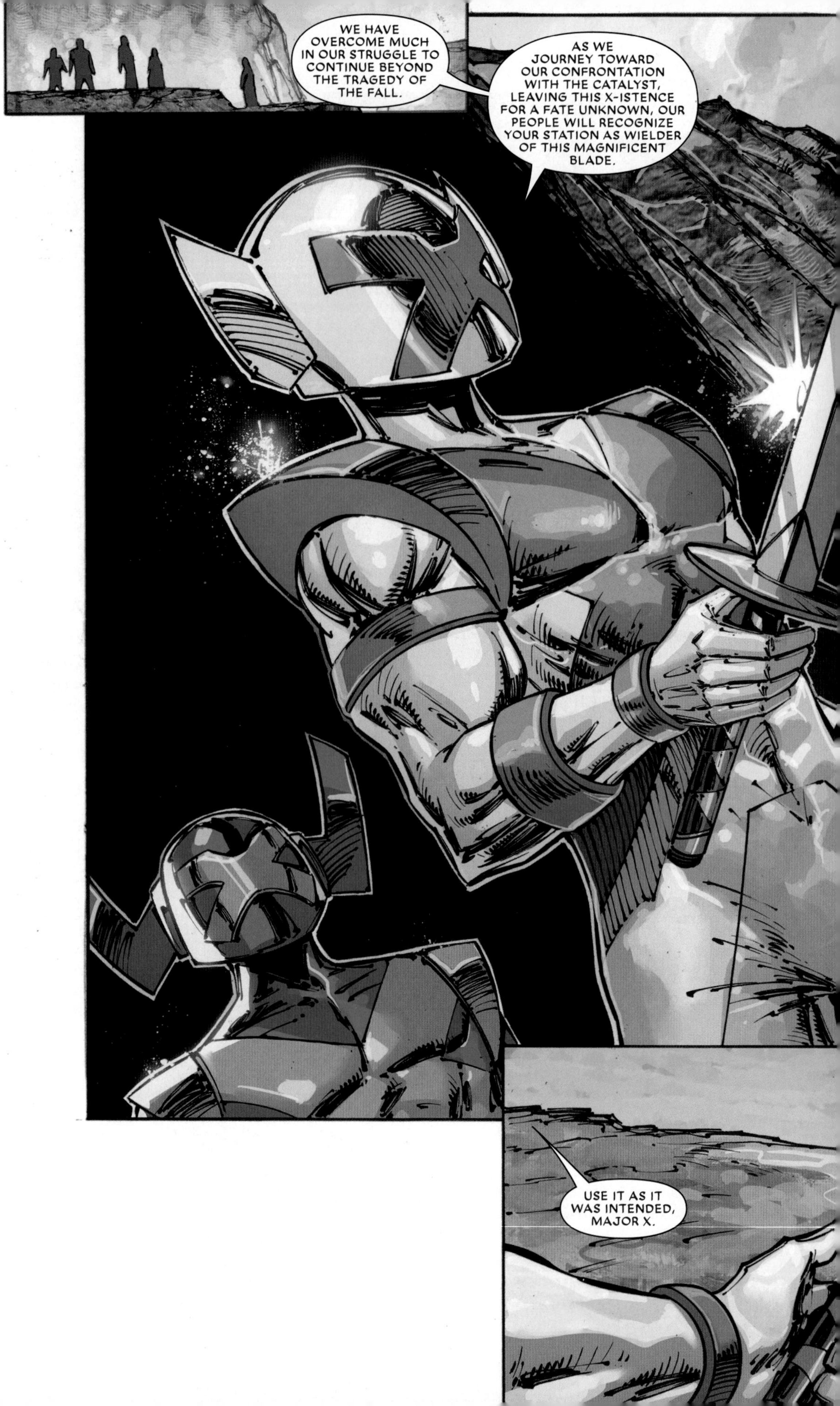
WE HAVE OVERCOME MUCH IN OUR STRUGGLE TO CONTINUE BEYOND THE TRAGEDY OF THE FALL.
AS WE JOURNEY TOWARD OUR CONFRONTATION WITH THE CATALYST, LEAVING THIS X-ISTENCE FOR A FATE UNKNOWN, OUR PEOPLE WILL RECOGNIZE YOUR STATION AS WIELDER OF THIS MAGNIFICENT BLADE.
USE IT AS IT WAS INTENDED, MAJOR X.

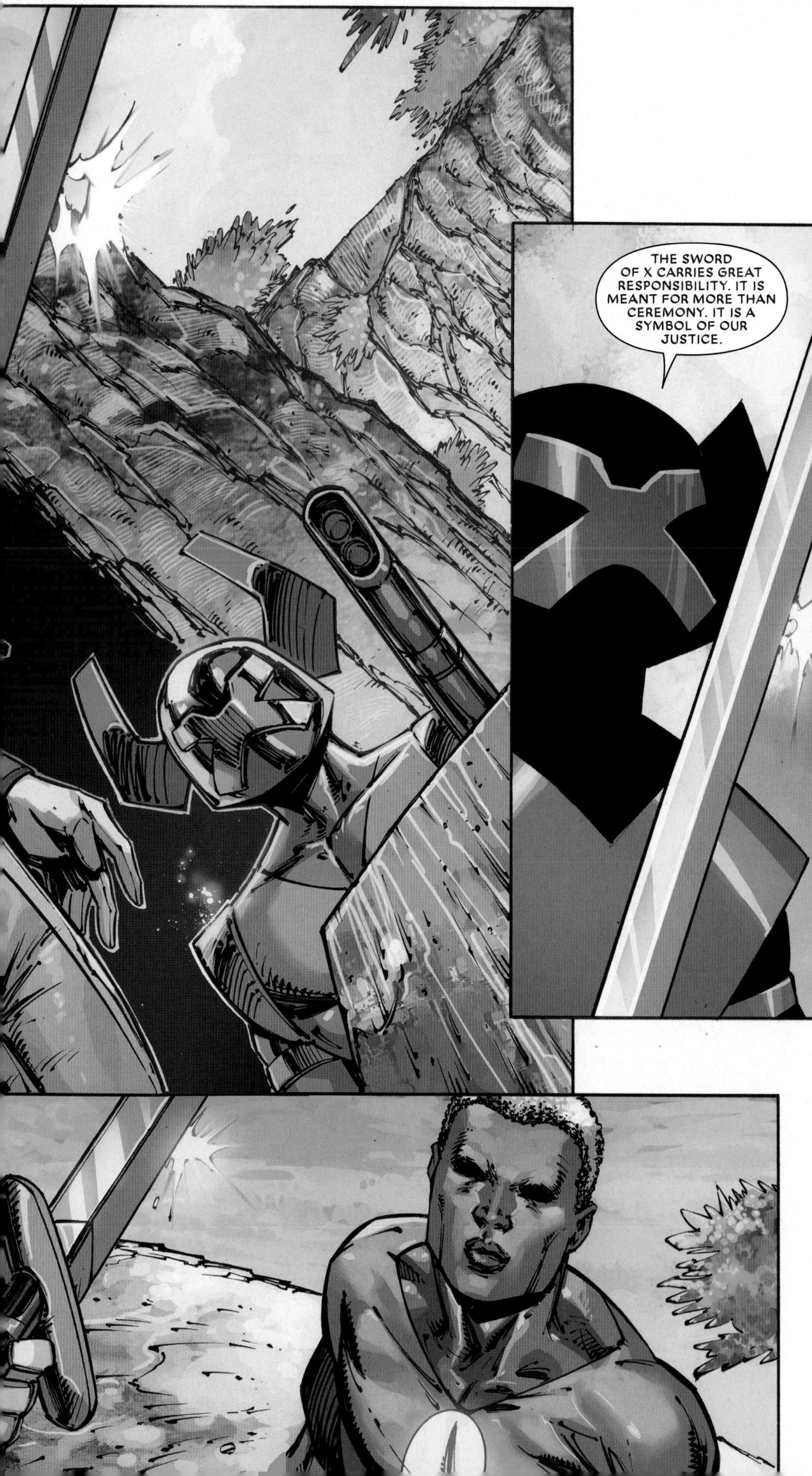
THE SWORD OF X CARRIES GREAT RESPONSIBILITY. IT IS MEANT FOR MORE THAN CEREMONY. IT IS A SYMBOL OF OUR JUSTICE.

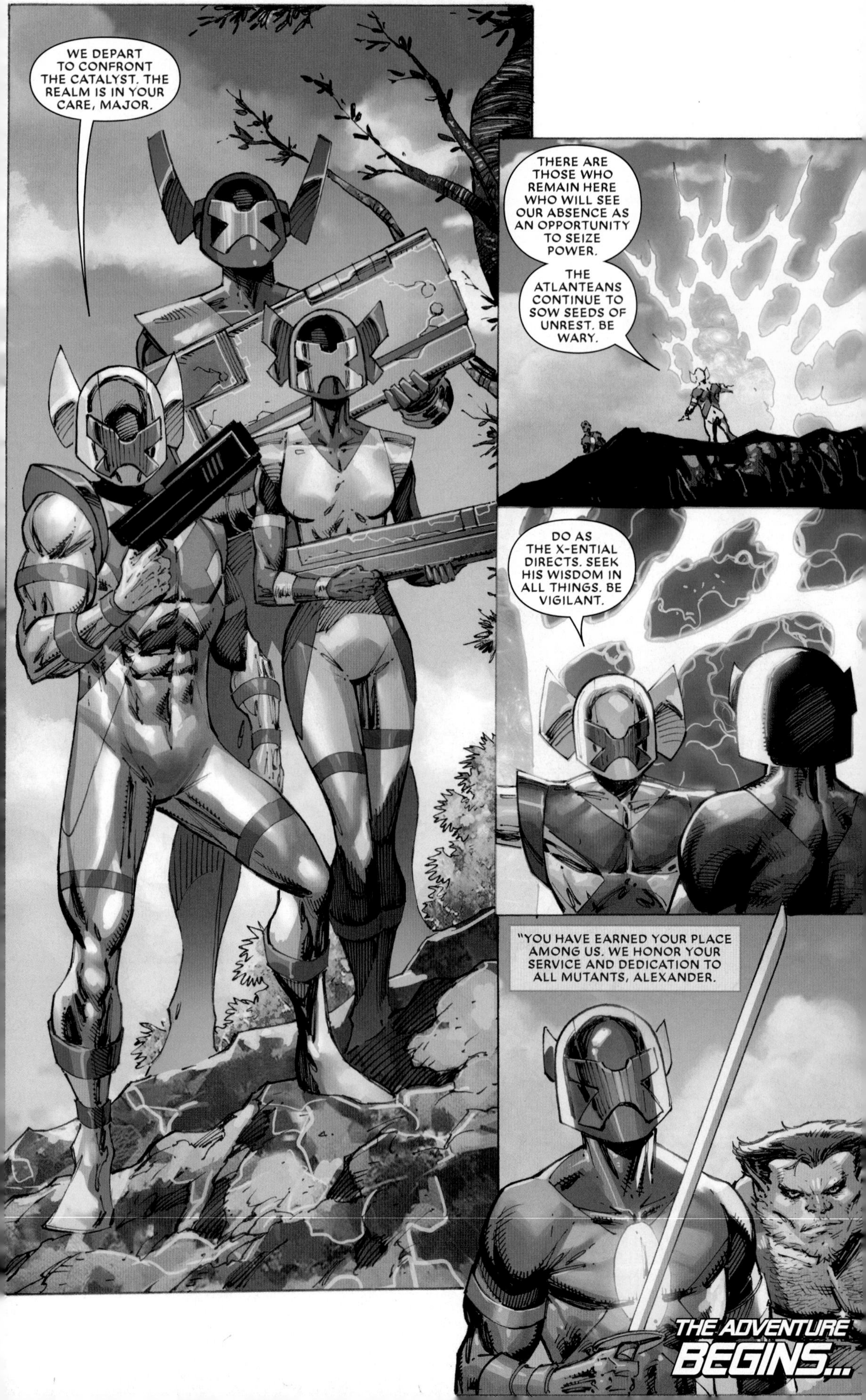
WE DEPART TO CONFRONT THE CATALYST. THE REALM IS IN YOUR CARE, MAJOR.
THERE ARE THOSE WHO REMAIN HERE WHO WILL SEE OUR ABSENCE AS AN OPPORTUNITY TO SEIZE POWER.
THE ATLANTEANS CONTINUE TO SOW SEEDS OF UNREST. BE WARY.
DO AS THE X-ENTIAL DIRECTS. SEEK HIS WISDOM IN ALL THINGS. BE VIGILANT.
"YOU HAVE EARNED YOUR PLACE AMONG US. WE HONOR YOUR SERVICE AND DEDICATION TO ALL MUTANTS, ALEXANDER.
THE ADVENTURE BEGINS...

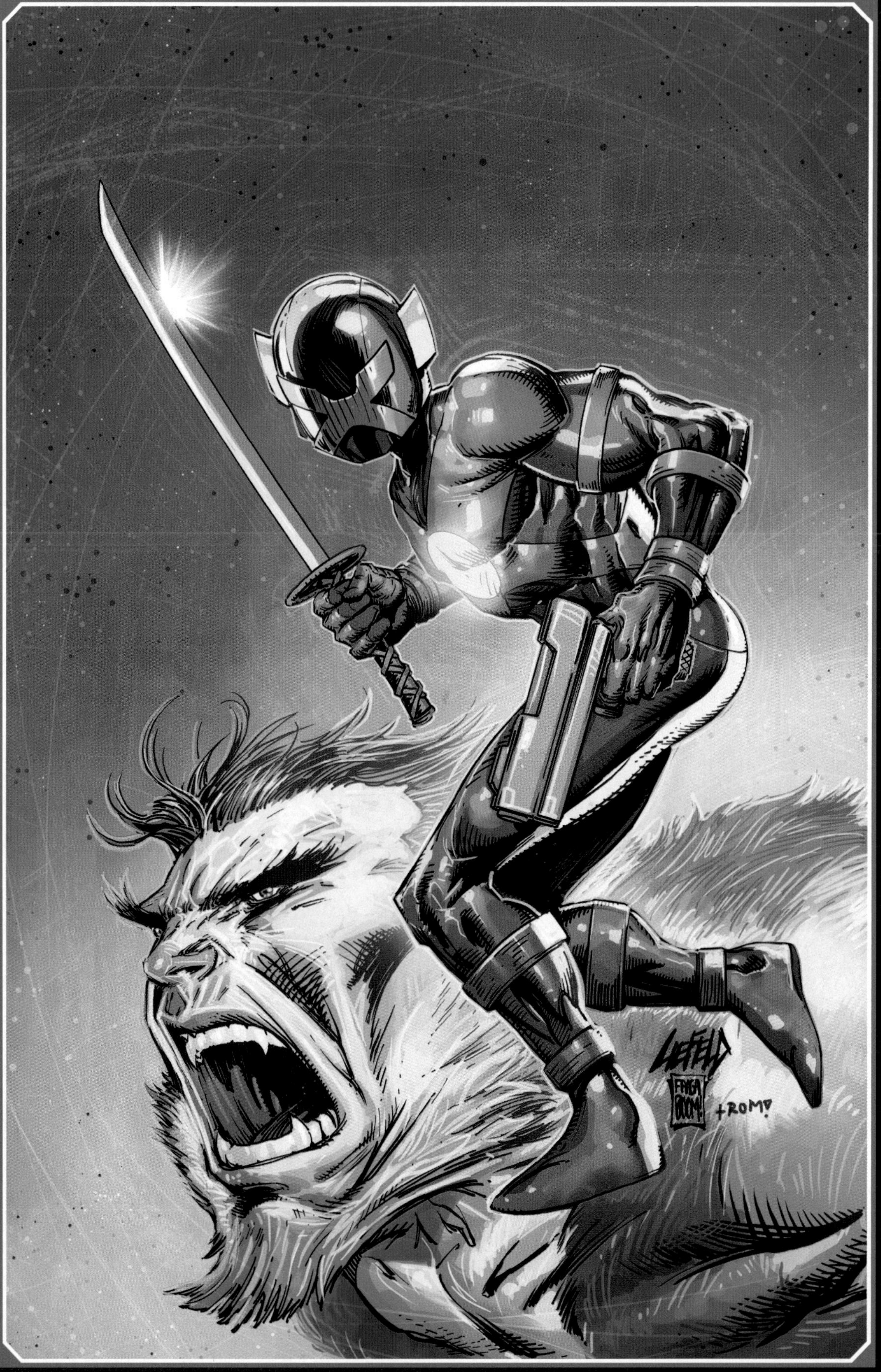

ROB LIEFELD, DAN FRAGA & ROMULO FAJARDO JR.

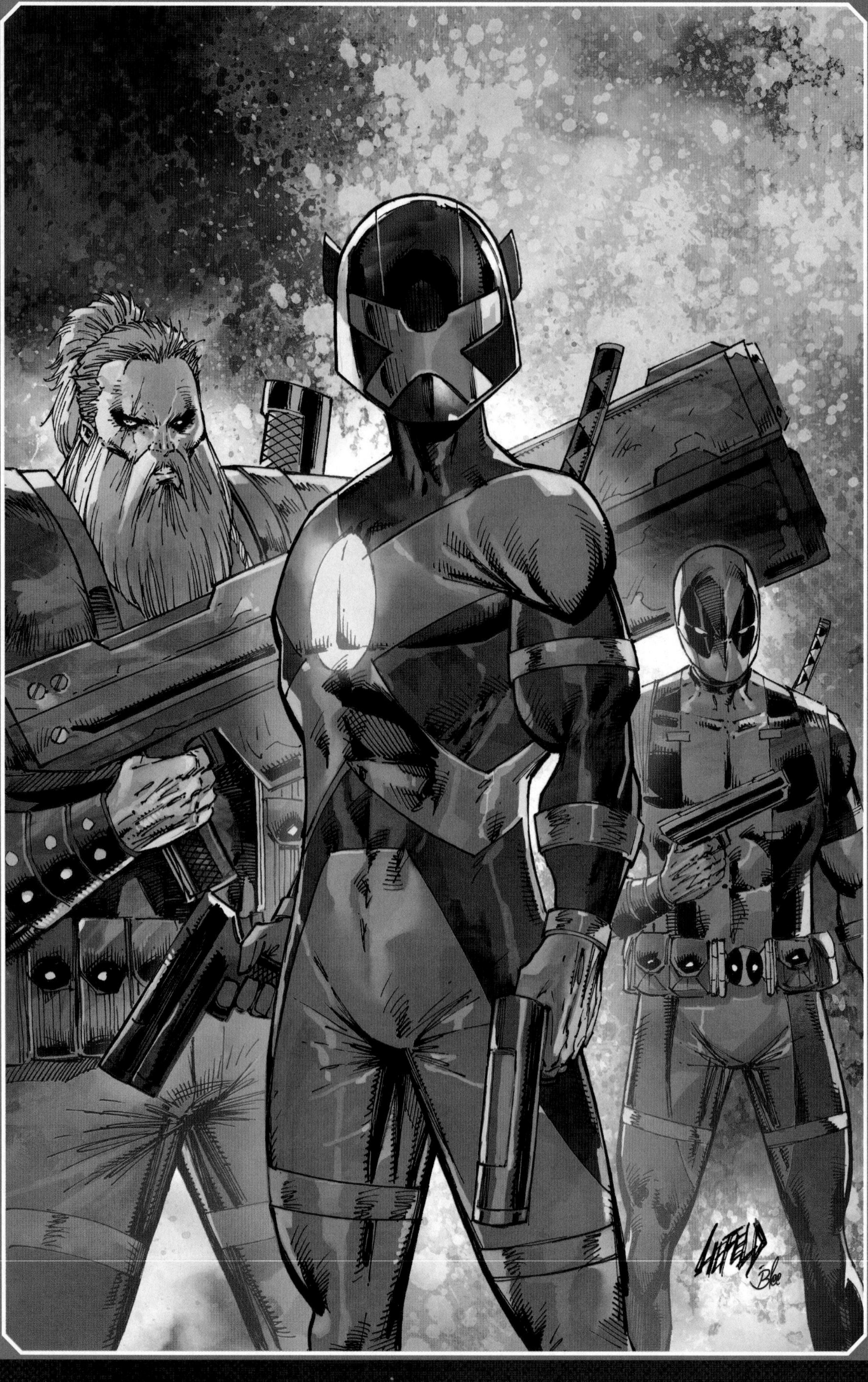
LIEFELD
Blee

ROB LIEFELD & FEDERICO BLEE

#6 SECOND PRINTING COVER

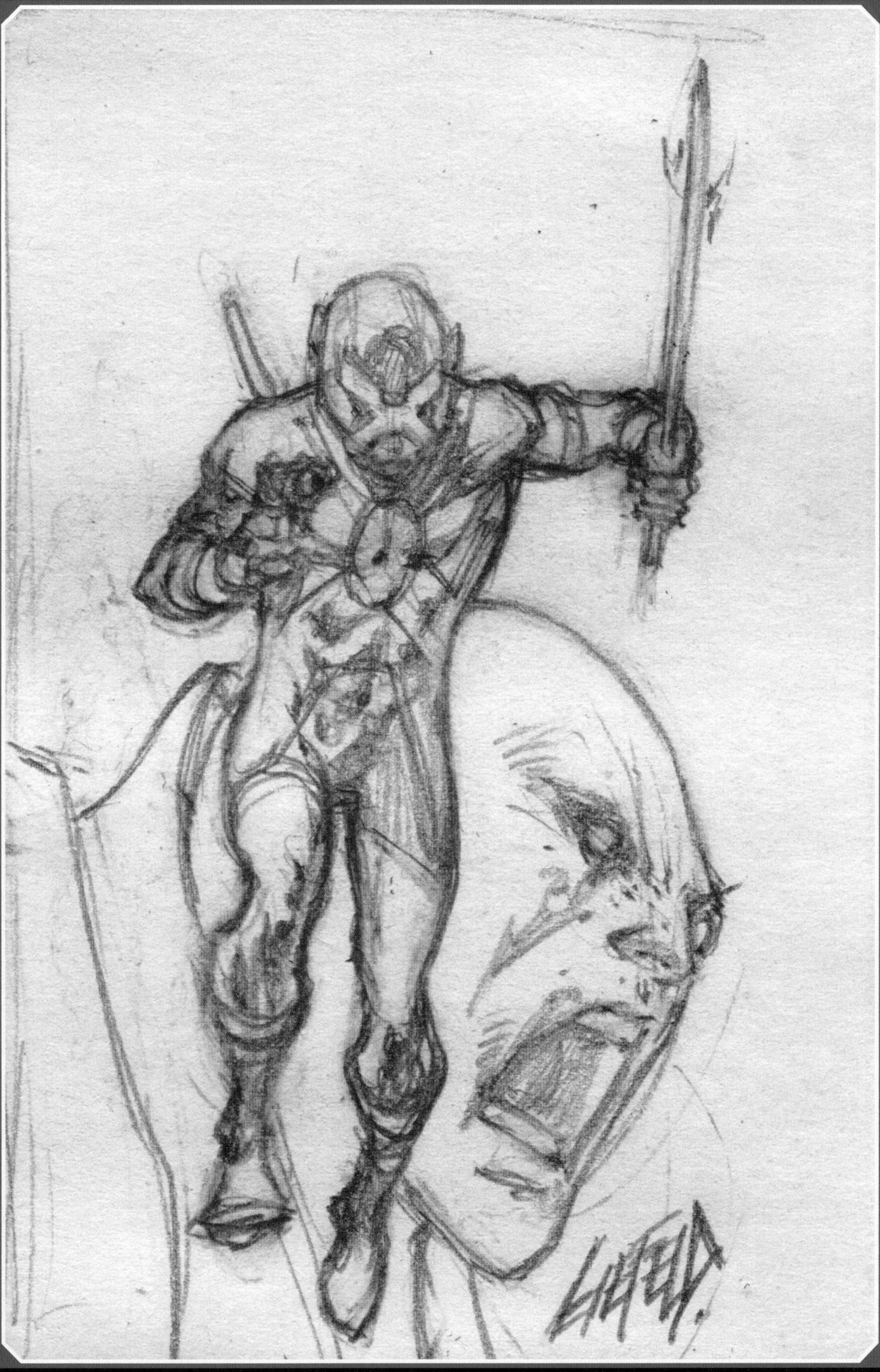

ROB LIEFELD

#0 SKETCH VARIANT

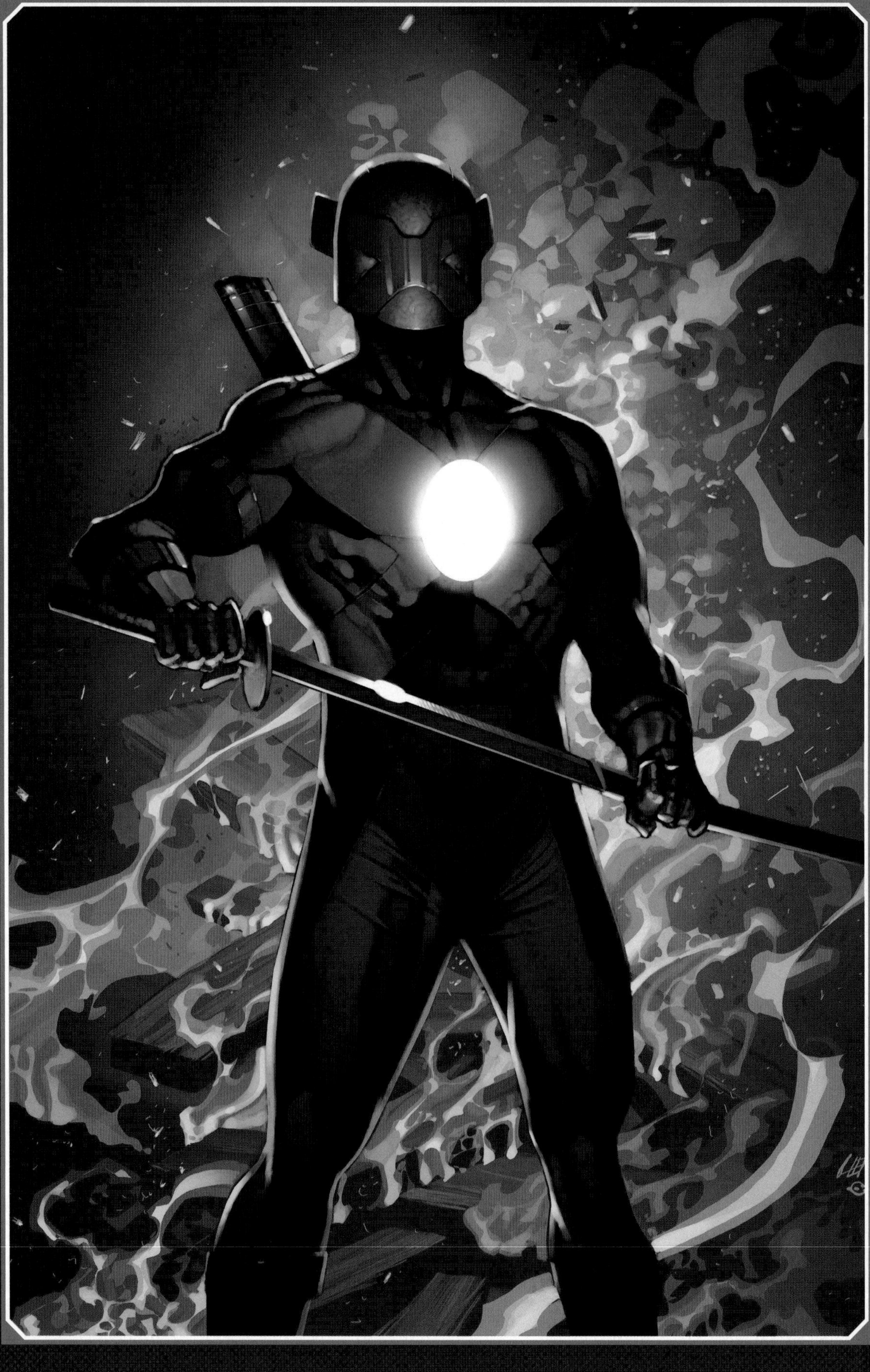

ROB LIEFELD & CHRIS STEVENS

#0 VARIANT

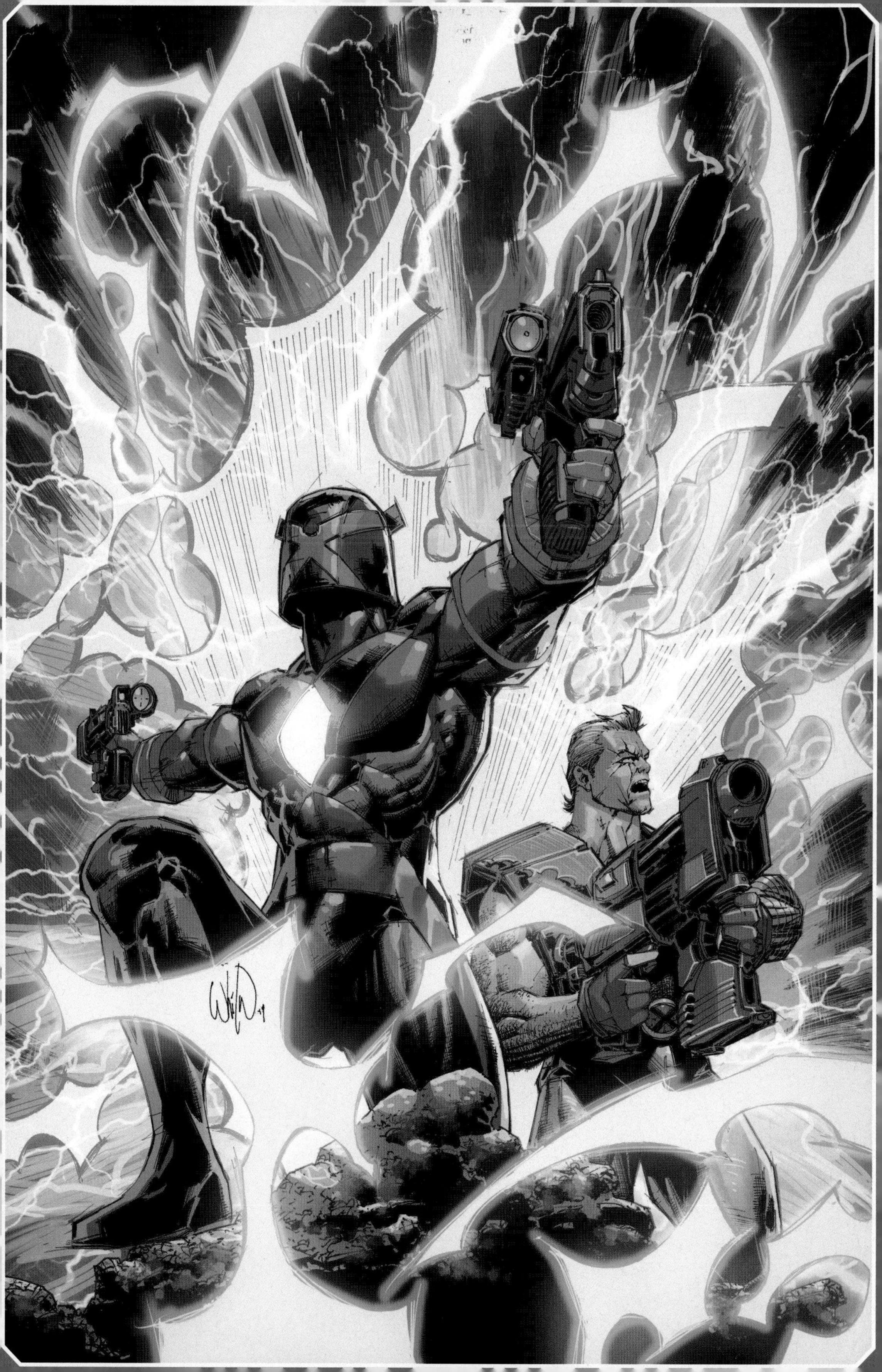

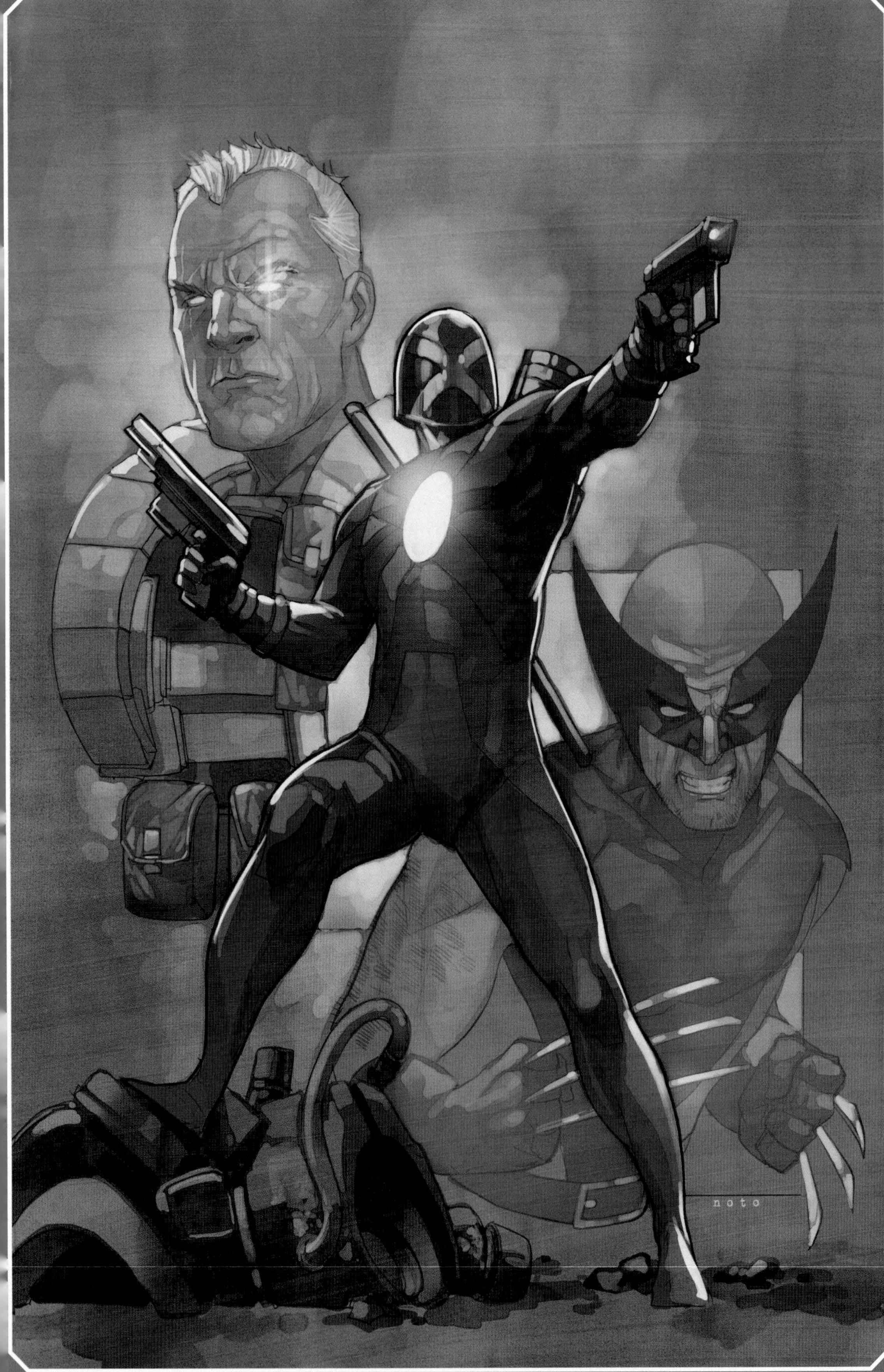
noto

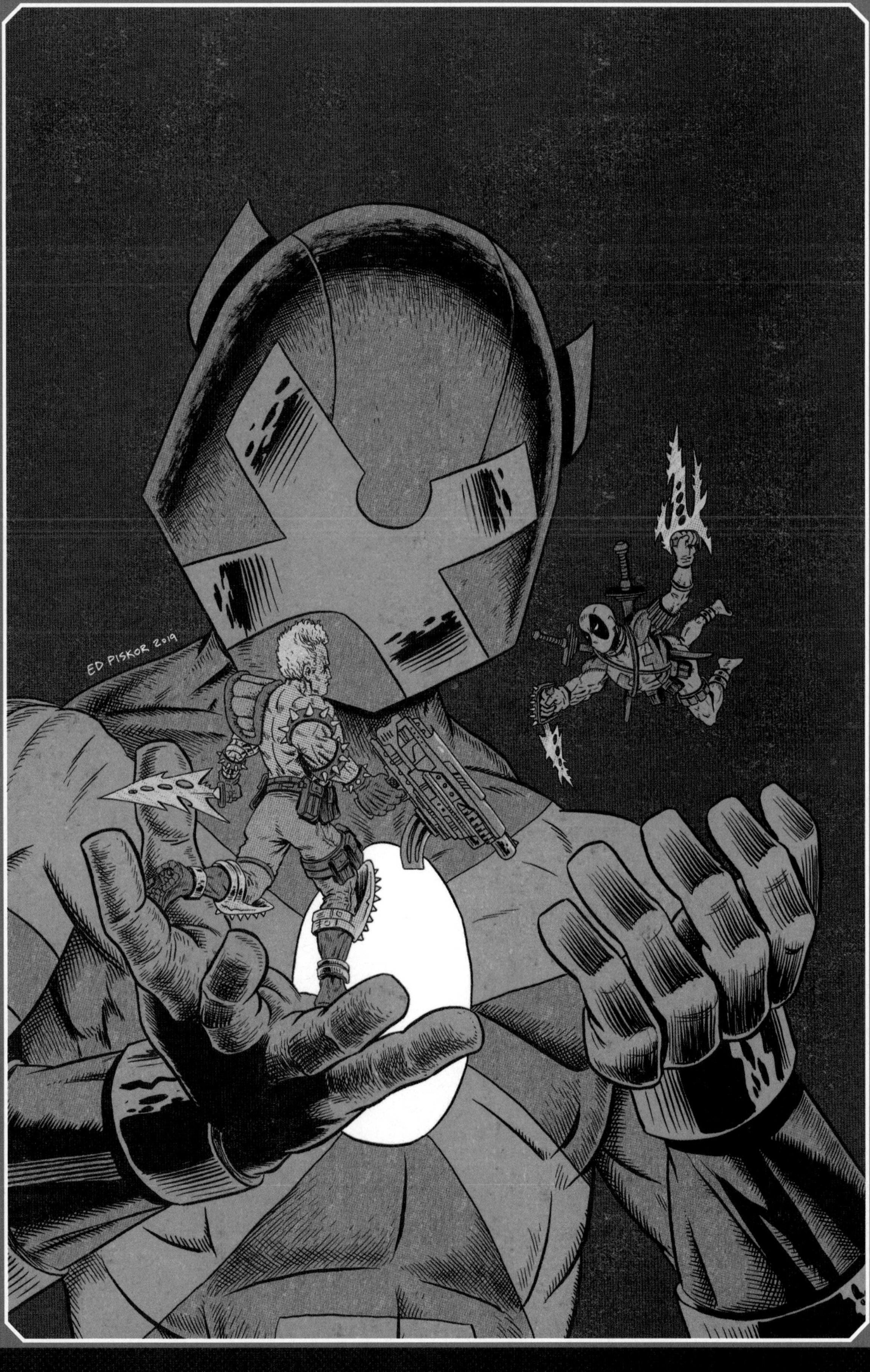
ED PISKOR 2019

ED PISKOR

#0 VARIANT

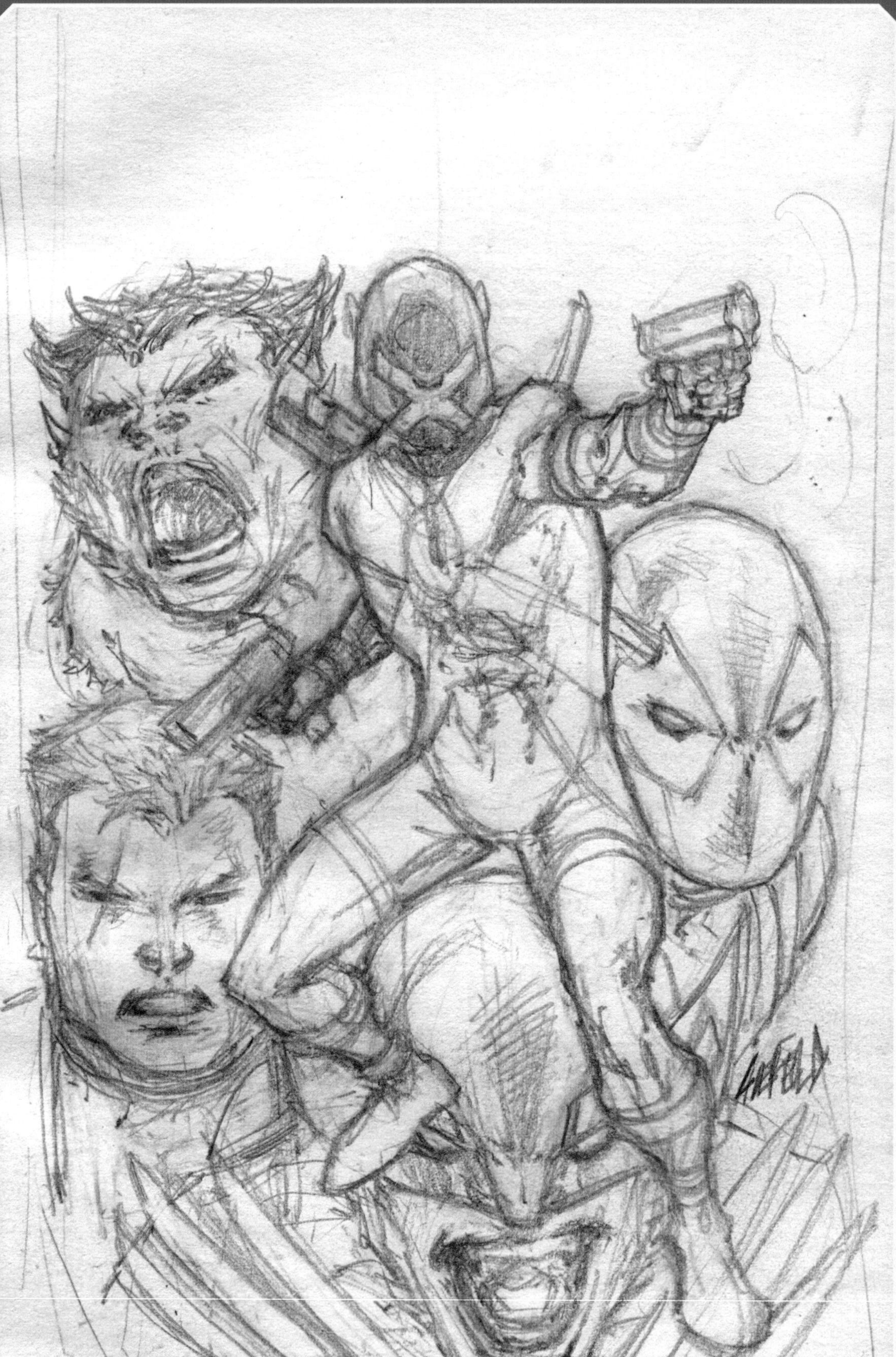

ROB LIEFELD

#1 COVER PENCILS

ROB LIEFELD

THE VIEW FROM THE WATCHTOWER

by Dugan Trodglen

As you'll see in this exclusive interview with **ROB LIEFELD**, *the* Major X *saga is not a random thread being pulled from a past story but is based on a concept he's wanted to expand on ever since his original* Wolverine *story was published in 2000. And not only that, but Rob assures us that there is more to come from our hero, as well as the Watchtower and the Administrator!*

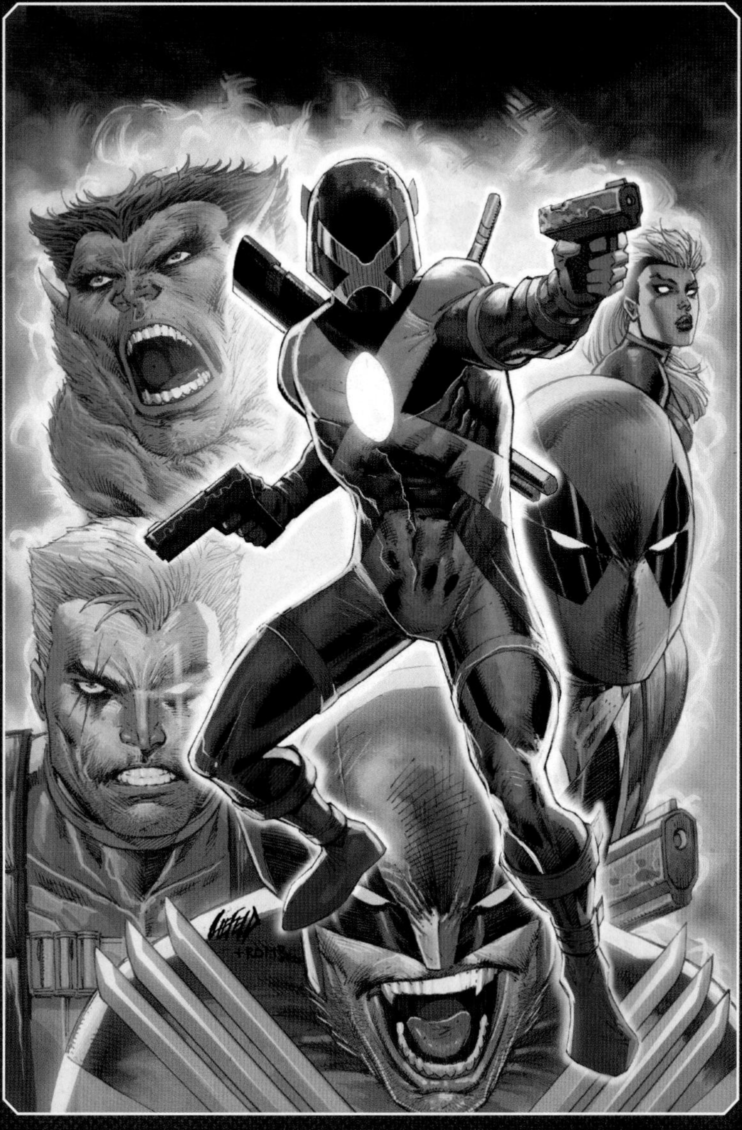

Major X #1 cover by **ROB LIEFELD** & **ROMULO FAJARDO JR.**

It seems like you were given carte blanche when it came to this series. Was the idea that it was going to feature a new, original character always part of the plan?

LIEFELD: Yes. Marvel EIC C.B. Cebulski approached me and asked me if I wanted to tell some X-Men stories. I told him I've been looking to do *Major X* since my original *X-Force* run. I shared with him the story, the mystery, the motivations, the entire saga, and he gave me the green light to run with it. I think it turned out okay. The time was right for Major X!

How did you come up with the idea of tying this in with the Wolverine/Deadpool story from back in the day?

LIEFELD: When I first produced these *Wolverine* stories back in 2000, the idea was always to establish the Watchtower and the Administrator as a creepy organization that exploits mutantkind in the hope of scientifically replicating and harnessing their DNA for their own nefarious purposes. I revisited them again in my *X-Force* miniseries a few years later. I believe there is a lot of creative juice in the Administrator as well as the Watchtower, and he's a character that I'll continue to revisit and expand on.

Making Major X the son of Cable is another nice way of tying into your X-legacy. Was that something that you hit on early in the process?

LIEFELD: It is the only reason he exists at all. I always wanted to expand Cable's legacy in this way and provide another fold in the wrinkles of his ongoing saga. That said, Alexander has turned out to be compelling in his own right, and readers have really responded to his finding his own voice and courage and resourcefulness. In all my years, no character has seen such an immediate surge since I introduced them. Maybe Deadpool. The mail on *New Mutants #98* was staggering. The social media reaction to

The Administrator from *Wolverine #145*, page 17-18 art by **ROB LIEFELD**, **NORM RAPMUND** & **DIGITAL BROOME**

The Watchtower from *Major X #3*, page 10 art by **WHILCE PORTACIO** & **ROMULO FAJARDO JR.**

Major X is similar in its enthusiasm.

What does revealing that Storm is his mother say about the character?

LIEFELD: It says there was more than a passing flirtation that Cable and Storm shared back in their late '90s interactions. Longtime fans will remember that they revealed a waning attraction to each other and, as far as I am concerned, they share a deep respect for one another. BUT, and this is a big one, while the parentage is firmly in place, the actual reasons for Alexander's existence have not been fully established or revealed as yet. What

is the nature of the union that generated him? I'm keeping all of that really close to the vest right now.

You're known for some classic character design work, and Major X is certainly striking. Do you come up with ideas a lot even when not working on specific projects?

LIEFELD: Yes, my sketchbook is always filled up with new characters and designs that I'm looking to introduce. I'm always creating new stuff, new characters, names, designs and plotting where it can be planted. Just like when I worked on *New Mutants* back in 1989.

visually, Major X fits in with your classic aesthetic perfectly. What went into the design process?

LIEFELD: This one was really among the easiest as I wanted to have a guy rocking an X on his head, but not in the manner we've seen it portrayed before. The motorcycle-styled helmet was the best option, and then putting the X across his chest and trunk, adding the "skirt" design, just playing with a pleasant aesthetic. This one worked out early and turned out for the best. As you can see in this #0 issue, we establish that it's a uniform design for most everyone in X-Command.

The X-Men have spent a lot of their career trying to prevent dystopian futures. You turned that concept around by having Major X's mission preventing a utopian mutant future from being erased. What was the inspiration there?

LIEFELD: Yes, as you said, I wanted a peaceful existence, or in this case, X-Istence, a paradise that they had dreamed of, a place of harmony, until it wasn't. Until it was selfishly ripped from them. The loss of their home and the threat of the Catalyst will be explored further in our next installment. Are there others who survived and made the leap before the purge?

You got to play around with an alternate-future Atlantis. Is that a corner of the Marvel Universe that you've always wanted to...dive into?

LIEFELD: My first Marvel comic was *Fantastic Four #147* with the cover depicting Namor exploding out of the depths to challenge the Thing, and it still takes my breath away. That comic had a profound impact on me. I absolutely love Prince Namor and all he represents. In my first *New Mutants* job, *Annual #5*, I introduced some Atlantean teen warriors named Surf; they fought alongside Namorita. I used them in *Major X* as well, as they presented a natural tether to Namor as well as my own past with the X-Men. So yes, I have always fancied Namor and all things Atlantis. A *Fantastic Four* story featuring them all would be a dream come true.

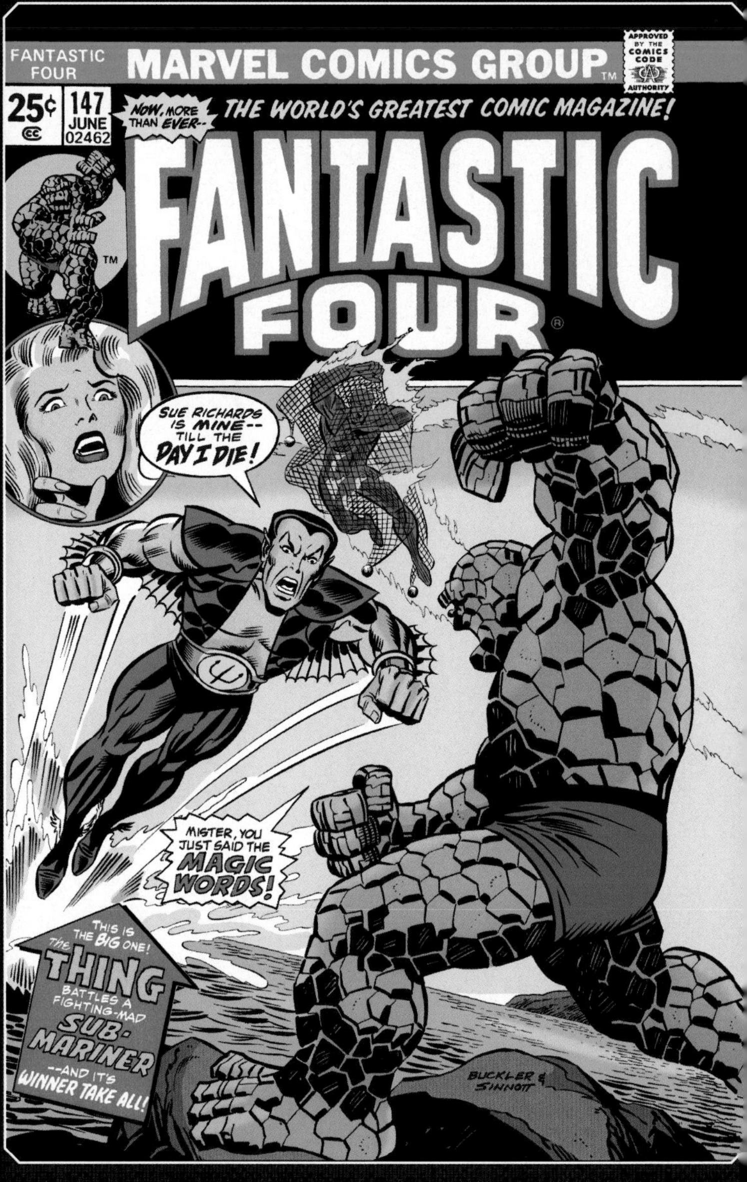
FANTASTIC FOUR
MARVEL COMICS GROUP
APPROVED BY THE COMICS CODE AUTHORITY
25¢
147 JUNE 02462
NOW, MORE THAN EVER--
THE WORLD'S GREATEST COMIC MAGAZINE!
FANTASTIC FOUR
SUE RICHARDS IS MINE-- TILL THE DAY I DIE!
MISTER, YOU JUST SAID THE MAGIC WORDS!
THIS IS THE BIG ONE! THE THING BATTLES A FIGHTING-MAD SUB-MARINER --AND IT'S WINNER TAKE ALL!
BUCKLER & SINNOTT

Fantastic Four #147 cover by RICH BUCKLER & JOE SINNOTT

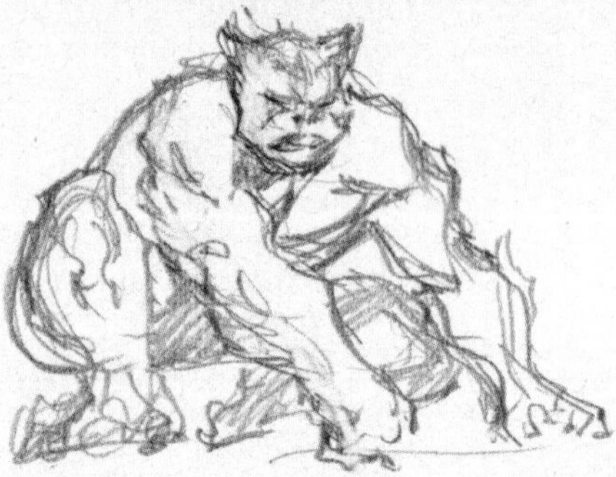

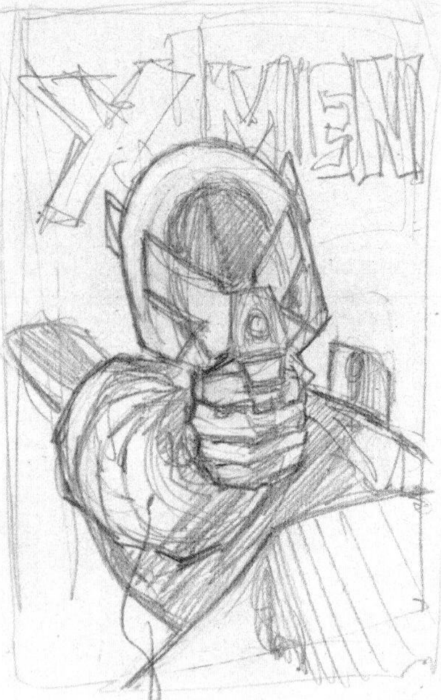
X MEN

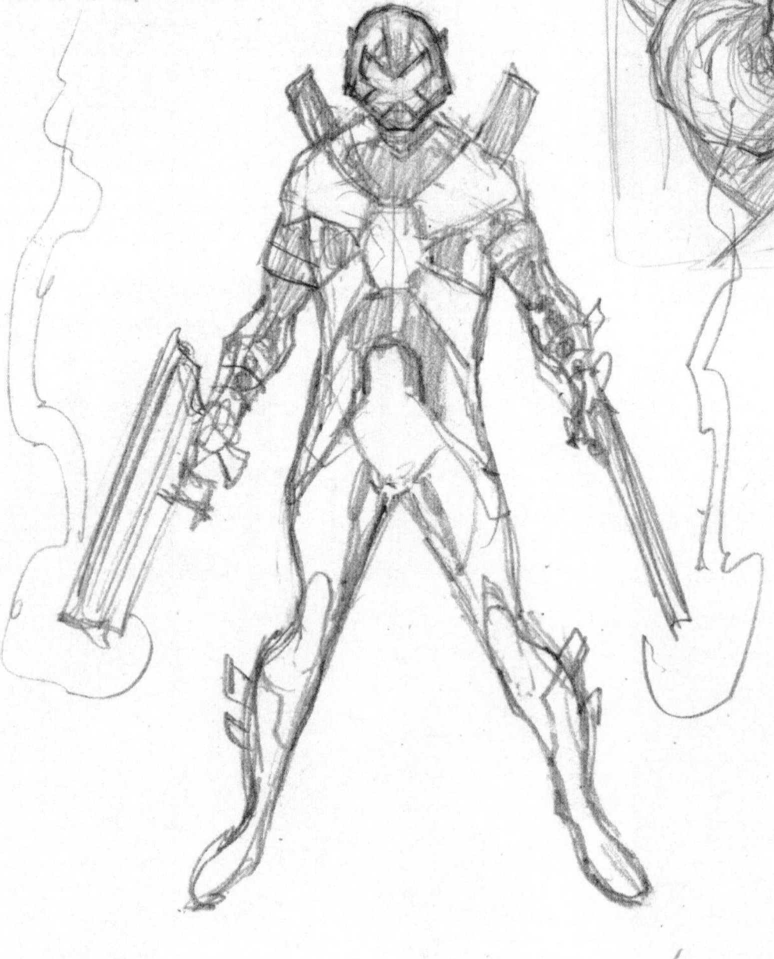

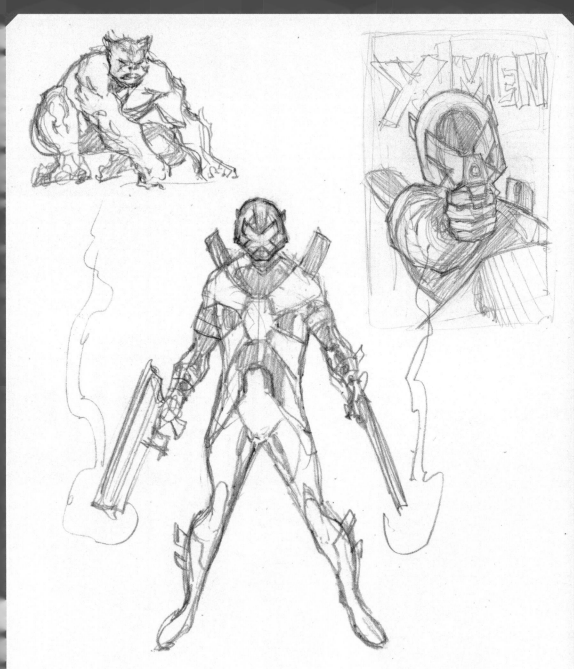

COMMANDER X

COME TO PROTECT THE SANCTITY OF THE MUTANT PLANET!

SYSTEM X

THE XISTENCE

REALM X

PLANET X

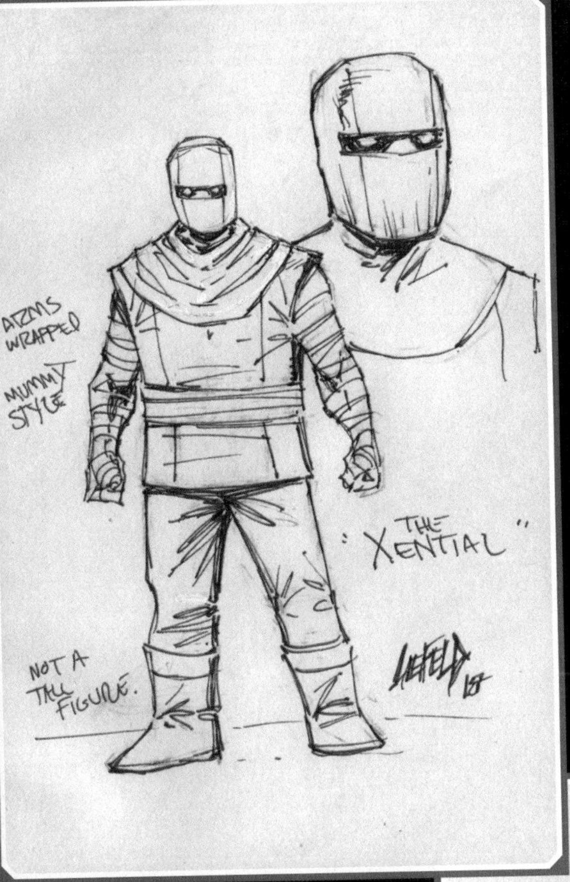
ARMS WRAPPED
MUMMY STYLE
"THE XENTIAL"
NOT A TALL FIGURE.
LIEFELD

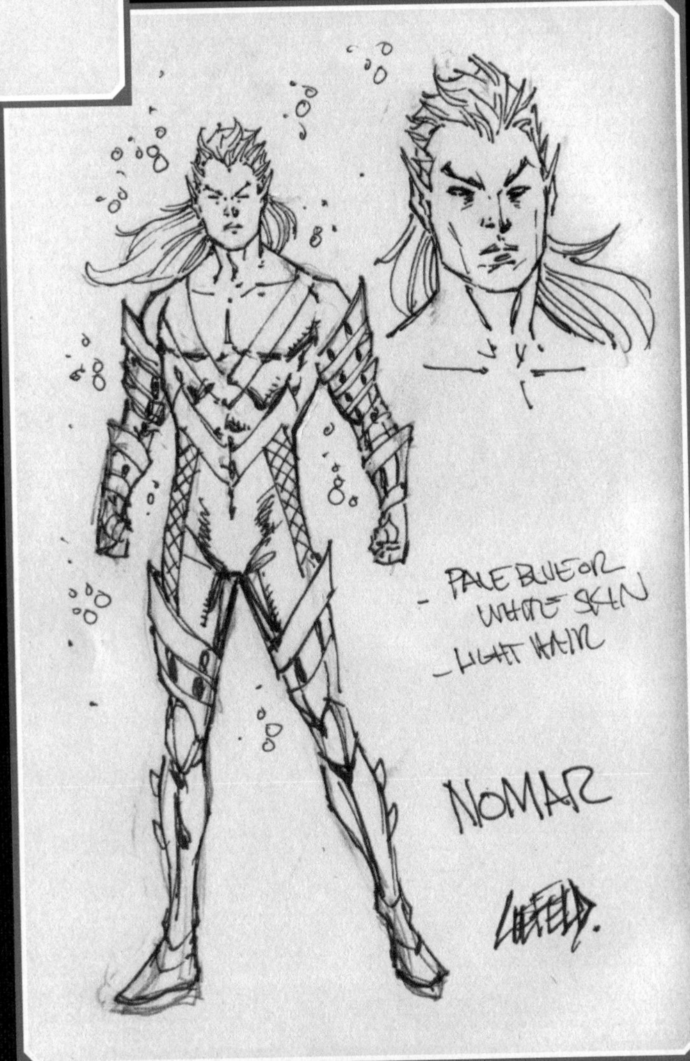
- PALE BLUE OR WHITE SKIN
- LIGHT HAIR
NOMAR
LIEFELD.

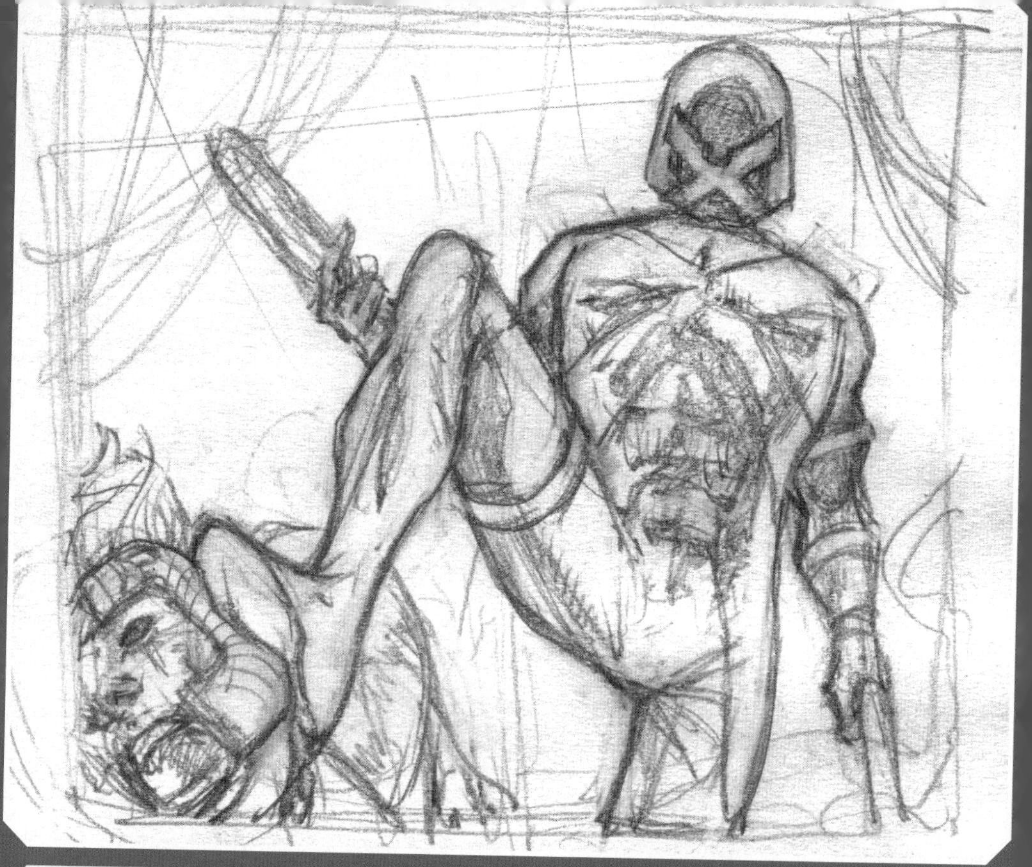

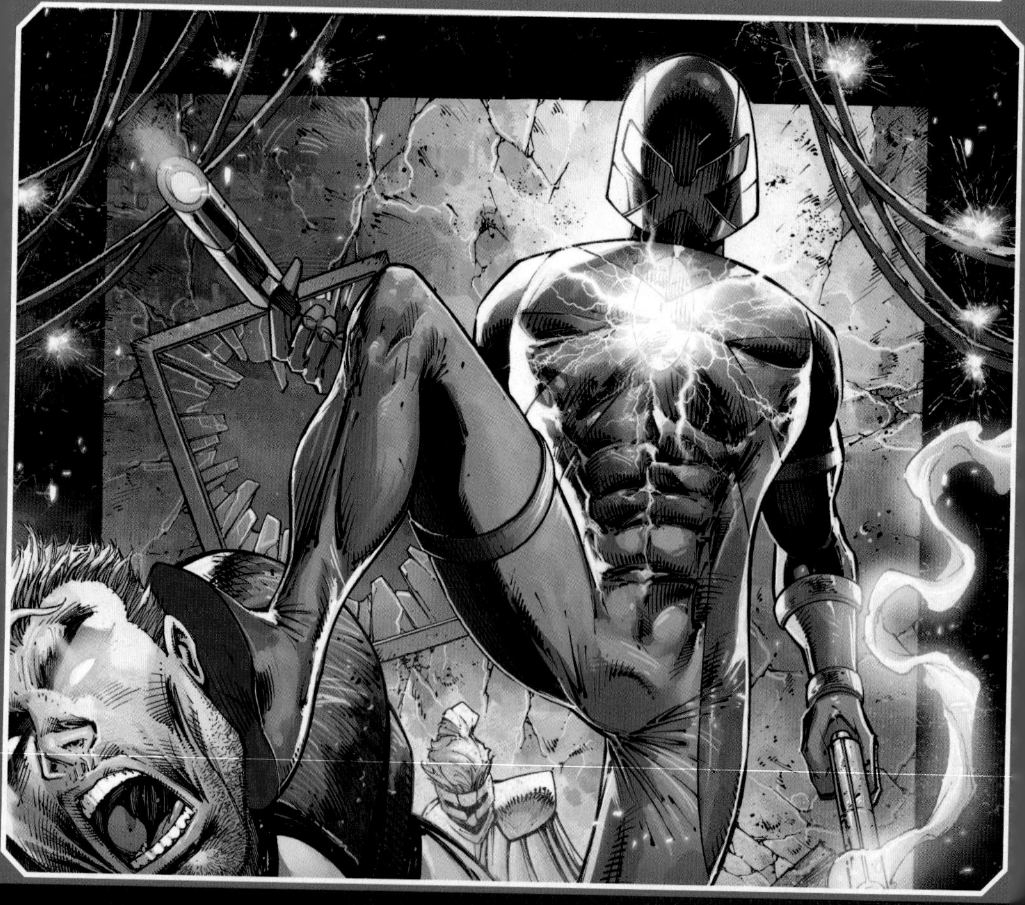

OB LIEFELD, ADELSO CORONA, DAN FRAGA & ROMULO FAJARDO J

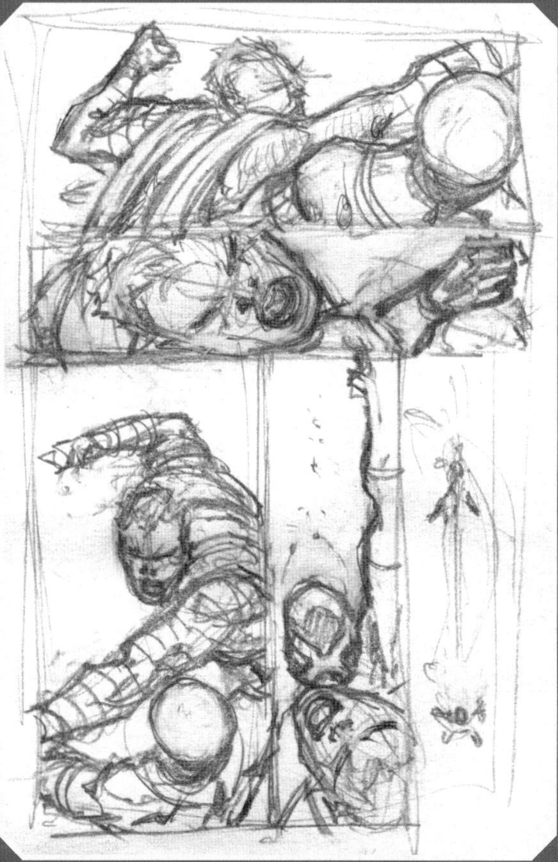

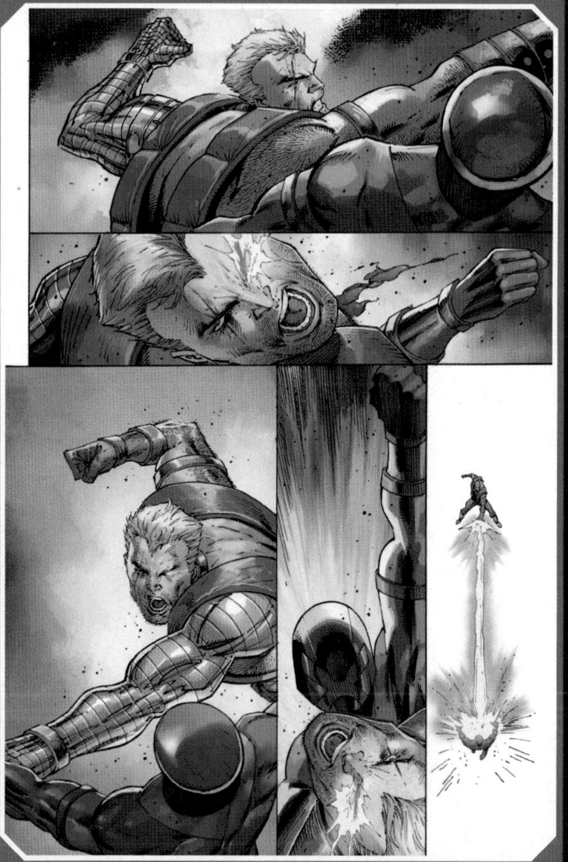

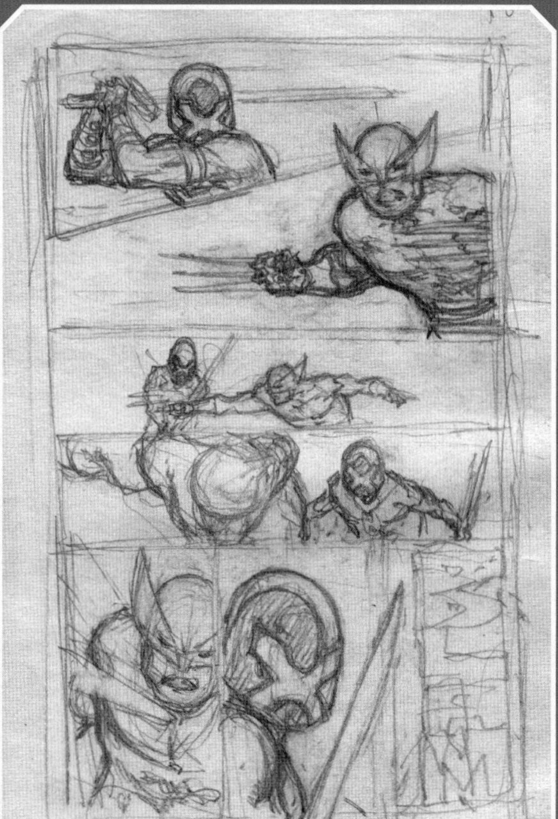

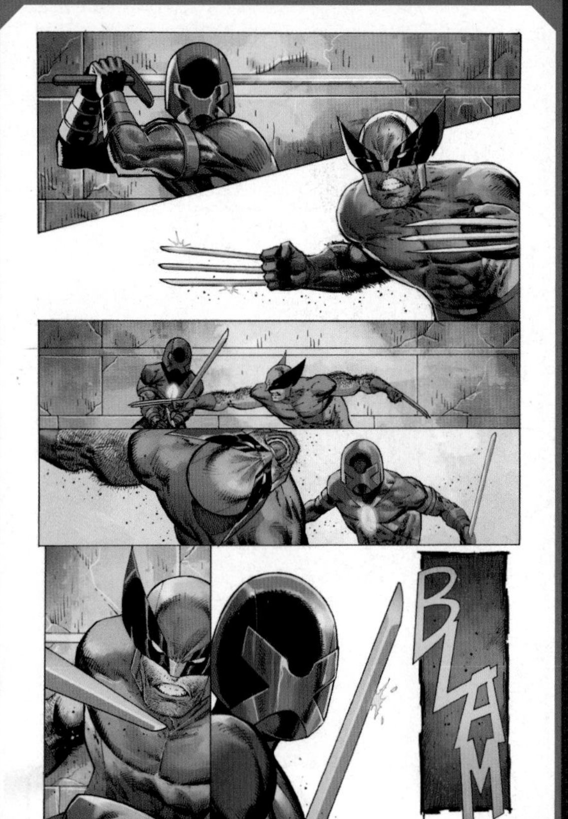
BLAM

ROB LIEFELD, ADELSO CORONA, DAN FRAGA & ROMULO FAJARDO JR.

MAJOR X #1: PAGES 5 & 18 SKETCHES AND FINAL ART

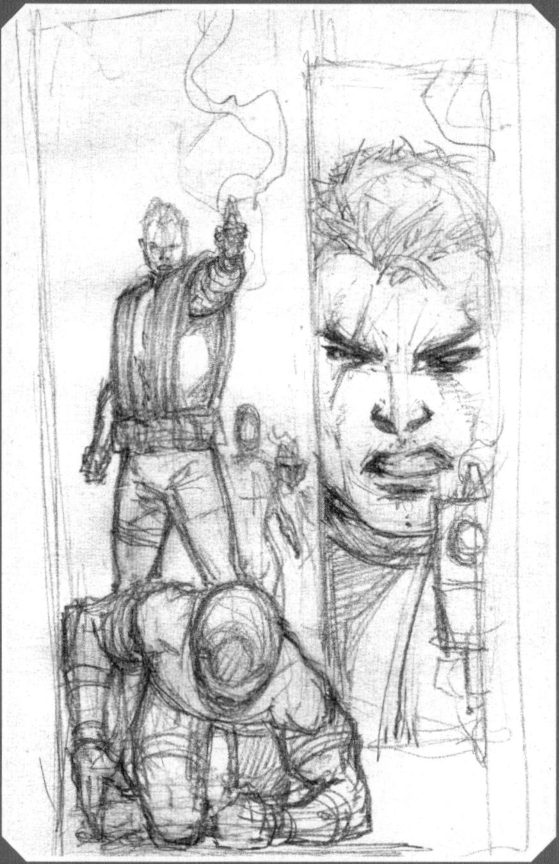

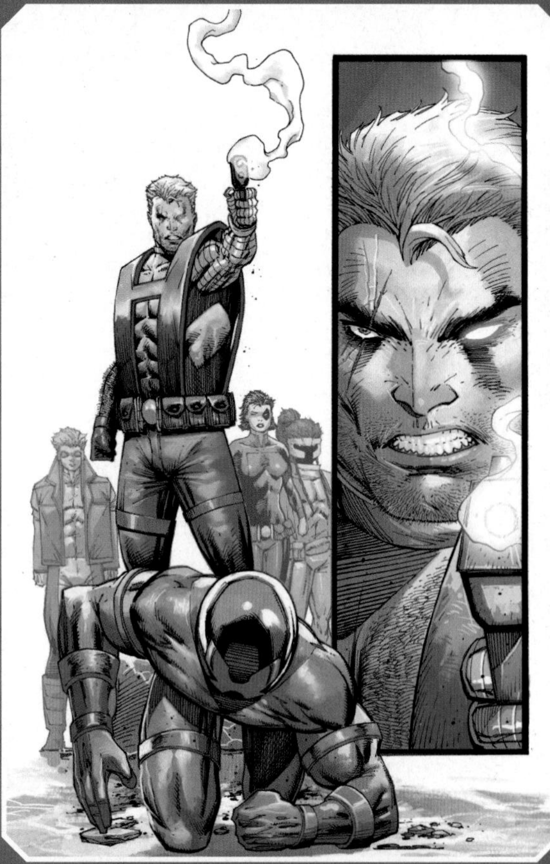

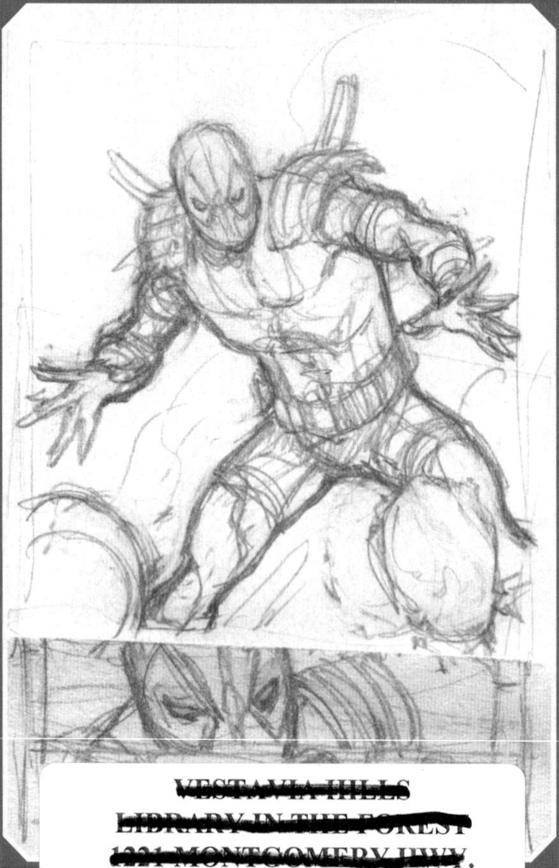

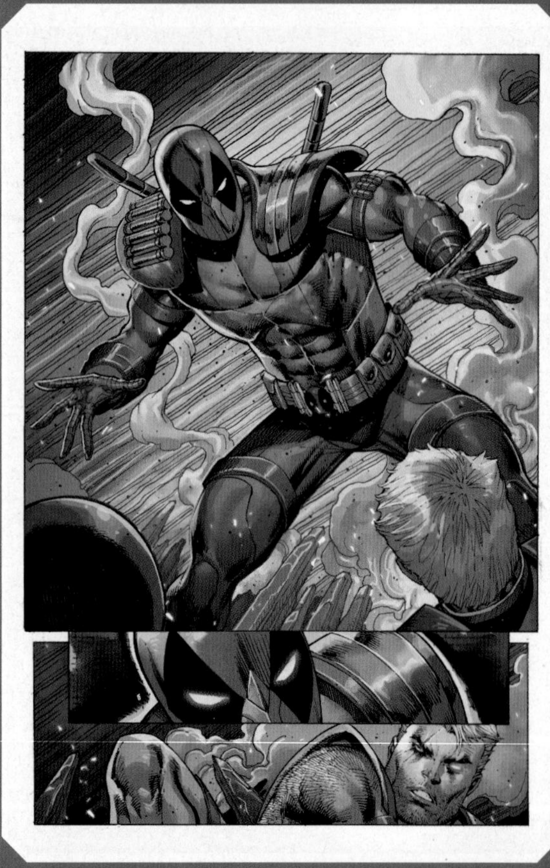

DAN FRAGA & ROMULO FAJARDO JR.

19 & 21 SKETCHES AND FINAL ART